To Dan Bailenson
on his Bar Mitzvah --
someday *you* may have
a chapter in this book!
With love from
Bruce, Marian & Emily
Weiss

THE JEW IN AMERICAN SPORTS

THE JEW IN AMERICAN SPORTS

New Revised Edition

by

Harold U. Ribalow

and

Meir Z. Ribalow

Hippocrene Books
New York

AUTHORS' NOTE

When this current revised edition of *The Jew in American Sports* was compiled, it became clear that numerous distinguished athletes could not have their careers included if the book was to be kept to a length less than that of a massive tome. This was especially true of the many fine baseball players—a number of whom have been included in earlier editions of this work—from the pioneering stars like Johnny Kling and Erskine Mayer to the diamond aces of the current age like Ken Holtzman and Steve Stone. There were so many of these men whose admirable careers warranted recording that the decision was made to give them a book of their own, *Jewish Baseball Stars*. This separate volume, published in 1985 by Hippocrene Books, examines the memorable legacies of eighteen Jewish baseball stars, including the four immortals who represent the national game and their fellow Jewish stars in the book you are reading now.

The other sport which was included in earlier editions, but which is absent from this one, is chess. This most cerebral of games, which has had more than its share of Jewish champions—including the chess geniuses Lasker, Reshevsky and Fischer—will be treated in a separate book called *Great Jewish Chess Champions*.

First Edition, four printings, 1948–1952.
First Revised Edition, 1954.
Second Printing, 1955.
Second Revised and Enlarged Edition, 1959.
Third Revised and Enlarged Edition, 1966.

Fourth New Revised Edition by Hippocrene Books, Inc., 1985.

For information, address: Hippocrene Books, Inc.,
171 Madison Avenue, New York, N.Y. 10016

ISBN 0-88254-995-2

Printed in the United States of America

To the memory of my beloved parents
who were my first readers and who
would have been delighted with my collaborator.
H.U.R.

To my parents
to whom I owe far more than can ever
be conceived, let alone repaid;
with admiration, love and thanks
from the most fortunate of sons.
M.Z.R.

Contents

Acknowledgments ix
Preface xiii
Introduction xvii
Why *Jewish* Athletes? 3
The National Game 7
Hank Greenberg — *Bomber From the Bronx* 13
Al Rosen — *Indian Chief* 33
Moe Berg — *Diamond Scholar* 47
Sandy Koufax — *Hall of Fame Pitcher* 71
The Romance of the Ring 129
Joe Choynski — *Frisco Flash* 137
Abe Attell — *Ring Wizard* 147
Benny Leonard — *Immortal Lightweight* 155
Benny Bass — *Featherweight Fury* 179
Jackie "Kid" Berg — *Whitechapel Whirlwind* 187
Al Singer — *Glass Jaw Champion* 195
Barney Ross — *The Frail-Waisted Champion* 203
Football Frenzy 219
Phil King — *Little Big Man* 225
Benny Friedman — *Michigan Marvel* 235
Harry Newman — *The Second Coming* 245
Marshall Goldberg — *Backfield Blaster* 251
Sid Luckman — *Hall of Famer* 263

Beguiling Basketball 291
Harry Boykoff — *Big Man* 299
Adolph Schayes — *Pro Star* 313
The Tennis Court 325
Dick Savitt — *Wimbledon King* 329
Harold Solomon — *True Grit* 343
Brian Gottfried — *Reliable Star* 355
Scattered Stars 365
Sidney Franklin — *Bullfighter from Flatbush* 375
Irving Jaffee — *Olympic Speedster* 383
Henry Wittenberg — *Lord of the Mat* 393
Mark Spitz — *Seven-Medal Olympian* 399
Bernie Wolfe — *Hockey Netminder* 411
Herman Barron — *Links Master* 419
Shep Messing — *Goalie for the Cosmos* 427
Nancy Lieberman — *They Call Her "Fire"* 443

Acknowledgments

This book has grown out of many sources. Many of the facts and background material were culled from record books, daily newspaper accounts, magazine stories, sports books, personal interviews whenever possible and, now that this edition has been written by two writers, talks with personal friends who follow sports closely and have offered valuable insights into individuals and events.

Our gratitude goes to:

Arthur J. Horton of Princeton University, who made available records on Moe Berg, one of that university's most unusual graduates;

Benny Leonard, who was so gregarious and friendly in offering details of his career, but who died tragically before the book appeared in its first edition;

The late Ned Fleischer, founder of *Ring* magazine and foremost authority, for the pictures of the boxers which appear in this book and for *Ring* itself, without which no one can write about boxing;

Harry Boykoff, who took the time to answer many questions;

Herman Barron, who cooperated in every way possible on the story concerning him;

Susan Irvine of *Tennis* magazine, who helped so much on the stories about Harold Solomon and Brian Gottfried;

Chuck Creesy and Steve Dujack of the *Princeton*

Alumni Weekly and the Mudd Library of Princeton University for aid in writing the story on Phil King;

Pierce Gardner of the Washington Capitals for cooperating on the chapter about Bernie Wolfe;

Dr. Edward Craig and Stephen J. Spaulding for sharing insights on baseball and basketball;

Robin Herman of the *New York Times* for background material on Bernie Wolfe and her informal discussions on hockey in general;

And to the various people and organizations who helped in the gathering of the hard-to-get photographs of the sports personalities included in this book.

Most of the sources used and quoted appear within the pages of this study and it would be repetitious to name them again, except that some of the books have been of special meaning and importance in organizing and writing a book of this kind. Let us, then, offer special thanks to the following sports books:

The Jew in Sports by Stanley Frank, for historical surveys and overviews;

Moe Berg: Athlete, Scholar, Spy by Louis Kaufman, Barbara Fitzgerald and Tom Sewell, an original and exciting study of the Princeton scholar and baseball catcher, and spy;

Morris Berg: The Real Moe by Ethel Berg, an interesting collection of memorabilia about the author's brother;

The Great No-Hitters by Glenn Dickey, for its accounts of Sandy Koufax;

How the Weather Was by Roger Kahn, for its special insights into the baseball career of Al Rosen;

Famous American Athletes of Today: Twelfth Series by Frank Waldman, for its interesting story on Sid Luckman;

Koufax by Sandy Koufax and Ed Linn;

The Summer Game and *Five Seasons* by Roger Angell, for their general excellence and brilliant accounts of some of Sandy Koufax's feats;

Dock Ellis in the Country of Baseball by Donald Hall;

The City Game by Pete Axthelm, a brilliant account of big-city basketball;

Encyclopedia of Jews in Sports by Bernard Postal, Jesse Silver and Roy Silver, an absolutely invaluable book for *all* sports fans, and particularly for historical information on prize fighter Abe Attell, Phil King, Harry Newman, Irving Jaffee and Henry Wittenberg;

as well as reference volumes like *Current Biography*, and librarians at the New York Public Library at 42nd Street and the Donnell Branch and at the Firestone Library at Princeton University.

Other credits are strewn throughout this work.

The footnotes "H.U.R." and "M.Z.R." that appear from time to time in personal eye-witness passages, indicate which of the two authors was the "witness" at the moment.

Preface

When Harold Ribalow gave me the galley proofs of this book and asked me to write its preface, my first reaction was wonder . . . wonder that anyone should write a book called *The Jew in American Sports* and wonder that any publisher should consider it sufficiently saleable to risk the publication costs. After glancing through the galleys, I discussed the matter with a few of my friends. We all agreed that the act of singling out one particular group . . . social, racial, religious or even fraternal . . . and writing a book about its ability in some particular field seemed more of a chauvinistic indulgence than a contribution to either literature or history. My feeling was one of resentment that a book should have to be written to recognize the abilities of my fellow Jews in sports.

I can assure you that I pondered this problem for some time. Finally I decided to read the galleys more carefully and really see what Ribalow had to say. I discovered that he had written about Jews in sports, not to glorify them, nor to point with pride and say, "Here, see what the Jews have done. Are we not acceptable?" Instead, through long and arduous research, he has collected a number of anecdotes and personality sketches about many famous figures in the world of sports. That all of these names are Jewish was the prerequisite of his title; but the book contains more than misplaced jingoistic inventions, as one might infer from that title. It is an interesting, sometimes thrilling record of the achievements of American athletes who had an even harder struggle than usual in their climb to the top simply because they *were* Jews. Perhaps many of you will say "But the important thing about these people is that they were fine athletes. It matters not at all that they happened to be Jewish athletes!" And if you say that, you will be wrong. For it does matter that these men were and are Jewish athletes. I know from my own experiences that every Jew who enters a competitive sport (indeed, any field of endeavor) carries with him more than the burden of acquitting himself well as a human being and as a specialist in his field . . . he carries, too, the burden of being a Jew. It is a burden he carries in common with other minorities, which affects all of his behavior, and of which he is constantly reminded as he travels from city to city pursuing his occupation.

Apart from my realization that Harold Ribalow should be congratulated for putting together a new record, a record of Jews in sports, I am pleased to write this introduction because the book that follows it contains some of the most interesting anecdotes about the sporting world that I have ever heard . . . and I have heard many. For instance, there's the story about Joe Choynski (if I may select an example from my favorite sport). It's a portrait of Choynski that no one else has ever written about. Sure, we've all heard about Joe's fight with Corbett, but this is Choynski's own story, independent of Corbett.

Then there are stories about Jewish baseball players, football players, boxers, basketball players, golfers, chess experts, ice skaters and even a chapter about a Jewish bullfighter! There are names like Hank Greenberg, Benny

Leonard, Sid Luckman, Marshall Goldberg, and I won't pretend that I am unflattered by the pages concerning the career of Barney Ross.

In short, this is a collection of stories about Jews in all sports. They are interesting, new stories that I enjoyed reading. I think there are many people in this country who will enjoy reading them as much. And if any of them object to the title as I did at first, let them pick up the book and discover for themselves that it contains a lot of fine reading about some of America's greatest athletes.

BARNEY ROSS

[From the first edition, 1948]

Introduction

The Jew in American Sports was conceived in 1942, during World War II. Because the original author served in the United States Air Force for three-and-a-half years, the book began to take shape only in 1947 and was first published in 1948. It exhausted four printings in its initial edition and was revised in 1954, 1959 and again in 1966. The current edition has a co-author, a son not yet born when the book first was published, and it is quite different in its contents from all other editions.

Some of the older athletes included in the earliest edition were dropped in later editions. A few are now back. New stars, who came to prominence in the ensuing years have, of course, been introduced here. Some chapters have had to be altered because of continual changes in the fortunes of the athletes whose careers are traced in this book. This edition blends the long-forgotten stars of the past with contemporary sports stars.

The structure of many sports has changed and one has to take this into account to offer an up-to-date volume. In the 1940's, football was primarily a college sport; today, it is largely a professional game. Basketball was an urban, white sport. But now most of its stars are black, the game's professional aspect has overwhelmed the college competition and the players are extremely tall and come from small hamlets and inner ghetto regions of the nation.

When the 1948 edition was published, Sandy Koufax was a Bar Mitzvah boy and his achievements were described for the first time in the 1966 edition, just prior to his retirement. By that time, he was already a candidate for the Baseball Hall of Fame, which he entered as soon as he became eligible. This edition rounds out his career and makes a judgment on his remarkable diamond accomplishments.

After his death, it was revealed that Moe Berg, the ballplayer who was a scholar and linguist, had served as an intelligence officer for the United States, a spy, while he wore a baseball uniform! His exciting double life inspired the publication of a book on his exploits and his sister also has written a memoir on Berg. The new chapter in this volume takes into account the new and intriguing material on Moe Berg, one of the most unusual athletes in American history.

Abe Attell was a great fighter and was omitted from earlier editions because of some unsavory aspects concerning his career after his boxing days were over. However, it is now felt that his achievements in the ring do not deserve to be overlooked and a short sketch of his ring activities is included.

Harry Newman, the football player who followed Benny Friedman at Michigan University, was, long ago, considered a carbon copy of Friedman and the tendency was to downgrade him for that reason. With the passage of the years, it has become clear that Newman was a unique athlete on his own and so a history of his comparatively brief football career is given.

The younger partner in this enterprise is himself a graduate of Princeton University and is partial to his old school.

Through his research, he discovered that one of Princeton's greatest all-around athletes — and football stars — was Phil King, a man scarcely recalled at the start of the 1980's. The story of Phil King, however, is too exciting and satisfying for it to remain in the archives of the Princeton Alumni office.

When Mark Spitz emerged as the greatest star of the 1976 Olympic Games, one was reminded of the accomplishments of an earlier Jewish Olympic star, Irving Jaffee, so here are chapters on each of these two men, uncommon in their own special way and men who glittered in international competition.

Once, tennis boasted very few Jewish players. Dick Savitt was the finest when *The Jew in American Sports* was planned. He had won the Wimbledon championship, which automatically made him a major tennis personality. Since that time, tennis has become an explosive and popular mass entertainment and is no longer elitist. There are Hungarian, Rumanian, Black, Polish, South African — and Jewish stars, including Harold Solomon and Brian Gottfried, both of whom are included here.

Toward the end of the 1970's, soccer became a major American sport. For years the most popular game around the world, it had not attracted American audiences and fans. That has changed and one of its leading figures has been Shep Messing, once the goalie for the New York Cosmos. The game, and Messing, deserve attention, and they get it in this book.

Wrestling is a peculiar sport. The professional "game" is an entertainment, not a contest. It is exhibitionist, not a game of skill. But the amateur sport remains pure and difficult. One of its greatest practitioners has been a New

York City policeman, Henry Wittenberg. His career is outlined here.

Hockey is not really an American game, but a Canadian game. As a result, few Americans are stars in hockey but all of the stars play and are known in the United States. One of them, the only Jewish professional hockey player, is Bernie Wolfe, goalie for the Washington Capitals. While he has not been a "star," he has won a degree of prominence and he is therefore entitled to a chapter in this edition.

Nancy Lieberman is the most prominent Jewish woman athlete to have emerged in recent years and so there is a chapter devoted to her. Amy Alcott, the golfer, also deserves passing mention.

It should be stressed that when this book was first conceived, it was difficult to gather information on Jewish athletes, for most sports information appeared only in the sports pages of the daily newspapers and there were few outlets for features or long accounts of sports careers. There were not many sports magazines and the communications industry was not nearly as well developed as it is today. Nowadays there are dozens of sports magazines, general and specialized, available to all. One can see on television tennis matches, live, from the West Coast, Texas or New England. Football games, basketball games, baseball games, fill the airwaves and one can make his own judgments without the aid of sports reporters.

There have been full-length books published on Sandy Koufax, Al Schacht, Red Auerbach, Red Holzman and chess masters Samuel Reshevsky, Bobby Fischer and Emanuel Lasker. A film was made on the life of Barney Ross and, years before he died, Ross wrote his autobiography.

There are excellent books on baseball by Roger Angell and Roger Kahn, which include material on Jewish players. There are histories on the no-hit baseball games, with running accounts of the achievements of Koufax and Holtzman. There are official histories of major league ball teams, again with pages on their Jewish players. Elsewhere there is included a list of acknowledgments and the reader will be able to judge how many sources there are to draw upon at the present time, including the invaluable *Encyclopedia of Jews in Sports* by Bernard Postal, Jesse Silver and Roy Silver.

While *The Jew in American Sports* does not attempt to be encyclopedic in its approach and does not name every American Jewish athlete in history, it does attempt to convey the excitement and thrills in the lives of men who were outstanding in American sports. There also are historical surveys of the major sports which are not focused on individuals but on sociological developments and trends in American Jewish history. It is hoped that this volume is both interesting on its own and as a contribution to that history.

THE JEW IN AMERICAN SPORTS

Why *Jewish* Athletes?

"Why," a well-meaning friend asked, "are you writing this book? Does it really make a difference that Al Rosen and Sandy Koufax were Jewish, Joe Louis or Joe Morgan black or John McGraw an Irishman?"

The best answer would be that it shouldn't make any difference, but the sports fan, like the average citizen (who is the sports fan in another guise) likes to know all about his idols; he wants to know their history; he wants to be able to attach himself to them. Sports lovers are really dreamers. One of the attractions of sports is that the spectator can and does project himself into the shape of his heroes and makes believe that it is he, and not they, who are performing the great deeds which make all America cheer wildly. Therefore, the Negro, or black, fan feels closer to the black athlete than he does to the white one. Italian fans have a tendency to root for Italian ball players and Jewish fans take a special interest in Jewish players. It is hard to deny this conclusion, for life is not an isolated thing and neither is the sports world. The tie between the individual and his society is strong and so is the tie between the sports fan and his hero.

All men are gregarious. They are proud of their relatives, of their townsfolk, of their co-religionists, if these people do something outstanding. And because the world of sports is a great leveller, because there is a greater degree of equality between contestants in sports than in most battles in life, the sports world is, in a very true sense, one of the best of all possible worlds.

The sports world is a simple place in which to live. There are few complexities in that universe. There is the hero — and there is the villain. There is the champion — and there is the challenger. There is the big guy — and the little guy. There are drama and tragedy and disillusion and passion and hysteria, but they are starkly simple. Few sports heroes are contemplative people. And the fans, complex as they may be, shed their worries, their phobias, their complexes as they enter the sports arena. Games are fast and physically skilful. The cleverness of a boxer, the grace of a baseball player, the keen analytical mind of a football quarterback are unlike the cleverness, grace and keen analysis necessary in other spheres. There have been some exceptionally clever baseball players — unlettered men who never threw to the wrong base — who were rather stupid in other fields. Conversely, there have been intelligent, educated men who, playing a game, have been slow-witted.

So in considering the sports world, one must realize that it is a world entire unto itself. And the sports personalities described here are placed in their sports niche and are compared on a sports level.

Thus it must be realized that in the sports world the fan and the athlete are sometimes aware of bonds which would be overlooked by those who are not sports lovers. When there was a swelling of black pride upon the accomplishments of Jackie Robinson and the hundreds of black ball players who followed him; when Jews took pride in Benny

Leonard, or Hank Greenberg, or Sandy Koufax, it is to be taken seriously.

Here is why.

In the simple world of sports, victory is all-important. The word "champion" has wonderful connotations. It means just that, "champion," the one man at the head of the class. The "champion of the world" in boxing means that the champion can beat any other fighter in the world at his weight. It is a thrilling and all-embracing thought.

Therefore, when a Jewish prize fighter wins a title, as Benny Leonard, Barney Ross and Abe Attell did, it means to sports fans that Jews can fight. They don't need lengthy, scientific treatises to show them that Jews have guts; they don't need long histories to show them that Jews have participated in national wars; Israel has given enough evidence of that. But if they see a Jewish fighter wearing the Star of David and showing courage in the ring, they have proof enough of bravery.

And when they see a Jewish baseball catcher stand up to flying spikes and tag out a desperate runner, they know it is a lie to call Jews cowards.

Hank Greenberg, hitting the pennant-winning home run in the last game of the season in 1945, taught baseball followers that a Greenberg is as dangerous in a pinch as Babe Ruth or any super-star.

Larry Sherry, coming into a World Series, game after game, and stopping his opponents in their tracks, personified grace under pressure.

Sandy Koufax, pitching a perfect game while suffering from arthritis, demonstrated a remarkable degree of courage as well as skill.

Al Rosen, who grew up fighting Jew-baiters with a combative tenacity and fierce spirit that forced even his opponents to regard the tough ballplayer with respect and admiration, summed it up this way: "I wanted it to be, Here comes one Jewish kid that every Jew in the world can be proud of."

And so it goes.

The sports world is a spectacular world, an interesting world, and always a dramatic world.

That it and its followers are, in essence, tolerant and basically democratic, is proved by the very success of the headliners included in this volume.

The National Game

In the reams and reams of paper written about baseball, the sport's basic attraction is seldom stressed. It is this: baseball is America's most democratic game. The ball park is where everyone comes with his hair down, so to speak. The fans take off their jackets, roll up their sleeves, jeer or cheer at the players and forget their outside troubles, worries and tensions. In a sense, the same could be said for any sport, with this difference: one of the main attractions of baseball is to be part of the crowd. That is to say, it is not only the game itself which attracts the fan; it is the comforting knowledge that you know your neighbor, like you, is interested in the game itself and that he is, if only for a few hours, your buddy.

The fight crowd is, generally speaking, a pretty cynical body of fans. The gamblers, the people with primitive instincts and willing to display them, go to the fights, which cost more than baseball seats. One can pay hundreds of dollars for a seat at a prize fight and only a few dollars for a baseball seat. The football crowd is mainly a young group, especially collegians at the college games, and perennial collegians at the professional games, although in recent years pro football has grizzled fans as well. Here, as at baseball games, you get a cross-section of the nation, but somehow the camaraderie of baseball is lacking. The tempo is different; there is no time element in baseball.

Perhaps, also, the reason is that football is played once a week and too many people try to squeeze all their thrills into a short period of time.

Some of the best sports writing in recent years has been about baseball and its unique fascination. Donald Hall, a distinguished poet, happens to be a baseball follower and he published a book on the pitcher Dock Ellis, entitled *Dock Ellis in the Country of Baseball*. Hall phrases with eloquence the magic of the sport: "In the country of baseball, time is the air we breathe, and the wind swirls us backward and forward, until we seem so reckoned in time and seasons that all time and all seasons become the same." Hall continues: "Baseball is a country all to itself. It is an old country, like Ruritania, northwest of Bohemia and its seacoast . . . It is a wrong-end-of-the-telescope country, like the landscape people build for model trains, miniature with distance and old age. The citizens wear baggy pinstripes, knickers and caps. Seasons and teams shift, blur into each other, change radically or appear to change, and restore themselves to old ways again. Citizens retire to farms, in the country of baseball, smoke cigars and reminisce, and all at once they are young players again, lean and intense, running the base paths with filled spikes . . . In the country of baseball, men rise to glory in their twenties and their early thirties — a garland briefer than a girl's or at least briefer than a young woman's — with an abrupt rise, like scaling a cliff, and then the long meadow slopes downward. Citizens of the country of baseball retire and yet they never retire."

Probably the best of all baseball writers is Roger Angell, author of two classic volumes, *The Summer Game* and *Five Seasons*. He describes games in careful and loving detail;

he devotes a remarkable chapter to the baseball itself; to a baseball scout scouring the country for talent; to upcoming players, to stars on the decline, on the exhibition games, on key games, on the World Series and, from time to time, on the beauty and poetry of the game itself.

Read this magnificent passage and you will begin to understand the attraction of the game to an intelligent, sensitive, cultured man:

"Always, it seems, there is something more to be discovered about this game. Sit quietly in the upper stand and look at the field. Half close your eyes against the sun, so that the players recede a little, and watch the movements of baseball. The pitcher, immobile on the mound, holds the inert white ball, his little lump of physics. Now with abrupt gestures he gives it enormous speed and direction, converting it suddenly into a line, a moving line. The batter, wielding a plane, attempts to intercept the line and acutely alter it, but he fails; the ball, a line again, is redrawn to the pitcher, in the center of this square, the diamond . . . In time, these and other lines are drawn on the field; the batter and the fielders are also transformed into fluidity, moving and converting, and we see now that all movement in the baseball is a convergence toward fixed points — the pitched ball toward the plate, the thrown ball toward the right angle of the bases, the batted ball toward the as yet undrawn but already visible point of congruence with either the ground or a glove."

Angell remarks, after further descriptions of batting and fielding, "It is neat, it is pretty, it is satisfying." Then, like Donald Hall, he also notices the element of time. "The last dimension," he writes, "is time. Within the ball park, time moves differently, marked by no clock except the events of the game. This is the unique, unchangeable feature of baseball, and perhaps explains why this sport . . . remains somehow rustic, unviolent, and introspective. Baseball's time is seamless and invisible, a bubble within which players move at exactly the same pace and rhythms as all their predecessors . . . Since baseball time is measured only in outs, all you have to do is succeed utterly; keep hitting, keep the rally alive, and you have defeated time."

Baseball is a pastoral sport, a leisurely game. To the uninitiated it is slow-moving. The non-baseball fan does not appreciate the background of the game. He cannot understand the struggle between a pitcher and a batter because he doesn't know, for example, that the pitcher may be striving for a strikeout record and that the batter is swinging for, say, his fiftieth two-base hit of the season. In a word, the person who comes to a ball game for the spectacle value alone, misses the backbone of the game: the facts and figures, the statistics, which make every single play an important one in the overall context of the single game and the overall season and the entire career of the athlete.

It is this understanding which brings baseball fans together. You can root for any one of some fifty players on the two squads during the course of a game. You can quote the batting averages of your favorites and a loud-mouthed fan can come back with statistics about his own men. The fan pays his money, yells at the players, the umpire, at his heroes. He argues with the guy sitting next to him, he buys a cold drink, a hot dog and a score card and for a few hours he is transported into another world. The weather is good (baseball games are not played in heavy rains or in the snow or in zero temperature, like football games), the game is played outdoors (not in a smoke-filled arena, like basketball or hockey) and time stands still (none of this two minutes left to play, as is the case with football, hockey, basketball and other sports).

Unfortunately, comparatively few Jews have made the major leagues. It is an outdoor game and the Jews in America have lived in the large cities. If you were to read about most major leaguers, you would discover that they come from small towns and hamlets of the United States. Amazingly few come from the crowded urban areas. Nevertheless, there have been a substantial number of Jewish baseball players. Some rank with the top stars in the game; others were mediocre; some lasted a very brief time in the big leagues.

Baseball is a hard profession. A man has to be exceptionally talented to reach the big leagues and then a combination of skill and luck keeps him there long enough for him to win recognition as a star. Not many Jews went in for professional sports, because there was not much encouragement at home. Baseball did not become "respectable" until after Babe Ruth's homeric feats with the bat attracted all elements of American life to the ball parks of the nation. It is also clear that in the early, pioneering days of the game, Jewish players were given a hard time. Some changed their name. Others had to fight their way, literally, into the lineup. Al Rosen said as much. Saul Rogovin felt the lash of anti-Semitism. It is possible the same happened with Ken Holtzman in a more recent period. Yet Jewish players were looked for in the 1920's and when Andy Cohen broke into the Giant lineup, he won publicity throughout the United States. A Jewish star, it was obvious, would draw additional fans in the big cities where Jews lived. But baseball was prejudiced for a very long time. Black players did not come into the game until Jackie Robinson broke the color bar, and then the gates were opened and now it is almost impossible to keep up with the constant flow of black players.

Jews have had other options. Constantly seeking an education, Jews in the United States preferred medicine, the law, other professions, teaching, business, to the athletic field. This is why the number of Jewish basketball players diminished. It is why there are scarcely any Jews in professional football.

But history remains and looking to the past and even the immediate past, we find that Jews have made a significant contribution to baseball. It is the national game and the Jew is part and parcel of the national life of the United States. To that extent, Jews and baseball are tied together.

HANK GREENBERG IN HIS TOP TIGER FORM

Hank Greenberg

Bomber from the Bronx

It was the last game of the 1945 pennant race and the whole baseball world was waiting tensely to see what would happen. The Detroit Tigers had to win this game from the pestiferous St. Louis Browns, the 1944 American League champions. The Tigers were not far enough ahead of the Washington Senators, and here it was, the last game of the season and Nels Potter, the ace of the Brown staff, was twirling.

The score was deadlocked and it was the last of the ninth inning. Somehow the Tigers had filled the bases on infield hits and a bit of wildness on the part of Potter, a smart old campaigner.

And the batter was Hank Greenberg, the mightiest right-handed slugger in baseball. But Hank was rusty after a long hitch in the Army. Fans turned to one another, some in hope, some wishing that Greenberg had suddenly grown blind in the Army.

And then, with a count of one ball, Potter grooved a medium-fast pitch. Greenberg swung hard. The ball began to climb towards left field. Because it was two out every Tiger on the base paths ran with the crack of the bat. But they didn't have to. The ball grew smaller and smaller as it rose and when it disappeared among the patrons in left field 351 feet away, the Tigers had won another American

League flag, Hank Greenberg had re-established his reputation as a great money player and once again the city of Detroit went quietly mad.

* * * * *

It was the fifth game of the 1940 World Series. The Detroit Tigers and the Cincinnati Reds were tied at two games apiece. Gene Thompson, right-hander, was pitching for the National League champions. There were two runners on the bases. It was a crucial moment.

Swinging three heavy bats, a husky figure emerged from the Tiger dugout. A roar like the pound of surf greeted the tall player who took his careful stance at the plate, after having dropped two of the bats. Thompson looked at the base runners. He wound up and blazed one in there. It was a strike. The count went to two strikes. The Redlegs pitcher measured his opponent. He breathed deeply, took a long windup and pitched. The batter swung. Bang! The ball took wings and disappeared over the left field wall. Pandemonium reigned. The noise shook the park.

Hank Greenberg had hit another home run.

For hitting home runs at such times, Hank Greenberg was paid more money than any other player in baseball in 1940, again in 1941 and in 1946, his next complete year in baseball. The reason for this is obvious. Hank Greenberg, a Jewish boy from the Bronx, had become the favorite of millions of baseball fans all over the country. Hank was unable to play as many years as he could have, because in 1941 he became one of the first major leaguers to join the Army and play the grim game of war.

Leaving one of the most lucrative spots in sports, handsome Hank Greenberg shouldered a rifle instead of a bat and trained as a private instead of a $60,000-a-year baseball star. Within six months he became a sergeant, and then, because he was nearing the age limit, was given his military release and placed on the reserve lists. But Pearl Harbor made history and Greenberg immediately returned to service before the Army called him. The war years dragged on and Greenberg became an officer, finally being sent to the China-Burma-India theater, where he was placed in charge of a Headquarters squadron of the 20th Bomber Command.

When the war ended Greenberg was discharged and returned to the Tigers. He was older than thirty-four, which is generally the beginning of the road down for a major league ball player. But Hank showed that his eye was still deadly when he began to swing his mighty bat. In half a season, rusty from lack of work, Hank hit .311, slammed thirteen home runs and, from the day he came back, led to victory after victory.

Henry Greenberg was born January 1, 1911, in the Bronx, the son of Orthodox Jewish parents from Rumania. They were ordinary, simple people, to whom the idea of a famous son was strange at first. But they must have sensed years ago that Hank would be something special, for he grew into a huge young man, six feet four inches tall. Even though Hank loved baseball, he had the good sense to turn down many cheapening, but financially good, offers after he became a star. He never took show bookings. He lived quietly and, unlike many other ball players, he never spent the winter hunting, which never was a Jewish way to spend free time. Instead Hank played handball, lived with his folks and did not marry until he was nearly thirty-six.

Hank attended James Monroe High School in the Bronx

and became a four-letter man. He was especially adept at baseball, for his big frame carried a lot of power. True, he was awkward, but he hit the ball tremendous distances. Then Hank began to play for the Bay Parkways. One day, when Paul Krichell, clever New York Yankee scout, watched a game in which Hank hit three home runs, the big Jewish player was given a offer by Krichell to join the Yankee organization.

"I'll give you $1,000 if you come with us," Krichell told the eager young man.

But Hank had New York University in mind, for he wanted an education.

"No," he said, "I want to go to college."

Krichell wanted Hank badly, and so he said, "I'll give you $1,000 down and $500 a year while you go to school, $3,000 all together. What do you say?"

And before Hank could say anything definite, the wily Krichell had Hank see Ed Barrow, the Yankee general manager, who lunched with Greenberg and tried to talk him into joining the Yankee system. Hank's parents liked the idea and they told him to go ahead and sign with the Yankees. But Hank remembered that Lou Gehrig, the great and powerful first sacker on the Yankees, would be impossible to replace. So he did not give Barrow a definite answer.

Then Hank began to play with a baseball team in East Douglas, Mass., a mill town. He grew homesick and after doing no work for three weeks he announced that he was going home after the next game; this was July, 1929. Hank played that day. He slammed a home run and a double. Joe Engel, Washington Senator scout, was impressed with what he saw and offered Greenberg a $10,000 bonus for signing up with his club plus a salary of $800 a month, immediately. Hank still had NYU in mind and said "No." But the Detroit Tigers played it smarter. They offered Greenberg $9,000, $3,000 immediately and the rest after he left NYU.

Realizing that he could go to college, Hank said, "I'll take it." And so he signed up with the Tigers.

* * * * *

But after one semester at NYU Greenberg became uneasy and unhappy when the spring training season started. He dreamed of playing ball, and the lure became too strong. He wired the Tigers that he would like to join them at once. He was given the rest of his money and got $500 a month to play with Raleigh, in North Carolina. So far all the breaks were going his way. Major league scouts had been fighting for him and Greenberg was getting lots of money. Now the grind began. Up and down the minor league circuits, in bad hotels, travelling on poor roads in rumbling buses, Greenberg followed the hard trail taken by anyone who wants to be a star in baseball. The big crowds, the big money and the cheers and headlines look good but they don't come easily. First there is the training in the minors, the day-by-day sweating it out, the bad breaks, and the good ones, learning how to hit the good pitchers and how to evade the wild pitches of the tyros just breaking in. With Raleigh in the Piedmont League, Hank began to learn. He hit .314 and he felt better because a bit earlier he had played seventeen games with Hartford in the Eastern League and had done badly. But Hank had power. He weighed more than 200 and his lumbering awkwardness at first base was overlooked. He was learning.

Then, in 1932, Greenberg's coordination and power and ability began to crystallize. With Beaumont in the Texas League Hank hit well. He drove in one hundred and thirty-one runs, drove thirty-nine home runs out of the park and was voted the most valuable player in the league. He could no longer be overlooked. He was on his way. The Tigers brought him up and in 1933 he was a rookie trying to make the majors.

* * * * *

Hank had a hard time in his first season. He happened to break into the lineup in the face of obstacles few talked about after Greenberg made the grade. Baseball is a peculiar game. There are always personal struggles and prejudices, even if they don't appear in the box scores. Bucky Harris, then the Detroit Tiger manager, had been nursing along a promising first baseman named Harry Davis to play first for the Tigers. Davis cost the club $50,000. And when a player costs that much a manager must stick with him, even if a tall, lumbering player with a lot of power stumbles into the training camp. So Harris paid no attention to Greenberg. He moved big Hank to third base. Hank was never what can be called a natural player. He worked hard to master a position. He slaved and practiced and worked in his mind as well as his body. He did not expect to be moved to a new and strange post as he worked his way up. He looked very bad at third.

Than one day Harris had to leave the club and Del Baker, a coach and later a manager at Detroit, ran the team for a while. He saw that Greenberg was no third sacker and he moved Hank to first in an exhibition game against the Giants. Eager to prove that Baker was doing the right thing, Hank got three hits that day, a single, double and triple. He felt better. He thought he had proved where he belonged. But when Harris rejoined the team, Davis returned to first. At this stage Greenberg grew morbid and decided to see Frank Navin, the popular and fair owner of the Tigers.

"I am a first baseman," Greenberg told him, "And I want to play there."

"Wait," Navin advised him. "We'll use you against lefties and Davis against right-handers."

But when the season began and the Tigers faced their first southpaw, Lloyd Brown, Davis was announced by Harris as the starting first sacker.

But he had not reckoned with Navin. As soon as he read off the batting order, Harris got a phone call. Then he returned to the dressing room.

"There is a change in the batting order. Greenberg will play first base," the manager said.

Nervous, upset and tense, Greenberg had a hitless day at the plate. Grimly, Harris replaced him with Davis and for three weeks Hank sat on the bench as he watched the graceful but light-hitting Davis play first. Then, in Boston, Hank got a break. Brown, who had been traded to the Red Sox, was pitching. Greenberg got into the batting order. This time the story was different. Hank got two hits. That year he played 117 games, despite Harris' attempt to install Davis as his first baseman and justify the $50,000 price tag for the Fancy Dan. Greenberg batted .301 in his first full season, breaking into the charmed circle of .300 batters. He hit twelve homers, showing potential power and, more significant, he batted in eighty-seven runs, which is the true sign of the valuable player.

* * * * *

But Hank did not find it all easy. Davis was smooth around first base. Greenberg was clumsy. The fans booed his lack of grace. They liked his batting, but they were critical and their chatter drove Greenberg to morning sessions at the ball park. He came to the park at ten o'clock and practiced spearing grounders. He learned how to stretch for wide throws. He became death on pops to the infield. He learned how to make the double-play and how to move his feet smoothly. He became a real major leaguer, and only through hard work and the knowledge that his own manager did not think much of him.

But in 1934 Harris was replaced by popular Mickey Cochrane, a great catcher and fine leader of men. Hank and Mickey hit it off from the beginning. Cochrane showed his confidence in Greenberg by selling Davis. Hank had the first base job to himself. He relaxed and played better ball. He had a tremendous year and began to assert himself as one of the top sluggers in the game. Hank batted .339 and led the league in doubles with sixty-three. He more than doubled his homer total of the previous year by slamming twenty-six. He batted in 139 runs. He was a baseball star, and no longer "promising." Hank Greenberg had arrived.

Nevertheless, he was aware of his Jewishness all along. The Tiger infield was setting a record of having played all season long without a substitution. But when Rosh Hashanah came Hank refused to play. The *Detroit Free Press* printed Hank's picture with Happy New Year

Greetings in Hebrew captioned above the photo. And nine days later Yom Kippur came. The day before Yom Kippur Hank hit a home run to beat the Yankees 2-0 in a tense pennant race. He did not play on Yom Kippur and the Tigers lost. When he returned to the lineup the club perked up and took the flag. The entire city respected Hank for his attitude. Edgar Guest, America's most popular verse-maker, devoted a long poem to Greenberg's action. Hank was acclaimed not only as a fine player but as a sober, religious citizen who was setting a fine sportsmanlike example for everyone to follow.

* * * * *

In the World Series that year Greenberg tried his best against the Deans and the Cardinals, even though the Tigers couldn't win. He batted .321, drove in seven runs and showed that he did not tighten up in such an important sports event as the World Series. Many players do. The great Ty Cobb did badly in his first Series. But in the first game, in which the Tigers lost to Dizzy Dean by an 8-3 score, Hank hit a long home run in the eighth inning and got one other hit besides. In the fourth game, which the Tigers won to tie up the Series at 2-all, Hank was the batting star. Here's why:

In the third inning with a rally going, Dazzy Vance, onetime great pitcher, came in to relieve for the Cards. Greenberg singled and drove in a run. This was only one of his hits. He found Card pitchers for four hits that afternoon.

In the sixth game he drove in the tying run against Paul Dean and the Tigers went ahead to win it.

* * * * *

Greenberg's power developed as the years moved along. He discovered that his seriousness about baseball was paying off. In 1935 Hank was voted the most valuable player in the American League, one of the highest honors paid to a baseball player. And no wonder! He hit .328, led the league in homers with thirty-six and led in runs batted in with one hundred seventy, which was an amazing figure. And for the second year in a row he connected for more than two hundred hits, a feat usually reserved for light hitters, not sluggers like Greenberg.

Hank did not try for home runs, even if he did hit them. A line drive hitter, he said that "I am tall, heavy and reasonably strong," when asked about his power. He was also modest. After his fine 1935 year he was compared with the great players of the game. Naturally enough he was placed against players like Foxx and Gehrig, two phenomenal sluggers.

"It's a mistake to compare me with either Foxx or Gehrig," Hank said. "They are veterans with years of service. I am only a beginner."

Perhaps he sensed something, for when the World Series came that year, Greenberg had a tough break. He played in only two games, for he broke a wrist sliding into the plate. In the second game, however, Hank pulled his famous home run act. Facing Charlie Root, the Tigers teed off quickly. After the first three batters hit safely, Greenberg drove Root out of the box with a long home run. Happily, the Tigers won the Series.

* * * * *

The 1936 season was one of the worst Greenberg ever had. After twelve games he collided with Jake Powell in a base-line scuffle, and hurt his wrist again. The wrist gives leverage to a slugger and it meant the end of Greenberg in that pennant race. Hank seemed to be on his way out. Word spread that he was brittle, in spite of his fine body. But then one day, in an exhibition game the next spring, Greenberg got five hits in five times at bat. He was ready. And the fans knew it. That year Greenberg drove in one hundred eighty-three runs, the second highest in the entire history of the American League. Only Gehrig in the American and Hack Wilson in the National League ever bettered that. Babe Ruth and other legendary sluggers never came close to this figure. On top of that Hank hit .337, nearly the highest he had ever soared in his attacks against major league pitching.

From here on in Greenberg was considered the best of all the right-handed sluggers in the game. And if there was any doubt at all, it vanished the next year when Hank again battered at established records.

In 1938 he hit fifty-eight home runs.

Babe Ruth made baseball what it is today when he slammed sixty homers in one season. That mark intrigued all America. Men and women who never showed any interest in the game started to come to baseball parks to see the Babe. As a personality he transcended the game itself. He became a great figure in American life. No one else ever approached his home run rampages. But Greenberg came mighty close; he hit nine homers in one week and was sixteen days ahead of Ruth's schedule. He worked hard. During a batting slump he paid some kids a few cents to practice with him on a sandlot, at a time when he was the greatest slugger in the game. Instead of choking up with tension toward the end of the season, as some baseball writers said he did, Greenberg did nothing of the sort. The facts are these: in his last twenty-four games he hit twelve homers, an average of one every two games. And if he would have maintained this pace all year he would have hit seventy-seven home runs! It must also be remembered that Ruth was left-handed and aimed at a 296-foot wall at the Yankee Stadium most of the time. The park was built for him. Greenberg, right-handed, aimed at a fence 340 feet away. And despite this handicap he fell only two shy of Ruth's record! Years later, in 1961, Roger Maris managed to hit sixty-one homers in a lengthier schedule of games.

Hank did shatter one Ruthian mark, when he hit two homers in one game eleven times. All but one of the games ended in a Tiger victory, which is another indication of Greenberg's value to his team.

* * * * *

The 1938 season was Greenberg's peak year, even if he did hit .340 two years later and win the most valuable player award for the second time and lead the league in home runs for the third time. In 1940 he led the team in doubles, with fifty, in homers with forty-one and in runs batted in with one hundred fifty. In the World Series that year he batted .357. In the fifth game he hit a home run off Gene Thompson, the home run described earlier in this story. But when a man drives fifty-eight homers in one year no accomplishments can dim them. That was Hank's year, the one which established him in the immortal class with

Babe Ruth and Jimmy Foxx, who also hit fifty-eight one year.

* * * * *

Normally statistics are uninteresting, but they are the lifeblood of baseball. The fans at the park always talk in figures. Educated and illiterate voices roll off statistics with equal glibness. And even if figures do not always tell the entire story, they are the best proof of accomplishments in baseball. To those who are casual ball fans, the mysterious figures in the box scores, the record books and the sports columns do not mean much. To the dyed-in-the-wool fan, they mean nearly everything. To them the way to prove Greenberg's greatness is to show that his one hundred and eighty-three runs batted in in one season was only one behind the record; that after his first year with the Tigers he drove in more than one hundred a year every full year he played; that day-in-day-out he has been a great performer. His records and accomplishments mark him as perhaps the greatest Jewish baseball player in the history of the sport and a star who ranks with the greatest simply through his deeds on the diamond.

And toward the end of the 1946 season of play, in the hot climate of August and the dog days of September, Hank Greenberg accomplished some startling deeds, all with the stamp of greatness. Grantland Rice declared that, "In my opinion Greenberg's September surge was one of baseball's greatest achievements when you consider all the angles involved."

In 1946 Greenberg, flushed with his remarkable comeback of 1945, knew that the season was going to be a hard one. He was thirty-five, and his legs were beginning to go back on him. He wasn't able to unwind himself until August, a month in which most old players begin to feel the years. In September his home run bat began to flail. Within a short time he was again the Hammering Hank of old. He hit sixteen homers in September and batted .345 that month. He ended the season with the title he most coveted — that of runs-batted-in leader. He smacked across one hundred twenty-seven runs, four more than the highly-publicized Ted Williams and sixteen more than Nick Etten drove in to lead the league a year earlier. It was the eighth time in his career that he had knocked in 100 runs or more a season, and the fourth time that he led the league in RBI's. His homer splurge netted him forty-four, to lead the majors in homers. He slammed six more than Ted Williams, although for most of the year Williams held a wide lead over Hank. On August 31, Hank had hit twenty-eight homers, most of them early in the season. Within less than a month he had his forty-four.

And then the 1946 season ended and on January 18, 1947 one of the most surprising deals in major league baseball was completed. Hank Greenberg, a top Tiger for a long, long time, was sold out of the league, to the Pittsburgh Pirates in the National League.

When the deal was first announced, the entire sports world was aghast. And for weeks the sports pages were loaded with stories about the Tiger management, Greenberg's reaction, the attempts of the new owner in Pittsburgh to inject power into a fading team.

General Manager Billy Evans of Detroit said that the seven other American League clubs had declined to claim the slugger at the $10,000 waiver price — but later it developed that the Yankees wanted Hank, and passed him up only because the Tigers had sworn that they would withdraw their waivers on Hank if New York claimed him.

Upon hearing the sudden news of his sale, Hank was deeply shaken. He issued many statements and debated retiring. But finally, he decided to go along with his new owners.

When he was asked whether he would play for Pittsburgh, following his shock over leaving the Tigers, Hank declared: "Playing baseball just for what financial returns there may be in it for me does not interest me. I've been around a long time and anyone who knows me knows I'm not that kind."

And then came his official statement:

"The news that I was sold to Pittsburgh which I heard over the radio, came as a complete surprise. I signed with the Detroit Baseball Club immediately upon graduation from high school and played for them continuously for fourteen years, excepting the four years I served in the Army.

"When discharged from the Army in 1945, I returned to Detroit and have been with them ever since. My whole major league career has been spent in a Detroit uniform. I have always given the Detroit club and the fans my best efforts and my record speaks for itself. I am deeply grateful to the Detroit fans — the finest in the world — for their loyalty and encouragement and to the members of the press and radio for their fairness and support.

"I also regret leaving my teammates, many of whom are my close friends. Naturally, after this long and pleasant relationship, I am disappointed to be traded from the Detroit club and waived out of the American League."

This statement reveals how deeply hurt and disappointed Hank was when the Tigers released him. And Hank's following action showed that he was willing to give up the game. He informed the Pirate management that he was retiring.

"This decision," he said, "is not easy to make. I love the game and feel there is yet much good baseball in me as a player and executive. But after seventeen years and 1,150 games in a Tiger uniform, I always expected to finish my career in Detroit. Since it was decided for me that this could not be, I do not desire to start anew in a strange environment."

Frank McKinney, Pirate owner, expressed his chagrin, but never gave up hope that Greenberg would change his mind. The pain, however, was fresh in Hank's mind — and for a while he did nothing.

Meanwhile, the sports writers had a field day and they all praised Hank to the skies. Arthur Daley of the *New York Times* wrote that "the baseball writers will resent bitterly the way Greenberg presumably is getting pushed around in this latest switch in clubs. Big Hank has no firmer supporters than among the typewriter pounders. He always has been gracious and nice to everyone of them; talks intelligently and interestingly on every occasion; has always been overpoweringly friendly and has been a colorful personality down through the years — well, they're all in his corner to the very last man."

Other writers went to town on Hank. Dan Daniel, the *New York World-Telegram* baseball expert, pointed out that "the records at Briggs Stadium say that without Greenberg the Tigers have not been a big draw."

And Hal Newhouser, the Tiger ace southpaw pitcher, upon hearing of Greenberg's departure from Detroit, said,

"Hank's a great guy and it's tough to see him leave with that big bat of his. Those forty-four home runs last year meant a lot to all our pitchers, including myself, and I hate to see him go." Hal added: "I figured he'd get awfully tired as the 1946 season wore on, but as the weather got hotter, so did Hank."

Newhouser, without Greenberg's 1947 bat, experienced his worst season in four years and won less than twenty games.

Greenberg, in time, decided against quitting, and played with the Pirates in 1947. While talking to reporters one day after he joined the Pirates, Hank said: "I really meant it when I said I didn't want to play ball any more. It had been hard enough, getting into shape and playing last year. Being sold to the Pirates meant I had to start all over again. A new club, a new league and a new manager. It seemed too much. I didn't even want to try it. So I quit, but they came to me and said:

" 'Look. We need you in Pittsburgh. We have sound plans for the future. We're going to rebuild the club, bring in the best players we can get and give the town a real ball club. We want you. We don't care if you don't hit at all.' "

Than Hank laughed a little. "Well, that was stretching it a little far, I thought. But, anyway, they convinced me that the fans in Pittsburgh were counting on me to — what? Lead them out of the wilderness? I don't know what I'm supposed to do, but I would like to have a good year."

And here is the lead of the Associated Press story on the opening game between the Pirates and the Cubs:

"Big Hank Greenberg belted only one hit in his National League debut, but it was a screaming double that enabled the Pirates to nip the Cubs, 1-0, and settled a stirring mound duel between Truett Sewell and Hank Borowy before 29,427 thoroughly chilled fans."

In the second game of the season Hank hit his first National League home run off Hank Wyse — and he was off. But then he slowed up and although he had fifteen home runs in July, he asked to be benched after a protracted slump.

Throughout the rest of the season, Greenberg played in spurts. He ended the year with twenty-five home runs, plus a painful chip in his elbow which kept him inactive toward the last weeks of the season. During the heated Yankee-Dodger World Series, the Pirates announced that Hank had been given his unconditional release. Declaring he would first submit to an elbow operation, Hank said he would seek a job in baseball for the 1948 season.

He found one shortly, as the general manager of the Cleveland Indians. Within a brief period, Greenberg became one of the leading executives in the game, running, in effect, the Cleveland organization. He became a stockholder and a controversial personality because he continually came in second to the Yankees. In 1958 he finally sold his shares in the club and left the Cleveland organization after being ousted as general manager, and later became a stockholder in the Chicago White Sox.

It was almost inevitable that Greenberg should have been elected to the Hall of Fame for his impressive accomplishments during a brilliant major league career.

But the true sports fan remembers a player not for his statistical achievements alone, but for the kind of a job the player did when the fan watched him. Apart from the record books, what kind of a man was Hank Greenberg?

In the many years I* have been watching sports, Greenberg seemed a fine performer and equally fine person. Of course, as a New Yorker, I saw Hank most often in the Yankee Stadium, playing against great Yankee teams before his own home crowd. He pressed because he wanted to show the home folks that he was good enough to play in the Stadium as well as in Detroit. And when he was not relaxed, he did not hit. No one does.

It is good to remember that tall, husky figure, wiggling a bat, standing quietly while waiting for the pitch. Each time he came to bat, he was a potential homer. The pitchers suddenly screwed up their eyes and watched for the catcher's signs. Somehow, Greenberg at bat meant something more than just a hitter at the plate. He was power personified. I have seen him strike out vigorously. Later, in the same game, against the same pitcher he would send a screaming liner booming into the distant stands.

Once I saw Charlie Ruffing of the Yankees fan him twice in a row and the next two times at bat Hank drove the ball out of the park. I saw Joe DiMaggio rob him of a homer when he nabbed a 450-foot Greenberg drive. Yet later in the game Hank drove in the winning Tiger run.

To those men who were in the Army, baseball meant a lot because it was a symbol of home. When, in 1945, I found myself in Ceylon, serving with the Air Force, I listened to every World Series game on the radio. And when the boys got together and heard that Hank Greenberg was still walloping homers, they felt better because they knew that "home" was still the same. Greenberg was part of American life and a significant part of the national game.

*H.U.R.

AL ROSEN AND HIS STANCE

Al Rosen

Indian Chief

Of the many outstanding Jewish baseball headliners in the long history of the national game, few have ranked with the superstars of the sport. But in the winter of 1953 there occurred an event which indicated that a Jewish diamond ace named Al Rosen had the potentialities of becoming a legend in the game. On November 27, 1953 the American League announced that Al Rosen, slugging third baseman for the Cleveland Indians, had been named its most valuable player for 1953.

Other athletes had won a similar honor, so there was nothing extraordinary about the announcement. What made it remarkable was that all twenty-four members of the Baseball Writers Association, three from each American League city, had listed Rosen as the best player of the year. It was an unprecedented unanimous vote. Rosen received 336 points, highest in history — and in winning the award saw himself lifted to the ranks of the great players of his time.

It was no wonder that Rosen had been acclaimed in this fashion. He led the circuit with home runs — blasting forty-three; was first in runs batted in with 145 and missed winning the batting championship of the league by the proverbial hair. Casey Stengel, manager of the New York Yankees, called Rosen a great player. Marty Marion, once a slick major league shortstop, said that "As far as I'm concerned I have yet to see a better clutch hitter." Harry Brecheen, an astute veteran of the game, who had pitched successfully in both major leagues, said of Rosen, "He's the best hitter in the American League." After a pause, he added, "And there's none better in the other league." He amplified: "Rosen has no real weakness. Even when you get him out he usually hits the ball hard. I'd rather face any other player than Rosen in a clutch spot."

A former major leaguer named Buddy Blattner, who became a sports announcer, paid his tribute in this fashion: "If I wanted to try to teach a youngster how to hit I'd tell him to watch Rosen, day after day. Rosen has become a picture book hitter. Watch how he cradles the bat and how he never commits himself to the pitcher . . . and see how smart he is. He has very strong arms and quick wrists, yet he isn't afraid to choke up on his bat and make his stroke more flexible."

During the 1953 season, when Rosen was roaring along, leading the league in practically everything, he heard nothing but chimes of praise. His manager, Al Lopez, said "What I like about Al most of all is his determination. After a pitcher gets him out he'll come back to the bench and say, 'I'll get him next time.' And, by golly, he does. To him, each pitcher is a personal challenge."

Yet Rosen's rise was neither rapid nor expected. He was not the super-athlete all his life long. Instead, the peak he reached in 1953 was a tribute to his courage and his determination rather than to his innate ability. Blattner's remarks on Rosen's beautiful stance, Stengel's grim concession that Rosen was the best player in the game, and the chorus of applause from players and fans alike were the fruit of much hard labor. Rosen, like Hank Greenberg, had more ambitious spirit than skill and his emergence as a star proved that the will to succeed is often more compelling than any other element in sports.

Rosen had said that "everything about this game is a challenge to me. I don't want to accept mediocrity. I want to be as good as I possibly can in every phase of the game." Thus he concentrated on running and on fielding, as well as batting. A former teammate of his, Hank Bauer, who won headlines as a Yankee star, said, after watching Rosen perform in the majors, "The change in Rosen's fielding is amazing. I roomed with him at Kansas City and even Flip will admit he was a poor fielder in those days. Now the guy is polished. If you had seen him before, you wouldn't believe it's the same person."

The manner in which Rosen became a polished fielder was typical of his approach to the game. In the spring of 1952, the Cleveland Indians held a pre-season camp for rookies at Daytona Beach. Only the eager youngsters were expected, not the stars of the team. Nevertheless, one morning Rosen appeared as Hank Greenberg and Al Lopez were at the batting cage.

"You don't have to be there," Greenberg told Rosen.

"I know I don't," Rosen replied, "But I can use this time to work on what's bothering me."

"Go ahead," Greenberg said, "You might as well take your swings," thinking that, like all hitters, Rosen could hardly wait to get a bat in his hands. But Rosen was taking the long view. He had already improved with the bat. "That can wait," he replied. "There are some things I've got to do at third base first."

And Rosen, called "Flip" by his mates, practiced in the broiling sun with the Indian coaches and, in time, his work paid off. Between 1952 and 1953 he was the most improved man in the game — and that difference made him the best player in baseball in 1953. He lost the batting crown to Mickey Vernon by .001 of a percentage point, .336 to .337, but swept honors in homers, runs batted in and slugging (his percentage in this department was .613; Vernon's .518).

Even in the matter of batting, the story went beyond the statistics. Rosen refused to play ball on the High Holy Days. Had he done so, he might easily have made a few hits and, at season's end, attained a fatter average than Vernon. That, however, was only part of it. Going into the last day of the 1953 season, Rosen and Vernon were waging a close fight for the batting title. Rosen was aiming for the coveted triple championship: homers, runs batted in and batting. Two of the three already were his. He had only to beat out Vernon to make the sweep. But Rosen missed two ways: by a close play at first base and by the lack of sportsmanship of the teammates of Mickey Vernon.

This was how Arthur Daley of the *New York Times* described it (and it was told in substantially the same fashion by the correspondent for the *Sporting News*):

"It happened in Al's final time at bat. The prematurely gray-haired Clevelander dribbled a slow grounder to Gerry Priddy and scampered down the line toward first. He made a frantic lunge toward the bag. His foot fell inches short and he had to make a mincing half-step with his other foot to make it.

" 'You're out!' barked Umpire Hank Soar. The throw

from Priddy had beaten Rosen in the fraction it took him to switch steps.

"Down in Washington, meanwhile, Vernon was striving earnestly to hold fast to his lead. The Cleveland game finished ahead of the Washington game and Washington writers flashed word to the bench that Vernon was home free if he didn't get up to bat again.

" 'I was wondering if I should bench you, Mickey,' began Manager Bucky Harris. But he stopped and sighed. 'But I guess you wouldn't want to win the championship that way. Go ahead. And good luck.'

"That's when the Washington conspirators took over. Being good at arithmetic, they figured that Vernon would not get to bat if none of them reached base. Two were forgetful but they speedily made amends.

"Mickey Grasso, for instance, doubled in the eighth inning. So he promptly took so big a lead that the enemy pitcher couldn't resist. He picked Mickey off the bag. In the ninth, Kite Thomas, a pinch-hitter, singled, but compensated for it by trying to stretch a stretchless hit into a double. He was thrown out by a mile. Eddie Yost, possessed of the sharpest batting eye in the league, popped out by hitting a ball a foot over his head. Pete Runnels struck out and Vernon, who would have been the next hitter, never did get to bat."

That was Arthur Daley's account. The Associated Press, in another version, said that Rosen, in his race to the bag in his last time at bat, made it so close that "Most of the 9,579 fans thought Rosen was safe." Rosen himself declared, "I missed the bag. I had to take an extra step, and that did it. Soar called it right, and I'm glad he did. I don't want any gifts. Why, I wouldn't sleep at night all winter if I won the batting championship on a call I knew was wrong." Not only was this sportsmanship of the highest order; Rosen also played his heart out in that final game. In the first inning he singled, in the third, he doubled and in the seventh he bunted safely for a third hit, raising his average to .3355. If he had been safe on the final play (or Vernon would have come to bat and missed hitting safely), Al would have been the triple champ.

Still, his brilliant season did not go into the discard. The fans and the reporters knew that Rosen was top man of the game, and voted him just that.

Typical of the kind of ball Rosen played in 1953 were these games, chosen nearly at random. On August 21, 1953, in a double-header against the Browns, Al hit three home runs, driving in seven runs, helping his mates to two wins. His homer in the second game came with one man on base. The Indians won the game by a score of 3-2. On September 9, 1953, Rosen's fortieth home run of the year came in Boston against the Red Sox. It was a scoreless tie going into the top of the eighth inning, in a duel between Mike Garcia and Bill Henry. In that frame, Bill Glynn drew a base on balls. Rosen strode to the plate two batters later and lashed the game-winning homer off the left field light tower. In the final inning the Red Sox scored a run. Final tally: Indians the winners, 2-1. When Rosen hit homers forty-two and forty-three on September 25, 1953 against the Detroit Tigers, he broke a club record of forty-two originally set by Hal Trosky, and drove in four runs in the bargain, leading his mates to an overwhelming 12-3 victory.

That is why Al Rosen was the player of 1953.

As Milton Gross of the *New York Post* phrased it, in discussing the award Rosen won: "Against the background of provincialism usually shown in this voting, the landslide not only is unprecedented, but the most sincere sort of testimonial to the prematurely graying twenty-eight year old after only four full seasons of big league baseball."

The major league years, curiously enough, were the easy ones for Al Rosen. It was his fight up the ladder which was difficult for him. His sports career, like most others, had its ups and downs. His were rather complicated, however. Al was born on March 1, 1925, in Spartanburg, South Carolina. His mother and father were divorced when Al was a child and Al and his brother Jerry were brought up by the mother, who worked as a saleslady in a dress shop to support her family. While she worked, the boys' grandmother, Mrs. Gertrude Levine, originally from Poland, looked after them. Al's mother, unlike many Jewish mothers, encouraged her children to indulge in sports. When Al suffered from violent asthma attacks, his mother heeded the advice of the doctor that he be allowed to play outdoors as much and as long as possible.

His mother told Harry T. Paxton, who wrote an intriguing story about Al Rosen for the *Saturday Evening Post,* that "when he was little, I'd watch him playing with the other boys, gasping as if each breath would be his last. His grandmother was afraid he was going to drop dead on the spot. But he never would stop playing. He had those attacks from the time he was a year old until he was about sixteen, and finally cured himself."

The Rosen family had settled in Miami, Florida and Al was about fourteen when he was attached to a baseball school, which his grandmother permitted him to join. It was not a very happy experience, but Al's determination was already in evidence. He even earned some money playing semi-professional softball. When he was in Miami High School he became a pretty good player, winning a job at third base and being named to the all-city team.

That summer, the recreation director of the city of Miami asked Al if he would like to attend military school. Al was thrilled by the offer. He was accepted — with a full scholarship — at Florida Military Academy. At the school, Rosen was a four-sport man, excelling at football, basketball, boxing and baseball. He won the middleweight championship in the Florida high school tournament, but never gave professional boxing any serious thought. Baseball was his real love. At sixteen, he obtained a tryout with the Cleveland Indian Class A farm team at Wilkes-Barre. He did not show enough to stick with that team, but received an offer to play with Thomasville, a Class D Club in the North Carolina State League, at the munificent sum of seventy-five dollars a month. He was rather shocked at the small sum and decided to get some advanced schooling. He entered the University of Florida and later the University of Miami. In time, between baseball seasons, he continued to attend classes and managed to earn his degree.

With his characteristic aggressive determination, Rosen became an all-around college sports star. He played end on the football team, won the state intercollegiate boxing championship, and picked up his nickname "Flip" because of his talent in scoring with a basketball.

But in 1942, he thought once again of playing baseball. He connected himself with the Red Sox farm system, was eventually told he would never make a ball player, made contact again with Thomasville and there started his professional career. One day, however, that career nearly came to an abrupt finish. The manager said to him that he was planning to drop him. Rosen, amazed, asked why. The manager gave it to him straight. "I'll stick with anybody as long as he puts out, but you aren't putting out any more." Rosen begged for another chance, and got it. Years later he said, "Believe me, I know now that the real ball players are always hustlers. I've hustled ever since."

The war came and Rosen served in the U. S. Navy, emerging in 1946 as a full lieutenant. He returned to the Cleveland chain system, and moved around a great deal. He performed with Pittsfield, Mass., with Oklahoma City and with Kansas City. He hit with all these clubs, and with power. In 1947 he nearly tore open the Texas League when he starred with Oklahoma City. At one time, he hit seven doubles in a row and ended the year batting .349, being named the best player of the league. This won him a 1948 trial with the parent Indian club, but he did badly in the spring and was shipped to Kansas City. There he batted .327, hit twenty-five home runs and was voted the rookie of the year. In one game he got four hits in five times at bat. The last three were home runs. He drove in seven runs in that game. The very next night he hit two more home runs in his first two trips to the plate and a double later in the game, a hit which narrowly missed being another round-tripper. He drove in six runs, making it thirteen for two games. He naturally earned another Cleveland shot, but was unable to beat out the veteran Ken Keltner. He managed to get into twenty-odd games and hit practically nothing. This time, he was sent to the San Diego team in the Pacific Coast League. There, too, he blasted the ball well.

But when he came up to the Indians for his third attempt

in 1950, it appeared that this would be his last chance to make the big league grade. In spring training, Keltner showed that the years had caught up with him. But Lou Boudreau, the Indian manager, wanted to keep Keltner on the bag, hoping his aged legs would warm up in the sun. The Cleveland general manager, Hank Greenberg, argued Lou into giving Rosen a chance. He said that Al was ready. Perhaps Greenberg remembered how he was ready with the Tigers and Bucky Harris, then the Detroit manager, insisted on going along with the fancy-fielding Harry Davis at first base. In any case, Al was given his opportunity.

On opening day, before 65,744 Cleveland fans — a hard, tough bunch of baseball followers — Rosen came up in the eighth inning with a man on base and his club trailing, 6-4. He hit a home run to tie the score. He slipped soon thereafter, but then perked up again, hitting eight home runs in the first month of the season. Later, as the season progressed, Rosen gained confidence in himself and let his bat do his talking. By July 4 he had twenty-five home runs, an astonishing total for a rookie. In one stretch, he hit six home runs in eight games and then seven in another streak of nine games. But he was now a major cog in the Indian machine, and there was little doubt that his minor league record as a hitter was an authenic indication of his skills with the bat.

His thirty-seven home runs, and his 116 runs batted in made him the slugging king of the league, although he did not attain a mark of .300. In 1951, as in his first year, he drove in more than 100 runs, but his average slipped to .265 and his homers to twenty-four. In 1952 he was back in stride, batting .302, hitting twenty-eight home runs, and driving in 105 runs. He became known not only for his averages but his spirit.

Though a strong man, the big third baseman was no stranger to injury, and an accident ultimately shortened his brilliant career. One May day in 1954, with a baserunner screening his view of the ball, a hard line drive crashed into the fingers of his right hand. Unwilling to stay out of the lineup for long, he returned before the hand had fully recovered. Each time he hit an inside pitch, the contact further damaged the index finger. The injury never did heal, and today Rosen retains only half the use of that finger. But the fierce competitive nature of the man was such that in the 1954 All-Star game, with his right index finger stiff and useless, Rosen smashed consecutive home runs, and drove home five runs to lead his team to an 11-9 victory.

Al continued to perform well, with blazing spirit and with a hot bat. But during the 1956 season he slowed up considerably because of his physical pains. As the season was ending, Hank Greenberg stated that "I think he would be better off playing with another team." Rosen's reaction to the statement was, "I'm just a ball player. If those are his feelings then they're his feelings. He has a right to his own opinion."

This was a cruel twist to an unusual story. Al Rosen had been an enormous star for the Indians, appreciated by his foes on the field more than by anyone else. In 1956, however, the fans of Cleveland — famous for their violence generally — got "on" Al, and once they reacted in a disgraceful manner. Rosen had made a try for a difficult infield grounder, stumbled and hurt himself. As he lay on the ground, in agony, the fans cheered his misfortune.

Shocked, Al Lopez, the team manager, blew up and said that the Indian fans did not deserve to have a big league team. This act of theirs was the beginning of the campaign against Rosen in Cleveland.

Rosen chose his own way out. He quit baseball and said, "I've seen other players get to the end of the line with nothing in mind for the future. I didn't want that to happen to me." And it didn't, as he joined the investment house of Bache & Co., where he became a successful securities executive, and later a top executive with the New York Yankees and then the Houston Astros.

Rosen always was a fierce competitor, and friends of his continually stressed his willingness to take on foes of all sorts. Tim Cohane, writing in *Look* magazine, once said, "An opponent, now friendly with Rosen, slurred Al's religion — Al's a Jew. Rosen dropped his bat, stalked to the enemy dugout, invited the fellow under the stands — and everybody else who wanted to come along. Trouble was averted when a couple of the fellow's teammates, just as incensed as Rosen at the off-base crack, advised the offender to stow that stuff."

In 1951, the popular New York columnist and television star Ed Sullivan wrote that "Al Rosen, Cleveland third baseman, is a native of Miami, Fla. Of Jewish parentage, he is Catholic. At the plate, you'll notice he makes the sign of the cross with his bat."

Rosen entered a bitter denial of that story. He said that ever since he had been a kid he made an "x" mark on the plate before stepping up to bat, a superstitious gesture not uncommon to many players. He asked for a retraction of the Sullivan statement and insisted that he was a proud Jew. He told this writer that "I have belonged to a synagogue for most of my life." When Rosen was the recipient of a Bible from a Philadelphia congregation, he accepted it with humility and with pride and said as much in a telegram to the members of the congregation.

In an expressive interview with writer Roger Kahn in Kahn's excellent book *How the Weather Was,* Rosen explained that he first took boxing lessons in the gyms of his youth so that he would be able to defend himself against the anti-Semitic remarks that so often came to the athletic "Jewboy."

"I wanted to learn how to end things," he remarked tersely. "That was important. I wasn't starting trouble in those days, but when it came to me, I wanted to end it, and damn quick."

Once, when he went out for football at a Miami high school, the coach was curious as to why he had come out for the violent sport. When Rosen replied that he loved to play the game, the coach told him, "Rosen, you're different from most Jews. Most Jewboys are afraid of contact."

All of his career, Rosen fought against that image of the timid Jew. He observed to Kahn that when he was struggling to work his way up through the minor leagues, he sometimes wished his name was one less Jewish than Rosen. But once established as a star, he wished his name were more Jewish, "perhaps Rosenthal or Rosenstein," Kahn writes. "He wanted to make sure that there was no mistake about what he was."

Kahn then reflects that "One suspects that even now, as parent, businessman and tennis player, he would react to an anti-Semitic remark by shedding the tweed jacket, along with the broker's manner, and punching hard, to end it fast, the way he used to in Miami, Florida, so that whoever started this, and whoever was observing, would remember, next time they were inclined to pick on a Jew."

The career of Al Rosen, like that of Hank Greenberg, was created by hard work, for few things came to him without difficulty. Like Greenberg, Rosen overcame his flaws and developed into one of the finest stars of the game.

Moreover, his awareness of the name he bears and the faith he carries has made him a proudly self-aware American Jewish athlete. "When I was up there in the majors," the big slugger told Kahn, "I always knew how I wanted it to be about me.

"I wanted it to be, Here comes one Jewish kid that every Jew in the world can be proud of."

In the summer of 1980, Rosen was inducted into the Jewish Sports Hall of Fame in Beverly Hills, and told the audience what already had become typical of his thinking, "At no time have I been so deeply moved as I have been this evening to be recognized a Jew by Jews."

MOE BERG, BACKSTOPPING

Moe Berg

Diamond Scholar

One of the most fundamental attractions of sports are the personalities that get involved in the various games. In a very basic way, the endeavor of professional sport reduces all men to competing on terms of natural equality. A white second baseman from the Deep South can turn the double play with a black shortstop, and both men gain an understanding and a mutual respect new to both of them. A shy country hick like Mickey Mantle can become fast friends with a slick city sharpie like Whitey Ford, though the two might have never met were their talents not joined on the Yankee team.

Avid sports fans obtain rich enjoyment from the differentness of their athletic heroes. Devotees of the great New York Knickerbocker basketball team of 1969-73 delighted in the fact that the stars were so different in temperament and background: the muscular stockbroker DeBusschere, the stylish black clotheshorse Frazier, the studious Rhodes Scholar Bradley, the Louisiana country boy Reed. Yet all these men, once on the court, blended into a single, smoothly functioning unit of precision and intelligence.

The history of sports includes a great number of striking figures and unusual personalities, several notable for standing out in their chosen world. Gene Tunney was an intellectual who quoted Shakespeare in a sport, boxing, which was filled with tough, semi-literate brawlers, many with criminal records, who would probably assume that Lord Byron was the name of a contending fighter. (When asked what he thought of Shakespeare, Two-Ton Tony Galento replied, "I'll murder the bum.") Bill Bradley, the Princetonian banker's son from the Midwest, was a source of curiosity to his fellow basketball players, most of whom were products of the urban black slums.

In virtually every sport, there have been several outstanding personalities, men who seemed unlikely candidates as professional athletes. But no man in the history of any sport was as unusual a phenomenon as Moe Berg, a major league catcher in the years before and after the second world war. In a sport where men with any kind of advanced education were relatively rare, Berg was an intellectual giant by any standards. His education included degrees from Princeton, Columbia and the Sorbonne. He was a successful lawyer and businessman. As a radio personality, he became famous for his ability to answer obscure questions on any subject. A master of some dozen languages, including Latin and Sanskrit, he was a brilliant linguist of international renown who made phonetic and scholarly contributions to Japanese and other languages. And in recent years, the fact has emerged that before and after the war, he was America's top atomic spy, playing a major role in the counterintelligence that helped the allies win the war.

Born in New York at the turn of the century to Russian immigrant parents, Moe startled his family by being interested in baseball from the very beginning. "Moe was simply a genetic deviant," says his brother Sam, himself a doctor. "The Berg family tree shows it produced about twenty-five doctors in North and South America during the first half of this century, but Moe didn't like the sight of blood. Ever since he was two years old it was 'Hey, Sam, let's catch.' It could be a ball, an orange, anything."

After graduating from Barrington High School of Newark at the top of his class (his family had moved to Newark, where his father was a pharmacist), Moe was accepted at Princeton University, an extraordinary achievement at that time for a poor Jewish boy. He rapidly became a famous figure on that campus: both as a marvelous linguistic scholar who spoke numerous languages fluently, and as the star shortstop for the baseball team. The Princeton nine was so good that in Moe's junior year, they played an exhibition game at the Polo Grounds against the world champion New York Giants, and the Giants were lucky to win, 3-2, coming from behind in the last of the ninth.

In his senior year, Moe hit .337 and led the team to a record eighteen straight wins. The *Princeton Alumni Weekly* characterizes his play this way: "He was slow and lacked hitting power but had a slingshot arm and an ability to hit in the clutch."

A Princeton classmate named Crossan Cooper, who played second base on the team, also studied Latin in Moe's class. The two often bewildered their opponents by communicating with each other on the ballfield in that ancient tongue. "Moe and I would shout 'your turn' or 'my turn' in Latin so that the other side would not know which of us was going to cover second base on a given play. Of course, we assumed the first base coach for the other side didn't understand Latin," Cooper recalls to Kaufman,

Fitzgerald and Sewell, the co-authors of *Moe Berg: Athlete, Scholar, Spy,* a study of Moe's life.

Moe graduated *magna cum laude,* and received votes in his class poll for the "Most Brilliant" member of the class. Although Princeton offered him a teaching post in the Romance Languages, Moe wanted to go to Paris to study experimental phonetics at the Sorbonne, but he did not have the necessary funds. Baseball also beckoned: he was offered a contract by the Brooklyn Dodgers. Uncertain what to do, he sought advice from his Princeton coach, Bill Clarke, who pointed out to him that the money he got for playing ball would pay for his courses at the Sorbonne when he took them in the off-season. Still unsure that he could last long in the major leagues, Berg spoke to Dutch Carter, a successful lawyer who had been a legendary hurler at Yale.

"Take the baseball career," advised Dutch, according to Arthur Daley's account in the *New York Times.* "The rest can wait. When I was your age I had a chance to pitch in the National League. But my family looked down on professional sports and vehemently opposed my accepting. I've always been sorry I listened to them, because it made me a frustrated man. Don't you become frustrated. At least give it a try."

So Moe decided to give baseball a whirl, and joined the Dodgers immediately. In his first major league at-bat, he singled to drive in a run against Philadelphia. He played with Brooklyn for the rest of the season, fielding beautifully at shortstop but hitting rarely. Actually, Moe's shortcomings at bat were responsible for one of the classic remarks in baseball history. A scout named Mike Gonzales, told to wire a report on the young infielder, had sent the deathless four-word message: "Good field, no hit." It was a reputation that Moe carried with him for the rest of his career.

In the off-season he went to Paris; when he returned he spent the next two seasons in the minors, having a great year in the International League in 1926, when he hit .311 and drove in one hundred and twenty-four runs. He was called up to the Chicago White Sox, and arranged his schedule so that he could attend Columbia Law School when he wasn't playing ball. Despite his hectic schedule in pursuing both vocations as well as linguistics, Moe went on to place second at Columbia in a class of more than a thousand students.

For most of the 1927 season, Moe rode the bench with the White Sox, seeing limited action at short. But then came a day in August that was to alter his entire career. In a series against Philadelphia, the first and second string Chicago catchers had been injured in successive games. Now, playing in Boston, the White Sox faced disaster when their last backstop, Harry McCurdy, was hurt in the fifth inning. Player-manager Ray Schalk, himself one of the injured catchers, roared on the bench in confusion and disbelief, and ordered his road secretary to "get us a catcher, quick!"

Berg turned calmly to his distraught skipper and said, "What do you mean, get a catcher, we have a catcher on this bench."

Schalk whirled on the youngster. "Okay," he snarled, "get in and catch, wise guy."

"The funny thing is," Berg mused later in recalling the incident, "that when I said we had a catcher, I didn't mean myself. Earl Sheely, a first baseman, was a pretty good backstop and I had him in mind."

But as it was, Moe, eager for a chance to play, hustled out to the field and donned "the tools of ignorance," as catcher's equipment is sardonically known. He did astonishingly well for the rest of the game, although his first throw to second base got wedged between the bag and the ground. When he returned to the dugout, his mates needled him, explaining that the ball is meant to be thrown above the base. "Now you tell me," Moe deadpanned.

Chicago's next game was in New York against the mighty Yankees, and White Sox ace Ted Lyons asked for Berg behind the plate. When Babe Ruth, who became a good friend of Moe's, came to bat for the first time, he glanced down at the neophyte catcher and assured him that he'd be the fourth wounded White Sox catcher by the fifth inning. "That's all right," Moe responded, "I'll only call for inside pitches, and we'll keep each other company at the hospital." They both laughed, and Moe proceeded to catch an excellent game. He had found his natural position, and he never again returned to the infield, becoming one of the best defensive catchers in baseball.

"I'm elated over becoming a catcher," Berg confessed. "Being allowed to catch is the best break I've ever had. I'm not fast on my feet and my arm has saved me lots of times as an infielder. I've never been able to stay in the lineup long enough to develop as a hitter."

Casey Stengel offers this evaluation: "Now, I'll tell ya. I mean Moe Berg was as smart a ballplayer as ever come along. Knew his legs wouldn't cooperate in the infield and when the catching job opened up he grabs a mask and there he was. Guy never caught in his life and then goes behind the plate like Mickey Cochrane. Now that's something."

Ted Lyons, Moe's lifelong friend, accounts for some of Moe's success in his new position: "He had good reactions and a strong arm and great hands. His signal calling was flawless and in the years he was to catch me I never waved off a sign; few pitchers did. He became clinical in studying batters, knew their weaknesses and strengths. He took full advantage of this and pitchers simply felt confident with Moe doing the catching. And his shortstop experience showed behind the plate. No catcher could pick up short hops like Moe could."

While he became a shrewd and accomplished backstop, Moe still struggled at the plate. One day, after Berg trudged back to the dugout after another strikeout, a teammate and fellow catcher Buck Crouse drawled, "Moe, I don't care how many of them college degrees you got, they ain't learned you to hit that curve ball no better than the rest of us."

Still, Moe hung in and worked hard at improving. In the 1929 season, he reached the peak of his career. He led all catchers defensively, making only seven errors all season. His improved hitting earned him a thoroughly respectable .287 batting average. He even received votes for Most Valuable Player and was considered to be the best at his position except for the great Bill Dickey himself.

But in spring training the next season, a serious injury crippled all the bright promise of his career. Hustling into a base, Moe's spikes caught and the ligaments in his right knee were ruptured badly. He realized that he would never again be able to approach the standards he had set in 1929. But with intelligence and application, he continued to be one of the truly valued catchers in the league. Over the next years, he was traded to Cleveland, then went to Washington and Boston; and he was welcome wherever he went. He always played the game with enthusiasm, no matter how rarely he was put in. He became a legend in the bullpens around the league: he would not only help develop young pitchers and catchers, but keep them spellbound with tales of travel, history and women from all over the world.

He contributed on the ballfield in every way he could. As a part-time catcher, he went four seasons (1930-33) without making an error. When he joined Washington in 1932, manager Joe Cronin put him into seventy-five games, and Moe came through with several clutch hits as well as a steadying influence on the young pitchers. One of the key hits he had, which won an extra-innings game against the White Sox, was against his old buddy, Ted Lyons. Ted chased Moe into the Washington locker rooms. "He was doubled up with laughter," Lyons remembers fondly. "I gave him a couple of friendly punches. I said, 'Why'd you have to pick on me? You haven't had a hit in twenty years.' I told him he would have to pay for dinner that night."

In 1933, Berg realized the dream of every ballplayer when he played on a pennant-winning team. The Senators upset the powerful Yankees and won the championship of the American League, though they lost the series to the Giants.

Moe's fame as a person and as a ballplayer already extended well past the shores of his native America. In 1932, he went on a tour of baseball-mad Japan with Lyons and slugger Lefty O'Doul. They gave baseball clinics to enthusiastic Japanese players, while Moe astonished the delighted Japanese with his knowledge of their language. Though he declined an invitation to lecture at the University of Osaka, he did teach a Japanese waitress to tell O'Doul, in English, "You're a lousy hitter and lucky to be a major leaguer."

During his long major league career, Moe Berg anecdotes abounded through the sport. Reporters loved him because he was always "good copy" for their stories; and his unlettered colleagues on the field were equally fond of the Princeton scholar. Berg himself appreciated being treated as an equal, and never looked down upon his uneducated companions. "In baseball," he said, "a player stands on his own feet, and the fact that he can talk in five or six languages avails him nothing when he is up there at the plate with the bases filled and two out."

Stengel, in his inimitable style, put it this way: "It was amazing how he got all that knowledge and used all them penetrating words, but he never put on too strong. They thought he was like me, you know, a bit eccentric. He was very well liked."

Always fascinated by the origins of names, Moe would sometimes tell a teammate things the man didn't know about his own history. "Costello, you're an Irishman now but you weren't always Irish," Moe would say. "You were Spanish until Drake beat the Spanish Armada in 1588." With his phenomenal ear for dialects, Moe could identify a speaker's home town just by listening to him talk. Kaufman, Fitzgerald and Sewell describe incidents where stunned onlookers saw Berg correctly identify strangers as being from Marseilles, France and Coffeyville, Kansas.

One day, one of Moe's Washington teammates, an uneducated but power-hitting outfielder named Sheriff Harris, showed up in the hotel lobby looking pained. According to columnist Larry Merchant in the *New York Post,* when Moe asked what the trouble was and told Harris to stick out his tongue, "Harris did, of course, because for all anyone knew Berg had a degree in medicine too."

"You have a touch of intestinal fortitude," Berg diagnosed. "Go upstairs to your room, take it easy, don't eat anything heavy and you'll be fine." The next day, Harris appeared again in front of Berg; this time, the outfielder looked much healthier. "It worked," he reported to the amused Moe. "I got rid of that intestinal fortitude."

Another time, Al Schacht, the Washington third-base coach who was a friend of Moe's, took over the team while Cronin was absent. Al put Moe in to catch the first game of a double-header, although Berg had been doing very little playing for a while. Then, according to Schacht:

"We win 6-5 and he's beat, and I have to start him in the second game because of injuries. We have a big argument over it but he goes out and plays. By the fifth inning he can hardly get off his haunches, he's so tired. It's really hot. Then the pitcher and the batter, Whitehill and Cramer, have a staring contest — on the mound, out of the batter's box, in the batter's box, off the mound. Four or five times. It's killing Berg. Finally he takes off his mask and his chest protector, puts them on home plate, walks back to the dugout and says, 'That's it. I'm going in for a shower.'

" 'Here's your shower,' I say, and I throw a bucket of water on him. Then I tell him about injuries and he says, '*Now* you tell me.' He goes back and Whitehill is laughing so hard he throws a wild pitch on the first pitch. Berg just sits there and says to him, '*You* get it.' "

Later on, when Berg, Schacht and Cronin were all with

the Red Sox, Cronin one day called for a pitcher named Jack Wilson to be summoned from the bullpen to bail out his faltering starter. Schacht informed Cronin that Wilson was unavailable. When Cronin inquired what his coach was talking about, Schacht explained that Berg, spinning another of his famous tales, had Wilson somewhere in Russia at the moment, and the pitcher couldn't leave the place without a passport.

In another well-documented incident, the team bus once got lost on side roads after exhibition games in the Deep South. Night had fallen, and the driver was lost, the players helpless. Moe got outside, studied the stars in their constellations for a moment, and then informed the driver that he was heading in the wrong direction. When Moe told the driver precisely which way to head, the startled driver asked how he knew. "So say the stars," was the catcher's reply. Moe and the stars, naturally, turned out to be accurate.

Moe's legendary intellectual accomplishments, well-known to the baseball world, received national attention when, in February of 1938, he was persuaded to make a guest appearance on "Information Please," a popular radio show on which panelists answered questions on any number of esoteric subjects. Moe amazed all of America with the depth and breadth of his knowledge, and shattered the image of the universally dumb ballplayer. He was a sensational success. Tens of thousands of calls poured into the show's offices, as people asked who this extraordinary fellow could be. Moe was urged to make a second appearance in April, which he did; he was, if anything, even more of a hit.

In a final effort to stump baseball's resident genius, a

group of reporters got together and prepared a list of questions. Berg agreed to this one last round of queries, and was asked to identify the Seven Sleepers, the Seven Wise Masters, the Seven Wise Men, the Seven Wonders of the World and the Seven Stars. Moe fully and correctly identified all of them, and added that it was really impossible to know the true number of stars in the Seven Stars, as the Pleiades, or Pleiads in the constellation of Taurus were bunched too closely together for anyone to tell how many there were.

In a final effort, the reporters asked Moe to identify the Black Napoleon, the modern Hannibal, Poppea Sabina and Calamity Jane. He did, flawlessly.

Moe was now a national celebrity, with admirers from one end of the country to another. The *New York Times* even took out an advertisement in which they pointed out that one day in Detroit, when the paper had been late to arrive, Berg's newsboy had brought him the *Times* in the Red Sox dugout. The incident gave rise to more anecdotes and cartoons.

Even while constantly furthering his intellectual pursuits, Berg was always doing his best as a ballplayer in the game he loved. When he joined the Red Sox in 1935, he played as a part-time catcher and hit .286. "Moe lived up to every expectation," said Joe Cronin, the manager. Tom Yawkey, owner of the Red Sox, insisted that Moe "had a tremendous impact on our players," and called his acquisition one of the best moves the Red Sox ever made.

In the 1939 season, Moe showed the sharpness of his baseball judgment by insisting to reporters that Boston rookie Ted Williams, who seemed like a brash busher to many, was destined to be a great player. "They call him screwy," said Moe. "Well, he isn't any screwier than a college sophomore, or any kid of 20. And he asks more sensible questions than most kids coming up. He's always eager to learn something.

"A little while ago, for instance, he came over to me and said, what will Ruffing throw with two strikes and no balls on a left-handed batter? How does his fastball break? Questions like that."

Moe was, of course, right, as Ted Williams became the greatest hitter of his time. But according to sports writer John Lardner, the veteran catcher and the cocky rookie did not hit it off at first sight. Lardner wrote in the *Newark News:*

"Moe Berg, the scholarly catcher, picked a conversation with Williams one day.

" 'So you come from San Diego, eh, young man?' said Mr. Berg, who, if he pooled his information with Einstein's, would have all but about 2 per cent of the information there is.

" 'So what?' said Mr. Williams suspiciously.

" 'San Diego,' mused Mr. Berg. 'County seat of San Diego County, about 15 miles north of the Mexican border. An excellent harbor. Largest naval and marine base west of Chicago."

"Mr. Williams made a dive for Mr. Berg. The strong arms of his teammates caught him in time and held him back as he yelled, "Lemme at him! I'll tear him apart!"

" 'What's the trouble?' the boys asked Theodore.

" 'He can't knock my home town,' "snarled Mr. Williams, and continued to gnash his teeth.

Later on, Williams grew to admire and like Moe. He referred to Berg's "special uniqueness" and "real man's guts," and tells of the time Moe slammed one of his rare hits and, returning to the bench, told the slugging Williams, "That's the way you're supposed to hit them, Ted. I hope you were watching."

1939 turned out to be Moe's last year in the major leagues as a player. On the rare occasions that he would be summoned to catch, he would hustle in from the bullpen and don the catcher's gear to the delighted applause of his teammates in the dugout. Sometimes he would amble over to his teammates and ask in a confidential tone, "Gentlemen, does everyone still get three strikes out there?"

Moe ended the season with a .273 average, giving him a lifetime mark of .243. In the last game he ever played, against Detroit, Moe slammed a home run; it was only the sixth of his whole major league total. Still, despite his struggles at the plate, Moe's defensive ability, hustle, intelligence and popularity had enabled him to be a major league ballplayer for sixteen years, an exceptionally long career.

Among the admirers of the intellectual catcher was a Red Sox bat boy who was destined to become better known in future years as the President of the United States. According to Ethel Berg, Moe's sister, in her book *My Brother Morris Berg: The Real Moe,* John Kennedy "spoke with Moe every time the team was at home, Fenway Park. They both met often even through the years in the White House."

Kennedy was hardly Moe's first acquaintance in government circles; but it wasn't for many years later that the public knew the extent of his work for the government. In 1934, he had visited Japan for the second time, this time as part of a barnstorming team of major league all-stars that included the likes of Babe Ruth, Lou Gehrig, Lefty Gomez and Charlie Gehringer. But Moe Berg was the only man on the team who carried with him a letter of introduction from Secretary of State Cordell Hull; and unknown to anyone in Japan, including his teammates, Moe was engaged in undercover work for the U.S. government. One of the most popular members of the enormously idolized American band, Moe was a guest speaker at Meiji University, where his eloquent speech was delivered in Japanese; but on another day, while his mates were playing ball, Berg skipped the game and took carefully selected pictures of Tokyo from the top of one of the city's tallest buildings, a hospital where he was ostensibly visiting an American mother who had just given birth. Berg never met the woman he had supposedly come to see, but his photographs were later among the chief ones used by Gen. Jimmy Doolittle's pilots in their attack on the Japanese mainland in 1942.

After his retirement in 1939, Moe spent two years as a coach with the Red Sox; but by 1941, the war that he had foreseen so clearly had arrived, and he felt an obligation to help his country in any way he could. "All over the continent men and women are dying," he told Arthur Daley of the *Times*. "Soon we, too, will be involved. And what am I doing? Sitting in the bullpen telling stories to the relief pitchers."

Not for long, though. When the season was over, Moe accepted a request from Nelson Rockefeller, the Coordinator of Inter-American Affairs, that Berg become a Goodwill Ambassador to Latin America. The papers, as might be expected, played up the story with enthusiasm.

"Berg without a doubt is the most remarkable man baseball has ever known," Frank Graham wrote. Tom Meany asserted that "Berg is destined to do a great job for his country. When the final victory of the United Nations is achieved, I venture that Moe's contribution will outweigh that of any other athlete." The *Washington Post* said that Moe's "diplomatic mission is almost without parallel in the annals of diplomacy."

Before he left for Latin America, though, Moe first made an extraordinary broadcast to the Japanese people over the radio. In fluent Japanese, he pleaded at length, "as a friend of the Japanese people," for the Japanese to avoid a war "you cannot win." He invoked examples of historical American-Japanese friendship over the years. Berg's address was so effective that several Japanese confirmed afterwards that they had wept while listening. President Roosevelt called Moe the next day, thanking Moe for the speech on both his own behalf and that of the American people. Within a year of Moe's speech, Japanese officials banned baseball, referring to it as a decadent American sport.

Relations between the United States and her neighbors to the south had been strained for decades, and the strain had lately been increased by Nazi Germany's skillful propaganda campaign aimed at discrediting the U.S. Moe's official task was to improve the welfare of U.S. servicemen stationed in Latin America, and the relationships between them and their hosts. His unofficial function was to assemble secret, high-priority assessments of leading political figures, as well as simply to win friends by the sheer charm and magnetism of his considerable personality, and his unusual background (baseball is highly popular in sections of Latin America, and some of today's finest major leaguers come from south of the border).

Moe's report on his mission reflected the skill and concern with which he had invested his efforts; he was particularly concerned about the fact that American soldiers were not taking adequate advantage of the opportunities available to mingle with and understand the native populations. Rockefeller was highly pleased with the results of Moe's trip, and wrote to him that his work "has contributed greatly to the inter-American programs. Only someone with your experience and knowledge of international as well as human problems could have handled this situation with such tact and effectiveness."

Moe's subsequent work for the Office of Strategic Services was considerably more vital, and far more secret. He was one of the very finest American undercover agents. Michael Burke, himself an OSS agent and later president of the Yankees and of Madison Square Garden, says of Berg:

"Moe was absolutely ideal for undercover work. Not by design; just by nature. One, because of his physical attributes. He could go anyplace without fear. He had stamina. Also he had that gift for languages. In addition, he had an alert, quick mind that could adapt itself into any new or strange subject and make him comfortable quickly. He was immensely involved intellectually and active in international affairs through reading and travel. He had the capacity to be at home in Italy or France or London or Bucharest. He was on familiar ground in all those places. He also possessed a great capacity for being able to live alone, and could do this for long periods of time. The life of an agent sometimes is a lonely one and some people aren't suited for that."

Berg's first mission was to assess the political and military situation in embattled Yugoslavia. He slipped into the country, probably by parachute, and spoke to the forces under Tito and to the Serbian camp of Mihajlovic. Moe's report that the Yugoslav people supported Tito turned out to be prophetic.

After Moe's successful work in Yugoslavia, his commander, General William Donovan, decided to send him on the crucial and sensitive mission that would determine the degree to which Germany had perfected the atomic bomb. When Moe was named to undertake secret work in Italy, a Donovan aide, seeing Berg's name, asked the general, "Do you know who they gave us for this mission? A ballplayer named Moe Berg. You ever hear of him?"

"Yes," Donovan answered. "He's the slowest runner in the American League."

Moe performed a secret mission in Norway, providing the U.S. with information that Germany had a crucial plant there producing heavy water, a component of their planned bomb development. The plant was subsequently bombed and shut down for good. In Italy, Moe learned that another German atomic center was based in Duisburg; that, too, was then devastated with bombing raids that hampered Germany's progress on the bomb. Berg located several important Italian scientists and engineers, and helped arrange eventual passage to the U.S. His work in Italy was so important that the University of Rome awarded him an honorary Doctor of Laws degree in September, 1944.

Another of Moe's vital assignments was to determine the

extent to which Germany was planning and developing radiological warfare. His investigations led to scientists in Switzerland and France, and his reports were important aids in Allied assessments. With his extraordinary mind and concentration, Moe was rapidly able to become an expert on the fine technical aspects of atomic energy and radioactive repercussions; expert enough to discuss them on even terms with the world's top specialists in those fields.

Moe's most sensitive, and probably most dangerous, mission involved locating and somehow making contact with Germany's top atomic scientist, Professor Werner Heisenberg. Only Heisenberg would know whether Germany was virtually ready to produce an atomic bomb, or was still lagging in its research. According to the account of the mission in *Moe Berg: Athlete, Scholar, Spy,* Berg was even prepared, if necessary, to "eliminate" Heisenberg, "if it meant world survival." With an elaborate scheme, Berg lured the German scientist to Switzerland to give a lecture on quantum theory; Moe carefully evaluated the lecture, and then managed to attend the dinner party afterwards. With his polished German, no one knew Moe was an American agent.

One of the remarks Berg overheard was Heisenberg saying that he did not believe that Germany would win the war. Such a comment from a man in his position was strong evidence that the German effort was not an immediate threat. British Prime Minister Winston Churchill, President Roosevelt and the scientists working on America's Manhattan project (to develop a U.S. bomb) were all briefed on Berg's invaluable report. Roosevelt got the report from a General and responded, "Fine, just fine.

Let us pray Heisenberg is right. And, General, my regards to the catcher."

Moe continued to work on numerous secret missions, all vital and dangerous, for the duration of the war. Time and again, his mission was successfully accomplished. On one assignment in Germany itself to trace development of aeronautical work, Moe's trip, according to U.S. reports, "produced the collections of approximately eighty percent of the information of the German development work on high speed aeronautical designs and tests."

In 1945, as the war drew to a close, America had a new concern: they were anxious that the U.S., and not Russia, capture Germany's top scientists. The Americans knew that the Soviet Union was anxious to utilize the best German brains for their own purposes. Moe Berg's detailed reports on the secret whereabouts of the top German scientists enabled American investigators to find and capture them.

But while Berg was one of America's most valuable and effective secret agents, he always remained a ballplayer at heart. One day, while visiting a front-line hospital in Germany, he saw a couple of American soldiers standing on a grassy bank, wearing baseball gloves and tossing a ball back and forth. According to Russell Forgan, OSS commander in the European Theater, this is what happened:

"Moe went down and said, 'Look, do you fellows mind if I catch with you?' The guy with the catcher's mitt said, 'Sure. Take this.' He handed Moe the mitt. So Moe put it on and started throwing the ball with that short, quick flip, like that, you know. And this kid, the one who had given him the catcher's mitt, kept looking at the way Moe threw the ball. The kid kept looking and looking and looking and said, 'Hell, I know who you are. The last time I saw you was in Sportsman's Park. You're Moe Berg.' And Moe came back and, boy, he was the happiest guy. Imagine, the middle of Germany with a war going on and this guy recognized him. It pleased him tremendously."

In coming back to the United States after the war, Berg escorted Paul Scherrer, a top Swiss physicist. The two men went to visit Albert Einstein at Princeton. During their visit, Berg told the great genius that he had read Einstein's article on atomic war, which had been published in the *Atlantic Monthly.* Much to his pleased amazement, Einstein answered, "I read your baseball story, Mr. Berg, in the *Atlantic,* also. You teach me to catch and I'll teach you mathematics." Indeed, Moe's article on the nuances of the national pastime had described in literate and fascinating terms the struggle between the pitcher and the batter in baseball and the duties of the catcher on the diamond. It had been highly praised by literary, as well as sports, figures.

The war over, Moe resigned from the OSS. Colonel William Quinn of the Strategic Service Unit wrote a ten-page letter of recommendation suggesting that Berg be given the Medal of Merit, the highest honor given to civilians during wartime. Quinn cited Berg for his "many accomplishments . . . and for several times risking his life." The medal was awarded to Moe, but, apparently disinterested in formal honors for all his services, he politely declined.

In his later years, Moe continued his beloved scholarship, always delighted to make new discoveries in the world of linguistics, or indeed in any field. John Kieran, the *New York Times* columnist who was also a regular on "Information, Please" relates a telling incident in *This Week* magazine:

"As a Princeton alumnus he was naturally interested in the annual Princeton and Yale football disputes. Moe and I made a date to ride down to Princeton on a train from New York. Being well acquainted with his taste for literature I brought a book along. It was an old, thick, dog-eared Latin dictionary. During the train ride we pored over the quotations from Caesar, Cicero, Virgil and Horace. We traced words through their gradual change in spelling and meaning from the original Latin and French into English. We grubbed among the roots of the Romance languages. Just as the football special arrived at Princeton Junction, Moe looked up and said, 'John, imagine wasting time and money in a nightclub when you can have fun like this.' "

But however deep his love of the academic world, on the baseball diamond he only wanted to be known as a ballplayer. I* remember a game years ago at Yankee Stadium. The Yanks were hooked up with the Red Sox and I watched the game from the deep bleachers. Moe was working in the bullpen early in the afternoon, about an hour before game time. I yelled down at him and asked him what he thought of Bob Grove, who was scheduled to pitch that afternoon. He answered in a language that resembled Polish.

"You're in New York," I called. "Why not speak something we can understand?" He answered in Yiddish, and the spectators roared. I said a few words in Hebrew and he replied without hesitation, giving the crowd a real thrill. That same afternoon he caught the slants of Lefty

*H.U.R.

Grove, one of the greatest pitchers in the game's history, and got two hits himself. Trapping him on the way to the showers, I asked him about this game which was so much more physical than mental.

"I don't want to be known as a ballplayer who read a book," he told me. "And I don't want to be known as a lawyer with a bat on my shoulder. I practice law in the winter and play ball in the summer and I am careful to keep the two apart in my life. And I love baseball."

And baseball certainly repaid the compliment. Berg was one of the most popular players to play the game, and in his entire sixteen-year career was never once thrown out of a ballgame. Always extremely elusive to find in his private life, he could always be found in the ballpark at World Series time, buying his way in to the fall classic like any other citizen. However highly educated he may have been, he was always deeply delighted and privileged to be a major league baseball player.

Dr. W. Hardy Hendren is a doctor who met Moe at a World Series game in Boston in 1967. Hendren didn't know who the dignified stranger was, but quickly realized that this was no ordinary former ballplayer. Berg seemingly knew about every subject that came up, not least what pitch was going to be thrown next. Hendren, fascinated, invited the elderly stranger to join him for dinner. The doctor remarks:

"When he entered my house, he immediately began translating the Latin on a brass rubbing on the wall.

"That evening, we had several guests, doctors, who were in Boston to work with me. As we were sitting in the dining room I said to Moe I was amazed to see him predict what sort of pitch was coming next. He said it was easy for a professional ballplayer to do that.

"Then he mentioned that it was easy for professionals to make mistakes, too. He said, 'Occasionally surgeons make mistakes. For example, when a surgeon is operating for appendicitis and discovers it was Meckels diverticulum.' Well, the doctors dropped their forks. They could not believe their ears."

On May 30, 1972, at the age of seventy, Moe Berg died after suffering injuries in a fall at his Newark home. Before he died, he turned to a nurse and spoke his last words.

"How did the Mets do today?" he asked.

Many people who knew him are convinced that Moe Berg's intellect was of genius caliber; that this extraordinary man could have accomplished anything he wanted in life. Some feel he wasted these tremendous gifts; others admire his determination to enjoy his life to the utmost. John Kieran believes that had he applied himself to law, Moe could have gone all the way to the Supreme Court, and "could have been a Brandeis." Berg's brother never did understand why Moe wasted his time in baseball, remarking that "all it ever did was make him happy."

Friend and batterymate Ted Lyons says that "a lot of people tried to tell him what to do with his life and brain and he retreated from this . . . He was different because he was different. He made up for all the bores of the world. And he did it softly, stepping on no one."

Moe Berg remains in memory as one of the most remarkable men who ever lived, and certainly the most fascinating personality in the history of American sports. That's quite a legacy for a Jewish kid from Newark who had trouble hitting the curve ball.

SANDY KOUFAX, A GREAT PITCHER, RELAXES

Sandy Koufax

Hall of Fame Pitcher

In the long history of baseball there have been many great pitchers and so it is dangerous to call any one pitcher the most effective, brilliant, spectacular twirler in the annals of a game which has an army of statisticians. But an excellent case can be made for Sandy Koufax, the Jewish southpaw star of the Los Angeles Dodgers in the National League.

Let us begin with a night game between the Dodgers and the Chicago Cubs at Dodger Stadium, September 9, 1965. Koufax faced Bob Hendley, a tough opponent, and Sandy started off fast by striking out two of the first three batters in the opening inning. Byron Browne, a rookie playing in his initial major league game, solved one of Koufax' pitches and lined it hard to Willie Davis in center field for the final out in the second inning. This was the first time in the game that anyone had come close to hitting safely. But Sandy then "settled down" and his fast ball and curve had the Cub batters perplexed and puzzled. Throughout the proceeding innings, this game became one of the best-pitched any of the fans had ever seen. Bob Hendley kept pace with Koufax and it was a hitless, scoreless game up to the fifth inning. Lou Johnson, in the Dodger half of the fifth, drew a walk and was sacrificed to second by Ron Fairly. Johnson stole third and came home on a throwing error by rookie catcher Chris Krug and Koufax had a one-run lead over his brilliant foe.

It was a no-hit game for both pitchers going into the seventh inning and the 29,139 fans realized that they were in attendance at a remarkable game in baseball history: perhaps a double no-hitter. Who could tell, with a guy like Koufax being extended by a pitcher determined to match Sandy pitch for pitch?

In the seventh inning, Hendley yielded the first hit of the game, a double to Lou Johnson, but it proved to be harmless because it came with two out and Bob retired Fairly for the final putout of the inning. Koufax, meanwhile, had pitched like an absolute master. Going into the eighth inning, Koufax had struck out eight and only seven batters had managed to lift the ball to the outfield.

In that eighth inning, when the fans realized that Koufax had a no-hitter going, and a perfect game at that, the tension rose. The first batter was the dangerous Ron Santo, followed by Ernie Banks, the two toughest Cub batters. Sandy struck them both out and ended the inning with a flourish by fanning Browne.

In the ninth inning, Krug, unaccustomed to the big leagues and a pitcher like Koufax, followed the lead of his more illustrious teammates — and struck out. Joe Amalfitano, a pinch-hitter, was the next swinger, and he fanned on three straight pitches, swinging with futility at the last one. The score was 1-0 and Hendley had pitched a one-hitter. The Cubs were still in the game, or so they thought. Now they sent up another pinch-hitter, Harvey Kuenn, a former American League batting champion and a man who seldom struck out. Sandy had, at this moment, thirteen strikeouts for the game and five in succession. Kuenn proved to be no problem to Koufax, who struck him out, and recorded a perfect game, one of the extreme rarities of baseball. Hendley had been victimized by Koufax and this was the only game in professional baseball in which only one hit was given up by both sides combined.

This victory brought Koufax' record in 1965 at that phase of the season to twenty-two victories against seven defeats. It brought his strikeout mark to 332 and made him the only pitcher in the game to pitch *four no-hitters* in the major leagues.

It added another milestone to an incredible career, which included these highlights: struck out eighteen in two different games, to tie a major league strikeout record; pitched no-hitters in four successive years; struck out fifteen Yankees in the World Series and was a World Series star almost every time he was in the classic.

Even before his remarkable feats in the 1965 World Series, Koufax had gained the respect of his fellow players as the best pitcher they had faced. After his perfect game against the Cubs, Ron Santo said, "I've never seen Sandy throw as hard as he did when he struck me out in the eighth. He threw one fast ball right by me and I was waiting for it. He seemed to get a burst of energy in the late innings." Walt Alston, Sandy's manager, remarked that "I thought this was the best of all his no-hitters." Lefty Philips, a Dodger pitching coach, called Sandy "a better competitor than any pitcher in baseball. Most pitchers hate to be matched against a Juan Marichal, a Jim Maloney or a Bob Veale, but Sandy welcomes the challenge. And he pitches just as hard against the bottom clubs as he does against the pennant contenders." Ernie Banks chimed in with, "He was just great — it was beautiful," and Banks had struck out three times. "That guy will drive you to drink," another Cub said.

Koufax himself, tired after that history-making game, was calm about his feat. "I knew all along I was pitching a no-hitter, but it never crossed my mind that it might be a perfect game." As for Hendley, who was so good himself, he said sympathetically, "That's the best any guy has pitched against me in my career."

Leonard Koppett, writing in the *New York Times* a few days after the perfect game, wrote that "Koufax brings people into the park as no pitcher has since the heyday of Bob Feller." And he made this observation: "Thursday night's game was Koufax' thirty-fifth start this season, all advertised in advance. The attendance for those thirty-five games is 1,284,934. This represented more than ten per cent of the National League's total of 12,019,241 through Thursday's games — and the league total was on the threshold of a major league record. Another viewpoint on the same figures is more enlightening: in his appearances, Koufax has averaged 36,712 customers per game; for all other National League games, without Koufax, the average is 15, 247."

Obviously, baseball fans knew that in Sandy Koufax they were watching one of the immortals of the sport, a pitcher who was capable of throwing a no-hitter every time he went to the mound. It was no wonder that after eleven years as a major leaguer, Sandy Koufax had come to a point where baseball writers were speculating on whether there ever had been a better pitcher in baseball. He had won almost every award in the game that a pitcher could win. He had achieved miracles. He held strikeout records, earned run records and had won key victories for his team year after year, sometimes under physical handicaps. He had captured the imagination not only of the baseball world but of millions to whom baseball was of small importance. He had had books written about him, thousands of articles and hundreds of feature stories. He had his picture on the cover of the leading magazines in the United States and he had become one of the best-known names in the United States. Thus, he had also become one of the most famous Jews in America. If any athlete in this volume is "great," Sandy Koufax is that man.

There is no space in this volume to describe in full detail the entire career of Sandy Koufax, but a good place to start is not at the outset of that career but at the end of the 1965 season, for it was then that the sports historians had begun to analyze his accomplishments. There were two essays in particular that struck me,* in compiling a file on Sandy Koufax which I had begun just about when he came to the Dodgers. One is by Bill Libby in the 1966 edition of *True's Baseball Yearbook,* and the other is a feature by Dave Anderson in *Dell Sports* (March, 1966) entitled "Koufax: How He Compares With Six All-Time Greats." A summation of these two studies will offer some insight into the position that Koufax held after more than a decade of pitching in the major leagues.

Bill Libby asks, "How Great is Sandy Koufax?" and comes up with some conflicting answers. Libby quotes Atlanta manager Bobby Bragan as saying, "He is the greatest pitcher who ever lived," but Libby observes that Bragan was not yet born when some of the best pitchers had performed. Libby also quotes the retired baseball com-

*H.U.R.

missioner and former newspaperman Ford Frick: "The way he has pitched the last few years, his name belongs right up there with Cy Young as one of the great pitchers of all time."

But Libby then points out that at the end of 1965 Koufax had won only 138 games and had pitched only eleven years and had only two twenty-game seasons. Cy Young won 511 games and Walter Johnson 416. Warren Spahn, a contemporary of Koufax, had won 363, and, Libby remarked, of twenty-two pitchers in Baseball's Hall of Fame only one (Dizzy Dean) had won less than 190 games. Dean had won 150 and had his career cut because of injuries.

On the other hand, Libby writes, "Koufax is the only pitcher in history to ever pitch four no-hitters. Bob Feller and Cy Young had three each. Koufax has twice tied Feller's record of eighteen strikeouts in a single game. Last season, Sandy struck out 382 batters to surpass Feller's one-season mark of 347. And Sandy is the first ever to lead his league in lowest earned run average four seasons in a row. His recent accomplishments cannot be dismissed lightly. It does appear that at his best, he is as good as the best has ever been."

Libby goes on to examine the records of all the great pitchers and stresses that Koufax' early years were not impressive and that he came of age as a pitcher in 1961, when he began to live up to his promise. It was, therefore, only in his later years that Koufax began to bear comparison with the other outstanding pitchers. Libby makes clear that, to his way of thinking, Koufax had not been pitching brilliantly for enough years to be ranked with men like Cy Young, who won thirty-one, thirty-two, thirty-three, thirty-four and thirty-six games in single seasons, and Christy Mathewson, who won thirty, thirty-two, thirty-three and thirty-seven games. Walter Johnson won twenty or more games twelve times, ten years in a row. And Libby records the lifetime records of Spahn, Early Wynn, Robin Roberts, Whitey Ford and Lefty Grove to show that they won far more games than Koufax over many years of service to their clubs.

Yet Koufax' earned run average was 2.93, lower than Carl Hubbell, Grove, Spahn, Feller or Dean. And Sandy had thirty-five shutouts, eight more than Dean, only one less than Hubbell. But Grove had 135, Johnson 113 and Grover Cleveland Alexander 90. Thus the statistics are quoted and they do not, of course, stand alone, for baseball has changed. There are night games and more difficult schedules today than in the past. One cannot necessarily offer statistics as the only measurement of greatness, but Libby concludes that Koufax "is just about as good right now as any pitcher has ever been," which is a fair statement, for if a man is to be judged at his best, how can anyone improve on Koufax' accomplishments since he became a first-rank pitcher?

Dave Anderson is more aware of the differences in generations than Libby. In his investigation, he remarks, "Sandy Koufax outclasses his contemporaries. He is too good. It is meaningless to compare him with today's other star pitchers: Don Drysdale, Juan Marichal, Jim Maloney, Whitey Ford, Mudcat Grant, Dean Chance. They are the first to admit Koufax is better. The Dodger lefthander must be judged against the great pitchers in baseball history."

Then Anderson writes that "it is not fair, perhaps, to

compare pitchers of different eras. The game has changed. The ball has changed. But the size of the plate and the distance from the mound have been the same for Koufax as they were for the six premier pitchers of the modern era: Christy Mathewson, Walter Johnson, Grover Cleveland Alexander, Lefty Grove, Bob Feller and Warren Spahn."

Here is how Stan Musial, one of the best hitters of the modern age, compares Koufax and Spahn, both lefthanders. "Koufax," according to Musial, "is the most overpowering pitcher I ever faced. He overpowers you with both his fastball and his curve. Spahn never really overpowered you. Spahn would work on you. Pitch you in and out, low and high. Spahn was a scientist." About Koufax, Musial adds, "Sandy throws as hard as any pitcher I ever saw. In my time in the National League, there were some hard-throwing pitchers — Johnny Vander Meer, Rex Barney, Bob Veale. But none of them threw harder than Sandy and none of them had his curve. Sandy has one of the best curves I ever saw . . . That's what makes Koufax great. He has the great fastball *and* the great curve. He just overpowers you with them."

Ted Williams compares Koufax with Feller, but he never batted against Koufax. Still, he recognizes Sandy's skill and says he has the same tricky motion that Feller had. "There's no doubt," he says, "about Koufax being the best of today's pitchers. His curve is a big pitch with him. Feller used his curve as his strikeout pitch and I've noticed that Koufax does the same thing."

In comparing Koufax with Grove, Luke Appling, who is in the Hall of Fame together with Williams, reports, "I've never batted against him so I can't really say if he's faster than Grove or not as fast. I just don't know. But it seems that Koufax works on a hitter more than Grove did. Grove had good control. But he never tried to set you up. He didn't have the curve ball to do that."

Edd Roush, also in the Hall of Fame, remembers Alexander well and says that Sandy is faster, but that the eras in which they worked differed greatly and so he couldn't be sure just how Koufax would rate against Alexander. Roush does concede, for example, that Walter Johnson, considered the king of the speed pitchers, did not have a curve ball nearly as good as Sandy's.

George Sisler, another Hall of Famer, played against Johnson and, as a modern-day batting coach, also has seen much of Koufax. His opinion, therefore, is of particular interest. "It's hard to compare pitchers of different eras," he admits, "but Koufax is a great pitcher and would be a great pitcher in any era. He has a great fastball, a great curve, and he has poise and control. He has a better curve than Johnson. In fact, I don't think anyone has ever had a better curve than Koufax. It breaks down and it breaks sharply, but it breaks big, too. It's a great curve. I've always said that I thought Walter Johnson was the best pitcher I ever saw. And at his best he was tops. But if Koufax' arm stays sound, he has a chance to equal Johnson."

Max Carey, on the other hand, insists that Mathewson is the best he ever saw. Christy worked with his brains, according to Carey, a Hall of Famer. Mathewson could have been faster, if he wanted to be, but he did not operate along those lines. Carey does say, however, that "Koufax is terrific. He's got the stuff. Both the curve and the fastball. He's a natural."

Anderson concludes that, so far, Sandy's problem is

durability, for he has had trouble with his health. "But it is also the *only* flaw. He has everything else. He has something on all the premier pitchers except Feller. He is faster than Spahn, Alexander and Mathewson, and he has a better curve than Grove and Johnson. He has something on Feller, too. Koufax already has four no-hitters. Bob Feller had three."

At the height of Sandy's career, awed admiration was expressed by hosts of his contemporaries. "Hitting against Koufax is like mining hard coal with a toothpick," said Joe Garagiola, catcher and TV broadcaster. "The size of the ballpark means nothing to Koufax. He could pitch shutouts in a telephone booth," added Hank Bauer, the one-time Baltimore manager.

The immortal Casey Stengel made this dry observation: "Umpires often can't see where Koufax' pitches go so they have to judge from the sound of them hitting the catcher's glove. He's very tough for umpires who are hard of hearing." Sam Mele, former Twins manager, said of Sandy that "He's the only pitcher I'd pay my way into the park just to watch him warm up."

Two pitching colleagues offered these perspectives: teammate Don Drysdale said that "I expect him to pitch a no-hit, no-run game every time he starts. I'm only surprised when somebody gets a hit off him." And Twins hurler Jim Grant said flatly that "Koufax is the greatest pitcher alive. And maybe dead. The only thing I can do better than Sandy is sing and dance."

Paul Richards, longtime baseball executive who has seen so many of the sport's great players, feels that "Koufax is so good he could beat a team made up of the nine best players in the history of baseball." After Jack Mann of the

New York Herald Tribune watched Koufax massacre the mighty Yankees, he wrote, "the archaeologists . . . will review the films of the 1963 World Series and conclude that it was a tough league in which Sandy Koufax could lose five games." Comedian and baseball fan Milton Berle summed it all up when he announced that "Koufax is the greatest Jewish athlete since Samson."

It is obvious that Sandy Koufax had to be considered every time a list of great pitchers was compiled. He truly had won the admiration of the baseball world, of his own contemporaries, of former stars, of Hall of Fame players, of managers, coaches, fans and sports writers. In the course of this chapter, some of the great moments of his baseball career will be spelled out in greater detail. But meanwhile, one cannot conclude that Koufax attained baseball heights suddenly, that he came to the major leagues and immediately conquered them. In spite of his later success and his constant potential, he struggled hard to attain the eminence he later won. Pitchers are not born; they are developed. And Sandy surely did not start his career as though he was going to have any easy time of it in professional baseball.

He was born Sanford Koufax on December 30, 1935, in Brooklyn. He lived in various sections of the borough and spent his time with a group of boys to whom basketball was more interesting than baseball. Neither of Sandy's parents were baseball fans. His father was a lawyer and his mother worked and they did what they could to raise their children, but certainly did not stress professional sports. Sandy played ball at the Jewish Community House in Brooklyn, in schoolyards and at Lafayette High School. He played on Lafayette's basketball team but did not even think of trying out for baseball until he was a senior at Lafayette, and then he played first base! It was while he played sandlot ball that he attempted to pitch. His coach, Milt Laurie, admired Sandy's fastball and a Brooklyn sportswriter, Jimmy Murphy, told the Brooklyn Dodgers that he had just seen a fifteen-year-old sandlotter with a tremendous amount of speed. The Dodgers put a scout on the boy's trail. And it was a long trail, for Sandy won a basketball, not a baseball, scholarship at the University of Cincinnati. He made that team, too. He pitched some six games and he was so startlingly effective that he soon had a herd of baseball scouts watching him. In thirty-two innings, he struck out fifty-one batters. In two games in succession, Sandy fanned thirty-four, eighteen in one game and another sixteen in the next one.

After his first year at college, Sandy was invited by the New York Giants to work out at the Polo Grounds. Sandy was wild, as lefthanders often are, and the Giants lost any interest they may have had in him. But other scouts could not forget Koufax' blinding speed, and they kept after him. The Dodgers, following the Giant lead, invited Sandy to try out with them. Manager Walt Alston was among those who watched Sandy, but there was no serious talk after that. Sandy then tried out with Milwaukee and Pittsburgh, but no offers were forthcoming and Sandy returned to Cincinnati for his sophomore year.

Al Campanis, the Dodger scout, made Sandy a firm offer on December 22, 1954 — a $14,000 bonus and a $6,000 salary. The Koufax family, unacquainted with baseball values, did not know quite what to do. They waited for other bids for a while, but none came and Campanis was persistent. Campanis also said it would be nice if a

Brooklyn boy signed to play for a Brooklyn team. Finally, Sandy signed and he now was a professional player, although he had not pitched in more than fifteen or sixteen games and a total of 100 innings. What is more, being a bonus player, he could not be farmed out to the minors. He had to learn his craft the hard way, in the majors, with veteran players looking askance at bonus rookies.

Sandy joined the Dodgers in 1955 and was wild and unimpressive. "I was so nervous and tense," he remembered, "I couldn't throw the ball for ten days. When I finally started pitching, I felt I should throw as hard as I could. I wound up with an arm so sore that I had to rest it another week." The Dodgers were fighting for the pennant in 1955 and could not gamble with a bonus player without experience or control. He started his first game in July and lasted less than five innings against Pittsburgh. In August, the Dodgers were leading the National League by a comfortable margin and they gave Sandy another chance as a starter. On August 27, 1955, Sandy Koufax gave baseball fans a glimpse of the pitcher he could eventually become. He beat the Cincinnati Reds, shutting them out with two hits. He fanned fourteen and showed that when he had his speed under control, he was extremely difficult to solve. Somewhat encouraged, he started again, and Milwaukee knocked him out of the box in the first inning. The next time around, he pitched another shutout, against the Pirates, yielding five hits and fanning six. He was, as one can see, uncertain and undependable, and although the Dodgers won the pennant, Sandy did not feel he had contributed anything to the victory.

For the next few years, Koufax was learning how to pitch. In 1957, he won five games and lost four and split twenty-two decisions in 1958. Koufax, at this time, was merely another lefthander with occasional good days. It was in 1959, another indifferent year, that Sandy had one of his first great days, or nights. It happened on August 31, 1959. In June of that year he had struck out sixteen Phillies. Now, he was facing the Giants. There were 82,794 fans in the stands in Los Angeles and Sandy won, 5-2, but that was the least of it. Sandy felt loose and he struck out the first batter, Jackie Brandt, on three pitches. Willie McCovey was the next hitter and he did not do much hitting, for Sandy fanned him on a swinging third strike. That was the beginning. Sandy had control and speed and had the Giants popping out and fanning. In the sixth inning, he struck out the side and by this time had eleven strikeouts. In the seventh, Brandt and McCovey fanned again, for No. 12 and No. 13. In the eighth inning, with the score 2-1 in favor of the Giants, Koufax had to bear down harder than ever. He got Willie Mays when Roseboro, his catcher, held Mays' tipped third strike. And then Orlando Cepeda became Sandy's fifteenth victim. In the ninth, Koufax realized that if he fanned the side he would shatter the National League record of seventeen, held by Dizzy Dean, and the major league mark of eighteen by Bob Feller would be equaled.

Eddie Bressoud was the first batter in the ninth. Sandy struck him out on four pitches. Danny O'Connell was the next batter. The second baseman carried the count to 2-2 and then watched a curve break over the plate for strike three. This was No. 17 and Koufax had tied Dean's record, set in 1933. The batter was now Jack Sanford, the pitcher. There was no point in lifting him for a pinch-hitter because Sanford was all tied up with Koufax in a 2-2 game.

Sandy wound up and threw three bullets and history had been made. Sanford was the eighteenth strikeout and Koufax had tied Feller's mark. But the game was not yet over. And, as though this were a game out of fiction, the Dodgers won it in the last half of the ninth inning. With one out, Koufax, a weak hitter, shocked everyone by singling to left. Jim Gilliam also singled to the same area and now the Dodgers had their pitcher on second and Gilliam on first. Wally Moon then hit a home run and the Dodgers won the game, thanks to Koufax' brilliant pitching and timely hitting. With these eighteen strikeouts and the thirteen in his previous game against the Phillies, Sandy now had a two-game record of thirty-one, breaking another Feller record of twenty-eight in two games and a National League mark of twenty-seven, set by Karl Spooner, another Dodger pitcher, in 1954.

This game, a highlight in Koufax' career, was only one game. Sandy was not as effective in others. And in 1960, he was angry that he had not done better and that Buzzy Bavasi, the general manager of the Dodgers, had not given him more opportunities to pitch. He had lost a game in the 1959 World Series, but he was not, in his view, getting the chances he felt he deserved.

One night, in 1960, Sandy got into a fight with Bavasi, which was overheard by many reporters. "I want to pitch," Sandy yelled at Buzzy, "and you guys aren't giving me a chance!"

"How can you pitch," Bavasi responded to the challenge, "when you can't get the side out?"

"How can I get anyone out sitting in the dugout?" Sandy replied.

It was no wonder that Sandy was dissatisfied. By the end of 1960, he had won thirty-six games and had lost forty. One of his teammates had said of Koufax that "He has a bad competitive spirit. He never had to ride the bush leagues. He doesn't realize what it means to pitch and win in the majors."

During that winter, Koufax gave serious thought to quitting the game. He had been playing for six years and had little to show for it. He was not even a pitcher who could win as many as he lost. He was erratic and apparently did not have the stuff to become a star.

Joe Becker, the Dodger coach, said of Koufax that he was "overanxious," and Bavasi said that he tried to overpower the hitters and you cannot do that indefinitely against major league batters unless you mixed up your pitches.

Sandy Koufax began to develop into a real pitcher in 1961. He had the benefit of the advice of a Jewish teammate, Norm Sherry, one of the team's catchers and the brother of Larry Sherry, the Dodger pitching star in the 1959 World Series.

Riding in a bus together during training, Sherry said, "Sandy, I think your troubles would be solved if you would just try to throw easier, throw more changeups, just get the ball over."

Koufax was a man willing to listen, even if the advice came from a "secondary" player. He thought about it and decided not to attempt to overwhelm every batter with every pitch. "I used to throw each pitch harder than the previous one," Sandy later told a reporter. "There was no need for it. I found out that if I take it easy and throw naturally, the ball goes just as fast. I found that my control improved and the strikeouts would take care of themselves."

He got off to a fine start in 1961. He had won only eight games in 1960. In 1961 he already had won eight games in June. He had become a regular, steady pitcher. He was used in forty-two games and pitched more than 200 innings. He won eighteen games and lost thirteen. He struck out 269 batters, thus breaking a National League record of 267 held by Christy Mathewson for fifty-eight years. The batters said that Sandy now had control of his fastball and that his curve was more effective than ever before because his control gave him an opportunity to mix up his deliveries.

The baseball fan will recall that 1961 was famous for another reason as well. That was the year Roger Maris of the New York Yankees strained to beat the most famous record in the books: Babe Ruth's sixty home runs in a single season. The pressure on Maris was tremendous. Reporters followed him everywhere. Television cameras were fixed on him on the ball field, almost to the exclusion of the other Yankee stars. Maris got his sixty-one home runs, but he never came close again to being a superstar.

It was during this turmoil that Sandy Koufax was trying to break an older record than Ruth's, which had been set in 1927. The National League record for strikeouts for one season was Mathewson's 267, set in 1903 by one of baseball's greatest pitchers. Koufax, working hard to establish himself with the Dodgers, was having a good year, an especially fine one for him. On August 29th, he beat the Chicago Cubs for his fifteenth win. In the process, he fanned twelve batters, giving him, as of that date, 212 strikeouts and bringing his goal somewhat closer. It also was the eighth time in 1961 that Sandy had struck out ten or more men in one game. On September 15th, Sandy won from the Milwaukee Braves, chalking up his sixteenth victory. He now had 243 strikeouts, beating the record set for lefthanders by Rube Marquard of the New York Giants in 1911. In whipping the Braves, Sandy beat the great lefthander Warren Spahn, then seeking his twentieth win of the year. It was also the ninth time in the year that Koufax had struck out ten or more in a game. A few days later, on September 20th, Sandy won his eighteenth victory, licking the Cubs, fanning fifteen of them and bringing his strikeout output to 259. In another appearance he got three batters on strikes. He now was up to 262. On September 27th, Sandy pitched brilliantly against the Philadelphia Phillies. He received no batting support and lost 2-1. But he struck out seven, smashing Mathewson's record. Another point: Christy worked 367 innings to attain his mark; Sandy pitched in only 255 innings.

How did the wild, ineffectual, sometimes brilliant pitcher become so steady and so good? Sandy had an answer of sorts for Leonard Koppet, then writing for the *New York Post*. "In a strange sort of way," Sandy said, "I think the terrible season I had last year had a lot to do with it. I learned to lose. I used to want to win so badly that I couldn't get myself to stop thinking about the last thing that went wrong. If I lost a game, I'd be thinking about making it up in the next one. If a batter got a hit in the first inning, I'd still be mad and worrying about it with the next hitter, or the next inning. But last year I lost so often that something finally got through to me: that even when you lose, you start out the next game even. There's a certain number of times you're going to get beaten, and there's no sense worrying about it if you can just concentrate on the next thing coming up."

This kind of talk indicated that Koufax was maturing as a player and as a man. He now was twenty-five, finally a winning pitcher, a record-holder and a regular on a good team. The year of 1962 was one to which he and his fans were looking forward with confidence.

And 1962 was one of the most remarkable seasons ever experienced by a major league pitcher. Koufax proved forever that at his best, no one was better. But he also demonstrated that his luck was not always of the best. He won fourteen games and lost seven, which does not seem to be too impressive. The reason for the 14-7 record was due to an injury that nearly ended Sandy's career. But until he was stricken, he was brilliant. He struck out 216, walking only fifty-seven, and he won the earned run average title for pitchers with a low of 2.52. Notwithstanding his injury, he pitched a no-hit, no-run game and also became the first pitcher to have *two* eighteen-strikeout games in a career.

On April 24, 1962, Sandy Koufax again went into the record books as a strikeout pitcher when he beat the Chicago Cubs in Chicago by a score of 10-2.

While the victory itself was an easy one, Koufax had to work hard for his record. He fanned eighteen Cubs, to repeat his 1959 feat and to become the only pitcher to do this job more than once. It happened early in the 1962 season and the achievement proclaimed to all that Sandy's 1961 successes were by no means an accident. Sandy allowed the Cubs six hits, including a lead-off homer to Billy Williams in the ninth inning, when the score already was a lopsided 10-1. Sandy struck out nine of the first ten batters to face him. He also fanned the entire side in the first, third and ninth innings.

This performance led to an even greater one two months later, against the New York Mets, who had become the clowns of major league baseball, but who also had won a fanatical following in New York City, after the loss of the Brooklyn Dodgers and the New York Giants. Koufax, living as he was on the West Coast, remained at heart a New Yorker and he pressed more than usual when he played in New York. For example, he pitched against the Mets in the Memorial Day double-header at the Polo Grounds in 1962 and won by a score of 13-6. Surely this was not one of Koufax' finest victories. Yet he told Arthur Daley of the *New York Times* that "It was the most exciting game I ever pitched in my life." Daley was shocked to hear this statement from a man who already had pitched record-making games, for Sandy had had a ten-run lead and had pitched sloppily after that, yielding thirteen hits. The reason for Sandy's satisfaction went beyond statistics.

He told Daley, "Maybe it was just being back in the big town again. I was higher than a kite. It was an emotional jag and I couldn't relax. That crowd was unbelievable and it added to the excitement. It was such an enthusiastic crowd and it never stopped cheering for the Mets, no matter how hopelessly they were out of it."

Then Koufax reminisced. "The Mets, in a way, reminded me of the first Dodger team I ever saw. When I was a small boy, my father took me to Ebbets Field to see my hero, Pete Reiser. The other team had a ten-run lead, just as we did yesterday. But the Dodgers refused to quit. They kept pecking away and finally Reiser won the game in the ninth with an inside-the-park home run."

With this sentimental attitude about the Mets, Sandy Koufax must have had a special thrill on the night of June 30, 1962 at Los Angeles, when he pitched the first no-hit, no-run game of his career. He beat the Mets, striking out thirteen and winning 5-0. In retrospect, even this no-hitter was not the best performance of Koufax' career, but it was enough to make him an immortal of the mound.The Dodgers gave Sandy a four-run lead in the first inning, so there was no pressure on the pitcher almost from the outset. In the first inning he needed only nine pitches, all strikes, to eliminate Richie Ashburn, Rod Kanehl and Felix Mantilla. Two Mets fanned in the second; two more in the third; Kanehl again in the fourth; one in the fifth and two in the sixth. Sandy missed a strikeout in the seventh because with a man on base with one out, he forced Frank Thomas to hit into a double play. In the eighth Sandy got two more strikeouts for a total of thirteen. Meanwhile, not a single Met got a hit and no runner reached third base, although Sandy walked five.

After the game, many ballplayers were interviewed and, of course, Koufax was the man they talked about. Solly Hemus, who was a Dodger coach, needled Sandy throughout the game and perhaps kept him loose as pressure mounted. Once, in 1960, Sandy had pitched a one-hit game, against Pittsburgh, and so he knew what the feeling was like. After the three strikeouts in the first inning, Hemus said to Sandy, "It isn't really that easy, is it?" Halfway through the game, Hemus reminded Sandy that he had not yet given up a hit. "I've had one a lot later than this," Koufax replied, and went back to work.

In the second inning, the Mets almost hit safely, when Thomas drove a ball sharply to the right of Maury Wills, the fine shortstop of the Dodgers. Wills made a backhand stab and quick throw to first. Fortunately for Koufax, Thomas was a slow runner and so a threat did not materialize. That was the only time the Mets came close to a hit.

It is no wonder that after the game the players raved about Koufax. Gene Woodling, a former Yankee who pinch-hit in the ninth inning, said, "Koufax is the kind of guy who sends you back to the farm, and happy to go." Rod Kanehl observed of Sandy, "He throws the ball hard until he's got two strikes on you. Then he throws it harder." Richie Ashburn chimed in, "The way he was throwing, he had you completely at his mercy."

Sandy himself had a great deal to say. First, he denied that the no-hitter was "tainted" because he had thown it against the weak Mets. He also said he had trouble getting his curve ball over the plate in the middle innings and that his arm stiffened on him in the fourth inning. Still, the no-hitter was an exciting experience for him, as it must be for any pitcher. "It doesn't happen very often," he said, not knowing what the future held in store for him. "A lot of great pitchers never got one. Sal Maglie had to wait almost to the end of his career to get his. And he said it was the biggest thrill of his life. I remember thinking after the game, 'Now you've got it. Nobody can take it away from you anymore.' It's a hard feeling to describe."

At this point in 1962, Sandy had won eleven games and lost four. In his last five starts, he had given up only three earned runs, for a 0.63 earned run average. Over the season, his earned-run average was 2.33. Sandy was on his way to his best season. He was named to the All-Star game, and by that time had won thirteen and lost four. He had more than 200 strikeouts and his earned run average was the lowest in the National League. With Sandy to lead them, it appeared that the Dodgers were on their way to the pennant.

Why not? Koufax had been burning up the league with his pitching form. He had struck out eighteen in a game; he had pitched a no-hitter; he hit his first major league home run in a game to win from Warren Spahn, 2-1. In eight starts, from June 13th to July 12th, he had been as overwhelming as a pitcher can be. He gave up only four earned runs, and his strikeouts had mounted to 209.

Then tragedy struck. Sandy did not start another game that year, and made a few hapless appearances on the mound in September. The Dodgers, minus his talents, slowly fell back among the other teams in the league. The Giants caught up with the Dodgers and won the pennant in a playoff.

What had happened to Sandy Koufax? The entire baseball world was wondering. At first it appeared to be a blood blister on Sandy's index finger. The finger had been numb for a while, but it had not affected Sandy's pitching. Then it grew so numb that he could not throw a curve ball effectively. He could not spin the ball off his fingertips, and he noticed this after the All-Star game break. He saw his curve fail him in a game against the Giants; then he left a game against the Mets in the seventh inning. He started one more time but could not pitch and quit after the first inning. In August of that year, Sandy told Milton Gross, a *New York Post* columnist and a good friend, that his finger was "sort of useless right now. It doesn't hurt or anything, but there's a half inch of finger that's raw, virtually no skin on it. The skin had just died."

It was a blood clot, a dangerous one, and throughout the hot August month, when the pennant race was getting closer and closer, Koufax was visiting doctors. He learned later that he had been in danger of losing the finger. After the blood clot, infection had set in. Drugs and medication to repair the blood vessels had been successful. "All I care about," Sandy said, "is the future. I can't help being a little worried. Will it come back?"

No one knew. He hardly did any more pitching in 1962, although he made a final appearance on September 27th in a game against Houston. In that effort, Sandy pitched four scoreless innings and struck out four. Then he weakened and gave up a two-run homer. He left the game ahead, 4-2. His catcher, John Roseboro, reported that Koufax had his "usual good stuff." Sandy himself was relieved. "That game," he said at the time, "meant more to me than any other I had ever won, and that includes the no-hitter I pitched against the Mets. Although I wasn't as sharp as I would like to have been, I was satisfied. More than that, I was relieved. I had looked awful in two previous turns on the mound after the long layoff and I didn't want to spend the winter wondering whether I'd ever be able to pitch again. My finger wasn't completely healed — although there was no more pain — but I had to pitch and find out. I did."

The Dodgers lost the pennant and Koufax thought his finger would be all right. Could anyone tell about Koufax? The sports magazines and columns were full of stories about the Jewish lefthander. Bob Hunter, writing in the *Sporting News* in February, 1963, put the story in proper focus when he wrote: "Sandy Koufax, the man with the golden arm and the tinplate finger, without a doubt will be the most spotlighted Dodger when the club opens spring training in Vero Beach. He'll be the center, the key, the crux of the double comeback as both the Dodgers and Sandy strive to reach the goals that each barely missed last season." Hunter added that "Koufax was headed for twenty wins, easily, and his strikeouts would have just about rewritten the record books for keeps . . . Now, Koufax is the man being looked upon to perform the double comeback — for himself personally, and for the team as a National League entry."

Robert Creamer, writing in *Sports Illustrated* (March 4, 1963), on the subject of "An Urgent Matter of One Index Finger," reported that "The Finger cost the Dodgers the National League pennant, it will have a great deal to say on whether the Dodgers win or lose in 1963 and it had brought Koufax more publicity than his extraordinary pitching achievements ever did."

Koufax was constantly being asked — and the magazines and newspapers were dutifully recording his replies — whether his finger was still bothering him. "It feels all right. I don't think it's going to give me trouble," was his answer to all reporters. Would the pressure of the finger against the ball cause a recurrence of his difficulty? "No, it shouldn't," Koufax said, again and again.

The baseball fans of America waited for Sandy's first 1963 mound performance. It was a fine one. On April 10, 1963, he beat the Chicago Cubs in Chicago, by a score of 2-1. Sandy gave up only five hits and struck out ten. It was his first complete game since the previous July and he was in excellent form, for he walked only two batters. "The finger didn't bother me a bit," the southpaw stated to reporters. "The one thing that pleased me was that I had no trouble with the cold weather and I was making good pitches in the last few innings. There was a little numbness in the finger, but that was due to the cold."

Two starts later, Sandy gave the Cubs two hits and shut them out 2-0, fanning fourteen. All seemed to be well with him and the Dodgers. But on April 23rd, Sandy was working against the Milwaukee Braves and yielded only two hits in six and two-thirds innings. He suffered a muscle spasm and left the game, with a 1-0 lead. The Dodgers won the game, but Koufax' condition was far more important to the club than a victory in April. Dr. Robert Kerlan, who had worked on Sandy's finger the previous year, analyzed his new trouble as an injury to the "posterior capsule of the left shoulder joint." Sandy had stretched or torn the membrane which covers the muscles there."I'll try not to let it get me down," Sandy said. And he did not. After a two-week absence, he pitched an 11-1 win over the St. Louis Cardinals. Alston, Bavasi and Sandy relaxed and made jokes. Koufax was back in the shape that assured the Dodgers of a serious run at the pennant.

At Los Angeles, on the night of May 11, 1963, Sandy Koufax pitched his second no-hit, no-run game, and it was a better performance than his no-hitter against the Mets. He retired the first twenty-two men he faced and then walked Ed Bailey, the Giant catcher. Jim Davenport then hit into a double play. Sandy walked one other man and faced twenty-eight batters in all, only one more than the minimum of twenty-seven. He had walked Willie McCovey with two out in the ninth, as the pressure grew. The final batter was Harvey Kuenn, who hit the ball back to Koufax on the mound. Sandy tossed the ball to first for the putout. More than 55,000 fans screamed in admiration and

Koufax had had another night to be remembered.

As though repeating a recording made again and again, Koufax told the reporters hovering over him, "This was my greatest thrill. To pitch a perfect game would really have been something great. I'm sorry I had to walk those two guys. But it's still my biggest thrill."

That game was, of course, Koufax' best of the 1963 season, but it was by no means his only excellent performance. Throughout the year he demonstrated the kind of skill that propels a player into the Hall of Fame. On June 17th, Koufax won his tenth game of the year against three defeats, by shutting out the Giants 2-0, for his sixth shutout of the year. On July 6th he had his eighth shutout of the season and his seventh straight victory. Already, his shutouts were the most marked up by any National League pitcher in any season since 1942. Sandy kept rolling along. By July 15th, he was the leading winner in the major leagues, with sixteen victories. By mid-year, *Time* magazine reported that Koufax was the best pitcher of the year. He had pitched a no-hitter, two two-hitters and four three-hitters and he had nine shutouts. "His fastball," *Time* said, "comes in like a 20-mm. cannon shell; his curve breaks so sharply that it acts, says Dodger catcher John Roseboro, 'like a chair whose legs suddenly collapse.' Control? 'When an umpire calls my pitch a ball,' says Koufax casually, 'that means it is either high or low. It's never outside or inside.' All in all, agrees St. Louis Cardinals' slugger Ken Boyer, 'Koufax is just too damned much.' "

Through July 23rd, Koufax was the major league's standout pitcher, the *Sporting News* concluded. On the basis of a point system for low-run games, in which a shutout is worth five points, Koufax had a twenty-point bulge over his nearest competitor and his great pitching was bringing his club closer and closer to the National League flag. But he had difficulty in winning some of his best-pitched games. For example, he pitched one-run ball twice in succession and failed to win either decision. He did not lose, but neither did he gain victories. He gave up one run in twelve innings against St. Louis and left before the game went one way or the other. A few days later, he tried for his twentieth victory of the year and limited the Milwaukee Braves to three hits in eight innings. His eleventh shutout was also in the offing. But Sandy weakened in the ninth. With one out, he allowed Eddie Mathews a double and with two out Gene Oliver tied the score with another double. The Dodgers eventually won but the decision went to Bob Miller.

In spite of his brilliance, Koufax never had a twenty-game victory season until 1963. On August 28th, he finally made it, with an 11-1 win over the Giants. He thus became the second Jewish twirler in major league history to win twenty games in a season. Erskine Mayer had been the first. Mayer won twenty-one games with the 1914 Phillies and repeated in 1915.

Koufax did not cease to win after achieving this goal. He set a major league record of eleven shutouts in a season for lefthanders, when he blanked the Cardinals for his twenty-fourth victory. Again, it was one of Sandy's most masterful efforts. He made a 1-0 lead hold up until the seventh inning. He did not give up a hit until Stan Musial singled in that frame. He allowed three more hits only after the Dodgers stretched their lead to four runs.

What made this game especially significant from a

Jewish point of view was that Sandy had altered his pitching schedule to avoid working on the Jewish High Holidays. He had pitched in Philadelphia with two days rest and in St. Louis with three days off so that he could miss working during the holidays. In winning, Koufax added to his National League strikeout record, bringing his total to 288. His twenty-four victories was the most any lefthander in the league had won since Carl Hubbell had twenty-six in 1936.

Koufax ended the year with twenty-five wins against five losses. He started forty games and completed half of them. His twenty-five wins and eleven shutouts were tops in the majors for the year. His earned run average of 1.88 was the lowest in the league since 1943, when Howie Pollet finished with 1.75. Sandy yielded only sixty-five earned runs in 311 innings. He also averaged nearly a strikeout an inning, with 306 in the 311 innings he pitched.

It was Koufax' performance in 1963, against his shortened 1962 season, that made the difference for the Dodgers, who won the pennant in 1963. As Larry Sherry, his Jewish teammate, said of him in the midst of the 1963 season, "He has incredible confidence. He should have, of course, he's that good, but it's more than that. He just doesn't seem to have any doubts at all. He knows, he just plain *knows,* he's going to get them out. It's made a tremendous difference in him."

As exceptional as Koufax was during the year, he attained new heights during the 1963 World Series against the New York Yankees. No matter how a player performs in the course of the long baseball season, he is best remembered for his World Series feats. And even Sandy Koufax, who entered the Series as the pitcher who could make all the difference in the world in a short series, was not expected to be as overpowering as he proved to be. After all, the Dodgers were facing the Yankees, the most feared team in the game, with sluggers like Mickey Mantle and Roger Maris and a pitcher like Whitey Ford. Moreover, the Yankees had the reputation of seldom losing to the National League in the World Series; when they did, it was considered to be an accident.

Some experts favored the Dodgers because of Koufax, Don Drysdale and Ron Perranoski, the relief pitcher. Others continued to believe that Ford, Jim Bouton, a promising new righthander who had won twenty games, and Ralph Terry, with the support of Mantle, Maris, Tresh, Elston Howard and other Yankee regulars, deserved backing as ultimate winners.

Dan Daniel, a veteran baseball expert, always had been a Yankee man and if ever he had an opportunity to favor anyone, it would be the Yankees. Prior to the World Series, Daniel, comparing Koufax with Ford, implied that Ford would prove to be the better pitcher, but that the Series had "the makings of one of the greatest southpaw battles of classic history between Whitey Ford and Sandy Koufax." While Koufax had won twenty-five games, Ford was a twenty-three game winner. Ford, according to Daniel, had a wider variety of pitches, with Koufax being primarily a fastballer. "Sandy is muscle bound," Daniel told his readers. "He has the back of a blacksmith. This makes for strength but not for fluidity. The bachelor from Brooklyn never worked in a mine. He never had a construction or road job. . . . Some critics fault Koufax for what they allege to be a lack of color . . ." and so on, and on.

Milton Gross, a competing columnist, had a different attitude. In analyzing the Dodger chances for the World Series, he wrote a column entitled "It All Depends on Koufax." In it, Gross said, "If Koufax loses the opening game, forget it. The Yankees will do what they customarily do in the Series." John Podres had beaten the Yankees before, but now he was older and less impressive. Drysdale was a righthander and the Yankees "ate them up." Or so it was said. "The Dodgers," Gross insisted, "have come to regard Sandy as a super pitcher. He is the one responsible for this NL pennant, just as he was the one who could have won it last season if not knocked out of action by the circulatory ailment in the index finger of his pitching hand. When Sandy works the Dodgers feel that they must win." Gross quotes Don Drysdale as saying about Sandy, "He's the only pitcher I've ever seen who wouldn't surprise me a bit if he pitched a no-hitter every time he went out there. I am surprised if he doesn't strike out everybody or if someone hits the ball off him." Podres, who had made World Series history himself, said of Sandy, "I think he is the greatest." And Casey Stengel, who had seen them all, said, "The fella is positively amazing and it almost takes a miracle to beat him." Stengel made this observation immediately after Koufax won his twenty-fifth game of the year, beating the Mets, 1-0.

The first game of the World Series, on a pleasant day on October 2nd at Yankee Stadium, saw Ford and Koufax locked in what at first seemed to be a pitching duel. Who was the better lefthander?

On this day, Koufax bested Ford as, before and later, he proved to be better than other great pitchers in the game. More than 69,000 fans settled down to watch these two stars. In the first inning, Whitey retired the Dodgers in order: two strikeouts and a bouncer to third. Well, then, here was good old dependable Whitey, at his best in the World Series, when it counted. Koufax showed the Yankees that his strikeout record was no freakish thing, that the Yankees were merely batters and not supermen. He merely struck out the first five Yankees, as though he were eliminating gnats! Tony Kubek was the first Yankee batter and he struck out, swinging. Bobby Richardson, a cute batter who was known for his good eye, was no more effective. Sandy also got him swinging, fooling him badly. Tom Tresh took a called third strike and Koufax had demonstrated to the Yankees they were in for a rough afternoon.

Ford, however, was not in good enough form to keep pace with the National League lefthander. Frank Howard, with one out in the second inning, hit a long drive down the middle lane of Yankee Stadium. It went 460 feet in the air in front of the center-field bleachers. Mickey Mantle chased it and chased it but had no chance to make the catch on the fly. Howard, a 255-pounder, was slow around the bases and so had to settle for the longest double in Yankee Stadium history. Moose Skowron, who earlier had been a Yankee star and now was playing for the Dodgers, singled over second and Howard scored the first Dodger run. Dick Tracewski, a rookie, also hit safely and then John Roseboro hit a drifting fly to right field which came down just inside the foul pole. It was a home run and Koufax had a four-run lead over Ford, who had won ten previous World Series games.

Mickey Mantle was the opening Yankee batter in the second inning. Like Tresh in the first inning, Mantle took a called third strike. The next batter — and victim — was Roger Maris. He went down swinging on the final strike and Koufax had now fanned five Yankees in a row! Sandy's curves, fastball and floaters had confused the great Yankee hitters. He had imposed his will on them and, one could guess, this series of outs made its impression on the Yankees. They now knew that they were facing a pitcher the like of which they had not met on their path to the American League pennant.

Joe Pepitone struck out in the third inning, and by this time Koufax had a five-run lead. In the fourth frame, Koufax repeated his exploits of the first inning: he retired the side on strikeouts, with Kubek and Richardson swinging vainly and Tresh again being fooled on a call. In the fifth, Mantle struck out and Maris was retired. Sandy had a perfect game and the fans began to buzz. But Elston Howard singled, Joe Pepitone did the same and Clete Boyer beat out an infield hit to fill the bases. Now the Yankee fans woke up and called for their team to knock Koufax out of the box. It may be that the Yankees were not listening, for Hector Lopez, batting for Ford, went down swinging and the side was retired, with Koufax marking up his eleventh strikeout.

With one out in the sixth, Richardson drew a base on balls and Koufax was a bit disturbed by this temporary loss of control. He walked Tresh and the Yankees again had cause to hope, with Mantle and Maris the next batters. Koufax, however, regained his form and forced both muscle boys to pop out to infielders. Sandy was on his way to a shutout and had a chance to better Carl Erskine's record of fourteen strikeouts in a World Series game, set ten years earlier.

In the eighth inning, the Yankees finally scored. Kubek singled. Richardson fanned for the third time and then Tresh hit a home run into the lower left-field stands. The shutout was gone, but the game was still in hand.

In the final inning, Koufax already had his fourteen strikeouts and three outs to go for victory. Howard lined out. Pepitone singled, Clete Boyer flied out and Koufax had one more out to nail down and he needed a strikeout to set a new World Series record. He faced a pinch-hitter, Harry Bright. A dangerous long ball hitter, Bright swung desperately at a third strike, missed, and Koufax had his record and the Dodgers had won the first game.

"Everything they were writing about him is true," Mantle said after the game. Richardson, who had fanned only twenty-two times in 630 times at bat during the regular season, had been victimized three times. He asked, "How come he only won twenty-five? If Koufax is this consistent, I've never seen anyone like him." Bright had a semi-joke. "I wait seventeen years to get into a World Series and I strike out. That isn't bad enough, 69,000 people were rooting against me." Howard was calm, saying, "He can't pitch every day." Koufax said he got a little tired around the sixth inning, but then regained his strength. Like a gentleman, he said that he was a little sorry he had broken Erskine's record for Carl had been a Dodger pitcher himself, but Sandy admitted that "I wanted that last strikeout so badly, I could taste it."

Apparently, Dan Daniel was not correct when he thought Koufax did not have the "fluidity" a great pitcher needed, and Sandy did not have to work in the mines to overpower the Yankees.

The Dodgers had shown the Yankees their best pitcher.

Johnny Podres, who pitched the second game, was only a trifle less effective. He beat Al Downing 4-1 in the second game at the Stadium. He tired in the ninth, yielding one run and being saved by Perranoski. The Dodgers had won both games in New York and returned home as the favorites to win the Series. Everyone knew that Koufax would pitch again in the fourth game and that was enough for most fans to know. Meanwhile Don Drysdale, who had been the big Dodger winner before Koufax came along, pitched an even better game than Koufax and Podres. He faced Jim Bouton, the Yankee twenty-game winner, and the Dodgers scored one run in the first inning. It was a cheap run. Bouton walked Jim Gilliam, who advanced to second on a wild pitch, and Gilliam scored on a single by Tommy Davis. The Davis hit bounced off the pitching mound toward Richardson, who partially lost sight of the ball against the shirts of the crowd, the ball then bouncing off Richardson's left shin. It was enough for Drysdale, who pitched a shutout and won 1-0. The Yankees, already proud, were now faced with the humiliation of losing a World Series in four straight games, and it was a distinct possibility with Koufax on the mound.

This time, Whitey Ford was much better than he had been in the opening game. There are those who believed he was better than Koufax on this afternoon in Los Angeles, but you pay off on the score.

Koufax got the first nine Yankees, four on strikes, and it began to appear that the Yankees never would solve his serves. Ford kept pace with Sandy, facing only twelve batters in the first four innings. It was 0-0 and this one was a grim pitchers' duel. Frank Howard had singled in the second inning and Skowron had hit into a double play.

Whitey then got the next seven batters. He did not have the same luck with Howard, who had hit that long double off him in the first game. In the fifth inning, Howard lashed another one of his powerful drives, this time 450 feet into the left field stands, for the first run of the game.

In the fifth inning, Richardson hit a pop fly that fell for a double when two infielders and an outfielder messed up the play. It was a lucky hit, but Koufax was not invincible. In the seventh, Mantle finally got a hit off Koufax. He hit the first pitch into the left-field bleachers and the score was tied 1-1. The tie did not last long. Gilliam, in the bottom of the seventh, hit the ball to Boyer who stretched, caught it and threw perfectly to Pepitone. Joe lost the ball in the crowd and it bounced off his chest. When the scrambling was over, Gilliam was on third. Willie Davis hit a long fly to Mantle, who caught it but could not throw Gilliam out at home. Now the score was 2-1 in favor of the Dodgers. Koufax held that lead to the end. Richardson began the ninth with a single, and Koufax, who had fanned only six batters, now struck out Tresh and Mantle for a total of eight. It seemed to be all over when Howard grounded to Maury Wills, but Tracewski dropped the ball on a force play on Richardson and the Yankees had two runners instead of the last out. Koufax, however, was not fazed. He got Hector Lopez to hit a dribbler to Wills, who made the final out by tossing the ball to first.

Koufax had won two of the four games; the Yankees had dropped four in a row and the Dodgers were the world champions, thanks to Koufax' season and World Series performance. Now the praise rolled in like waves. Koufax won a Corvette from *Sport* magazine for being the outstanding player in the World Series. The City Council of

Los Angeles passed a resolution commending the Dodgers for their showing and the County Supervisor, in a moment of excitement, proposed that Fairfax Avenue be renamed Koufax Avenue, at least for a while. Sandy was the only United Press International 1963 Major League All-Star player chosen overwhelmingly. He received sixty-eight of seventy-one votes. The *Sporting News* named Sandy the No. 1 National League pitcher. And he became the winner of the Cy Young Award as the outstanding hurler in the major leagues. He won this honor unanimously, getting all twenty votes cast by a committee of the Baseball Writers Association of America. It is interesting to note that this vote was conducted before the World Series.

Late in October, Sandy won the National League's Most Valuable Player Award. Twenty members of the Baseball Writers Association did the picking and fourteen of them chose Sandy as their first choice. In the total vote, Koufax received 237 points to Dick Groat's 190. This was only the seventh time in thirty-three years that a pitcher had been named for this honor. Koufax, when informed of the vote, said, "I'm awfully surprised to win this. I honestly never thought they'd name a pitcher most valuable. I'm especially proud of this honor. I feel it is the most important one in baseball." Sandy's manager, Walt Alston, said that Koufax "had a great year and he deserved every honor he got. I haven't done much else than pat Sandy on the back all year long, so I think he knows how I feel about him."

In its February, 1964 issue, *Sport* magazine named Koufax its "Man of the Year." In an editorial, Al Silverman, editor of the magazine, wrote, "In a pitchers' year, one pitcher stood above them all. In a year of heroic performances in all sports, one man stood above them all.

Not since 1934, when Dizzy Dean blazed to thirty victories plus two more in the World Series, had a pitcher enjoyed such a year as Sandy Koufax." Then Silverman gave the details of Sandy's 1963 season and concluded, "*Sport's* Man of the Year for 1963 — the Dodgers' Sandy Koufax — without argument."

Life magazine, in a close-up on Koufax, called Sandy "the best pitcher in the past decade," and called attention to his "remarkable year, following his finger injury."

What could Koufax do in 1964 after having conquered all possible worlds in 1963? Milton Gross asked this question in a magazine article between seasons: "What do you do after you've won twenty-five games, set a National League strikeout record of 306, pitched eleven shutouts, had a 1.88 ERA, won the Cy Young Award by unanimous selection and the National League's Most Valuable Player Award?"

It should be borne in mind that no matter how successful Koufax was, ill health dogged him throughout most of his career and 1964 was no exception. It was a year of some brilliance, but it ended on a question mark, for before the season was over, Koufax had another injury and baseball fans were asking if this great pitcher was not brittle, if his sports life was going to be a long one.

He won his first start of the year by shutting out the St. Louis Cardinals, 4-0. It was his tenth consecutive victory, counting the two World Series wins of 1963, and his twentieth in his last twenty-two decisions. It appeared that he was going to be as good as ever — if not better. He hurt his arm on April 22nd and then recovered, winning from the Chicago Cubs 2-1 in ten innings, and striking out thirteen batters. But he also was losing games and had five victories against four defeats when he faced the Philadelphia Phillies on the night of June 4th. He had been worried about a soreness in his elbow, but on this night he pitched the third no-hit game of his major league career, facing the minimum number of twenty-seven batters. Richie Allen drew a walk in the fourth inning and then was thrown out trying to steal second. He fanned twelve batters and by striking out ten or more men for the fifty-fourth time in his career, he tied a record held by Bob Feller and Rube Waddell. Only Feller had three no-hitters before Sandy tied him. Koufax won the game when Frank Howard hit a three-run homer in the seventh. The fantastic lefthander was so invincible that only four balls were hit to the outfield by the Phillies. Sandy was as strong in the ninth as he was in the early innings. He struck out the initial batter, made the second one pop to the first baseman and then only a pinch-hitter, Bobby Wine, stood between him and his third no-hit game. The count went to two strikes and one ball. Then Wine struck out.

By June 13th, Sandy was on his 1963 schedule of victories and there was no doubt in the minds of the fans that he was going to reinforce his reputation as the premier pitcher in the game. On the last day of June, he won his seventh straight game and his eleventh of the year, and for the fifty-sixth time he fanned ten more hitters. In his next start, he ran his streak to eight in a row, getting his fifth shutout and his twelfth victory, by defeating the Mets. He had yielded only eleven earned runs in his last ninety-five innings. And so he rolled on and on and by mid-August he had nineteen victories. How much better could anyone be? Was he meeting the challenge of 1963? Of course!

But he remained injury-prone. In a game in Milwaukee

on August 8th, he hurt his elbow sliding into a base. He continued to pitch, but the pain persisted and it became clear at the end of the month that he was through for the year. It was a terrible blow to the Dodgers who were unable to repeat their pennant victory of the year before. And so the 1964 season ended on a sour note for Koufax. He had won nineteen games and lost five. He led the National League with seven shutouts and had 223 strikeouts in 223 innings. Don Drysdale finally overcame this mark by pitching steadily all year long. Sandy's earned run average was 1.74. Brilliant, of course. But what could one do? Jimmy Cannon, the sportswriter for the *New York Journal-American*, in a sensitive series on Koufax, said of his injuries, "It came at him again, like a tiger who lulls the trainer into temporary serenity by acting like a house cat . . . He awakened one morning and the elbow was swollen and stiff, like a snake in death. The doctors examined him and could not recognize the symptoms of any injury or disease. He had won nineteen by then and requested they allow him to try to get twenty but they persuaded him that leisure would repair it."

Koufax remembered that August morning when he discovered the bad elbow. "My arm was as big around as my knee. I didn't know what it was. But we got the swelling down. I started to throw and it started to swell again. I possibly could have pitched at least one game. But the season had ten days to go. I had won nineteen, and would have liked to have won twenty. But the club wasn't going anywhere. The doctor said forget about pitching. The rest would be beneficial and I wanted to be right."

It was not surprising that Koufax started the 1965 season with the feeling that he would go as far as he could, pitching from day to day, hoping against hope that his arm would not collapse. True, he had been wonderfully good. He had gained national acclaim for his feats. He had proved his ability under pressure of a tight pennant race and he had shown his staying qualities in the World Series. He had demonstrated that he was more than a strikeout pitcher, that he was a winning pitcher. But had he pitched himself out? Did he have the stamina required of the truly immortal hurlers of the game? Or was he going to break down every once in a while, during critical moments, and become an uncertain player, one who might — or might not — break down? How would he rank when compared with those steady pitchers who lasted for ten or fifteen or more years? After all, his early years were indifferent. Now, when he finally had learned the art of pitching, when he had shown the skill of the best pitchers in the game, was he going to be like Herb Score, who had started well and then, following an injury, faded away? Of course, he had done more than Score and even Dizzy Dean, but he still was young enough to accomplish even more. What was to happen in 1965?

Sandy proved, if ever further proof were needed, that in spite of his uncertain arm, he was a great and dazzling pitcher. In spring training, the baseball world was watching him closely. He pitched two complete games and seemed as good as ever. But he knew that at any moment, his career could end. Yet he hoped to be a regular starter, regardless of the arm flare-ups.

On April 18, 1965, Sandy had his first start of the season, against the Phillies in Philadelphia. He had pain earlier in the spring and his ailment had been diagnosed as "traumatic arthritis." According to the Associated Press,

"A struggling Sandy Koufax, showing definite signs of his pitching ailment," beat the Phillies 6-2. The AP reporter said that Sandy appeared to be far from the invincible lefthander of the previous season. But Leonard Koppett of the *New York Times* had a different view. He wrote, "Accounts of the game in Philadelphia say Sandy 'struggled' — but only by the superhuman standards people have been imposing on Koufax since his record-breaking performances of 1963. Actually, Sandy pitched a five-hitter against the team that almost won the pennant last year; he struck out seven, which is about normal, and walked five, which is high for him but not surprising in view of his interrupted training schedule."

The important thing was that Sandy had no after-effects following his opening victory. And he retained his form throughout the year. On June 12th, he shut out the New York Mets for his ninth win of the season against only three losses, and a week later Sandy again won from the Mets, 2-1. He had twelve strikeouts and marked the seventh time in 1965 that he fanned ten or more, and the sixty-eighth time in his career that he had accomplished this feat. By mid-July he still had only three losses, against sixteen victories, with three shutouts. He had completed fifteen games in twenty-two starts and, for the fifth consecutive year, had marked up a minimum of 200 strikeouts, which was a National League record. This was rather impressive for a pitcher who did not know, from one start to the next, whether his arm would blow up on him — and on his team, which was fighting for another National League pennant.

By the end of July, the Dodgers — and Koufax — were flying high. But at the end of the month, the pitcher and his team had another scare. Sandy had won eleven in a row and had not missed a turn all year, when he lost a night game to the Cincinnati Reds, 4-1. Sandy pitched eight innings, striking out eight and allowing five hits. In the early innings, he experienced a stiffness in his left arm and his doctor, Robert Kerlan, admitted that "I would say the arthritic condition in his elbow, which is chronic, was perhaps a bit worse last night."

Sandy had a response. "I haven't missed a turn this year and I don't intend to." He was scheduled to pitch against the Cardinals in his next start and he did not let his team down. He went all nine innings for a 3-2 win. He yielded only five hits and fanned eleven batters. He won his twentieth game when he beat the Mets 4-3 on August 10th and a few days later chalked up his twenty-first victory, in a ten-inning, 1-0 game over the Pittsburgh Pirates. Again, Sandy was in strikeout form, getting twelve Pirates.

Already, the 1965 season was a successful one for Sandy Koufax. His arm, while not always strong, was good enough to serve him through a difficult season. He was winning and striking out batters as in the past. It was all quite satisfactory. But on the night of September 9th, he achieved a pitching performance better than any in his life and equaled by very few pitchers in the history of the game. He pitched a perfect game against the Chicago Cubs and thus became the first twirler in baseball history to pitch four no-hitters in a career. What made the game even more remarkable was that Sandy's opponent, Bob Hendley, gave up only one hit. But the reader will remember that this chapter began with a description of that game, Sandy's "finest hour." Up until the moment Koufax pitched this history-making game, he was one of only four hurlers to have three no-hitters: Larry Corcoran beginning in 1880 and then Cy Young and Bob Feller. Now Sandy stood alone, the only man who put together four no-hitters — and four years in succession!

Meanwhile, quite apart from Sandy's exploits, the Dodgers were engaged in one of the hottest, closest pennant races in many years. This was an unusual Dodger team. It had the pitching of Koufax and Don Drysdale, but Tommy Davis, one of the team's best players and finest hitters, was injured in May and never came back in 1965. Jim Gilliam, who had started as a coach, was reactivated as a player and minor leaguers were brought up to fill various holes in the lineup. The Dodgers fought their way to first place in early July, then faltered and recovered enough to keep the lead into mid-August. On September 6th, the Dodgers led the Giants by a single game, and then the Giants ran off a fourteen-game winning streak and appeared to be "in" as the next National League champions. On September 16th, the Giants held a four-and-a-half-game lead over the Dodgers and hardly anyone held any hopes for the Los Angeles club, which had Maury Wills stealing bases, Koufax and Drysdale winning, but the rest of the team lagging behind them.

At this moment in the race, the Dodgers took hold of themselves and started to play brilliantly. They won five in succession, including three shutouts. In thirteen games, Dodger pitchers held the opposition so tightly, that seven of those games were shutouts. Claude Osteen and Ron Perranoski joined Koufax and Drysdale and the race became so tight that on September 30th, with only four games left to both the Dodgers and the Giants, the Dodgers held a two-game lead. Sandy won his twenty-fifth game of the year the night before, shutting out the Cincinnati Reds and fanning thirteen and bringing the Dodger winning streak to twelve. On October 1st, the Dodgers lost to the Milwaukee Braves and the Giants also were defeated, so with the race that close, no champion would be declared until almost the very last day of the season.

Sandy had pitched steadily all year and now he was called on by Walt Alston to nail down the pennant. Sandy was pitching with only two days of rest. He was bone-tired, but now, if ever, he had to win. The Braves were a tough team, and eager to play the role of spoilers. But Koufax was not going to allow *this* season to end sourly. He rose to the challenge and won, 3-1, striking out thirteen and giving up only four hits. The pennant was won, Koufax had won twenty-six games and the Dodgers were now in the World Series. Koufax had an earned run average of 2.06 and set a major league record with 369 strikeouts for a single season. He surely had made a major contribution to the 1965 pennant chase. And his personal records kept coming. Not only did he have his perfect game and his strikeout record. He also fanned ten or more men in a game eighty-one times (a new mark), twenty times in 1965 alone. His last four victories of the year, coming at moments of extreme pressure in the race, were shutout wins.

The 1965 World Series opened in Bloomington, Minnesota, October 6th, with the Dodgers trying to win the world championship from the Minnesota Twins, a new power in baseball, a team that had easily beaten back the challenge of the once-great New York Yankees, and every other American League team as well. Normally, Koufax, the Dodger ace, would have been the first Dodger pitcher to take the mound. But it was on Yom Kippur and Sandy already had told Alston — and the sports world — that he would not play ball on the Jewish holiday. This act of faith made for a good deal of discussion throughout the nation, but Koufax won the admiration of almost everyone by making clear he did not think that even a baseball game, a World Series game at that, was as important to him as observing Yom Kippur. After this game, Alston permanently kept a Jewish calendar on his desk so that he would always be aware of any upcoming holiday.

Don Drysdale opened the Series and, to the surprise of many, lost 8-2 to Jim Grant. The Twins showed both power and speed to lick Drysdale, but the Dodger fans remained confident, for Koufax was scheduled to pitch the next game, and who could beat Drysdale and Koufax back-to-back? Hardly anybody, was the usual reply to that question. But the Twins did it and consternation took over among the Dodgers.

Koufax lost to another southpaw, Jim Kaat, in what started out as a close game but became a rout when Sandy left the mound. For the first five innings, Sandy pitched shutout ball, although he later said that he had control trouble. Kaat was quoted after the game, saying, "Nobody expected me to beat Koufax. When I saw him throw after an inning, I thought I'd better not give up a run." And he did very well, keeping pace with Sandy for those five scoreless innings. In the sixth, Zoilo Versalles, the aggressive Minnesota shortstop, hit a ball to Gilliam, which took an unexpected bounce, hit Gilliam's right shoulder and caromed into left field. It was called a two-base error and Koufax was in trouble. Struggling for control, he allowed Tony Oliva to hit safely and then Harmon Killebrew singled Oliva home and the Dodgers were two runs behind.

In the Dodger seventh, there were two singles and then a sacrifice, advancing both runners, and Alston lifted Sandy for a pinch-hitter, after John Roseboro singled to drive in one Dodger run. The Twins stopped the rally and Koufax was out of the game. Dodger pitchers gave up another three runs to allow the Twins 5-2. When Sandy had left the game, the score was 2-1 in favor of the Twins.

Now it seemed that the Dodgers were in deep trouble. Their two top pitchers had been beaten. But Claude Osteen pitched a 4-0 shutout in Los Angeles and then Drysdale won an easy game 7-2, with his teammates running wildly and effectively on the bases and showing the old Dodger style of run, run, run. The World Series was all tied up with two victories apiece.

In the fifth game, the last one at Los Angeles, Koufax faced Jim Kaat and Sandy was back in his "normal" form, which meant that the Twins could not score a single run off him. Sandy won a 7-0 shutout and gave the Dodgers a one-game lead in the World Series, three victories to two. Sandy was again almost perfect. He faced only twenty-nine batters, two above the minimum, and pitched perfect ball until the fifth inning, when Killebrew looped a hit into center field. He yielded only three other hits, walked one and struck out ten — a standard performance by the southpaw. It also was Sandy's twenty-eighth complete game of the year and the twenty-second game in which he struck out ten or more batters. Jim Grant said after the game, "There should be one Cy Young Award for him and another for the rest of us to shoot at." But Koufax amazed not only the opposition players; he also astonished the medical profession. The team physician of the Twins, Dr, William E. Proffitt, Jr., said, "You would never have thought that Koufax could pitch consistently with that arthritis condition in his elbow. At least he might've had to rest every three or four pitching starts. But the way he's performed this year is amazing."

Jim Grant, who had won the first game of the Series and lost the fourth, came back for a third start — and won the sixth game, by a score of 5-1, hitting a three-run homer to clinch the victory. This brought the Series down to a fateful seventh game, and again it was Koufax who carried the hopes of the Dodgers and the National Leaguers. He had only two days rest and he was tired, as he had repeatedly said during the week. He had not missed a turn in the regular season and already had pitched twice in the Series. But he was the man who had to do it.

He showed, in the first inning, that he was not as sharp as usual. With the first two batters retired, Sandy walked Oliva and Killebrew. He met this opening challenge by striking out Earl Battey. In the third inning, Versalles got the first hit for the Twins. The following inning gave Sandy a two-run margin on which to work. Jim Kaat yielded a home run to Lou Johnson. Ron Fairly doubled and scored on a single by Wes Parker. It was a thin lead, but Koufax nursed it along. He had his troubles in the fifth. Frank Quilici doubled and Rich Rollins walked. Sandy was upset by the umpire's calls and showed some temper — which was rare for him. Versalles then hit a sharp grounder toward third base. Gilliam, old as players go but a veteran who did not panic, made a good catch and barely made a force play at the bag. That was the last time the Twins had a real chance to score.

It was still 2-0 when the Twins came up for their last chance against an exhausted pitcher fighting to keep a shutout, to win a game, clinch a World Series. Oliva was the first batter and Koufax got him on a grounder to third. Sandy was pitching a two-hit game and had eight strikeouts. The game was one of his patented ones, but the fans realized that here was a pitcher fighting fatigue as well as the Twins. Killebrew singled and the crowd, rooting hard for Minnesota, screamed with anticipation.

Now Battey was the hitter. The first pitch was fast and over the plate. Battey looked at it. On the second strike, Battey swung and missed. Sandy had him puzzled. The next pitch was a curve, and as it hooked the plate, Battey stood there, bat on shoulder. He was the ninth strikeout victim of the day for Koufax.

Killebrew remained frozen to first base as Bob Allison strode to the batter's box. It was Allison who had homered in the sixth game to tie the Series and bring it down to this seventh contest. He fouled back the first pitch for the initial strike. Then Sandy was low and then high for two balls. Again, Allison swung and missed for a second strike. Koufax reached down for another fastball, threw it — and Allison missed it one more time, a final time, and the World Series was at an end. Koufax had his second shutout, another game with ten strikeouts, and a world championship for his mates and himself.

Walt Alston, the Dodger manager, had to make a major decision for this seventh game. He had Drysdale ready and a well-worn Koufax. Whom was he to pitch? The fans buzzed over it, but Alston made the winning choice. It was no wonder that after that last game, he said that Koufax was the best in the world. "If there ever was a better pitcher, it was before my time," Alston told reporters. Sam Mele, the losing manager, agreed. "He's in a class by himself."

Newsweek magazine called it "Sandy's series." *Sports Illustrated* said that "the best pitcher in baseball proved to be the difference between two very different ball clubs." Tommy Holmes, writing for the *New York Herald Tribune,* reported that "there was only one story as the long baseball season came to its end. That was Mr. Koufax." He also pointed out that in this World Series, Sandy had pitched twenty-four innings, allowing one earned run and striking out twenty-nine.

The honors came frequently for Koufax after the season ended. He won a Corvette from *Sport* magazine for being the outstanding player in the Series. *Sports Illustrated* named him "Sportsman of the Year." On the same day, January 8, 1966, he was named to receive the Sid Mercer Memorial Award (for player of the year) and the Babe Ruth Award (for being the top World Series star) by the New York Chapter of the Baseball Writers' Association. He was the first player to win the Ruth Award more than once and only Joe DiMaggio, Ted Williams and Mickey Mantle had repeated as Mercer winners. The *Sporting News* selected Sandy as "Player of the Year," and the pitcher was chosen "Male Athlete of the Year" for 1965 in an Associated Press Poll. He also had won this honor in 1963. Sandy also won the Van Heusen Award "for grand performance in baseball," outpolling Willie Mays and other fine players. And, to make it just about unanimous, he won the Cy Young Award for best pitcher in baseball by unanimous vote of a committee of the Baseball Writers' Association and was the first player to win the award twice. The committee stressed that Sandy had led the major leagues in total wins, with twenty-six; most innings pitched, 336; most strikeouts, 382; and lowest earned run average, 2.04.

After the remarkable 1965 season, Koufax entered into financial negotiations with the Dodgers, and once again he won national headlines. He and Don Drysdale attempted to deal with the management not as individual players but as a team — a tactic never before used by baseball players. They asked for a $1,000,000 three-year package. It shook the baseball world, not only because of the huge sum of money but also because the two outstanding pitchers were negotiating in tandem. The two men held out for more than a month and finally settled for record-breaking sums, Koufax for a reported $125,000 for 1966 and Drysdale for a reported $110,000.

"Our fight," Koufax said later, "was to establish ourselves at a certain plateau salarywise. That's the battle of every ball player." He added that "We accomplished what we set out to accomplish, and that is the right of a baseball player to bargain."

Fans wondered whether Koufax would be effective in 1966, without the benefit of spring training. "Don't let anyone tell you spring training isn't necessary," he told reporters. But one week-end before the season opened, he pitched six innings of no-hit ball against the Cleveland Indians. He began the year a bit uncertainly. Soon, however, he hit his normal stride. On May 19th, he pitched a shutout over the Giants, for his sixth win of the season. Almost as usual, he struck out ten in this victory. On June 1, he pitched another shutout, this time a 1-0 win over the St. Louis Cardinals, for his ninth triumph. He ran off an eight-game winning streak and by mid-June, he led the National League with a pitching record of 11-2 and in earned run averages and strikeouts. Obviously, the long holdout had no effect on his ability.

Yet shadows did not pass over the great pitcher. As the 1966 season continued, Koufax kept winning, but, for a while, he was no longer overpowering. He did not overwhelm the batters. He struggled for control, even though he added to his victory list and strikeout victims piled up. At the end of July his arthritic elbow acted up again and he required, for the first time in the season, heavy shots from his doctor. On July 23, he won from the Mets, 6-2, but he was wild and unhappy with his performance. It was victory No. 17, but Sandy, a perfectionist, knew that something was wrong. As Maury Allen of the *New York Post* phrased it, "Sandy is 17-5 on the season with a 1.70 ERA but has not been the same, smooth overpowering pitcher in the last few weeks."

It was thought that Sandy would have to miss his next mound turn. He didn't. Instead, he was his brilliant self again. On July 27, he went eleven innings against the Phillies. He yielded one run, four hits and scored sixteen strikeouts! He left after the eleventh inning and his team won 2-1 in the twelfth. His fourth strikeout of the game was his 2,267th of his career, moving him ahead of Lefty Grove and into tenth place among the lifetime leaders. His fifteenth strikeout, which came in the ninth inning, was his 200th of the season. This was the sixth year in a row he reached that high figure. Clearly, Koufax, when healthy, was extraordinary. Equally clearly, his arm had its uncertainties.

Before the season had ended, Sandy had decided to make this his last year in the game; but the team was in the thick of a pennant race, and the decision remained private.

The pain in his arm grew worse all the time. The doctors had warned him that on any given pitch in any game, the elbow might stop working, and Sandy would lose the use of his arm not only for pitching, but for doing anything at all. He risked becoming a cripple, but he felt obliged to finish the season as best he could. He wanted to honor his commitment to his team and his teammates.

Writing in *Sport* magazine, Milton Gross observes: "It wasn't generally known that as the season progressed into the tight stages of the pennant race, Sandy had begun to receive injections directly into the elbow two days before every pitching assignment. In the days immediately following each game, the pain was intense. In the day following each shot, the pain was even worse, but Koufax continued the pretense that he was going about his daily routine normally."

On the final day of the season, the Dodgers played a doubleheader against the Phillies. Los Angeles needed to win one of the two games to win the pennant. They were losing in the first game, and Sandy went to Alston in the eighth inning and volunteered to go to the bullpen and pitch relief if he was needed, and then pitch the second game as well if they couldn't win the opener. Alston had no intention of relieving with Sandy, and the Dodgers did drop the first game. The second game simply had to be won or it was goodbye pennant. Despite the aching pain in his arm, Sandy went out to the mound for the nightcap.

The Dodgers gave him an early six-run lead, and normally, with Sandy on the mound, that would have been the ballgame right there. But in the fifth frame, with one out, Sandy threw a pitch and heard a crack as he felt a sharp pain rocket into his back. Despite his agony, he got the third out of the inning, then went into the clubhouse while the Dodgers came to bat.

Sandy had slipped a disc. The trainer snapped it back into place while Sandy literally fell off the table. Then Koufax returned to the field and grittily hung on to finish the game and save a 6-3 win that won the pennant for his team. Afterwards, Sandy confessed that he really didn't even know how much he was hurting during the game "because I was full of codeine. It was the only way I could pitch." The pain-killer was added to the dosages of cortisone and butazolidine with which he had already been injected.

Koufax retired after the 1966 season because he felt he simply could not pitch without pain or up to his established standards. But it is a telling tribute to his brilliance that in this last season, during which he toiled in unremitting pain, he compiled statistics that would be awesome in any day or age. In leading his team to another pennant, he won twenty-seven while losing only nine, compiled an E.R.A. of 1.73, and struck out over 300 batters for a record-breaking third season. All this while gravely handicapped by a serious injury.

In the fall classic that year, the Dodgers were swept in four games by the Baltimore Orioles, a result that shocked the baseball world. Sandy lost his last game in professional baseball when centerfielder Willie Davis lost two consecutive fly balls in the sun, adding a wild throw on the second misplay for an unforgettable three errors on two plays. The two ruinous plays gave the Orioles three unearned runs and, ultimately, the ballgame.

"When Davis returned to the bench," Gross relates, "the rest of his teammates avoided Willie as though he were unclean. The centerfielder fled to the corner of the dugout as if he were trying to hide. He was hurt by the hoots and the boos. Koufax was hurting just as much, physically as well as mentally, but he went directly to Willie.

" 'Don't let them get you down,' Sandy said.

" 'Sandy,' said Willie, near to weeping. 'I'm sorry.'

" 'There's nothing to be sorry about,' Sandy said, trying to console his teammate. 'These things happen.' "

When Koufax retired after the season, accolades for the great southpaw poured in from everywhere. Leonard Koppett, in an article bluntly titled "Why Koufax belongs in the Hall of Fame," wrote these observations:

"In January, 1972, Sandy Koufax will be voted into the Baseball Hall of Fame. He'll have to wait that long because of the rule that forbids a vote until five years after the player's retirement. But it will be a formality; everyone recognizes that . . .

"He led the National League in earned run average for five consecutive years. No one else ever did that in either league. Only three men who won more than 150 games in modern times have better won-lost percentages: Christy Mathewson, Lefty Grove and Whitey Ford. In strikeouts, Koufax was in a class by himself. Only Sandy was able to strike out 300 or more men in three different seasons. Only Koufax, in the whole history of baseball, struck out more than one batter per inning pitched throughout his career. Only Sandy pitched four no-hitters, in four consecutive years.

"So Sandy will go into the Hall of Fame at the earliest possible moment for the simplest possible reason: he belongs."

Baseball fans everywhere, even the most sophisticated, marveled at the Dodger ace's feats; and their appreciation increased when they considered the physical difficulties that plagued his pitching arm. Mel Durslag, in the L. A. *Herald-Examiner,* called Sandy "the pin-up boy of the Arthritis and Rheumatism Foundation." But that arthritic arm struck out ten or more batters in a record ninety-seven games.

In *The Great No-Hitters,* Glenn Dickey notes that in the start prior to his fourth no-hitter, Sandy had been removed for a pinch-hitter in the eighth while trailing Houston, 2-1; Koufax had been so frustrated that he had picked up a rubbing table and tossed it against the wall. The next day, his elbow improved, and when he pitched the no-hitter the elbow felt as good as it had all year. "Maybe it was the exercise he got throwing the table," Dickey says dryly.

Arthur Daley of the *Times* makes the point that "the Dodgers begged Sandy not to announce his retirement when he did. They didn't want to be hung over a barrel at trading time, nor did they want to risk impeding the flow of their advance ticket sale. He could have taken a $150,000 salary for the next season for doing nothing. But Sandy had too much character for that. His high ethical standards could not permit him to be a party to such deceit. So he quit with his head held high."

Without question, Sandy went out a winner. His dazzling record in the last pennant-winning season capped his marvelous career. Just as impressive as his regular-season feats were his marks in interleague competition. Along with his four World Series wins, his cumulative E.R.A. in Series play was 0.95, the fourth-best in history (Babe Ruth, better known as a hitter, was second-best). Despite being in only three Series, his sixty-one strikeouts is the fourth best mark ever. He is second only to Bob Gibson in compiling the most Series strikeouts per nine innings (9.63), and his paltry allowance of only 5.68 hits per nine inning game puts him seventh in that category. He was also the winning pitcher in the 1965 All-Star game, and started the 1966 classic which his team won, 2-1. One can only imagine the dizzying heights to which his career might have led had his arm remained healthy.

In January, 1972, Sanford Koufax was elected to Baseball's Hall of Fame in Cooperstown, New York. At thirty-six years old, he was the youngest man ever so honored. He joined an elite group of only nine men who had ever been elected in their first year of eligibility. He led everybody on the ballot with three hundred forty-four of a possible three hundred ninety-six votes; his total of votes was the highest ever received by any player in baseball history. His judges had awarded him the highest possible accolade, and had confirmed what everyone always suspected: that there had never in the history of the game been any pitcher any better than Sandy Koufax at his peak.

Observing Koufax hurling against the Twins in the World Series, Roger Angell, in his splendid book *The Summer Game,* offers these reflections:

"I concentrated on watching Koufax at work. This is not as easy as it sounds, for there is the temptation simply to discredit what one sees. His fast ball, for example, flares upward at the last instant, so that batters swinging at it often look as if they had lashed out at a bad high pitch. Koufax's best curve, by contrast, shoots down, often barely pinching a corner of the plate, inside or out, just above the knees. A typical Koufax victim — even if he is an excellent hitter — having looked bad by swinging on the first pitch and worse in letting the second go by, will often simply stand there, his bat nailed to his shoulder, for the next two or three pitches, until the umpire's right hand goes up and he is out. Or if he swings again it is with an awkward last-minute dip of the bat that is a caricature of his normal riffle. It is almost painful to watch, for Koufax, instead of merely overpowering hitters, as some fast-ball throwers do, appears to dismantle them, taking away first one and then another of their carefully developed offensive weapons and judgments, and leaving them only with the conviction that they are the victims of a total mismatch. Maybe they are right, at that; the records of this, Koufax's greatest year, suggest as much. In the regular season, he won twenty-six games, struck out three hundred and eighty-two batters (an all-time record), and pitched his fourth no-hit game — a perfect game, by the way — in as many years, which is also a new record. In the Series, he won two shutouts pitched within three days of each other, and gave up exactly one earned run in twenty-four innings. He was the difference between the two clubs; he won the Series."

Other great hurlers and strikeout specialists always have been and always will be part of baseball's lore, and sooner or later most all of Sandy's many records will fall, as records are made to do; but Koufax has left his mark indelibly upon this sport. The Jewish boy from Brooklyn had become much more than a baseball star, more even than a Hall of Famer. He had become, as Angell puts it, "maybe the best pitcher in the whole history of baseball."

The Romance of the Ring

"Give me a Jewish fighter who can be built up into a challenger for the heavyweight championship and I'll show you the man who can bring back the $1,000,000 gate." — Tex Rickard.

"Benny Leonard had done more to conquer anti-Semitism than a thousand text books have done." — Arthur Brisbane.

Somewhere between these two statements lies the significance of the Jew in boxing. And the Jew in pugilism has been a tremendous figure. From boxing's infancy, when Daniel Mendoza founded the modern school of fighting and won the heavyweight crown and held it from 1790 to 1795, Jews have won many titles and have added lustre to the old, savage ring game.

It is generally acknowledged that the Irish, the Jews and the Blacks have contributed the greatest champions, the most spectacular ringmen, the best everyday pugs. There have been more than twenty Jewish ring champions and many of them, like Abe Attell, Benny Leonard and Barney Ross rank with the top names in the sport. But even on the lower levels there has been a steady list of Jewish fighters.

Boxing is a hard racket. Tough people make a living out of it and, by and large, people with primitive instincts pay good money to see bouts. It is true that within the past fifty years boxing has become "respectable." Now the ringside seats are bought by society folk, who come to see blood and boxing in ermine wraps and in tuxedos. But the fight game and the real fight fans symbolize the rougher aspects of American sporting life. To the uninitiated it is amazing that the Jew — considered by the average American as a quiet, peaceable sort of fellow — has been so prominent in boxing.

When Tex Rickard said that a Jewish fighter would bring back a heavy gate, the cool-eyed gambler who brought boxing into the big money meant that in the large cities and in New York in particular, which was the boxing center of the world, Jews would flock to the fights. And the shrewd Brisbane understood that the Jews, reviled and sneered at, would gain added dignity if a fellow Jew were to win a title. When Benny Leonard reigned as lightweight champion, all America admired him. And because Benny was as conscious of his dignity as Joe Louis was of his in a later day, the Jews were given new respect, just as Negro prestige was enhanced in Louis' era.

Most fighters come from poverty-stricken homes or from the slum areas of the nation. Joe was born in a poor cotton-picking area of Alabama; Benny Leonard and many other outstanding Jewish fighters were born in the ghetto of New York's East Side. Most fighters have known hunger and lack of decent clothing and shelter. They were brought up with pinching need at their side. They know that money means salvation for them. They see a quick fortune in the ring. Most of them never make it; but they become punch drunk and woozy through trying.

A boy who knows real poverty is not afraid to take a

beating if he has to, in order to earn a few dollars and to try to earn more. The spectre of always remaining in a slum area, for example, is much more powerful than the most dynamite-laden fist of a ring foe. Thus you find that the fighters who reach the top are a combination of cruelty and sentimentality. A champion is rough in the ring, for it is his bread-and-butter; once outside the ring he is generally a soft touch for beggars, for hangers-on and for fair-weather friends. The champion is good to his family, builds a house for his aging mother and takes care of the brothers and sisters. This is sometimes press agentry; often it is the truth. Ring Lardner, who wrote a classic short story called "Champion," which is a bitter portrait of a fighter who is exceptionally thoughtless and cruel to his family and is played up in the papers as though he were the kindliest of men, had more than a germ of truth in his tale. But the opposite is also true. Men like Jack Dempsey, Joe Louis, Benny Leonard and other champions, were known for their soft hearts — but only out of the ring. Within the roped area they were merciless. It is their background, their hard lives and their bitter memories that made them like that.

And of course there is another reason for this harshness. Boxing itself is a merciless game. It is not at all the "manly art of self defense" that some of its addicts make it out to be. The fan who loves to watch a good and clever boxer rather than a crude and heavy puncher is rare. For no fight fan likes anything more than the sight of blood. Fighting appeals to men all over the world. It would be senseless to deny it. It is raw conflict, dramatized and brought into the open where thousands can watch it. Here are two men, with their gloved fists as their only friends and a neutral referee between them. Who is the better man? Punching prowess and cleverness will tell. And millions of fans are willing to watch this sort of a struggle, mostly on television, every day in the week. Today, the fights rank with the major events on television and as many as 60,000,000 persons watch a heavyweight championship bout.

Why?

It is sheer conflict. No man can win because of his father's background or because his mother is a society woman. The "Aryan" supremacy idea means nothing in the ring. All of Hitler's anthropologists could not make Max Schmeling superior to Joe Louis when they met for the second time and the American Negro butchered the Nazi champion. The Jew who fights the non-Jew in the ring is considered the equal of his foe, unless his opponent manages to lick him. Conversely, the Jew is better than the other guy only if he wins his fight. Thus racialism, bias and background poisons vanish for the moment. The fight fan has to consider only one thing: Who is the better fighter?

For many years the race angle was important. The Negro was always discriminated against; decisions went against him; white champions drew a color line and refused to fight Negroes. When Jack Johnson won the heavyweight crown a hue went up and a search was started for a "white hope," as though the Negro were an alien, a non-American who somehow was not fit to be the champion. Joe Louis proved himself as good an American as the best of us. And when Jim Corbett met Jewish Joe Choynski, Jews and Irishmen nearly started riots in San Francisco, arguing who would win, the Irish or the Jewish boy.

Jewish fighters took Irish names. Mushy Callahan and Al McCoy, for example, were Jewish boys. But the Irish had a fighting reputation and the Jews tried to take advantage of it. Later, many Irishmen took Jewish names, and returned the compliment. But these were the raw days in boxing, when sheriffs broke up fights and sent the boxers to jail. Today things are different and fight fans are slightly better.

It is impossible to write adequately about every Jewish fighter or Jewish champion. Sometimes it is difficult to determine who is and who is not a Jew. Max Baer, for example, wore a Jewish star on his trunks and said that he was Jewish. But later it was discovered that he was supposed to have been Jewish on his father's side. And wise boxing writers believe that this, too, was strictly from Max's fertile imagination. Baer must have thought that the *Mogen David* would win him supporters. He may have had something there. Harry Greb, a wonderful fighter and a very hard character indeed, about whom a fine book was written a while back, was no Jew, but for years the legend had it that he was Jewish and that his real name was Harry Berg (which is Greb, spelled backwards). Greb was great. But he was not Jewish, even though the *Universal Jewish Encyclopedia* lists him as a Jewish fighter.

Nevertheless, there are some fighters who proclaim their faith and many of the Jewish immortals were among them. Jackie "Kid" Berg, for example, who came from the Whitechapel area in London, wore a *Mogen David* on his trunks and had the Hebrew initials of his name sewn into the center of the star. Benny Leonard was always interested in Jewish affairs, aligned himself with Jewish causes and worked for Zionism.

Some of the fighters who are not treated at length are Maxie Rosenbloom, who held the light-heavyweight title for years and who later went to Hollywood, became a succesful comedian and then branched out in night-club work; Battling Levinsky, who also held the same title and who beat top-notchers for years; Sid Terris, Ruby Goldstein, Leach Cross and Lew Tendler, exciting little lightweights who won headlines for years before they faded out. These men all added to ring history and fought brilliantly at times. Tendler was a near-champion; Terris and Goldstein mere flashes. But they were like rockets — once seen, always remembered, even though they plunged quickly into obscurity. Goldstein later won added fame as an outstanding referee. Another notable fighter was Sam Mosberg, the first Jewish Olympic boxing champion who won the lightweight title in 1920.

The fighters included in this book are representative of the sport. Apart from the great champions described, Al Singer symbolizes the champion who rose to prominence and then faded fast. His story is the tale of Goldstein and Terris, except that he was at the top, if for a little while. Jackie Berg was a phenomenal fighter, a journeyman who is the backbone of the game. He is included to represent all such fellows, who have the game in their blood and never give it up. And Benny Bass is there because of his fight with Red Chapman, whose real name was Morris Kaplan. It is a bout that is the essence of all fighting. And it deserves to be in any chapter on boxing.

In recent years there were some heavyweight threats around the ring, who, had they beaten the champion, would have given Jewry its first real modern heavyweight champion. The bravest of these men was Abe Simon, who fought Louis twice and was knocked out both times. Then Simon was beaten badly by a Negro named Lem Franklin, who later met a tragic death. But the story of Franklin brings to mind a boxing tragedy which is a superb example of the hard game and its inherent fascination.

This story deals with another fighter named Franklin. This boy was Walter Franklin, the son of a rabbi from Yemen, and a *yeshiva* lad himself before he decided to follow a pugilistic career. In a two-year period Walter, a handsome middleweight with a powerful left cross and right hand, with an ironcast jaw and a marvelous body, changed from a contender for the crown to a common variety of Fistiana's cruel appellation, "the stumble-bum."

I'll never understand how it happened. I* saw the first eight bouts in which Walter engaged. He was tremendous. He could take it; he dished it out; he was a crowd-pleaser. Many fans came to see Franklin. Starting out as a club fighter, Walter soon moved into the mecca of boxing, Madison Square Garden. Having followed his career from its inception, I eagerly watched his Garden debut. There was nothing to worry about. He won by a knockout in the first round. Considering that a few weeks previous to this fight he had beaten Babe Risko, a former middleweight champion, with ease, Franklin was acclaimed as a coming champion. Then suddenly he lost a fight to a tough boy named Cal Cagni. Cagni had hit Franklin with a terrible blow in the first minute of the bout. From that moment on Walter fought on instinct alone. He nearly won out in a battle which will long be remembered by the crowd which saw the slaughter. Cagni won the decision; Franklin shared the cheers with him.

For three months Walter did not fight again. When he returned to the ring he won his first bout quickly. But then

*H.U.R.

he lost. Again he lost. His once iron frame crumpled under attacks which he used to laugh at. He was easy to hit, but still able to take punishment. Something was wrong and it was this: Franklin had lost the art of hitting back. The dynamite in his fists exploded no longer. Rapidly, tragically, inexplicably, Walter Franklin had slipped. The young man was a loser. He fought hard and well, but did not win.

Then, in an exciting fight he was knocked down and in the following round he was knocked out. I saw him go to his dressing room. His head was the size of an overgrown pumpkin, his ears were blown up like small balloons. His eyes cut, his lips swollen, the man who had been a champion in the making looked very much as though he had met up with a threshing machine.

I knew then that he was through. Subsequent events did not shock me. In small type on the inside sport pages were notices during the following year that Franklin had been put away in one round, or two, or three. Unknowns were beating him to a pulp.

I lost sight of him. I have no idea where he ended up. He might be a tramp today, or a businessman, or a soldier. I do know that he is a ring tragedy.

It is in this sport that the Jewish champions excelled. It was tragedies like this one that they skirted. They had to beat their environment, their opponents, their bad breaks and a variety of little things which one seldom thinks about. A Benny Leonard might have disappeared into oblivion if he was badly beaten during his first year, when he was still unknown and unskilled. Luck was with him, and with these other champions. And because tragedy stalks and fate puts in a harsh finger at any moment, boxing is a sport with its own special thrills, its private passions and its endless fascination.

JOE CHOYNSKI, RIGHT, SQUARES OFF AGAINST JIM JEFFRIES, JIM CORBETT, IN THE CENTER, LOOKS ON. (A VERY RARE PICTURE.)

Joe Choynski

Frisco Flash

Whenever heavyweights are mentioned in sports talk, the dialogue invariably turns to Daniel Mendoza, the first great Jewish heavyweight. But he fought so long ago, when boxing was in its swaddling clothes, that Mendoza is more of a legend than an actuality. It is fascinating to look at old sporting prints and see the heavyweights of old, in their now-funny stance, with their hands stretched out in the old-fashioned way which won the admiration of the spectators. Mendoza was one of the first heavies who made history in England, where the annals of boxing really began, or at least where modern boxing began. The Marquis of Queensberry rules are the ones which dominate the game today, and the Marquis was an Englishman.

But Mendoza was a personality of long ago and most of his fights are hidden behind a veil of the past; so well hidden, that most accounts are colored by time and by the impressionable reporters of that age, amd most of them were not trained, unbiased sports writers, as are today's experts in the field. The first real heavyweight of modern importance who was also probably the greatest of all Jewish heavyweights, was Joe Choynski of San Francisco. Although Joe never held the heavyweight crown, he was acknowledged to be one of the foremost fighters of any era. What made his successes even more remarkable was the fact that he was not a large or a heavy man. At his peak Choynski weighed no more than 155 pounds. But for twenty years he met and defeated some of the outstanding fighters in history.

It is not difficult to understand why Choynski was a tough fellow. The San Francisco of his day was a spectacular place, full of rowdies and of toughs who settled most arguments with their fists. Anyone who fought did so out of necessity and those who were successful fighters were the roughest men among a hard breed. In those days Frisco did not have its veneer of gentility with which it prides itself today. The West was really wild in its early pioneering days and Choynski, whose greatest fights took place in the 1890's and the early 1900's, was another tough guy who seldom bowed to anyone.

Today's fighters seldom go more than fifteen rounds and each round is three minutes long, with one minute rest between rounds. In a word, a fifteen-rounder takes, in all, no more than an hour. In the old days a round ended when a man was floored. Thus the business of fifty-round fights is a bit confusing. On the other hand, the old fighters fought for hours at a time, and the conditions under which they fought were difficult. To begin with, fighting was not allowed in most states. So the crowds used to gather at night, on the sly, and always tense because the sheriff might come along and arrest all the "sports." Purses were slim and a man had to fight long and hard for the money he earned. And he really earned it.

The point that must be made is that boxing eighty years ago was a cruel, hard sport which never had the approval of the Americans whose children now sit transfixed before their television sets and watch countless fights between mediocre champions. Fighting was a man's game in those days, and broken hands, busted jaws and bloody eyes were more common than otherwise.

And when people say that Jews never excelled in sports, or when they say, in modern times, that a Jewish fighter has the support of some mysterious "interests," they should remember the boxing era of Joe Choynski and they should recall that in the toughest boxing age of all, a Jewish heavyweight took them all on for twenty years and eventually emerged as one of the top heavyweights of all time.

Today Joe Choynski is best remembered for his historic fights with James J. Corbett, who was one of the finest heavyweight champs in boxing annals and is considered by many to have been the best heavyweight in history. Hollywood has glamorized the life of Corbett in a movie called "Gentleman Jim," in which Errol Flynn played Corbett. One of the key scenes in the picture was Corbett's success against Choynski. They fought many times and it was Corbett's success against Choynski that won him a chance at the biggest match in boxing, the title shot against the legendary and immortal John L. Sullivan.

Jim Corbett, in an authorized story of his life, told how he met Choynski, but like many a boastful champion, Corbett sometimes over-exaggerated. But part of what he said is true and reveals some interesting boxing history.

"There has been much discussion relative to my meetings with Choynski," Corbett wrote. "I'll tell you all about it. My brother and Choynski's brother were both employed in the City Hall," he added, and said that they argued about the abilities of both fighters.

The upshot was that Corbett and Choynski decided to

fight. According to Corbett he got cold feet about the entire matter, but finally decided to get into a ring with Choynski. "I walked ten miles over to the sand hills and we went at it with bare knuckles. I knocked him out in two rounds," Corbett said. Nat Fleischer says it took one round. According to the record book, it says that in 1884, the two men fought to no-decision in four rounds. This was before Choynski turned professional. In 1888 the fighters fought four torrid rounds on a pier before it was stopped by the police. This was the bout which the Hollywood version of Corbett's life played up. Even in that fight Corbett did not get the better of Choynski.

Originally, Choynski and Corbett fought only because they liked to fight. There was no "grudge" angle to it. And they were very closely matched. The year they fought on the pier they met again and this was the classic fight which entered Choynski's name in the boxing records for all time. In what was Corbett's roughest fight in his brilliant career, except perhaps for his last fight with Jim Jeffries, the Irishman went twenty-eight hard rounds against Choynski before he could eke out a victory. Choynski was fast, game and hit hard, but Corbett was one of the shrewdest boxers in history. It was a story of two good boxers, who were familiar with each other's style, and both of them were not yet at their peak. But Corbett had a bit more stamina and outlasted Joe Choynski. Nat Fleischer, in his biography of Corbett, called this bout "a genuine ring epic of savage slaughter."

Nat Fleischer, indefatigable ring historian, in *Gentleman Jim, The Story of James J. Corbett,* has reproduced Corbett's account of the fight. You are now listening to the great Corbett, with a bow to Nat Fleischer:

"I never dreamed as I waited for Referee Hogan to send us into action, that I would receive more punishment than I would absorb in any subsequent battle, and that the punishment to be inflicted would be more than ordinarily seen in a round dozen of present-day heavyweight contests.

"We started off at a fast pace, you might call it furious, for it was a whirlwind go right from the initial call of time. Choynski knew that my right thumb was practically out of commission, and he meant to give me no rest, but force matters from the beginning. A sturdier, more determined chap than Joe never stepped under the ropes, and that day he was at his best. I don't think he ever again put up such a brilliant exhibition of scrapping as he did that eventful day.

"I jabbed and jabbed persistently in the first two rounds, got home frequently with that driving left, and soon had his face cut up . . . Then came the third round. I led for his face, landed plumb on his hard forehead, and distinctly felt something give in my left hand. In the fourth session I damaged the injured right thumb again and things didn't look any too bright for me. I kept on jabbing and landing but Joe never slowed up. He kept coming in, rushing and mixing, determined to put over a kayo."

Corbett stopped in his narrative for a moment to reflect on the kind of fighter Choynski was. "Choynski was really stronger physically and could hit harder. I was the taller, had a weight advantage, 178 to 170 and had him buffaloed on speed. We were both in the very prime of youth . . . We were bitter rivals, enemies . . . There never was such a perfect setup for the working off a personal grudge."

Corbett then went to telling of the fight. "And so the fight went on at terrific speed, round after round. As it progressed, I suffered more and more from the pain of that broken thumb, yet there was no letup. In the fourteenth round I caught Joe with a stunning blow to the head, and he, in turn, smashed a wicked left to my right eye, almost closing it. There was a swelling that went clear around my cheekbone."

At this stage both Corbett and his brothers thought he was finished, but Jim added, "If I hadn't been right in the pink of fine condition, I could never have lasted out the fourteenth round. But I managed to stall through, and my shattered senses gradually struggled back to normal."

"Choynski," Corbett said, "was tired from his exertions in vainly trying to put me away. I rallied and went at him like a tiger. In the next few rounds Joe's claret flowed so freely that we were slipping around the deck in the blood."

Revealing the manner in which the spectators took the bloodshed, Corbett said, "Before the battle was half over, some of the spectators were so sickened by the sight of the red carnage, that even hard-boiled ring fans looked away from the ring at intervals."

"You might say," Jim told Fleischer, "that it was anybody's fight from the eleventh to the twenty-fourth round . . . In the twenty-fifth, Joe was fairly masked in blood, and seemed to be fading fast from the heat and his many injuries. I was but little better off. My blistered feet, my broken thumb, the strained tendon in my left hand, my bruised body and the steady suffering caused by the burning sun, formed a combination of agony, almost beyond human endurance. Sorry looking sights were we as we came out for the twenty-sixth round. Still, in that session and the two following, I had by far the better of the going."

Now Corbett gets to the climax of the bloody bout. "In the twenty-eighth frame, which proved to be the finale, I could do little but hit with my arms and forearms, for both of my hands were out of commision for striking purposes. I could scarcely close my right hand, so I determined to let one desperate wallop go with the left, in a dying end to finish up matters.

"As luck had it, I got that punch home. It crashed squarely on Joe's jaw, over he keeled, and lay prostrate. I stood like a man in a dream while Referee Hogan counted him out. Actually, I was almost out on my feet, and could hardly realize that it was all over. I was dazed when I collected my senses, so much so, that I asked Billy Delaney, who was by my side, what had happened.

"You knocked him out, Jim," said Delaney exultantly.

"A few years later, when a newspaper man asked Delaney which was the hardest fought battle he ever saw — and Delaney, it must be remembered, handled two heavyweight champions, Jeffries and myself, Bill replied:

"The fight between Corbett and Choynski. For cleverness, endurance and gameness displayed, I've never seen its equal.' "

Even if the Corbett fights were the most spectacular in the Choynski record, they do not indicate completely the mastery of boxing which was Choynski's. Against Corbett he was brilliant but, after all, Corbett was the winner in their major fight. Choynski was able to beat more than one great fighter. In 1901, years after he met Corbett, Choynski kayo'd Jack Johnson, the Negro champion who led a spectacular life and who died in 1946 in an automobile accident. Johnson, the first Negro champion, together with Jim Jeffries and Jim Corbett, are considered the top fighters of all time. But Choynski was able to knock Jack out in three rounds, some years before Johnson won the heavyweight crown. It was especially significant because Johnson suffered only two knockouts in his career. The other came when he lost his title to Jess Willard, and there were many witnesses who said that he threw that fight and was not knocked out honestly. If that is true, it meant that Joe Choynski holds the only honest kayo against one of the best fighters the world ever saw. Surely, that is enough to prove his own greatness. Especially when it is realized that Johnson outweighed Choynski by forty-two pounds!

There is an interesting story about the Choynski-Fitzsimmons fight which took place in 1884. They fought on Bunker Hill Day in a five-round exhibition. Like veterans who knew a good thing when they saw it, they agreed not to fight too hard, but Choynski saw an opening and bam! Down went Fitz, the great Fitz who was to win the heavyweight title from Corbett three years later. He was unable to move at the count of four and it seemed that Choynski had a tremendous win in his grasp. But the freakishly-built Cornishman was made of heart. He began to lift himself to his feet and at eight was standing on rubber legs. Choynski chased him hard but Fitz was too fast for him. He stayed away until he recovered and at the end of the five rounds was giving as well as he was taking. It was a no-decision fight.

To some purists it may seem that Joe Choynski took unfair advantage of Fitzsimmons, who had a punch like an ox but was built awkwardly, with a heavyweight's torso and with the slender legs of a lightweight. But boxing has never been a goody-goody sport. And in the days when the giants of boxing showed their wares, nothing was unfair. This was the jungle of sports and everything was fair. When Fitz went down he knew that Choynski was out for blood and when he rose he tried to retaliate. No doubt he got in some good blows. That was the sport and when it was all over the two men respected each other a great deal. They had fought and found each other a stalwart foe. In a period when there were no great sums of money involved in boxing, personal pride meant everything. When John L. Sullivan went into a saloon and roared his famous challenge that "No man alive can lick me and any man in the world is invited to try!" he was pounding his own chest and exclaiming his defiance of any man in the world. Fighting in those days was not big business. It was restricted to a small group of tough men and they all knew they were tough. When Choynski fought brilliantly against Corbett, kayo'd Johnson and knocked down Fitzsimmons, he knew just how good he was, and he was plenty good.

To the students of boxing, to the veterans who have been watching heavyweight fights for a long time, the greatest name among champions is that of Jim Jeffries, the huge boilermaker who was champion for years and retired undefeated when there was no one left for him to beat. The word "great" is tossed around a great deal in these pages because we are dealing with the most outstanding figures in boxing. The dozen or so champions we are writing about represent thousands of fighters over a long period of time. Now and then — as is the case with Joe Choynski or Lew Tendler — a really great fighter never entered the ranks of the champions. But when we call Jeffries the best of the entire group of champions, we are only reflecting the opinion of the most observant reporters and fighters. There are degrees of greatness. But Jeffries was the king of them all because he beat everyone who faced him and was born with the physical gifts which made him invincible before anyone except Time. He was six foot six, and was built like a giant. He hit very hard, was exceptionally fast on his feet and had a jaw of rock. His reflexes were amazing and often he picked off blows in mid-air. And if a blow did manage to reach him, his system shook it off with ease.

But he found in Joe Choynski a foe whom he could not outfight. In 1896, a few years before Jeffries won the heavyweight title which he never lost, he hooked up with Joe Choynski. Those veterans who saw the fight spoke with excitement about it. It was that kind of a fight. Both men were fast. But Jeff was forty-seven pounds heavier than Joe. Choynski weighed in at 159; Jeff at 206. His muscles bulged as he went after his lighter foe. Lightning fast himself, Choynski evaded all of the rushes and rapier-like lefts and rights of Jim Jeffries. It was a true boxing match, unusual among heavyweights who usually are ungainly, slow afoot and heavy hitters. These men carried dynamite in their gloves and wings on their feet. There was little to choose between them.The immortal Jeffries had to be satisfied with a draw. And if ever Choynski needed a final stamp of greatness, this was it. He had met the finest of his or any other day and had held his own against all of them.

The list of Jewish boxing champions is a long one. But there has never been a Jewish heavyweight champion. Choynski was the best of them and he was a champion in deed if not in official rank.

Abe Attell

Ring Wizard

Abe Attell grew up as a small, poor, Jewish boy in a world populated by people who were bigger, richer and gentile. But despite these disadvantages — or perhaps because of them — he learned how to defend himself and fight, and went on to become one of the greatest boxers ever to step into a ring. He held the world featherweight championship for more than a decade at the turn of the century, and after retirement was elected to the Boxing Hall of Fame.

"I was a conceited fighter," Attell admitted. "I thought I could lick anybody. For a long time I was right." Sports columnist Joe Williams says that Abe was the greatest featherweight of them all. Famed author and sports buff Damon Runyon identifies Attell as "one of the five greatest fighters of all time." Nat Fleischer, publisher of *Ring* magazine and the world's foremost authority on pugilism, names Abe as at least the third greatest fighter his class has ever produced, behind only Terrible Terry McGovern and Britain's Jem Driscoll, with whom Abe once fought a ten-round no-decision bout, with Attell retaining his world crown.

Born on Washington's Birthday in 1884, Abe found himself fighting almost from birth. Indeed, he liked to joke that one of the few fights he ever lost was when he took a swing at the doctor delivering him. As the sixteenth of nineteen children, he was constantly in scraps with his siblings. As a poor Jew living in a tough Irish neighborhood, he learned quickly that survival meant knowing how to fight.

"My folks were small and I took after them," Abe recalled. "We were Jews living in an Irish neighborhood. You can guess the rest. I used to fight three, four, five, ten times a day. On the street, in the vacant lots, on the docks. A little of Abie's blood stained every street in Frisco." At the tender age of seven, the aggressive Abie was hauled off to jail and reprimanded for taking a swing at a policeman.

He engaged in his first formal bout when he agreed to meet a neighborhood bully in a ring. Though Abe was only thirteen years old and small even for his age, he was determined to show his larger opponent that he had no fear of him. His mother was vehemently opposed to the confrontation. "My mother, she was set against me fighting," Abe said. "She told me not to worry about coming home if I fought. But I and my brothers talked her into letting me go out by promising I'd never fight again."

The actual fight was held at Alex Gragain's arena in Frisco, and Abe "slaughtered the bum," demolishing his enemy in the second round. The impressed ring promoter, ignoring Abe's amateur status, rewarded him with $15. When Mrs. Attell saw the money, she reconsidered her opinion about boxing as a worthwhile occupation, and permitted Abe to keep fighting as long as he kept winning and bringing home cash. "My mother was my biggest fan," Abe remembered fondly. "She thought I couldn't lose and bet on me in every fight. Every time I'd fight she'd ask, 'Who's Abie fighting this time?' They'd tell her, and she'd say, 'Bet two dollars on Abie for me.' " Once, a lighthearted reporter told the Jewish mother that her son's opponent was going to be James J. Jeffries, the world heavyweight champion. The matron never hesitated, replying, "Bet two dollars on Abie for me, please."

Mrs. Attell's faith was well-placed. Abe swept through the ranks of available amateurs, and in 1900, made his official professional debut by knocking out Kid Lennett in the second round. He whipped eighteen straight opponents in Frisco, stiffening sixteen of them. He then headed for the Colorado mining towns, a great center of boxing in those rugged days. He won twenty-four of his first twenty-nine pro fights by knockout in establishing himself as a deadly slugger.

"In the beginning," Abe said, "I was rough and ready and tried to knock out everybody I fought. Then I discovered I was getting hit too much. So I decided to learn to box." He was particularly admiring of the great Joe Gans, whose style was as clever as it was successful. "Gans was the greatest. After I saw him fight, I decided to start boxing. I got tired of busting my hands knocking guys out."

In fact, though Abe weighed under one hundred twenty-two and stood only 5'4", he sometimes fought three times in the same week, and frequently spotted his rivals as much as thirty pounds. But he won anyway. In fact, he had fewer problems with his ring counterparts than with his first manager, a mean Colorado roughneck known aptly as "Bad Jack" McKenna, who "handled" the seventeen-year-old boy's bouts.

"After every fight they paid us off," Abe reminisced wryly, "and that mean cuss McKenna would sort it into two piles, one big, one small. Then he'd sit there with his big cane and say, 'Jew, which pile do you want?' I wasn't dumb. I'd take the small one." Abe ran away from McKenna three times; the first two times Bad Jack caught up with him, but the third time Attell escaped to St. Louis and resumed his career. His later managers included both the famed Jack Kearns and the legendary western gunfighter, Bat Masterson.

In October of 1901, the seventeen-year-old Attell fought George Dixon for the vacant featherweight title (champ Young Corbett could no longer make the weight) in Cripple Creek, Colorado, and the two men battled to a twenty-round draw. They set a return for eight days later in St. Louis; and on October 28, 1901, the Jewish teenager became the featherweight champion of the world when he thrashed Dixon in fifteen rounds. Thus began Attell's reign as champion, which would last more than ten years and provide a steady stream of colorful and eventful fights.

Attell was particularly skilled at carrying opponents in fights, making them look better than they were so that he would be able to clean up on side bets in a rematch. A wonderful defensive fighter, Abe was also a marvelous attacker when he wished to be. Crafty and quick, he was able to nail his rivals with precise, crisp blows while controlling the bout with brilliant ring generalsmanship. Williams wrote that "it takes a superlative skill to make a bad fighter look good. Attell made them look good. And then there'd always be a demand for a return bout — which was the main idea from the start. Then, if the return was a betting fight Attell would send it in and go to work on the startled young man in front of him."

Abe explained that such a philosophy was responsible for his draw with Driscoll in 1909. "I was saving him for Frisco," Attell remarked. referring to the site of a proposed rematch where Attell planned to dismantle the great Englishmen. But when the rematch approached, Driscoll sent a cable that he was ill, and the bout never came off. Attell observed that he was also ill: "I had $20,000 to bet on myself."

Abe was renowned for his success in gambling as well as for his ring expertise. The day he was to meet Harlem Tommy Murphy in the ring, he won $36,000 in a sixteen-hour non-stop poker game. Then, exhausted and nineteen pounds lighter than Murphy, he fought Tommy to a tough twenty-round draw. After all, a loss would have cost him the $6,500 he had bet on himself.

Once, Abe carried a young fighter eight rounds so that the boy could win a bet and buy his mother a house. Another time, he had a bet that he would knock out Tommy Kaufman in the eighth round, but Kaufman stymied him by abruptly leaping out of the ring in the seventh and disappearing into the bewildered crowd.

In 1904, Abe fought Tommy Sullivan in St. Louis and was knocked out in the fifth. Attell vehemently protested that Sullivan was well over the weight limit for the division, and should not have a claim to the title. The press agreed. The next time the two men met, Attell kayoed Sullivan in four rounds and all dispute about the rightful champion was ended.

Attell himself considered his "masterpiece" to be his classic confrontation with Battling Nelson. The two men faced each other on March 31, 1908 in San Francisco, boxing skillfully and slugging viciously throughout the entire fifteen-round match. The bout was called a draw, though Abe thought he won, and many agreed; in any case, the fight was one of the ring's greatest, and Attell retained his crown.

"Abe reigned for over a decade but he never let boxing interfere with romance, drinking or gambling, which eventually became more of a profession than a hobby," writes Bill Verigan in *Boxing Illustrated.* "Finally, on his 28th birthday, Abe's carefree life caught up with him, and he lost the title on a twenty-round decision to Johnny Kilbane."

Actually, the decision given to Kilbane was highly dubious. Abe always maintained that he was "robbed," and Jim Jeffries, who saw the bout, called the verdict for Kilbane "atrocious."

"Kilbane should have been ashamed of himself," Abe insisted. "He was the challenger but he wouldn't do anything but lay back and play it cute." Still, a younger, fresher Attell could have demolished Kilbane; Abe's condition was no longer what it had been. "I would have made the fight," he admitted, "but I couldn't go forward. My legs were gone."

Despite being awarded the questionable decision, Kilbane still accused Abe of rubbing his body with chloroform so as to stun Kilbane with chemical warfare. Abe responded indignantly to the bizarre charge.

"It was an outright lie. It would have put me under before him," he observed pragmatically. "Johnny never would give me a return," he added many decades later, "but I met him around 1954 in Madison Square Garden and challenged him to fight me then. He thought I was kidding and maybe he was scared. Anyway, he wouldn't fight."

Still, Abe was clearly on his way downhill after losing his

title, and he made two ill-advised comebacks. Two years after relinquishing the crown, he lost to two men he would have dispensed with easily in his prime. Then, in 1917, he tried to make a comeback after a five-year absence, but he lost his first bout.

Even including these tacked-on losses late in his career, Abe was only defeated ten times in one hundred sixty-eight professional bouts, and he himself claims to have fought three hundred and sixty-five times. At his peak, there were few if any fighters in history who could match him pound-for-pound; rare is the pugilist who holds a world title for a decade on his way to the Hall of Fame. Despite his many bruising conflicts in the ring, he emerged with only one physical scar: a broken nose that he received, ironically, not from anyone's fist but when he was accidentally struck by a brick hurled by middleweight champ Stanley Ketchel.

A truly great champion in a rough-and-tumble era of boxing, Abe Attell continued to live to a ripe old age, a living reminder of former greatness to the generations that succeeded him into the ring. He remains to this day one of the most formidable names in the history of the fight game: a cocky, brash Jewish kid who proved over the years, against the very best there was, that he was every bit as good as he always said he was.

BENNY LEONARD, AT HIS LEGENDARY BEST

Benny Leonard

Immortal Lightweight

The greatest single name in Jewish sports history is that of Benny Leonard. Happily, the name of Leonard is also the greatest in the annals of lightweight boxers in the world. Thus Jewish pride in the accomplishments of a sports star runs parallel with the reputation of the athlete concerned. For Benny Leonard is a legend in boxing. The outstanding lightweight of all time, Benny Leonard retired the undefeated champion of the world after eight years as titleholder. In two hundred and ten bouts he lost only four times; once on a foul, once after he made an ill-advised comeback long past his prime and twice when he was first learning the wisdom of the ring.

But Leonard goes past statistics. When he died, the newspaper reporters recalled the glorious days of the neat-haired, slim young master boxer who, at his peak, was the finest boxer and one of the most effective punchers in fighting history.

Benny Leonard passed away on April 18, 1947, the way he would have chosen to die — in the ring. While refereeing a minor bout in dusty, smoky St. Nicholas Arena in New York, Benny collapsed. A few minutes later he was dead, at the age of fifty-one, of a hemorrhage of the brain. Leonard often said, "I'll be in boxing until I breathe my last." But no one dreamed that his fate would be to die in a ring. And then the tributes of all Americans poured in. For during his lifetime Benny had been written about in reams of paper. He had been loved, honored, praised and admired by boxing fans, by Jews and by all sports lovers. He was the idol of the East Side, the adored figure beloved by thin-faced little Jewish boys who, in their poverty, dreamed of themselves as champions.

Benny Leonard was the first Jew in America to reach the heights in both boxing and the love of his own people. He won the lightweight title from Freddy Welsh in 1917 and retired without a blot on his record in 1925. During that period he became the most famous Jew in America.

When a people is beaten, persecuted and frustrated, it finds more than mere solace in its champions, in its men and women who become outstanding in other fields, among strangers who might otherwise reject them and their personalities. In boxing, where basic emotions are aroused and where conflict is made clear-cut, people feel themselves as part of the combatants.

The Jews of New York, in the early twenties, lived mainly in New York's East Side. This was a rough, tough section, bitten by poverty, with few moments of glory of any kind to alleviate the misery of living. The people were Orthodox, the men wore beards and the women were properly humble. Children were given a strictly Orthodox education, and they obeyed their parents just as children used to in the old country. It was not often that the young folks stepped out of their background and became fighters or actors and actresses. And when they did, the older folks nodded their heads sadly and admitted that the new, fast life in America was making things difficult for the real Jews.

Yet, when Benny Leonard reached the heights in boxing he aided not only himself, but the entire American Jewish community, which, in a subtle sense, needed the shot in the arm which a champion gave them. When Leonard was accepted and admired by the entire fair-minded American community, the Jews of America felt that they themselves were being accepted and admired. Leonard, therefore, symbolized all Jewry. And he knew it. He could not help knowing it. His own parents were Orthodox and Benny was aware of his meaning to his people.

To begin with, he was a model son. Originally, his mother was upset when Benny decided to become a fighter. She looked at him when he told her his decision, and she said, weepingly, "A prizefighter you want to be? Is that a life for a respectable man? For a Jew?" And Benny became emotional and explained to her that he had thought about it, that he was good at fighting and that he could make a lot of money for the two of them. Of course he was right. He could fight; and he made a fortune. But wherever he went, no matter which tank town or whistle stop he stayed at, he took his mother's picture with him. One of his close associates said, "This is no gag, and we don't say it for publicity. But Benny never goes anywhere without taking out his mother's picture from his bag first; and the last thing he does is put the picture back again before he leaves. He just sits and looks at her."

Together with his intense love for his mother, Benny was himself an observant Jew. His love for his mother was too great for him to be anything else. He never fought on a Jewish holiday. He was acutely aware of his Judaism and after his fighting days he was connected with Jewish organizations, with the Jewish people and with problems of all Jewry. When he made his comeback, and he was about to face Jimmy McLarnin, who had beaten many Jewish stars, Benny said, "One of the reasons I want to lick McLarnin is that I want to wipe out his successful record against Jewish fighters." Perhaps this is not an unusual statement to make. Many Jews may think this way, but few Jews in public life, in sports life, would say something like this. Benny was different, and he acted that way too.

His attachment to his family was also typically Jewish. His father, very much like his mother, worried about Benny's fighting. So whenever Benny went to another city, he always called his folks after the fight. There is an amusing story connected with this habit of Benny's. One time he called his father after a bout in Cleveland, in which he made a couple of thousand dollars in whipping an opponent of not much ability. The conversation went something like this.

"Hello, Poppa."

"Hello, Benny, where are you calling from, Benny?"

"I'm in Cleveland, Poppa, and I just won another fight."

"In Cleveland, Benny, why so far? Tell me, how much is it to call from Cleveland?"

"A dollar a minute."

"Goodbye, Benny."

But stories like this always crop up about a legendary personality. There are tales about his prowess, his generosity, his parents, his ability. Sometimes the character is perfect in his dimensions; sometimes he is human, with the frailties of a human being.

Even the name of Leonard is buried in legend. When

Benny started to fight, the announcer mangled his last name, which was Leiner. It sounded like "Leonard," and the nervous Benny did not stop him, and it did not seem to make much difference at the time. Thus Benny Leiner, or more properly, Benjamin Leiner, the little Jewish boy from the ghetto, became Benny Leonard, the great lightweight champ of the world. In later years Leonard was becomingly modest about his role in boxing history. Here is an excerpt of a Frank Graham column in the *New York Journal-American,* which reveals the status of Leonard and the lightweights of his time:

> "Through the years in prize fighting, the lightweights have run second only to the heavyweights in public esteem and have furnished some of the most memorable fights and some of the greatest fighters the ring has ever known. Back there a long way there were Frank Erne, Joe Gans, Jimmy Britt and Battling Nelson and, later, Packy McFarland, Jack Britton, Benny Leonard, Tony Canzoneri, Barney Ross, Lou Ambers and Henry Armstrong.
>
> "Old timers still argue about whether Gans or Leonard was the greatest of the lot and there is plenty of room for argument there, as Gans had been dead for two years before Leonard fought his first preliminary bout and once, when Benny was in his prime and they asked him what he thought about it he shrugged and said,
>
> " 'I don't know whether or not I could have beaten Gans and neither does anybody else. But if they have to go that far back to find someone who might have licked me, I am satisfied.' "

This is the historic view, minus the emotionalism which came with Leonard's success. There have been many myths about his start as a fighter. And the East Side is the area where most of the legends arose. Benny, before he was champ of the world, was the champ of Eighth Street. And there are tales that tell of how Benny routed a group of "Goyim" who attacked an old Jewish woman, of how Benny went single-handed into a fray with a group of hoodlums who were trying to deface a synagogue, of how Benny was the knight in white armor in the East Side. Of course these stories all began after Leonard was famous; this is the way of legend.

Asked about how he began to fight, Benny laughingly said one time, "I got thirty cents for my first fight. The purse was fifty cents, thirty to the winner and twenty to the loser, I got the thirty."

But even this story has many versions. Another time, Benny told a group of young fellows who were taking boxing lessons from him, that he got $10. Here is how he related it:

"The first fight I got paid for, I got $10 and a black eye. As I came through the door my mother saw the eye and started to cry. My father was there and he said, 'You want to fight? For what?' I showed them the $10 but of course that didn't make any difference to my mother. My father took it though, and put it in his pocket and he said, 'It's all right, Benny. When are you going to box again?' "

In recalling the earliest days of his fighting career, Benny said, "I grew up around Eighth Street and Second Avenue, in a Jewish neighborhood. We had Italians to the south and Irish to the north — and the public baths were at the foot of our street. You had to fight or stay in the house when the Italian and Irish kids came through on their way to the baths. You fought with your fists and with sticks, stones and bottles."

Benny fought. He had to. But he didn't like this kind of

fighting. He often claimed that the worst beatings he ever took came in these kid fights. It was a lot more profitable to fight in the neighborhood clubs. He was sixteen when he began to box professionally and at twenty he was fighting the best the country had to offer. But Benny never forgot the ghetto in which he lived and the way he had to fight to live.

And then there was a legend about Benny which persists until this day. This is the story that in all of his more than 200 fights no one ever mussed Benny's hair. It is said that Leonard used to plaster his hair down and challenge his foe to muss it and that no one ever did. Of course this is a wonderful story. It reveals the daring of the man, and it shows that no one was good enough to touch him when he did not want to be touched. The legend is even richer. It goes on to say that if anyone took the challenge and *tried* to muss Benny's hair, the champion would grow very angry and then and there knock out his opponent.

What many of these story-loving fans refused to remember was that in a fight with Soldier Bartfield, Benny got into a clinch with his enemy and the soldier deliberately opened his glove and pulled at Benny's hair. True enough, Benny plastered his hair down, but when Bartfield got through with Benny, the champion did not look unmussed. He was a very much mussed-up fighter. More than that, Benny did not grow angry. He laughed, for he had a sense of humor and saw the joke in the situation.

It took Benny Leonard a long time to reach the top of his class, and it was no easy job. The fighters in his day were tough and there were lots of other Jewish boys who tried to get to the heights. An interesting sidelight of Benny's first year is that he fought a fellow who boxed under the name of Kid Ghetto. If nothing else does, this should indicate the power and influence of boxing in the East Side, where Orthodox Jewry was seeing its young men fall victim to the new crazes in this alien country.

In his first year, which was 1912, Benny was stopped by Joe Shugrue, when he was overmatched with the veteran. A year later Frank Fleming kayo'd him. From this point on Benny lost only one fight, and that was on a foul to Jack Britton, when he met Jack for the welterweight crown of the world. He never lost again until 1932 when he was old, worn out and far from the Leonard of old. He was stopped by Jimmy McLarnin in seven rounds and never fought again. But when it is considered that in an entire career Leonard was beaten so seldom, and he faced so many top-notchers, the record itself is amazing. In a word, after 1913, Leonard never lost a fight until his loss to Britton in 1922. Then he never lost again until he came back in 1932! It is a breathtaking record.

When Leonard made his mark as a lightweight contender, he earned and was given the chance to meet Freddy Welsh. On May 28, 1917, the title changed hands. Welsh had been a good champion, but he never saw the day when he could lick Leonard. The fight ended by a knockout with Welsh draped unconscious over the ropes. The East Side was wild with joy, but it was not at all unexpected. By this time Benny was already an idol of the ring, and he was the king of the ghetto as well as of Mr. Welsh.

Benny's career was filled with many more thrills, but his fight with Britton was a fairly black mark on his record. They met in May, 1922, two months before Benny met his arch rival Lew Tendler for the first time. Britton, thirty-seven years old, was the welterweight champ and he had been around. Although Benny was the lightweight titleholder, there was a good deal of doubt that he would win. It is not often that a lightweight can step out of his class and beat a heavier champion. Nevertheless, Leonard was favored. His reputation was dazzling and few had made championship bouts close with him. Benny could box like a master; he could hit with sharp effectiveness and he was canny in the ways of the ring. His years of campaigning had given him the sort of experience that goes wonderfully well with speed and with punch. He was a near-perfect fighter.

According to the yellowed pages of the *New York Times* of that date, Leonard was putting up a disappointing fight. His older foe was fooling him. Benny had won his crown at the age of twenty-one. He was now twenty-four and had found no one able to beat him. Maybe he had grown overconfident. It may also have been that he had listened to some well-meaning friends and thought that he did not have to train sharply for the fight. Whatever the reason, Leonard fought an unimpressive fight, one of the few in his career. Britton took an imposing lead. Benny began to come back after the first ten rounds were over. His youth began to tell. He slapped Britton around and handled him well in the clinches. It looked like he might salvage the fight. And then in the thirteenth round it happened. He hit Jack with a hard left to the stomach. Britton went down, contorted with pain. There was a scramble in the ring, some more blows tossed by Leonard, wildly, at the referee or anyone who happened to be around. And the fight was awarded to Britton. It was a poor performance; and there never was another like it in Benny's record.

Typical of Benny's modesty was his narrative of one of

his really tough fights, and he did not mention the Britton bout as one of his really bad ones.

"I'll never forget this fight as long as I live," Benny said. He was telling of a fight with a fellow named Ritchie Mitchell. The Mitchell name is not well known today but Ritchie figured in one of the bloodiest fights in which Leonard fought.

There is, first, some background history to fill in, before this fight can be understood in its best perspective. In 1920, the enactment of the Walker Law brought back professional boxing to New York. The one fight that installed the sport on a firm footing was the Leonard-Mitchell bout. It was a lightweight title fight staged by Tex Rickard in old Madison Square Garden on January 14, 1921. Up to this time, boxing was looked down upon by the "better elements," and in 1918 boxing had been banned in New York. But after the soldiers of the first World War showed how much they liked the sport, Jimmy Walker, the big city's popular mayor, then a state senator, pushed his law through and once again boxing was legal.

But the "blue-noses" were still unwilling to admit they were licked. That is, until Anne Morgan of the famous Morgan family, decided to help restore the war-devastated lands of France. She realized that money and publicity would be forthcoming through a major boxing bout. As a result, Leonard and Mitchell were signed to fight for the worthy cause of France. All kinds of people were there, the rich and the poor, the workers and the millionaires. So this bout marked a landmark in boxing's history, apart from what happened in the ring itself.

A year earlier Leonard had met Mitchell in Milwaukee. On the train to Milwaukee Benny became sick and, turning to his manager, Billy Gibson, he said, "I'll have to knock him out." And Benny, who often called his shots, chilled Mitchell in the seventh round.

Naturally, Leonard thought that he would win a quick victory this time. For one thing, he was not a sick man tonight and for another, Mitchell would remember that first defeat. To make sure of his victory, Benny indulged in a smart bit of psychology.

As the referee gave the fighters their instructions in the center of the ring, Benny made his move. "Just a minute," he interrupted. "Let me get this straight. As I understand it, I'm to return to a neutral corner every time I knock Mitchell down." The trick worked, for Mitchell began to sweat. Pleased with his maneuver, Benny got ready to go to work.

The fight began with a blast. Fifteen seconds after the first bell, Mitchell was down! Leonard, moving with the class of a great craftsman, had stepped into his man and had downed him with a sharp right to the jaw. Mitchell was a sturdy boy and came groggily to his feet at the count of six. Benny went after him with speed and with cunning. He feinted Mitchell into position and hit him again, with rights and lefts and a barrage of heavy blows to the stomach and jaw. Mitchell fell on his face and it looked like another fast kayo for Benny.

But Ritchie was courageous. He fought against the fog that clouded his brain and he looked at his superior foe with blood in his eyes. He came to his feet, weaving helplessly, but standing erect. Benny went for him once again. Mitchell tried to get away from the accurate-punching champion. He evaded a few, but not all the blows. Weakened by punishment, Mitchell reeled under the attack and for the third time in the first round Mitchell hit the canvas. The referee waved Leonard to a neutral corner and Benny smiled confidently at his handlers. Again Mitchell shoved himself into position to fight back. He stood there, smeared with his own blood, heavy-legged and weary from the beating he had taken. Another punch would finish him. Leonard coolly moved forward and set himself for what should have been the final punch. As Benny measured his game foeman, Mitchell instinctively fired his right hand. From the recesses of his mind, with the instinct of the true fighter, Mitchell drew upon every bit of reserve strength within him and blindly threw the punch. It caught the unsuspecting champion under the chin, lifted him in the air and dumped him to the canvas! Benny was badly hurt. He strained to rise and managed to get to his knees as the referee tolled seven. His head ached, his eyes were bleary and his brain was foggy. He remained on his knees as eight was counted off. He heaved up at nine and clung to the ropes. There were only forty seconds to go, but if he fell down again, it would take only ten seconds to count him out.

He fought blindly. On rubbery legs he avoided his bleeding foe. He was out on his feet but somehow he kept moving, ever shifting . . . to the left . . . ducking from blows . . . pulling away from a roundhouse right. The round ended, thankfully. Leonard's handlers were frantic. They gave him ammonia, ice-packs and advice. They worked over him like fussy old women. Too soon, the bell rang for the second round.

Benny managed to keep away from Mitchell and then, in the sixth round, Mitchell, a bloody wreck, was hung over the ropes, and out like a child after midnight.

It was one of those oddities of the ring, when one blow changed a fight and then another punch reversed it again. After his long career was over, Benny still considered this one of his nightmares of the ring.

A few months later, Benny hooked up with Lew Tendler, the left-handed fighter who, next to Leonard, was the best lightweight of his era. A southpaw is always a hard man to figure out in the ring, for the unorthodox stance is a puzzler to the average fighter. But Tendler was a great fighter no matter from which side he fought. It was unfortunate that he came along at the same time as Benny Leonard. He would have been a champion almost any other time. A Jewish boy from Philadelphia, Tendler was a crushing hitter, a shrewd boxer and a veteran campaigner who had fought all the top men around — except Leonard. To this day there are experts who call Tendler the best southpaw in history.

The story of that first fight between these men is an old story now. It is the story of how a champion, on the verge of defeat, talked a challenger out of the title.

Years later, Tendler, who became a successful restaurant owner, said, "Funny thing about that fight. People still come in here and ask me about it. They won't let me forget it. They won't let me forget what a prize chump I was. You know, I did have some good fights and beat some good men, but nobody ever seems to remember that."

The story is wrapped in legend. It was July 27, 1922, in Boyle's Acres, Jersey City and the fight brought in $367,862, a tremendous haul and an indication of what an attraction it was.

Although it was a fifteen-rounder, Tendler started early and hit Benny a vicious blow that tore off one of Leonard's eyebrows. That punch also taught Benny that he was in for a tough and rough evening. He fought back hard, for he knew that in Tendler he was facing a ringman worthy of his skill. But Lew did not have Benny's lightning-fast reflexes. During a rapid exchange Tendler showed Benny a fast left hand and a right-handed punch which was enough to blast Benny into never-never land. From that moment on, Benny began to think of how to outsmart his foe. But Lew kept him hopping. Tendler wore Leonard down and then, in the eighth round, it happened. Tendler hit Leonard so hard that Benny gasped with pain and staggered forward. Tendler was ready to come in for the kill, but Benny twisted the pain off his lips and forced a smile to his agony-ridden features. He faced Tendler and talked to him. No one really knows what he said, but here are the versions. One report has it that Benny whispered, "That was pretty good, Lew, but you'll have to do better than that." Dan Parker, a top sports reporter, published this version: "You're too fresh, kid. I was going to let you stay the limit but I guess I'll have to give you the works next round." Jersey Jones, another expert, claimed that Leonard said, "Keep your punches up," And when Tendler argued, "That wasn't low," he lost his big chance.

Nobody really knows what Benny said. It is known that he had a chance to clear his head and momentarily halt Tendler. Years later, Benny denied that he talked to Lew. "What did I tell Tendler?" he said, with a broad smile. "I told Tendler if he didn't stop hitting me so hard, he'd knock me out." But then he added soberly, "I couldn't talk. I just tin-canned until my head cleared."

Hidden in legend though this fight is, the result was that Benny Leonard just managed to win. And when the two fighters met again a year later, they attracted a gate of nearly $500,000, at prices far below current ones.

Leonard said of the second fight, which was a lot easier for him, "I knew Tendler pretty well by this time but I wasn't letting him get close enough to say hello."

Grantland Rice, the lyrical sports writer who saw them all, said of the second Leonard-Tendler bout, "The greatest boxer of the present age gave his challenger a lesson in ringmanship the world will never forget. Tendler saw ten million stars here tonight and one left hand did it all."

These two fights were top moments in sports in the Golden Age of the twenties. Benny had no more fields to conquer and as he became rich and unconquerable, he grew restless. And irritable. Little things began to bother him and he forgot the spectacular moments of his boxing career. And before he quit, there were fights which many boxing fans never forgot.

Here are a few of them.

In fighting Charley White, one of the best left-hookers in the game, Benny fought so interesting a fight that Joe Williams, nationally known sports columnist, called it "one of his most remarkable performances. Perhaps his most remarkable of all." Benny had been in Hollywood and had not fought for five months. On the way home, Benny stopped in Chicago to discuss a bout with White. Even though Leonard was not in the best of condition and White was an excellent fighter, Benny accepted the terms, though a few days before the fight Benny twisted an ankle and didn't tell his manager and trainer about it. But in preparing for the fight, he had to pretend that he was doing road work. White made it a tough fight. In the fifth round a series of vicious blows by the left-hooker drove Leonard out of the ring. But Benny was shoved back into the ring by his brother and managed to weather the storm. In the eighth round he floored White three times. Having a bad ankle, Benny fought a heady bout, making White come to him. As White thought he was a winner, he came toward Benny — and was dropped thrice in the eighth round. In the ninth, Benny kayo'd White. And the funny part of it is, the next day White gave an interview to the press, in which he said, "How can you call that fellow a great champion? He doesn't know the first thing about foot work."

And then there is the time Benny met Johnny Kilbane, the great featherweight titleholder. He had fought Kilbane a ten-rounder the previous year, and there was little to choose between the two. But Benny had an uncanny brain and after the fight he learned how to handle Kilbane. Just before their second bout, Benny said, "Johnny's a great boxer, tricky as they make them and dangerous. But I know just how and when to beat him. He has a sort of double feint shift but he leaves himself open for a flash of a second when he tries it. And that's when I'll get him."

Benny did "get" him when Kilbane left himself open. He battered Kilbane into helplessness in the third round — the first time anyone ever knocked out the crafty Kilbane.

After Kilbane's death, Lewis Burton, then a sports writer for the *New York Journal-American,* revealed an angle of that fight which had not been known previously to the general sporting public. It offered an interesting insight into the Jewish consciousness of Benny Leonard.

Kilbane was a fast-talking, rough little Irishman, who often baited his opponents in the hope that they would see red in the ring and, consequently, fight with diminished effectiveness. So Kilbane, at the weighing-in ceremonies, began to tease Leonard and, finally, taunted him in outright anti-Semitic phrases. Leonard, up to that moment, was willing to make an ordinary exhibition of his meeting with Kilbane. He had fought him before and did not hold a personal grudge against him. Now, however, he burst with anger, and swore that he would ruin the featherweight.

For the first time in many years, Leonard entered the ring in fury, not unlike the bitterness which propelled Joe Louis against Max Schmeling in their second fight. Just as Louis destroyed Schmeling, Leonard battered Kilbane, feeling, as he was pounding his man, that he was repaying him in part for Kilbane's remark against Leonard, the Jew.

Another big moment came when Leonard refused to draw the color line and gave a Black a chance at his title. The best Black fighter around at that time was Leo Johnson. In what was a shock to most followers, Benny gave Johnson a crack at his crown. Yet in one minute and forty-nine seconds Johnson was knocked unconscious. But what mattered was that Benny was willing to meet all comers, regardless of race, color or creed.

In fighting Willie Ritchie four rounds in a no-decision affair, Leonard took things easy and when the fight was over, Ritchie adherents claimed their man was the better of the two. The publicity led to a return bout. And as usual, Benny had noticed a weak spot in Ritchie's defense.

"If I can get Willie to peg that looping right of his," Benny said, "leaving himself open just long enough for me to drop in a left hook, I'll beat him."

When they met, Benny watched for his opening. In the second round Leonard stepped under that looping right and staggered Ritchie with his own left hook. A right to the body and another left to the chin dropped Ritchie, who seemed ready for the cleaners. But the bell saved him. He learned his lesson and kept himself out of danger until the eighth and final round. Perhaps Ritchie became careless because it was the final session, but he tried that right swing, leaving his jaw unprotected for a fleeting moment. Crack! Benny's left thudded against Willie Ritchie's chin. A series of blows dropped Ritchie. He tottered to his feet at the count of seven. Now Benny was blazing away at him. Bleeding profusely from nose and mouth, Ritchie was helpless on the ropes. With only forty seconds to go, the referee stopped the fight. Again, Benny Leonard had called his shot.

But Benny forgot these thrills after nearly a decade of championship fighting. He had used all his skill in the ring to beat everyone. He had come back from the verge of defeat many times. He had talked youngsters out of victories and had applied psychology to beat men who would otherwise have made a lot of trouble for him. He had seen everything in the ring and was about ready to move into new fields. He had discovered that there wasn't much else left for him in the field of boxing. He had made his mark. But he was looking for something new, and the way he quit the ring was symbolic of his new attitude. He signed up to fight Pal Moran, but Benny hurt a finger while training for the bout. Naturally, he asked for a postponement. Through some stubbornness on the part of New York State officials, they refused to allow him a respite. Suddenly angry, Benny decided to retire from the game. His mother never liked boxing and now that he had made a fortune and was tired of the sport, he listened closely to his mother. He showed how much he meant his decision when he refused an offer of $150,000 to meet Mickey Walker for the welterweight crown. His mother said, "Remember your promise, Benny," and Benny remembered.

And now there began for Benny Leonard, the star of the ghetto, a new career. Famous everywhere, Benny decided to put his reputation to work for him. It should be stressed that Leonard was a true personality of this day. He felt strongly about patriotism to America, for he saw that in this country, all people could get a fair shake if they put their shoulders to the wheel and worked. Thus he became a Lieutenant and was a bayonet instructor and boxing teacher to thousands of men. He also refereed many fights in the service, thus picking up the background for a career which he followed years after his retirement. He had never wanted to get away from boxing and, in a sense he never did, even when he went in for jobs in other fields.

For example, Benny, from 1926 through 1931, bought a hockey team, played in vaudeville, wrote sports and taught boxing in CCNY. He taught the history of the sport, its regulations and, no doubt, some of his students decided to learn from him how to make a million with their fists. But the call of the ring was still strong in Benny. And then he made his first real mistake. He decided to make a comeback. He had been away from the ring for seven years and, like many an old-time master, he saw very little talent in the current crop of pugilists. He said, in effect, "I can lick most of these bums." No doubt he could, but he was looking at the new men with the eyes of the old Leonard. He must have forgotten that the keenness of eye, the sharpness of condition and the powerful punch vanish with the years. He was no longer the old Benny Leonard, but he was still able to teach some of the boys a few tricks.

And Benny was fat. He had let himself go. He was, pugilistically speaking, an old man of thirty-six when he came back. It was old age in boxing, especially when he had begun in 1912. You can't fight for twenty years and expect to be as good at the end as you were at your peak. But Benny took a whirl at it. He had some hard times. "I fought some yokels in whistle stops and took greater punishment than I did in many a fight at my peak," he said. Eventually, however, he worked himself into some sort of decent shape. And as he did not lose, the picture of a new, even though an older, Leonard, spread over the sports pages of the land. And the inevitable upshot of it all was a bout with Jimmy McLarnin.

Now Jimmy was a great little fighter who, through some oddity, had knocked out many Jewish boxing stars. He was too honest a fighter to really want to fight Leonard because he knew he would be fighting the shadow of a former great in the game. If he won, it would be said of him that he beat an old man; if he lost, it would ruin his reputation. McLarnin had kayo'd Jackie Fields in two rounds, Louis "Kid" Kaplan in eight, Sid Terris in one, Ruby Goldstein in two, and now he was faced with the chance to beat the greatest Jewish fighter of them all.

Leonard was aware of the "race" angle. He told reporters that among other things, he wanted to beat McLarnin to wipe out the record of wins Jimmy had made against Jewish boys. The drums of publicity thumped hard and the fight was made.

It was an odd fight. At the start it seemed that Leonard might spring a spectacular surprise. He was fast and evasive. The hard-punching McLarnin, at the top of his game, pressed Leonard but found the former champion too smart for him. And Benny found that he had not lost his punch. Thus for three rounds it was an interesting fight, with exciting possibilities. But in the fourth McLarnin dug a hard right hand into Leonard's midsection. Benny gasped, fought back hard and utilized all of his wiles to escape another such blow. But the punch marked the beginning of the end. McLarnin began to hurt him more often. He could not really trap the ex-king of the lightweights, but he did not miss all his punches either. Benny remained hard to get. He ducked and swayed and pulled away from whistling drives. He became a shadow and a sprite. But the years told. In the sixth McLarnin caught up to Leonard and soon added him to his kayo list. When it was all over, Jimmy smilingly admitted that he was glad Benny wasn't younger.

Leonard never fought again. He became a referee, took an interest in Zionist affairs and was an active member of a group sponsoring Jewish Olympic games in Tel Aviv. He was a man who took seriously his role as an idol of the Jewish people. He was active in Jewish communal affairs and during the last war served in the Maritime Service, where he rose to the rank of Commander.

After he died tragically in the ring of the St. Nicholas Arena, the top sports writers in the land recalled his days of glory and paid him glowing tribute.

Joe Williams wrote that Leonard had "everything, plus that rare manner and presence which distinguishes a great champion from the stenciled product. It was a delight to watch Leonard in action and a delight to sit in his company."

Dan Parker wrote that "it's almost thirty years since I first saw the sleek-haired, good looking cocky chap who was destined to become one of the all-time greats of the lightweight division . . . He moved with the grace of a ballet dancer and wore an air of arrogance that belonged to royalty. His profile might have been chiseled by a master sculptor and there wasn't a mark of his trade upon it to mar its classic perfection."

Arthur Daley of the *New York Times* said that "Benny was a truly great fighter and a great person on top of it, one of the most creditable figures the sport ever had."

Lester Bromberg, boxing expert of the *New York World-Telegram,* wrote sincerely when he said, "But the real Leonard aleady is immortal — the artist of the ring canvas who glided up and back, the genius of punch-slipping, the counter-puncher of lightning reflex snap, the lion-hearted campaigner and the devoted believer in all that's good in boxing. And there must be some in a business that could produce a Benny Leonard."

After Benny's death, many tributes were paid him, and some have been quoted here. And to many Jews in America the name of Benny Leonard stands first when Jewish stars are mentioned. And here is a story told by Nathan Straus, the prominent Jewish leader and son of a great American Jew. Mr. Straus was the president of radio station WMCA, and this is the gist of his brief talk following a fifteen-minute dramatic sketch devoted to Benny Leonard.

Mr. Straus said: "Benny Leonard was a friend of my father, the first Nathan Straus. When my father was old and feeble and could go out but rarely, Benny never was too busy to come up to his home and tell him stories of the boxing world — which my father loved to hear.

"Benny Leonard was a friend of mine, a friend of many

years' standing. From the earliest days of my candidacy to the State Senate, I never entered a political campaign without calling on Benny to accompany me on speaking tours throughout the city — and he never refused. Some of my happiest memories of those hectic campaign weeks in October of many different years are the companionship and comradeship of Benny. He drew a crowd even in those places where few might have come to hear me.

"Later, as I grew older, the friendship was continued. When I wanted to give my growing sons an opportunity to learn the manly art, I asked Benny if he would undertake the task. I knew before I asked him what the answer would be.

"So a group of boys about the age of my two older sons met regularly once a week at my home in Westchester for Benny to teach them and coach them.

"Something quite typical of Benny occurred when my youngest son, only eight years old and far too small to take part with the older boys, started to cry because he could not get into the class. Benny immediately stooped down and said to him, 'Look, Peter, the others can only box with me — you're going to knock me out.' And sure enough, Benny rehearsed the kid, over and over again, in a routine which is preserved to this day in an amateur movie, now one of my most precious possessions. The movie shows Benny crouching down, being hit on the chin by the eight-year old, falling flat on the ground with his arms and legs stretched wide, and the movie ends as the youngster places one foot on the recumbent figure of the fallen champion.

"Benny made that boy happy as he made thousands of boys, some young and some not so young, happy over the years."

This story, told eloquently by Mr. Straus, offers a real insight into what made Benny Leonard a great man, besides being a great fighter. And Benny Leonard, the boy from the East Side who conquered the world, will always be loved and honored by the Jews in America and all others who knew of him.

Benny Bass

Featherweight Fury

In the history of boxing in America, there are many names which crop up for a moment and then sink back into obscurity. But the single second of glory is sometimes remembered for a long time and the obscurity is not really as bad as it seems to be. In a sports field where there are thousands of combatants over a period of, say, fifty years, there are many glorious names. But at times there are names which are not particularly outstanding yet are remembered for one deed.

Just as Tony Galento always will be remembered for his valiant effort against Joe Louis, when he floored the great champ with a left hook before he himself succumbed to the powerful Negro's chopping punches, so Benny Bass will be recalled by fans of pugilism, for his bloody, but winning effort against Red Chapman of Boston, in their fight for the featherweight title on September 12, 1927.

Benny Bass did not last very long as a champion. And it is doubtful if he will rank among the truly great titleholders of his day. In his fighting era there were great champs. Men like Jack Dempsey and Gene Tunney were grabbing the sports spotlight. It was the Golden Age of sports, the time when names like Bobby Jones in golf, Jack Dempsey and Benny Leonard in boxing, Babe Ruth in baseball and Bill Tilden in tennis became immortals in the annals of sports.

Today when a man is outstanding in his own field, there is always someone to whom he can be compared in the athletic world of the twenties.

No one really can explain why that era was so fruitful in producing stars. It has been said that it was an outgrowth of the first war, that the young men, tired of bloodshed but still interested in combat, took their ambitions to the playing fields and boxing rings of America.

In that age there were many athletes on the fringe of greatness. They never did crash the top rung and never climbed to the peak of stardom.But they did, now and again, produce an effort which ranked with the work of the best of them all. Such a man was Benny Bass, the slender Jewish boy from Philadelphia, who held the featherweight championship in 1927.

In our own day the champs of the lighter weights do not win much acclaim. This is an age for heavyweights. Only once in a while, when an amazing fighter like Henry Armstrong comes around, who can win and hold three titles simultaneously, does the crowd respond to his artistry and take an interest in him and his work. By and large, however, the heavy men get the money, the crowds, the applause and the headlines. A mediocre fighter who weighs 200 pounds will be followed more eagerly than a classy lightweight who, pound for pound, is much the better fighter. It has been thus nearly all the time. But in the Golden Age, the lighter men did well enough. They deserved the honors they won. The list included men like Tony Canzoneri, Benny Leonard, Billy Petrolle, Jackie "Kid" Berg and many others who are still recalled with respect by the men who go to the fights. A bout between Benny Leonard and Lew Tendler drew more money and more people than do most heavyweights of today. And when they fought the emotional thrills did not in any respect fall behind the thrills inherent in any heavyweight bout.

The reason Benny Bass is remembered is that the fight in which he won the featherweight championship was one of the best in the history of the ring. Its savagery, its skill and its pace have seldom been equalled by anyone. And when Bass was returned the winner, he and the fans sensed that the fight would go down in the pages of boxing as one of its top thrills.

The fight generally regarded as the No. 1 sports thrill of the century was the brawl between Jack Dempsey and the Argentine heavyweight Luis Angel Firpo. It lasted two rounds and Firpo hit the canvas at least eleven times. Dempsey was catapulted out of the ring and was pushed back in time to avoid the final count of ten in the first session. No one at the fight really remembered how many knockdowns there were; they were all transported into a world of savagery. Their emotions were overwrought and they were unable to think like civilized men.

But the fight between Benny Bass and Red Chapman was even more violent. It took place in Philadelphia before more than 30,000 boxing fans. That in itself is a story, for how many fans would watch two featherweights in this day and age? But as was said before, the lighter men drew heavy crowds in those days, for the fighters were the kind that drew the spectators. For two years there was no featherweight champ. The previous titleholder, Louis "Kid" Kaplan, another one of the Jewish boys who held sway in those days, had retired undefeated in 1925. Eliminations took place and Red Chapman and Benny

Bass were the two men who survived all of the bouts to meet for the title vacated by Kaplan. An oddity here is that Chapman was also Jewish and his name was Morris Kaplan.

Bass was a slight favorite, but the fight was so tense, up-and-down and bloody, that there should never have been any favorite. For the first two rounds they fought it was a "normal" fight. The men met and slammed at each other, felt each other out and tried to establish superiority. In boxing one man always tries to make himself the boss in the ring. And one or the other always does. His opponent knows it and feels it, and eventually loses because of it. But here neither man made himself top dog until late in the bout.

In the third round the men clinched and then Bass and Chapman butted heads. A hard head can take more out of a man than a heavy punch. When they parted, Bass' right eye was bleeding profusely. Chapman seemed to be none the worse for the blow. He went after Bass but Benny was too spry for him. He evaded Chapman's rushes and protected his eye with the cunning and skill of a veteran of the ring.

In the fifth stanza Chapman was still aiming for Bass' eye and it looked as though he would tear it out of its socket. Bass' handlers had cleverly patched up the bleeding optic, but in the fifth round Chapman tore the patch away and the eye opened up once more. Bass could hardly see as the blood poured over him. He was a study in scarlet and even though he was in strong shape, it looked like the end, for the referee had to watch the injured eye. But Bass was a clever fighter and try as Chapman did, he could not slam against Bass' eye long enough and often enough to beat him to the ground. Benny evaded the punches of Chapman and managed to land enough of his own to keep Chapman at bay. In the sixth round Chapman was unable to do anything with Bass and Benny used the respite well. In the seventh Bass came out with a rush, feinted his man into a pretzel and then landed a hard left and then a right to Chapman's eye. He opened a wide gash over the Boston featherweight's eye and now it seemed that both men would be able to fight through the bloody veil of only one eye.

The punch by Bass made Benny feel that he was on his way to a win. He fought hard and well and drove his man into a corner time and again and pounded the body with sharp blows and made Chapman wince with pain.

In the eighth round he went after his man as though he owned him. For a moment it looked like Chapman was weakening. And the crowd, which had been sitting in noisy fascination, was now calling for the kill. But the battering both men had taken slowed down the action. The featherweights were both bloody and the perspiration dripped from their bodies. They tried to do what they could but the flesh was unable to respond to the spirit.

The minute's rest between rounds gave them both a new lease on hidden energies. They came out at the bell and threw hard rights at each other. Both fell heavily. And the referee began to count over them. Bass rose first. He was groggy and nearly out on his feet. His action was an instinctive one, and the fans thought there was something inhuman about it. Then Benny looked for his opponent and saw him on the ground. Chapman stirred as Bass went to a neutral corner. Groggily, Chapman tried to lift himself to his feet. Finally he made it. The crowd was chanting in a sort of ecstasy. And the courageous featherweight came up to meet his enemy. This time Bass had the advantage of the clearer brain. He went after his nearly-collapsed foe but Benny found that the punch had taken too much out of him. He was the aggressor but he was not good enough to finish his man. He went after him with heavy legs and with a sodden brain and with arm-weary punches. Chapman retreated with wily cunning and with the instinct of a beaten man. He went backwards faster than Bass rushed him and then the round, the round which seemed to last forever, ended and both men fell on the stools in their corners, exhausted.

The tenth and final round was an anti-climax. The two fighters had been drained of everything. They had no energy left, only the spark which kept them upright. And like all fighters who are brought up in a hard school, they went for each other hammer-and-tongs. They moved in slow motion and were a caricature of their former selves. They clinched, breathed heavily and seemed to collapse into each other's arms. But they kept punching. Chapman stumbled down again but was up immediately. Bass just could not chase him any longer. Bass was in bad shape. His eye was badly bruised and his own blood was mixed with Chapman's blood. They both were nearly out on their feet. Chapman was completely covered with dried blood, which glistened where his perspiration met with blood. His teeth were out in a perpetual snarl and he moved with the deliberation of a sleep-walker. He threw punches he was unconscious of throwing and Bass ducked them with a casualness born of fatigue. Yet Bass seemed a bit more alert than Chapman and when the bell rang he seemed more human, more alive. The decision went to Bass and with it he won the featherweight championship of the world. He won it in blood and in winning it, he placed himself in that small group of men who, in one fight, won boxing immortality.

This fight took place decades ago and is hardly known to the new generation of fight fans, who read the record books and watch the bouts on TV. When one reads the yellowed back issues of the sporting pages in the newspapers, it is easy for one to see that the Bass-Chapman bout could never be forgotten even in a year when Dempsey and Tunney were the major names in pugilism.

Fighting is a barbaric sport and many psychologists have attempted to explain its hold on civilized man. Most probably it is a throwback to the time when man fought for everything he had and everything he wanted, and he battled with his fists. The spectator is transported to a primitive time and his mind reverts, for a brief moment, to an animalistic age. Thus the Dempsey-Firpo fight captured the imagination of all America. And this is why the sportsmanlike boxing of the light hitters is met with scorn. The fight fan is an individual with basic instincts. The veneer of civilization is ripped off for the moment of the fight. He wants blood and strife. And he gets it, or he doesn't come back to the arena. This is how Muhammad Ali and Joe Frazier fought each other. No matter what other fights they had, the Ali-Frazier fights stand out for their violence and fury.

What is remarkable about the Bass-Chapman fight is that the violence was so strong, the animalism so great that the bout stands as a classic of savagery all these years. And two slightly-built Jewish fighters were the battlers involved. If this story were written to provide "apologetic" literature for those sensitive Jews who feel that they have to show that Jews can do everything as well or as badly as their Gentile neighbors, the story of Benny Bass and Morris Kaplan would give them sufficient material. But to fight fans who judge only by what they see in the ring, this bout means only that it was a perfect example of the boxing courage of two young men who gave all their energy and all their strength in a fight against each other, a fight which aroused the emotions of 30,000 people. And it is because Benny Bass showed all the virtues of a high-class boxer, that he is included in this cavalcade of sports heroes.

JACKIE "KID" BERG, WEARING THE MOGEN DAVID WITH HIS INITIALS IN HEBREW

Jackie "Kid" Berg

Whitechapel Whirlwind

One of the international jokes in the world of sports is the caliber of the British boxer. Whenever an Englishman becomes a standout fighter, he comes to American shores to earn the Yankee dollar, and he finds that with the coin he picks up a bad beating from American fighters. British fistic annals of the past few decades reveals that the English fighter, with his old-fashioned, wide-open stance is easy prey for the rougher American pugilist, who is brought up in a tough professional school and who, before he reaches the top, takes a lot of punishment.

British boxing reputations are low in America largely because wily Jimmy Johnston once brought to these shores a heavyweight named Phil Scott, who made a lot of money by fighting so badly that he won the cognomen of "Fainting Phil" Scott. This fellow seemed unable to stand upright in a ring when he met an American. He won reams of newspaper copy and made a lot of money. His manager used to say that Phil won more money lying down than most fighters make standing up. But the cause of British boxing did not hold up very well with men like Scott to "strengthen" it.

Of course in the days of Fitzsimmons and Sullivan and Corbett the British had some pretty fair heavyweights. And now and again a brilliant champion in the lighter classes came to the fore. But an English fighter always has to overcome the handicap of being British. Somehow, the English never did turn out good fighters in wholesale lots.

There is another thing: the British fighters who were any good continued to fight in the non-rushing, non-aggressive style of the nineteenth century pug. It was mainly in this country that the whirlwind sort of fighter appeared. A man like Henry Armstrong, who was able to beat featherweights, lightweights and welterweights with the fury of his attack during a short period of time, was typical of the fighters developed in America. England produced the Fancy Dans, the clever men who had flashy footwork and quick fists.

But there appeared in England, in the late twenties, a Jewish fighter who to this day personifies the whirlwind fighter, the kind of guy who never let up for an entire fight, a fellow with lots of guts and the love for fighting which indicates tremendous spirit. His name was Jackie "Kid" Berg, and Jackie conquered the best fighters on both sides of the ocean. He was a thrill provider, a scrappy, eager foe who always gave the fans a run for their money. He was easy to hit and took a lot of punishment. But he waded in and was glad to trade punch for punch. He never hit very hard; fighters like him seldom do. They don't throw punches flat-footed, to get maximum power. They dance around and toss leather from all directions. They never stop punching and often their opponents fall down from sheer exhaustion. Fighters like Berg are seldom appreciated as "great" fighters. They take too many punches, they fall down too often and they are beaten too many times. But what is overlooked is the fact that their combative spark is astounding, that they take on all comers and on any given night they can beat the best men in the world at their weight, and sometimes over their own weight. They breathe rosin, and their veins are full of fighting blood. Their whole lives are wrapped around a bell, leather gloves and a willing opponent. They never quit until they have to. And even then they try to go on.

Jackie "Kid" Berg, born Judah Bergman, started to fight in 1926, when he was twenty years old. Born in London, in the Whitechapel area which is the British version of the New York East Side, Berg was brought up in a rough school. The slum areas of London are as dirty, as hard and as unscrupulous as the slum sections anywhere in the world. In Louis Golding's fine novel *Magnolia Street,* one can read of such a Jewish section in England. And there is a prize fighter in that story who undoubtedly must be "Kid" Berg, for Jackie won the following of Jews all over the world. He began to fight in 1926 and as late as 1941, he was swapping leather with professional fighters. Probably he had none of the spring in his legs and his reflexes must have been rusty. But he retained the spark that brought him to the top of his profession. The kind of passion he had for the ring generally pays off.

When Jackie came to the United States, after a few years of fighting in England, he did not do particularly well. But he showed the stuff which made him a great fighter, if greatness is measured by courage and the ability to stand up to the best fighters in the world.

In August, 1928 Jackie hooked up with Billy Petrolle in Chicago. Billy is another of those stupendous characters who make boxing the fascinating sport it is. Called the "Fargo Express," Petrolle was one of the hardest hitters who ever lived. He ruined many good fighters and his fights with Bat Battalino rank with the ring classics. After a few fights with Bat, Petrolle became known as a killer in the ring, and Battalino ended up in an insane asylum, driven mad by punches of the "Fargo Express." Somehow, Billy never won a title. And he was known, in his time, as the best fighter who never wore a crown.

It was against this same Billy Petrolle that Jackie "Kid" Berg tried to make an impression on American fight fans. Petrolle was an explosive hitter and the tactics of Berg did not annoy him at all. In the first round Petrolle came out and began to bombard his man. Berg went down. He was hurt but he was a gamester. Petrolle thought he would not have any trouble with the foreigner. Englishmen had bad reputations anyway, and when Berg went down the first time, it seemed to be the end. But he came up. And Petrolle knocked him down again. But no matter how many times Billy was able to floor his game foe, he could not knock him out. The crowd came to sneer at the English Jew, but they ended up howling for him. No one ever put up a more courageous fight against anyone. Petrolle went arm-weary in his attempt to kayo his man. And Berg showed that a knockdown did not mean anything to him. In that first round Petrolle floored Berg nine times! And Jackie kept coming back to plague his harder-hitting opponent. When the round ended the Chicagoans were able to say that this was one Englishman who did not have any yellow in his system. Berg proved that early in his career in America. Petrolle won that fight by a knockout. He floored Berg again in the third round before it was all over.

But Jackie showed enough to make him welcome in this country. He campaigned a few more years in the United States, picking up guile, but never needing to improve his courage. He met Petrolle one more time in his career and showed that he too, could win from the blasting hitter. And then Berg, like all fighters, had his peak night. He met Tony Canzoneri, who frequently was involved with Jewish fighters. The bout took place in January, 1930. More than 30,000 fans came to see the fight. Tony had already been the featherweight champ of the world and in a few years he was to go on to win the lightweight crown, which was taken from him by Barney Ross, another Jewish boxer.

Before the men entered the ring, Canzoneri was a 3-1 favorite. The experts and the fans remembered that Berg had been badly beaten by Petrolle and that Canzoneri was one of the finest little fighting machines around. Jimmy Dawson, of the *New York Times,* said that: "For action, excitement and savage, determined fighting, the bout has not been excelled here in recent years." The doughty little Whitechapel terror went after Canzoneri from the very start and subjected him to a vicious body beating. Dawson said that Berg gave Tony "one of the worst beatings he ever has experienced."

Every step of the way the English Jew outfought, outthought and outgamed the future lightweight titleholder. No one was braver than Canzoneri. Tony had the harder punch, he carried the heavier weapons and he brought with him the wiliness of many more years of fighting. But Jackie Berg had not taken beatings in vain. Every time he fought and lost, whenever he took a beating, he learned something. And now he was using all of his hard-earned wisdom. He caught Tony with chopping rights and cutting left hooks. He punished Tony in the infighting and he outwitted him on the ropes. The expert fight fan knows that it is in the infighting that a man takes his biggest beating. It is the punch in the stomach which takes the speed out of a man's legs and even if midsection drubbings are not spectacular, they can ruin a man. Canzoneri was too tough to be ruined, but in all of his years of fighting he never took a more severe licking.

A month later Berg, still riding the crest of his wave of power, met and won from Mushy Callahan, who was Jewish in spite of his name. In winning, he lifted Callahan's junior welterweight title. This was another typical Berg fight. With machine-like regularity he punched out a win over the champion. He did not kayo his man early, although he had him groggy in the seventh. And in the tenth round, Berg won by a technical knockout — which went in the books as a kayo. Callahan's seconds threw in the towel to save their man from further punishment. He was outclassed and beginning to see images which weren't there. Usually, a championship fight does not end in a technical knockout. But when a man is helpless on his feet and faces his opponent with bleary eyes, there is nothing else to do. And so the fight was stopped.

And now Berg tried to get a fight with the lightweight champion, Sammy Mandell. But Sammy was busy trying to hold on to his title. He avoided fights with dangerous contenders, but could not face the rumble of disapproval of the fight fans for too long a time. So he took his crown into the ring with him against Al Singer, who blasted Mandell from the ring in one round. Berg, who lost his big chance for the title, took on "Kid" Chocolate in August, a month after Singer became lightweight ruler.

Chocolate was to become one of the most interesting and graceful fighters of this period. He was at that time still undefeated and even the most dour of fight experts tabbed him as a coming star. The "Kid" was a Cuban with lightning reflexes, a whipping left hand and the lightness of a ballet master. He was completely unlike "Kid" Berg. He was a stand-off fighter, a jabber, a counter fighter. And Berg was a hustler, a fellow who put his head down, protected his chin with his gloves and went to work on his man. The bout attracted 36,360 fans and it marked Chocolate's first loss. Many of the fans booed the decision, but those who followed the game closely knew that Berg had been the winner in fact as well as officially.

It was a sizzling ten-rounder which Berg won by forcing the fight, never giving ground and always coming in on his foe. It was very close, and Chocolate, with his grace and his hard punching, won the eye of the crowd. But Berg took everything he had and kept coming back at his man. His body punches began to tell and the Cuban started to lose heart. He was accustomed to seeing his foes fall down when he hit them, but this fellow refused to roll over. His most robust blows had no telling effect on Berg and when he saw that, Chocolate began to fall apart mentally. Jackie kept at him, hitting from all directions, tossing leather without a halt, coming out at every bell with busy fists. Toward the end of the fight the Cuban faltered and Berg swept past him, hurting him, staggering him and otherwise making his superiority evident. At the final bell Berg won the decision. It was well-deserved.

The years of fighting take a lot out of a man like Berg. His stock in trade was taking a punch for a punch. And because many of his foes hit harder than he, Berg's campaigning began to tell on his stamina. In 1931 Canzoneri revenged himself and knocked out the man who had given him such a terrible whipping. Berg was not through yet. He beat the British lightweight champ Harry Mizler, who was a Jew, by a kayo in ten rounds and thereby won the Empire title, but the Empire is not America. Jackie came back to this country, without the power he used to wield. He seemed to be on his way out, and after ten years in the ring it was not at all surprising that he should begin to see the end of his trail. Jackie Berg, however, was an unusual man. Two years later he again fought all comers and lost only one bout that year, to Red Cochrane, who later became the welterweight champion of the world.

This was his last real whirl at the big time in America. He kept fighting all over the world, ready to give his best to all his fans. His face grew scarred and his features became indefinite. His name was still popular all over the world, among Americans as well as South Africans and Englishmen. He was welcomed everywhere. He is the symbol of the eternal fighter, this boy from Whitechapel, and in his time — which spanned two decades — he gave more thrills per minute than hundreds of champions and thousands of near-champions. In this sense, Jackie "Kid" Berg is the champion of them all. He was a fighter's fighter. A hard-headed, lion-hearted fighter who will be remembered by fight fans not only for his deeds in the ring, but for his passion for fighting.

AL SINGER, WHEN HE RULED THE LIGHTWEIGHTS

Al Singer

Glass Jaw Champion

After Benny Leonard captured the lightweight title and the hearts of American Jews, Jewish sports fans carried in their minds the victories of the smooth-haired Leonard and hoped that when his reign would end another Jewish boy would take his title from him. For a long time, whenever a likely-looking Jewish boy made a mark as a boxer, he was called, if he was a 135-pounder, "the new Benny Leonard." Benny was the symbol of the champion. He was, to the modern sport-minded Jew and to the Orthodox Jew who knew of boxing only through excited talk on the East Side, *the* Jewish champion. There was no other.

For years the East Side produced clever fighters, hard hitters and spectacular personalities. Yet somehow, each one lacked something. The long list of Ruby Goldsteins, Sid Terrises and other smart boys made boxing headlines for a short time and then met with obscurity as some rough kid from Nebraska or Vancouver knocked their brains out.

One of the best of this crop was Al Singer, who did manage to win the lightweight title. Today the fight fan is apt to belittle the abilities of Al Singer because, in his later fighting years he developed what is known in the trade as a "glass jaw." This is an occupational disease, which means that a man has a physical weakness in the jaw. A shot at the jaw affects his nervous system and knocks him out.

This is not a sign of cowardice, nor is it anything to be ashamed of. Some of the finest fighters in the world, big husky men with lots of intestinal fortitude, had that unfortunate handicap. The fight game, in its picturesque manner, calls it a "glass jaw." A man is born with it and sometimes he overcomes it. Al Singer did not seem to be afflicted with a "glass jaw" until he won the lightweight crown. Of course it could be that he had it with him all the time but that no fighter was good enough to connect with his jaw. But when, finally, some of the better fighters, like the scrappy Tony Canzoneri, who ranks with the top little men of all time, hit Singer the experts decided that Singer had everything, for even Canzoneri could not do anything to Singer. But then came Jimmy McLarnin, which is part of this story.

The point is that Al Singer is remembered today as something of a "cheese champion," a fighter who held a title when he wasn't really the best man in his class during his tenture as a fighter. The records, however, reveal that Singer was a sensation while he lasted — and that when he was conquered, it was a flaw of nature, not of Singer himself, that beat him.

Al Singer went from boxing obscurity to the world's lightweight championship in three short years, in an age when the light men were among the best fighters around and when lightweight bouts drew heavy crowds and lots of money. At the age of nineteen, Singer became a professional fighter. For his first fight he received $75 and for his second, $40. Two years later he fought Kid Chocolate and collected $44,227. This is an indication of the manner in which Singer jumped to the top of the lightweight heap. In July, 1930 he won the crown from Sammy Mandell, by knocking out the titleholder in the first round of a scheduled fifteen-rounder.

Al Singer was not quite twenty-two when he became the champion. He was born on September 3, 1908, on Broome Street, which is in the heart of the East Side. The Singers, however, moved to the Bronx when Al was a young boy, and when the lad won his crown, he and his family were living in the Pelham section of the Bronx.

Hymie Caplin, who managed many champions, was largely responsible for Singer's success. He managed Al even more carefully than he handled Sid Terris, one of the "near Leonards" of his time. Singer lost only five times in fifty-six bouts when he met Mandell, and Singer always gave Caplin the credit for much of his success.

It was in 1928 that Singer first won the respect of fight experts and established himself as a great box-office attraction. In his thirty-fifth fight Singer was matched with Tony Canzoneri. Tony was an aggressive, hustling, hard-hitting boxer, who had been fighting since the age of fifteen. A tough little Italian from New Orleans, he had, in his time, taken on and beaten nearly all the big shots of his era, in his class. Al Singer had leaped to the fore rather quickly and the fans as well as the experts wanted to know how Al would hold up against a tested little warrior like Tony. Canzoneri was a heavy favorite to win, but Singer, in a courageous showing, held the great Canzoneri to a sizzling ten-round draw. Jimmy Dawson of the *New York Times* grew eloquent and praised Singer to the skies. He called Al the new Leonard and this time it seemed that he was right.

A year later Al met "Kid" Chocolate. This Cuban flash was a ring tragedy; he was music in motion, with a great punch and with winged feet. For a while he seemed like the greatest prospect in the world. But he was unaccustomed to prosperity. He drank and caroused and spent his chances. He did become a champion, but he burned out fast. I* remember watching him fight in the Coney Island Velodrome when he was nearly finished. It was a mean night and it was drizzling. He fought a third-rater named "Buster" Brown. For a couple of rounds Chocolate was dazzling. His footwork was amazing. He lashed out with his left with tremendous power and accuracy. Then age began to weigh down on his feet, the rain made the canvas wet and he began to stumble. Of course Brown was not even good enough for a stumbling Chocolate and the fight went into the final round of an eight-rounder. Toward the end both men looked like tired dancing dolls. It was a long way from the days when Chocolate was fast and brilliant.

But the night the "Kid" and Al Singer drew a heavy crowd, Chocolate won the decision in a fast, sharp fight. There was little difference between them. And when Chocolate won the fight, the audience nearly raised the roof. The decision was debated for years and even after Singer won the lightweight crown, fighting experts recalled the fight and said that the "Kid" wasn't the real winner.

When Singer met Andre Routis, clever little Frenchman who held the world's featherweight title and kayo'd him in two fast rounds, everyone knew that Singer was a rather good copy of Benny Leonard. And then came the spectacular fight for the title in the Yankee Stadium, on the night of July 17, 1930.

More than 35,000 fans crowded into the ball park, paying $160,000 to see the fight between the Italian titleholder and his Jewish challenger. Mandell was twenty-six, with a

H.U.R.

decade of hard fighting behind him. Singer was a handsome, sprightly fellow of twenty-one, with only about three years of the boxing wars marked up against him.

The men came out cautiously, as befits pugs fighting for a treasured title. And then, when the fight was only one minute old, Singer startled the crowd by driving a hard left hook to the jaw and dumping the Italian, who had won the crown from "Rocky" Kansas four years earlier. Taking advantage of this blow, the young lightweight showed no respect for the champion. He crowded Mandell into the ropes and bombarded him with a fire of lefts and rights to the body and head. A long left hand was dug into Mandell's stomach and the champion gasped. It was apparent that Singer was concentrating on the midsection. Mandell tried to get away but Singer held him on the ropes and punished Mandell until the champion fell to the canvas once again. He rose groggily, and Singer came on once more. He was not to be denied. He levelled off against the tottering titleholder and slammed a hard left and a right against his head and ripped him in the body with telling drives. For the third time Mandell went to his knees. Gamely he climbed to his rubbery feet. His eyes were glazed and his breath came hard. A veteran in the ring, Mandell must have known in his heart that this was his evil night. Nevertheless, he faced his tormentor gamely and tried to swing back at him. But Singer did not allow overeagerness to overcome his efficiency. He easily brushed aside the weak blows of his near-helpless opponent and drove him to the canvas with a series of heavy lefts and rights to the head and to the body.

On the fourth knockdown, the Yankee Stadium went insane with joy. Arthur Donovan, the referee who in later years was the chief referee in Joe Louis' fights, tolled the final count of ten and the bedlam grew wilder. Hats flew into the air and thousands of voices acclaimed the new champion. It was Singer's greatest night.

In his first fight after winning the title, Singer tasted defeat, and it was a bitter pill because he suffered his second knockout. In 1929 a Filipino named Ignacio Fernandez knocked him out, but Al came back in a return engagement and reversed the result. And then he met Jimmy McLarnin, who was managed by old Pop Foster. Foster was like a father to the hard-hitting Irish boy and, therefore, seldom allowed McLarnin to meet a good fighter unless Jimmy outweighed the other man. This is not to say that McLarnin could not take care of himself. The records show that the Vancouver lad was among the best fighters of his day. But Foster liked the edge in the scales. His man outweighed Singer when they met in September, 1930. More than 25,000 fans came to see the fight and they saw a dazzling bout which revealed that both men had a good deal of courage, stamina and punching ability.

In the first round Singer started fast and dazzled McLarnin with fast left jabs. They mixed it a bit and McLarnin dug hard blows into Singer's stomach. It seemed that the lightweight champion was too frail to take all of those mean body blows, but he held up well and startled McLarnin with a right which dropped the Irishman to his feet. Singer must have been overawed by the reputation of the boy with the heavy right hand, for he didn't seem to know what to do when he had Mac on the floor. When McLarnin got to his feet, Singer was a bit flustered and didn't follow up as he should have. The heavier man escaped and then began to come back as he nursed his strength and cleared his brain which had been fogged by Singer's blow. At the end of the round the crowd roared with glee for the fighters were mixing it well and were giving a good show.

As the second round bell rang, the fighters came toward each other again and McLarnin didn't seem to be worried about Singer, even if Al did slam McLarnin with a heavy blow as the first round ended. This was a different story now. McLarnin's blows began to hurt and the ribs of the lightweight champion took on the hue of cherry-red. He began to slow down but fought back strongly even if he was faced with the prospect of final defeat at the hands of the harder hitter. McLarnin found that his blows had robbed Singer of his speed and he came in to slug. He slammed Singer with a hard right hand. Singer went down as if he were shot. Gamely he strove to regain his feet. He tried hard and managed it. McLarnin, whose baby-face was only a camouflage, came on after Singer for the kill. He hit Al on the jaw with a right hand. Singer went down again. This time he was a beaten man and McLarnin chalked up another victory over a Jewish boy, and only years later was Barney Ross to avenge all of the Jewish fighters who felt the awesome thunder of the McLarnin right hand.

Even after this fight Singer was the champion and retained a modicum of respect. McLarnin, after all, was no mediocre fighter. But Singer lost his title soon enough. Two months later he gave Tony Canzoneri another crack at him and this time Tony won from the fading champion and that was the end of Singer's glory trail.

Al showed good sense when he quit the game. He knew that his days as a fighter, or at least a top-notch fighter, were over. He could no longer take a punch in championship style and rather than become a punch-drunk relic of the ring, he went into business. Year ago, when I* attended a fight between Wesley Ramey and Maxie Berger, a Jewish boy from Canada, fight fans gathered around a nattily-dressed young man and asked for his autograph. I asked who he was, and I was told, "Why, that's Al Singer. He used to be lightweight champ in the days when the lightweights were more than just pretty good."

I sometimes think that Al would like this as his professional epitaph. And to those fans who think that there were no good Jewish lightweights other than Leonard, I would suggest that they re-read the newspapers of the 1930's and they will discover that Al Singer was one of a group of fighters who, for a moment, recaptured for the Jewish people of America, a bit of that glory which Benny Leonard held for so long for the Jews who were interested in sports. But what Leonard did for a long period of time, some of these younger and less talented young men did for briefer periods. And Al Singer, who was a real good lightweight champion, was built along true Leonard lines. His only trouble was that he didn't last as long because, with all his gifts, there was one flaw in his armor. It was the "glass jaw." But to his credit he overcame the handicap long enough to make a name for himself in one of the toughest businesses and sports in the world: prize fighting.

*H.U.R.

BARNEY ROSS, AT THE PEAK OF HIS CAREER

Barney Ross

The Frail-Waisted Champion

In February, 1943, a troopship pulled in on America's West Coast. The ship was jammed with soldiers overcome by emotion. They were not "high-point" men coming home at the end of a war; they were badly battered and wounded men returning to their homes because they were too shattered to fight on. As they began that happy, indescribable walk down the gangway to touch American soil for the first time in many agonizing months and years, sentimentality surrounded all the men.

And then a wonderful thing happened. A stooped, gray-headed,slim soldier walked safely to shore, got on his knees, kissed the earth and broke into tears. The other GI's tried not to look and they attempted to control their emotions. Some did not succeed and one could hear choked sobs in that crowd of wounded men who had been fighting the Japanese in the unknown islands of the Pacific.

The act of this old-looking soldier was a symbol of their thankfulness to be back home. But there was more to it than that. The soldier was not an anonymous, emotional GI; he had been a famous American before he went off to war. He was one of America's outstanding athletes. Now he was back — tired, scarred with wounds, sick with malaria and a hero of the battle of Guadalcanal.

When American newspapers splashed the picture of

Barney Ross kissing home soil, sports readers gasped with amazement. "This isn't Barney Ross," they said. "Barney is a young fellow, a strong, happy-looking boy. This man is old and gray."

But it was Barney Ross. And he was older. He had fought Japanese, fever and nightmares to live through the war. He was the first real hero of the war who had first made his mark on the sports pages of the newspapers throughout the land. He tried to forget the agony of his experiences on Guadalcanal, and, in time, succeeded. Surrounded by the enemy, Ross and a group of men thought they would never again return to their homes. Whining bullets, mortar fire and shrapnel filled the air that night on Guadalcanal, back in November, 1942. Ross, a Pfc. in the Marines asserted his leadership, and bravely led the fight against the foe. He saved the lives of three of his men. And he too was saved.

In an eloquent article in *Coronet* magazine, Barney told some of the facts about his war experiences. With three other men in his foxhole, Barney wrote that, "only one man at a time could fire from the rim, so I fired 200 rounds from the GI's Garand rifles. After we ran out of ammunition, I kept the Japs at a distance with the twenty-one grenades we had between us. When I tossed the twentieth, I fixed the bayonets and told the boys to pray. I did a little praying of my own too — in Hebrew." With bullets whining around him, Barney was scratched a few times and then, "a slug smacked my left foot." Then, "half-crawling and half-walking," Barney and his buddies reached safety.

He came home beaten by malaria and spattered with bullet scars. He was awarded the Service Cross and won the Edward J. Neil Memorial Trophy as the "Boxing Man of the Year." He went on speaking tours and collapsed time and again as malaria struck him with its notorious persistence. He found himself unable to continue and retired from public life.

Long before he fought at Guadalcanal he exhibited his raw courage in the ring. Of course most people don't think that both kinds of courage are the same; but they are. No man who fought as Barney Ross did against Henry Armstrong in 1938 could be anything but a hero in any war, at any time, in any age.

Barney Ross was a veteran of ten years in the ring when he faced the up-and-coming, amazing Henry Armstrong for the welterweight title of the world. Hammering Henry already held the featherweight crown and was to go on to win the lightweight title, to become the only triple-winner in boxing history. He beat Ross to take away Barney's crown, but the story is hardly in the fact itself. The tale lies in the telling.

Barney Ross was "whipped, undaunted but unfloored," as one boxing writer put it, in that fight with Armstrong. When the final bell rang the fans were crying openly, in pain and pride that any fighter could show the courage of Barney Ross. Early in the fight it was evident that the buzz-saw tactics of Armstrong would wear down the champion. Henry was young, eager and ambitious. He was on the way toward one of the greatest achievements in boxing history.

The two men, both real champions, set a blistering pace for the first few rounds. Armstrong always pushed forward, never letting up. Ross, a canny veteran, fought back hard. The years had not yet begun to tell on his system. For four rounds they stood toe-to-toe and pounded each other. Barney, the older man, began to tire first. And from that moment onward Ross was on the defensive against the windmill blows of his opponent.

Within a few rounds Ross looked like he had been put through a threshing machine. His right eye was closed, his face was puffed up and distorted and his thin waist was red with punishment. As Ross grew tired his blows became wild and he was nothing more than a punching bag for one of the most tireless punchers in boxing. Boxing critics have said that Ross could have quit with honor any time after the eighth round. The referee, Arthur Donovan, asked Ross many times during the fight if he wanted to quit. Through puffed lips and closed eyes, Barney wheezed a courageous, "No." Because he was the defending champion and could go out fighting if he so desired, Ross was permitted to continue. From the ninth round on, he fought on heart alone. In the twelfth he was helpless, and stood in the center of the ring with Armstrong raining blows on his beaten body. Henry, a fine person, attempted to let up on Barney. Like everyone else in the crowd, he understood that Ross knew he was going to lose his crown but wanted to go out fighting and was striving to finish the bout without being knocked out. It is a matter of pride in boxing for a champion to want to go out standing up. It is an admirable trait in any business. And Ross was an admirable man. But Henry was brought back to his practical senses when Ross, in desperation and weak with pain, threw a hard right to Henry's chin. At this point Armstrong realized that Ross did not want mercy. He wanted to last on his own merits. And he did last. No matter how hard he tried, Armstrong could not put away his game foe. Barney wobbled on rubber legs and took all those awesome punches. The crowd yelled, "Stop the fight!" But Ross waved away the referee and his handlers. They too understood the drama that was going on, and when the fight ended with Ross still standing, the huge crowd broke into applause, tears and hysteria. They had seldom seen such punishment meted out to one man; and had never seen anyone stand up to so much of it. When *Ring* magazine, the bible of boxing, ran a series of pictures on the fight, the editor titled the page: "Downfall of a Titan." That just about described it.

This was the end of the career of Barney Ross. It was an honorable career and presaged the courageous war record of Barney in the years to come.

But Barney's career was not loaded with pain and defeat. On the contrary, this slim Jewish boy who held both the lightweight and welterweight crowns, added lustre both to the Jewish people and to sports history in America. His whole boxing career was filled with victories, many of them brilliant.

Barney was born on New York's lower East Side, in 1909. His real name was Rasovsky and from early childhood he had a hard life. While still a child, his family moved to the Jewish section in Chicago, where his father opened up a grocery store. Soon tragedy hit the Rasovsky family. Barney's father was killed by a couple of holdup men, and he left behind a wife, four sons and a daughter.

In recalling the event, Barney said, "It was a crazy thing, this murder. Two poorly dressed men had come into the store and asked if they could warm themselves at the big stove. Pop said sure. Then a customer came in, an old Jewish woman who had known Pop for years. She eyed the men, became suspicious and warned my father in Yiddish." But after she left, they became panicky; one "pulled a gun on Pop and fired," Barney sadly remembered.

So to young Barney, in his early teens, came the responsibility of taking care of the suddenly bereaved family. He took on odd jobs, continued to go to school and managed to keep the family alive. He and one of his brothers closed the grocery soon after the death of their father, so that they could make a living in the way they knew best. Years later, after he won the lightweight diadem from tough Tony Canzoneri, Barney told a reporter, "My greatest ambition is to see to it that my mother, and the rest of the family, have everything that they want. If I could do that better in some other profession I would not hesitate to go into it in preference to boxing. But I thought I had some talent for the ring and could do better as a boxer than in any other profession and so I went in for boxing."

Recalling his early life, Barney said, "When my father was killed in a holdup of our grocery on the East Side of Chicago I figured it was up to me to do what I could for mother and my four brothers and one sister. My mother had a hard life for a long time, but at last things are going to be different. She's going to get some joy out of life."

And Barney did have talent for boxing, as he put it. He entered the Chicago Golden Gloves tournament, which also produced Joe Louis, and to his amazement walked away with the featherweight title. It was very possibly due to his environment that Barney was able to fight his way through all the tough kids who entered the tournament. In the Chicago ghetto Barney was always the fellow who was called upon to lick some tough boy. He was the leader of his group at all times. He played ball in high school while supporting his family. All these things added up. They made him tough without his being aware of it. So he waltzed his way through the amateurs. While still an amateur, Barney gave an impressive exhibition against a prominent professional featherweight named Earl Mastro. Earl's managers were Art Winch and Sam Pian. The reason this story is important is that the Winch-Pian team liked Ross and eventually signed him to a professional contract a short while after Barney gave up on his original manager. The team of Ross and Winch-Pian went far in boxing, as will soon be seen. "Pian was Jewish but looked Italian. Art Winch was Italian but looked Jewish. I was lucky getting them," Barney said.

Now Ross began to campaign in earnest. He beat a lot of good fighters, including Bat Battalino, Frankie Petrolle and Goldie Hess. He learned how to feint and box and shift and move about the ring. He was gaining ring wizardry. And then he fought Tony Canzoneri for the lightweight crown. At the time, in 1933, Barney was not too well known in the East. He had done most of his fighting out of Chicago and New York fight fans are never convinced about a fighter's class until they see him. It was true that as he moved into the Canzoneri fight, Ross had won twenty-three bouts in a row. But the question was: how would he do against the champion?

Ross, at this time, had fought some fifty times and had lost but twice. Naturally Tony was a heavy favorite. But the fight was rough, tough and nearly even. Barney took away Tony's title in a fight which was all uphill for Ross. Most of the critics gave the nod to Tony. And because the fight was fought in Chicago, the Ross victory was not taken too seriously. It seems that Canzoneri had the fight well in hand going into the seventh round. He had outslugged, outboxed and outthought the younger man. Going into the seventh, Ross had cuts under both eyes and had been staggered many times by Tony's powerful right. There were times when it seemed that Ross would fold up under this savage punching, but he always fought back hard. Yes, he was doing well but not well enough to win the title. Then Barney found his second wind. He started a blazing two-fisted attack. He pounded Tony and was never beaten back. Canzoneri, on the other hand, thought that he had the fight won, so he started to coast. He had the title for three years and did not think Ross was taking it from him. But Barney won the decision and New York fans, reading about it in the papers, decided that Barney was a cheese champion.

Like a real champion, however, Barney gave Tony a return bout a few months later. This one was fought at the Polo Grounds in New York and the fans of the metropolis were getting a good look at the man they called a cheese champion. They saw Ross beat Canzoneri with a perfect job of boxing. Nat Fleischer, editor of *Ring* and one of the foremost boxing experts in the land, said that Barney's left hand was as good as Benny Leonard's. Canzoneri went right hand crazy, which means that he tried to knock out Barney with a right hand blow and forgot to throw left hand punches. But Ross knew what he was doing and he won a convincing decision. This time fight fans in New York knew that the new titleholder was a good battler.

In his next impressive fight, Barney beat Billy Petrolle, the "Fargo Express." Billy has become a legend of the sport. Never a champion, he beat the best men of his time and offered some of the finest bouts within the memory of the oldest fight fan. Like Canzoneri, Petrolle is mentioned elsewhere in stories in this book. And for much the same reasons. He was too good a man not to be included in a history of boxing champions of his time. Billy was good, but Barney drove him into retirement. He peppered the veteran and tied him into knots. His boxing skill that night was astounding. He outguessed his man all night long. As one fight writer said, "If Barney had a real punch he would have been a wizard." But he had all he needed and his exhibition against Petrolle convinced even the cynics that this kid was a true champion.

Incidentally, Mike Jacobs first managed to obtain a foothold as a top-notch promoter, when his Ross-Petrolle bout successfully bucked the Garden setup. After this success, Mike was soon established as the top promoter in boxing. At this stage Barney Ross was outgrowing his field. He was growing older, filling out, gaining weight and eyeing the welterweights. The welter champion at the time was Jimmy McLarnin, whose record of knockouts was amazing. He was particularly good against Jewish fighters. He had at one time or another kayo'd a half dozen star Jewish fighters, and whether he liked it or not he was considered a nemesis to the Jewish pugilists of his era. Jimmy was a tremendous hitter and outweighed Ross, so when they finally signed up to fight, there was little doubt in most minds that Ross was biting off more than he could chew.

The interest in the first Ross-McLarnin fight was intense. This was only the third time in history that a lightweight was fighting a welterweight champion with the latter's title at stake. Benny Leonard had tried it against Jack Britton, but lost on a foul. Now Ross was trying it against a bigger, harder-punching, stronger man than himself. No wonder it attracted the attention of fight fans everywhere.

I* remember that at this time I was living in a section in New York where many European Jews — all young men — were attending *yeshiva* in the city. These boys knew little about boxing, but they could not miss the excitement throughout the city. And the fact that McLarnin had beaten many Jewish fighters made the event even more important to them. It was odd, watching these boys, with skullcaps on their heads, taking time out from their Talmudic studies to listen to a fight on the radio. And no matter how long I shall remember the famous trio of Ross-McLarnin fights, I shall recall the intense faces of the Jewish students who listened to each blow-by-blow account as though it were the most significant thing in the world.

The crowd was so huge that the great Long Island Bowl was the site of the fight. It was a sizzling bout, and Ross won a split decision. He continually fought his way out of danger and battered his foe whenever he saw an opening. He drew blood from McLarnin's nose early in the fight and showed absolutely no fear of the dangerous Irishman from Vancouver.

Each time Barney was stung he charged into his man and took the play away from him. Twice Ross was staggered and fought his way out of danger as his head cleared. In the ninth round McLarnin hit Ross with a good right and dumped him to the canvas. Barney hurried to his feet without taking a count. He had never been floored in his life and when he rose there was rage in his eyes. Again he rushed his man, disdaining the words of caution flung at him from his corner. Just forty-seven seconds later he wal-

*H.U.R.

loped McLarnin with two sharp left hooks and Jimmy hit the floor! McLarnin, too, refused to take a count and was up before the referee could start the toll. The fight continued along these violent lines until the end of the round. At the end of the first nine stanzas Ross held a wide lead, but then he tired. His foe was heavier and harder hitting. McLarnin's infighting had taken the steam out of Ross' legs. Barney was a slender boy, with a wasp-waist. He could take a lot of punishment, but it seldom helps to take a beating. So for the next five rounds McLarnin took the lead from Barney. He rushed his foe and pounded him. Of course Ross fought back hard, but the margin was clearly McLarnin's.

When the final round of this fifteen-rounder started, it seemed that if Ross did not hold his own the judges would be prejudiced in favor of Jimmy because even if Ross won most of the rounds, McLarnin was winning the last five or six. With bleeding lips and a puffed face Barney faced his tormentor. He attacked the feared Irishman with abandon but as soon as the round began McLarnin staggered Ross twice with right hands. It looked like the end for Ross until he showed his famous spunk and began to belabor his foe. At the end of the round both men were flailing away at each other. There was little to choose between them.

The decision was split. That is to say, the judges and the referee disagreed on the winner, but Ross was declared the victor. Harold Barnes, one of the best judges in the land, gave Ross eleven rounds, two to McLarnin, the rest even. Every newspaper reporter in New York agreed that Ross had won. He was the first man to win both lightweight and welterweight crowns and as of that moment Barney Ross was a ring immortal.

Mainly because the fight was so thrilling and vicious, it was natural that McLarnin be given a return bout. Barney, who never ducked a foe, gave Jimmy another shot at the title, and this time McLarnin was the winner in a bitterly-debated decision. Of the twenty-eight boxing writers who reported the fight for their papers, twenty-two thought the verdict a sour one. More than once McLarnin was shaken by Barney, who was confident after his first win over Jimmy. McLarnin closed Barney's eye early in the fight and pounded away at it all night long. Nevertheless, Ross staggered his man many times during the battle. At the infighting Barney was much the better man and pounded the Irishman viciously. At the end of the fight McLarnin was half-blinded with gore and with the effect of Ross' steady punching. The decision went to McLarnin and Nat Fleischer, who had predicted that McLarnin would win back his crown, announced in *Ring* that Ross was the real winner and that if they ever fought again Ross would win the title once more.

Nat proved to be a good prophet. In 1935, McLarnin and Ross met for the third and last time. Barney won a unanimous verdict over the boy who used to terrorize Jewish fighters. When the bout was over Barney was a spent scrapper. His nose had been split in an early stanza and he fought with a canny brain which guided him out of the way of McLarnin's crashing right hand punches. Barney cut Jimmy's left eye and evaded all the traps McLarnin set for him. Ross was a master in the infighting and was a demon around the ropes. This time it was evident that Ross was McLarnin's master and when the final vote was unanimous, the fans knew that Ross was the new welterweight champion once again.

It was now that all fans of fisticuffs knew that Barney Ross was a great champion and that his fights with McLarnin would become part of the classic series of boxing with which ring history is replete.

Nevertheless, Ross had many more brilliant performances left in his system. He beat all comers and showed fist fans a brand of boxing seldom equalled in his time. There were two fights, however, which remain vivid in the minds of boxing followers everywhere. One of them is his bout with Armstrong, where Barney showed greatness in defeat. The other was in his fight with Cerferino Garcia, the Filipino with the bolo punch, during the boxing carnival in 1937 in New York.

Mike Jacobs, who was trying hard to maintain his leadership over all other boxing promoters during the year 1937, concocted the idea of four world championship bouts in one night. Lou Ambers fought and defeated Pedro Montanez for the lightweight crown, thus retaining his title; Harry Jeffra won the featherweight diadem from Sixto Escobar; Fred Apostoli won undisputed control of the middleweight championship by licking Marcel Thil, French titleholder; and Barney Ross fought Garcia for the welterweight crown.

Even with such sterling performers, the bouts were dull. Montanez fought badly, Thil was stopped by a cut over his eye and Jeffra fought an uninteresting bout to uncrown Escobar.

But Barney Ross, with his guts, skill and brains, saved the night.

Garcia was a terrific hitter but not a clever fighter. He banked on his bolo punch, a curious sort of uppercut which was effective against most of his opponents. Strong, willing and dangerous, Garcia was one of the really hard men to beat during his tenure as a pugilist. He fought Ross more than once, but each time Barney managed to pull out a victory. Later, Garcia won the middleweight title from Apostoli.

In their fight on the night of the carnival of champions, Garcia was determined to whip the ghostlike, thin-ribbed welterweight champion. He never could understand how Ross was able to stand up under his powerful bolo punch.

In the first rounds, Ross outboxed the powerful Garcia and weaved cleverly out of the way of the Filipino's mad punches. In the fourth Cerferino slammed Barney in the stomach and doubled him up. Ross opened his mouth because of the pain but fought on gamely. In the sixth Ross warmed up and opened a cut over Garcia's left eye. But he paid for this blow, as Garcia staggered Ross, cornered and bombarded him with punches from all angles.

Showing courage and skill, Ross fought his way out of this bad spot. He maneuvered himself past the wicked body punches of Garcia and fought his way into the center of the ring, where Garcia could not reach him. The crowd roared with appreciation as the fast-thinking champion outguessed his hard-battering but slow-thinking opponent.

For the next few rounds Ross stayed out of the path of Garcia's heaviest punches and pecked and jabbed his way into a long lead on points. But in the eleventh round Garcia again caught up with the tiring welterweight champion. He buckled Barney's knees and pelted him freely. Barney's speed afoot was gone now and Garcia was finding it easy to get the range. He was unable to land the fatal blow and Ross kept his feet and head. During the next three rounds Barney took a bad beating. He fought with his mouth open, which gave away his condition. Only badly tired fighters open their mouths, to let air into their pounding lungs. Barney was fighting on instinct alone. He knew he held a margin over Garcia but he had to keep on his feet to win. He stayed erect throughout the thirteenth and fourteenth rounds, despite some terrible punishment. He heard the bell ending the fourteenth with relief mixed with determination to win the last round and save his title. But Garcia sensed that he was on his way to the treasured crown. He opened the final onslaught with a heavy barrage of rights and lefts that caught Barney off guard. Ross was a sight at this stage of the fight. He was bleeding from cuts on his face and his entire mouth was swollen. But he dug deep down into his reserves and rallied. For the last two minutes of that round he fought Garcia off his feet. It was as though he had said, "That's enough of that, chum. Now let's fight." He feinted and weaved and became a difficult target to hit. Meanwhile he slammed into his foe with hard driving punches. At the end of the round it was Ross who was carrying the fight to his man and the crowd gave him a tumultuous ovation. This rally saved Barney's title and gave fight fans another reason to remember him with affection.

But Barney was nearing the end of the trail. He had taken a lot of pounding in his day and his day was a long one. A year later Henry Armstrong came out of the Far West and knocked down all opposition facing him. Barney, a veteran by this time, was unable to stem the tornado that was Henry Armstrong and took a bad beating from the great black fighter.

Like most clever fighters, Ross knew he was all finished as a champion, so he quit rather than carry on with nothing more than a reputation. Life had been good to him; he had earned more than half a million in the ring and he was ready to call it a day.

Then war came and Barney, old as fighters go, but not as a warrior for America, joined the Marines. For a while no one heard of him or what he was doing and then suddenly his exploits made front pages of America's newspapers. When he came home to the country he so bravely helped to defend, he was given plaques, awards and other honors. He was too sick to accept a Government award himself and his wife accepted it for him from Mrs. Franklin D. Roosevelt.

In his autobiography *No Man Stands Alone,* Barney told the story of his life, his pride in his Jewish heritage and his battle against the drug habit. Published in 1958, this book emphasizes how a young boy, raised in the slums of a big city can come close to a criminal career — and how he can also attain international fame. Barney insisted that he managed to survive, to win in the right, to conquer a dread drug addiction because of his religious faith — and one can believe him.

When he passed away on January 17, 1967, a victim of cancer, Barney left behind him more than great boxing memories. He left a legacy of courage that men continue to remember.

Yes, Barney was a hero both in the greater war between the nations and in the small, intense battles in the roped ring. He won two titles, beat some of the finest fighters in the world to get to the top and was named to Boxing's Hall of Fame in 1956, when he received 100 out of a possible 111 votes from the nation's sports writers, in what was a remarkable tribute to him. He came a long way from Chicago's East Side to win the acclaim of all America.

Football Frenzy

As regularly as the seasons of nature, football follows baseball on the sports firmament of America. There is hardly a moment's respite. As the sports headlines scream forth the World Series scores, the gridiron stars already are involved in early season football games.

The football season is cruelly short. Few college teams play as many as ten games. The professionals perform in about eighteen league games. Still, for a few months, Saturdays, Sundays (and Monday night football on television), there is a madness over the land.

Why this intense interest in the game? Why this fall frenzy?

To begin with, football is a spectacular game; it is fast and furious. Pete Axthelm, in his excellent book on basketball, *The City Game*, comments on other sports as well. On football he remarks, "Its violence is in tune with the times, and its well-mapped strategic war games invite fans to become generals, plotting and second-guessing along with their warriors on the fields. With its action compressed in a fairly small area and its formations and patterns relatively easy to interpret, football is the ideal television spectacle."

You don't have to know much about it to enjoy its great moments. A slithering run, a long pass, a broken-field dash can be cheered by anyone who enjoys speedy action, well-executed. Baseball demands a vast background knowledge. You have to know comparative standings, batting averages, past performances, whether a pitcher throws the fastball or the curveball. Each play in baseball is a conflict, a slow-motion conflict, perhaps, but a fascinating one. Nevertheless, it requires a knowledge not only of the game but of the teams and the players. A true baseball fan is a walking book of meaningful statistics.

But a football fan needs only to know that his college or professional team is playing; that his boys, or hulking men, have to get the ball to the enemy goal and that any way they do it is exciting. Football is a bruising sport, a body smashing game and carries its own excitement.

Unfortunately for the college player, his reputation seldom outlives his college career, unless he turns professional, and only comparatively few players make the pro grade. A man goes to college four years and plays varsity ball the last three. Not too many schools allow a man to play varsity ball from the outset. If he is a remarkable athlete, he will become a star in his first season. At best, then, he is an outstanding figure for three football years.

Thus, in writing about football stars, one is handicapped in writing about those men who play only through their college career; the public memory is weak. But when a man stars for a decade in football, he becomes very well known. Especially if they are quarterbacks. Johnny Unitas, Joe Namath, Fran Tarkenton are among the quarterbacks who became as well known nationally as any baseball heroes.

Because football was basically a collegiate sport for so many years (and almost all the pros come from college teams), there have been many outstanding Jewish football players. One reason is that so many Jews do attend colleges and universities. Over the years, there have been hundreds of Jewish footballers, and many All-Americans.

The best way, in the beginning, to tell who the notable players were, was to follow the various All-American teams. Once, most of the good football was played in the East. And so, when Walter Camp, a great football expert, chose the eleven best players of each season, he generally saw most of them play, often against each other, and was able to pick the best of each year. The Camp choices were so famous that to be chosen by Walter Camp was the short way to football immortality. Still, there were extraordinary Jewish players even before those days, as the story of Phil King proves.

The next Jewish All-American picked by Camp was Joe Alexander of Syracuse. Joe was named twice by Camp, in 1918 and 1919. After Camp's teams, there seems to have been an outcropping of All-American squads, by the news syndicates, by individual sports writers and by sports magazines. It became impossible for a single individual to judge the players all over the United States. Out of the confusion and myriad of teams, there have emerged these Jewish All-Time All-Americans:

Benny Friedman of Michigan
Harry Newman of Michigan
Fred Sington of Alabama
Aaron Rosenberg of Southern California
Leroy Monsky of Alabama
Marshall Goldberg of Pittsburgh

There have been many other Jewish players who made some All-America teams, or who won honorable mention, or who later won fame in professional ranks. Most All-Americans are chosen from major teams. Sid Luckman of Columbia, for example, did not make the All-America teams in 1937 and 1938, the year Marshall Goldberg was a unanimous choice. Goldberg was playing with the powerful Golden Panthers of Pittsburgh, while Luckman was the star of a weak Columbia team. Luckman was as good as anybody, but playing with a losing team won him only honorable mention, not All-America fame. But when Luckman and Goldberg turned professional, Luckman joined the all-conquering Chicago Bears and Goldberg the luckless Chicago Cardinals. One result: Goldberg went into comparative obscurity; Luckman won recognition as one of the greatest quarterbacks of all time.

Other men who won some All-America mention were Izzy Weinstock of Pittsburgh; Barney Mintz of Tulane; Dave Smuckler of Temple (who became a professional star with a poor team); Sid Roth of Cornell and scores of others. Aaron Rosenberg of Southern California was a guard on one of the best college teams in the land in his time. During his tenure, his team lost only twice in thirty-three games. His savage line play won him All-America honors in 1933. In time, he became one of Hollywood's most successful and prominent film producers.

Leroy Monsky, like Rosenberg, played in the Rose Bowl when this Bowl was the only and greatest of them all. He was an All-America player for Alabama in 1937. Of course, there was Phil King, who is a member of the College Hall of Fame, was the first Jew named to any All-America team, and coached football at Harvard and Wisconsin. There was, during the Walter Camp football era, a brother combination which deserves mention. Arnold and Ralph Horween (born Horowitz) played for Harvard and from 1926 to 1931 Arnold was Harvard's coach. As for coaching and general administration in football, there have been a handful of Jewish notables. Allie Sherman of the Giants made an enormous impact for many years. Al Davis, a controversial figure, was the key personality in building up the Oakland Raiders and making them Super Bowl champions. Long before, Lucius Littauer, who became a Congressman and a noted Jewish philanthropist, had served as the first football coach of Harvard University and also as the first Jewish college coach. The prominent Reform rabbi, Rabbi Emil G. Hirsch, was a football player when he attended Pennsylvania University, and took part in the first football game ever played at Penn. A now obscure athlete, Samuel Jacobson, may have been the first Jewish pro football player, according to *The Encyclopedia of Jews in Sports*. He was a member of the Syracuse Athletic Association in the late 1880's, or early 1890's. Frank Glick of Princeton, who was a Tiger halfback in 1914 and 1915, was Princeton's captain in 1915 and, following in the distinguished footsteps of Phil King, Glick became a backfield coach for Princeton and then was head coach at Lehigh. Many years later, in the 1970's, Ron Mix was an outstanding pro and became a Hall of Famer. Sid Gillman, a long-time professional coach, became in his late years, an offensive coach with the potent Philadelphia Eagles in 1980.

It is almost impossible to list all of the fine Jewish gridiron stars, for thousands of Jewish students have attended institutions of higher learning and quite a few have made their mark in football, although far fewer in professional ranks. It is also true that a football player is easiest to write about if he is a spectacular backfield man. The backs do much of the scoring and it is around them that play revolves. A lineman gathers mud and bruised muscles and wins little attention or acclaim from the fans who fill the stadiums and watch the television screen. Only the coaches and enemy players know a good lineman. Still, it is the runners and passers and play-callers who win the headlines and it is they who in the final analysis make football spectacular. The demands on them are heavy. They need more than brawn and football intuition. They must be fast, know how to pass with pinpoint accuracy and, under tension, call the correct play.

Three of the finest quarterbacks in football history (college and professional) have been Jews: Benny Friedman, Harry Newman and Sid Luckman. One of the most powerful runners and line smashers has been Marshall Goldberg. Their stories are told here; but there are literally hundreds of Jewish stars whose careers cannot be outlined for lack of space and because their feats are not unlike those of the top men included here. In reading of this great quartet, remember that they symbolize hundreds of others whose names are now memories entrenched in the hearts of those who saw them and were thrilled by their startling feats on the gridirons of the nation.

PHIL KING, WHEN HE WAS A PRINCETON ALL-AMERICAN

Phil King

Little Big Man

Football before the turn of the century was a rough game. The 1890's were long before the days of the forward pass, let alone multiple option formations. It was a game of power, determination and courage. Yet, in this brutally physical pastime, one of the greatest stars in history was a short, slight gentleman from Princeton University.

Philip King's athletic prowess was extraordinary by any standards. He was not only a Princeton football immortal, he was one of the few four-time All-American selections the game has ever known; and he achieved his honors at two different positions. In addition, he was a magnificent baseball player, earning All-America distinction at that sport as well. In an era when the team captain was a virtual coach, King captained both the football and baseball teams at Princeton. Professional teams in both sports were anxious for his services, but instead he became a great college coach in both football and baseball. And all this from a man who, at the peak of his playing career, stood five foot five-and-a-half and weighed in at an underwhelming one hundred and fifty-five pounds!

Born in 1872 in Washington, D.C., King studied at Emerson Institute in that city to prepare for Princeton. According to Princeton University records, his standing in his class was "average." But at the University, he became a student of rare distinction. When he graduated with his class in 1893, it was as Class Salutatorian. He was also an editor of the *Daily Princetonian,* a member of Triangle Club, and a member of Tiger Inn, the campus eating club which, then as now, had its fair share of gridiron stalwarts. After graduation, King attended New York University Law School, obtaining his degree in 1896.

When the blue-eyed lad with the curly blond hair entered Old Nassau, no one really had a clear inkling of his athletic greatness, even after he made the freshman squad as a hundred and thirty-eight pound quarterback in an age of the flying wedge. When he joined the varsity in 1890, the *New York Times* evaluated the Tigers as the poorest Princeton eleven in years.

Phil got his chance with the varsity when the regular halfback was injured against Penn in the fourth contest of the season. In his first carry, Phil scampered around end for twenty-five yards; before the game was over, the Tigers had a new star halfback. According to the *New York Sun,* "King played a great game for Princeton, making several phenomenal runs, and two of them touchdowns."

He never left the lineup after that. His reputation rapidly became legend as he ripped off unstoppable runs against opponent after opponent. He ended the season with an astonishing twenty-nine touchdowns. In an incredible display, he faced Virginia and Columbia on successive weeks and racked up seven touchdowns against the former and eleven against the latter!

Though the Tigers suffered one defeat that season, a 32-0 thrashing in the final game against Yale, King was selected to the All-America team that year. He was already considered one of the most pile-driving line plungers football ever had. And his peers agreed that the game had never seen a more punishing, smashing tackler. Woodrow Wilson, prior to his days in the White House, was a fervent football fan who coached Princeton's squad in 1890. Wilson said flatly that Phil King was the greatest football player that he ever saw.

When the 1891 season started, King naturally started at halfback. But after only two games, it became painfully apparent that the Tigers badly required a skilled quarterback. King, the best player around, assumed the position. Quarterbacks rarely ran with the ball in those days; after scoring three touchdowns in his first two games at the new position, Phil didn't score again for the remainder of the year. But due to his unselfish, team-oriented efforts, the Tigers swept through the season undefeated and unscored upon until the final game when they again fell to mighty Yale, 19-0. The powerhouse Bulldogs played with three future Hall of Famers: Frank Hinkey, Bum McClung and Pudge Heffelfinger.

King was again named to the All-America team by selector Caspar Whitney in *Harper's Weekly,* and by Walter Camp, whose own list started that very year. Whitney remarked that "Last year Princeton lost a great halfback by putting (Phil) at quarter. Nevertheless his work in that position was very fine, especially his continued stirring up of his men, his interference and his tackling."

With the new season approaching, King was elected football captain and returned to his halfback post. Whitney observed: "He is the right man in the right place, for the Princeton football candidates have needed the past two years a captain with a sharp stick constantly in motion. I think King is about the best captain on the field I have ever seen. Nothing escapes his eye and when a player makes a mistake in practice he hears of it immediately, and is given instruction how to avoid it again . . . The best move captain King has made so far was to put himself at halfback instead of quarter."

In the 1892 season, the Tigers again rolled up eleven consecutive shutout victories before being upset by Penn, 6-4, for their first loss ever to the Quakers. The lone Princeton touchdown was registered by King (a touchdown was worth four points at that time). But King injured his ankle in the Penn game, and so he started at quarterback rather than at the running halfback position in the Yale game two weeks later. Princeton fans clung to the hope that Phil's injury would not cost them the long-sought victory over the men from New Haven, and the *New York Sun* commented before the game:

"One devout student yesterday determined to restrain his thoughts and keep to his Bible, but his eye lit on the passage, 'There shall be ten men, and a Jew shall lead them to victory.' When he learned that captain King is really of Jewish descent he was compelled to lay aside his devotions and speculate like the rest whether or not this passage were not a prophecy."

But sadly, the Lord preferred the color blue that day, not only for the sky but for the football game as well. Yale blanked the Tigers, 12-0.

King returned to Princeton for one last shot at beating the proud Bulldogs. As the two powerful teams drew closer to their inevitable confrontation, Princeton was once again unbeaten, and so was Yale. The Elis, in fact, had won thirty-seven straight contests over the years, led by the great Hinkey, of whom it was said that "no one ever turned his end."

For the Yale game, King devised a special strategy. He had not sought the captainship this year, but concentrated on coaching from his quarterback position. He put his ends back, in a precursor to the later double wingback formation. With defiant daring, King sent his attack directly into the teeth of Yale's strength — Hinkey's end. During the bruising classic contest that unfolded, King himself turned that end more than once.

"Attendance was the largest and most fashionable that ever witnessed a football game," reports the *Princetonian* of December 2, 1893, covering the confrontation that is generally regarded as the greatest game ever played to that time. The Tigers were "the strongest team Princeton had ever put in the field . . . unlimited praise is due the captain and coaches," added the *Prince.*

The Yalies, of course, knew whom they had to stop to win the day: Phil King. Bill Edwards, in *Football Days,* describes the scene: "On the kickoff Phil got the ball and all the Yale forwards began to shout, 'Here he comes, here he comes,' and then as he was cleverly dodging and evading Yale players, one of the backs, who was waiting to tackle him low, was heard to say, 'There he goes.' "

Phil began the game with a twenty-yard run, and continued to star throughout the hard-fought game. When Princeton finally crossed the goal line, Phil kicked the conversion. There was no more scoring that day. The final result was a 6-0 triumph for the orange and black of Princeton, completing a gloriously undefeated season. Praising Phil's magnificent efforts, the *New York World* observed that "in all around playing the doughty little Princetonian outplayed Frankie (Hinkey)."

During his college days, Phil's exploits on the diamond were as impressive as those on the gridiron. An exceptional second baseman, he is generally regarded as one of the greatest college ballplayers of the 19th century. An All-American in this sport as well, he captained the Princeton nine. An exceptional fielder who hit with power and was a dangerous base-stealer, he single-handedly whipped Yale in one contest that is still referred to as "The King Game." Vincent X. Flaherty, in the *Washington Herald,* writes:

"Built along the massive lines of Hans Wagner, King was a great infielder, endowed with large hands that smothered everything driven his way. He was a tremendous hitter and crashed out whizzing drives for amazing distance. And when he was graduated, be-whiskered big league scouts were around, eager to sign him for the infantile professional game."

But King shunned professional athletic endeavor, preferring rather to develop young collegiate talent and spirit. While pursuing his law degree at N.Y.U., he became Princeton's first paid athletic coach, handling both the football and baseball teams in 1894. The next year, he moved on to Brooklyn, N.Y. where he coached the Crescent Athletic Club football team. It was an amateur group composed of former Princeton, Harvard and Yale stars, and Phil's success was so impressive that he was immediately invited to become the head football coach at Wisconsin. By the time he left Madison in 1902, King's Wisconsin teams had won three conference championships, two of them in his first two seasons there.

King's teams were characterized by dedicated, aggressive defense, and the coach himself was known as a shrewd judge of character and motivation. In 1897, Bob Knoff wrote in *The Milwaukee Journal* that "King suspected a letdown or overconfidence. So he 'framed' the varsity with the officials in the alumni game and the decrepit old grads won by a touchdown. Then King soundly berated the team as a bunch of quitters, and they went out the next Saturday and beat Northwestern 22-0." The alumni defeat, by the way, was the only loss the team suffered during the entire season. King's 1901 team was also undefeated, and yielded a total of five points in the course of the season.

Coaching baseball as well, King led Wisconsin to two conference championships in that sport. In 1899, while still handling football at Madison, King took enough time off after the season to return briefly to Washington and coach Georgetown University's baseball team. Under his expert guidance, the Hoyas suddenly blossomed as a major eastern power, dominating all their competition in compiling a 22-2 record.

After 1902, King left Wisconsin and returned to Washington where he assumed controlling responsibilities in his family's department store, King's Palace. As successful in business as he was at everything else, Phil eventually won unanimous election as president of Washington's Merchants and Manufacturer's Association.

"It seems that King was equally proficient in every branch of athletics he tried," comments Flaherty. "He was one of Washington's first golfers and when golf was practically unknown in the Nation's Capitol, he was whamming out enormous drives. He was one of golf's first long-distance hitters, though he used a mid-iron rather than a driver."

But Phil retained his ties to the collegiate gridiron. In 1903 he coached Georgetown for part of the season, and he returned to Wisconsin for the 1905 campaign. He also continued his work with the Princeton eleven in an advisory capacity, and contributed his experienced and expert guidance to the Tigers' cause until 1916. When President Theodore Roosevelt called a special meeting of the most prominent football figures in an effort to save the game from excessive roughness and brutality, King was one of those who composed the rules that shaped the spirit of modern football.

King himself said of football that "Personally, the game has done me untold good. I have developed myself, have learned self-restraint, it has helped me when and how to act in a crisis, has given me self-possession, and I think better fitted me to take up the battle of life." A further insight into Phil's credo is evident in an evaluation he wrote of the Princeton baseball team's prospects for *Harper's* in 1895. The alumni All-American said of the collegians: "The general work of the team can be made superior to last year's if the old men will only waken from their lethargy, put their shoulders to the wheel, and work for all that is in them."

Phil King did his best to instill values of intelligence, hard work and dedication to all competitors with whom he came in contact, and his best was very good indeed. As a Princeton football star, he registered 55 touchdowns, 56 conversions, and a legacy of leadership. As a college coach, he compiled a 74-14-1 record. In *The Encyclopedia of Jews in Sports,* King has separate entries in the fields of football, baseball, and golf. In December, 1961, the phenomenon from Princeton was elected to the Football Hall of Fame.

When King died in 1938 at the age of sixty-seven, tributes resounded. Flaherty called him "the most thoroughly glamorous athlete of them all . . . whose feats of strength awed those who knew him in his prime. King was Washington's one football immortal . . . Back in football's formative days, Phil King towered over the field . . . In death, he stands alone, truly an immortal."

The *Princeton Alumni Weekly* remembered of King that "that stout warrior never flinched on the gridiron or diamond . . . football captain, captain of the baseball team, member of the *Princetonian* board, member of the Triangle Club, member of the track team, salutatorian of the class, winner of the Peace Cup for the Class, coach of football at Princeton, but most of all a good comrade, the University's and our debt to Phil is too great to measure . . . No gathering of the Class which he attended lacked for good fun and merriment; while his modesty and reserve, coupled with his innate sense of balance, helped to carry us through many a tough spot. To him our unstinted praise."

Indeed, there should be no stinting of praise for the awesome achievements of Phil King, the little big man of Princeton, whose place in American sports history is both secure and richly deserved.

Press Association

BENNY FRIEDMAN, READY TO THROW ONE

Benny Friedman

Michigan Marvel

Even now, decades after he ran wild on the football fields of the Midwest, Michigan University's Benny Friedman is remembered as the "perfect quarterback," the man who never made a mistake on the gridiron as he led his team tc brilliant conference victories in the Big Ten. Benny Friedman, one of the greatest Jewish football players in history, was a football immortal. It takes only a cursory glance at the yellowed newpapers of his era to prove that Benny was one of the top stars of all time.

In his time football was first becoming a national mania. Most fans probably think that football has an old and hoary tradition, something like baseball, which celebrated its 100th year in 1939. But the rah-rah of football, its huge 80,000-seat stadiums and its big business, aspects are a comparatively recent phenomenon. And in the blaze of football glory of those days, Benny Friedman was an honored figure.

Benny played football under the great coach Fielding "Hurry Up" Yost, who always used to say that Friedman was a man who never made a mistake on the field. This was a rare tribute, for Yost led some of the best teams in gridiron annals and it is generally agreed that Benny Friedman was his finest player.

This is no idle compliment, for Friedman starred in the

days when Red Grange won immortality; he was a clever quarterback in those days when the midwestern schools were building million dollar stadiums and were looking for — and finding — brilliant, husky men who could play like demons.

Friedman was picked by all football experts to the 1926 All-America team, in a day when these all-star teams meant a great deal. Today there are so many such teams that the whole business of All-Americans has become a mockery. But when Friedman starred, matters were different. There were not as many squads cavorting under the name of one school. In Friedman's day a man played football for sixty minutes and if he was good, he had to show it for a full, hard game.

Benny Friedman also pioneered as a professional football player. After dazzling college opponents for three years, Benny played pro ball for eight years, passing brilliantly, running his teams cleverly and making the All-Star teams with the same ease that he made the college All-America teams.

When his football days were done Benny became a coach of a weak CCNY team. He worked marvels with his players; in the final analysis he could not go out on the field and play for them. The result was that sports columnists wailed that the great Benny Friedman was wasting his time with a group of eager but untalented men. Of course when war broke out Friedman joined up with all the speed he could muster at his age and became a naval officer assigned to aircraft carriers.

Friedman later became athletic director and football coach at the Jewish-supported and sponsored Brandeis

University in Waltham, Mass. In time, he retired from this post.

This is the skeletonized story of his career. But how much drama and brilliance are left out!

And for those who really want to know about the great Benny Friedman, the footballing Benny, the passing Benny, the All-American Benny, here is the story.

Its beginnings are actually told in a newspaper story after the Michigan-Northwestern football game on November 8, 1924. Here is part of the account:

"Benny Friedman, former Cleveland High School star, who, at the start of the season was not regarded as of varsity caliber, forward passed Michigan to a 27 to 0 victory over Northwestern today. Three of the Wolverines' four touchdowns were the direct result of his passes."

This was only the beginning for Benny, who had been a substitute ealier in the season and had watched Red Grange lead his Illinois team to a humiliating victory over Michigan. Red had scored four straight touchdowns against a bewildered Michigan team when Friedman was pushed into the game. Years later Benny said, "I stopped Grange on his first play toward me, but the paper never gave me any credit for it. Anyway, it was my first real football thrill."

But it was in 1925 and in 1926 that Friedman really won his spurs. Early in the 1925 season Friedman led his boys to a win over Michigan State by a 39-0 score. Among other brilliant things, Friedman scored a touchdown on a 65-yard run and tossed a couple of touchdown passes. This, however, was only a warm-up. The following week Friedman gave one of the greatest performances any grid great ever offered his devoted fans. He drove the

Wolverines to a 63-0 count against Indiana. But that is not the whole story. Here is what Benny did: he scored one touchdown on a 55-yard run by dashing through the entire Indiana team, he passed for five more touchdowns and kicked eight points after the tallies. In a word, he was responsible for forty-four of the sixty-three points; of course this does not account for the tallies he set up.

At this point it should be mentioned that Benny Friedman was fortunate in having as his left end, the guy who caught his passes, a fellow named Benny Oosterbaan, who has also gone down in history as one of the finest pass-snarers and ends in football. The two Bennies, as they were happily called, ran riot for years. And whenever Friedman starred, Oosterbaan was right there alongside of him. But the way these two men played was a wonderful sight only to Michigan fans and Michigan players. Enemy teams dreaded and feared them. They had good reason for their fears. Especially Wisconsin. The week after Friedman went wild against Indiana, the Wolverines met the Wisconsin Badgers at Madison, Wisconsin. The final score was Michigan 21, Wisconsin 0. But let's go behind the score. Here is how the Associated Press ran the tale:

"It took just thirty-one seconds for Michigan to win the game at Madison and show the football world that Benny Friedman is destined for top rank among the great players developed by Yost."

Here's why. On the second play of the game Benny threw a 40-yard pass to Oosterbaan who ran the remaining twenty yards for the tally. The very next time that Wisconsin kicked off to Michigan Friedman swivel-hipped his way through the entire enemy team for an eighty-five yard run and another touchdown. In the third period he threw three passes almost in succession for a third tally. He kicked the three points after the scores.

All three games, however, were preliminaries to the great game of the year, the Michigan-Illinois battle. It was a conflict between titans. Red Grange, still considered the finest runner the game ever saw, was eager to repeat his sensational performance of the previous year, when he scored practically every time he handled the ball. Benny Friedman, who was Yost's ace to counter the flaming Grange, wanted to show that he could lead his team to victory over anyone, including Red Grange.

There were 67,000 fans in the stands. The game was phenomenal; it reeked with tension and with drama. And here is how it moved along, as told by the Associated Press the following day:

"Michigan, learning about Red Grange in 1924, presented Benny Friedman, the Wolverines' point-scoring ace, to Illinois today, to square accounts for the disastrous rout of a year ago.

"In one of the greatest football games of the Western Conference championship, Michigan defeated Illinois, 3 to 0, while 67,000 spectators, a record-breaking homecoming crowd, gazed down on the spectacle from Illinois' magnificent $2,000,000 memorial stadium . . .

"The Wolverines, humiliated by the 39 to 14 defeat of a year ago, achieved their victory near the finish of the second period, when Friedman, Yost's star quarterback, booted a field goal at a difficult angle from the 24-yard line after he and his teammates had advanced the ball from midfield.

"The Wolverines got possession of the ball when Oosterbaan intercepted Britton's pass. Friedman started a triple pass that was largely responsible for the gain that put him in position to boot the goal . . . With Gilbert holding the ball, the stocky nineteen-year-old Friedman stepped back while the huge crowd was deathly silent in the breath-taking excitement of the situation. The pass came perfectly from Captain Brown, Wolverine center, Gilbert grabbed it, held it to the ground, and in an instant Friedman's toe crashed against it, sending the ball hurtling through space and squarely behind the Illinois goal posts."

Red Grange, who was supposed to give Friedman competition, carried the ball twenty-seven times and lost a total of fifty-four yards. Years later Friedman recalled that "the Illinois left guard dropped out of line to run interference for Grange," and the clever Benny always sent someone in to charge the hole left by the guard. This was one reason for the Illinois defeat; it also showed the trigger reflexes of Friedman.

This was Benny's high spot in 1925. He had proved himself a real star. And he was more than that. He was an intelligent undergraduate who could talk about the significance of a Jew becoming a top footballer in a Midwestern school.

Friedman, who wrote many articles on his career for national magazines, once declared:

"There were times when I thought the grade was made harder for me on account of racial prejudice. I soon found out that was the bunk. The fact that I was a Jew didn't preclude social recognition for me on the campus. Indeed I was invited so often to frat functions that I came to suspect that it was because I happened to be rated the best quarterback on the squad."

That Friedman must have been telling the truth was indicated by the fact that a few years after his college career was over, Michigan boasted of another Jewish quarterback who is ranked by many as being better than Friedman. His name was Harry Newman, whose career is featured in another chapter.

Although Friedman starred in 1925, he made All-America ranking on the basis of his work the following season. And 1926 was, actually, the finest Friedman season in collegiate ball.

The Friedman-Oosterbaan combination swamped Oklahoma A and M to open the year, beating them 42-3. The week after that the Wolverines walloped Michigan State by a 55-3 score. Benny dazzled the enemy with his passes and with his running. He managed to get off one 47-yard sprint for one of the touchdowns, just to get himself into shape, as it were, for the next game, which was with Minnesota. Benny, who was the captain of the team this year, showed heady tactics in leading his men to a 20-0 win over the Gophers. The whole game, as a matter of fact, was a Friedman classic. Benny was daring, using passes and end runs to set up the scores and then, with victory in his grasp, settled down to a conservative game. Minnesota could not cope with him, as Benny outguessed, out-maneuvered and outplayed the foe.

And then came the important Illinois battle. The year before, Friedman had outsparkled Grange. What would happen now, with Friedman free to roam all over the gridiron, for Grange had turned professional and Benny was the most brilliant star on the football horizon? Benny showed 50,000 fans a complete bag of tricks as the Wolverines won 13-6. In a tough fight between the two lines, Friedman broke through two times by kicking field goals for six points, the equivalent of a touchdown. And when Illinois and Michigan both scored a real touchdown, Benny kicked the extra point for his side. In short, he scored seven points himself; that was enough to win.

After walloping Wisconsin 37-0 the next week, with Friedman scoring a touchdown, kicking a field goal and four points after touchdown, the Wolverines readied themselves for the contest with Ohio State.

Ohio State is known for its football frenzy. Always a strong team, the Ohioans put on a great show year in and year out, and when tney clashed with the Wolverines more than 90,000 fans showed up. At the time it was the greatest football crowd in history. A short while later more than 110,000 fans came to watch Army and Navy. But the week these teams battled each other, they set a new mark in attendance. And the game was worth the trouble.

It was a razzle-dazzle, exciting game which had the fans in a tizzy. Michigan won by a single point, 17-16. Here is an account of it, from a newspaper of the day:

"Michigan brought to Ohio Field a superb line that halted Ohio's running attack from the very start, and, of course, Michigan brought along the incomparable Bennies — Friedman and Oosterbaan. Anyway it was these two who forged a Michigan victory out of what at the start looked like a parade for Ohio State.

"Benny Friedman passed all afternoon like only Benny Friedman can, and Benny Friedman booted a goal from the 42-yard line that brought his team abreast of Ohio shortly before the first half ended."

Michigan finally won when Ohio, holding a three-point lead, fumbled late in the third period. Benny Oosterbaan recovered on the Ohio 7-yard line and the Wolverines went on to win from there.

Once again Friedman showed his coolness under pressure and his educated toe, when Michigan beat Minnesota the following Saturday. Outplayed most of the way, the Wolverines had to win this game if they were to tie for the conference championship. Minnesota took a 7-0 lead going into the final quarter. A desperate Benny Oosterbaan finally broke through with a 55-yard touchdown run before 60,000 frenzied fans. The score was all tied up. It was up to Benny Friedman to unravel the deadlock. He stood up there calmly and booted home the point that meant victory for the Wolverines. It was a spectacular exhibition of nerve.

And it was a fitting way in which to end his last season.

After he got his college degree, Benny Friedman came East where he was feted and admired by the countless Jewish fans who had followed his progress with interest and pride. At this time he was already connected with the Cleveland Bulldogs, a professional team. And fans everywhere waited to see how he would do with the play-for-pay boys. They need not have worried. He played spectacularly. And in connection with his pro football debut, there is a funny little story.

When Benny saw that his foes were such huge and formidable men, he must have looked a trifle worried. All of a sudden, he heard someone say, in Yiddish,

"Keep your chin up, Benny. It's a nice friendly game."

Benny wondered who his fellow Jew was. He looked across to the enemy line and saw a huge tackle smiling at him.

"What's your name and where are you from?" Benny asked.

"O'Donnell of Notre Dame," the big guy said.

But pro football was not particularly humorous to Benny. He played eight years of it and toward the end grew heartily sick of the game. It is interesting to listen to Benny's version of it.

"When I left college, he wrote, "I wanted, more than anything else, to be a stockbroker. Instead I became a pro football player, in Chicago, in Cleveland and in Brooklyn. For the past six years I've made $10,000 a year at pro football.

"It's been fun, hard-earned fun; but where has it got me? . . .

"My best advice to all gridders is to play the game as a college function — then forget it as a post-graduate career."

This was written long ago, and Benny Friedman has been a college coach, a naval officer and a businessman since these lines were first penned. But he will always be remembered as a college football star, a quarterback who has seldom been equalled and never surpassed. He was a real triple-threat player. He could run, pass and kick. And he was a brainy player, perhaps the cleverest team general in gridiron history. He ranks with the All-Time All-Americans. He'll be remembered as long as football remains a craze in America.

HARRY NEWMAN AS A PRO

Harry Newman

The Second Coming

One of the oldest cliches in the English language is that lightning never strikes twice. Yet, just a few short years after Benny Friedman had graduated college to bedevil pro defenses, Michigan's football opponents found themselves facing a seeming reincarnation of the fearsome Friedman. In 1930, Michigan introduced their new quarterback: a handsome, smart field boss, brilliant in both passing and placement kicking, and clearly destined to be an All-American stalwart before proceeding to fame and glory with the New York Giants in the professional ranks. No, it wasn't Friedman re-entering university for a second education — Benny was still calling signals in the pro ranks. The new Wolverine star was a Jewish athletic marvel, all right, but this one was a lad from Detroit named Harry Newman.

It is perhaps unfair but completely inevitable that Harry be compared to Benny throughout his career. Newman was a sensational football player in his own right, but there just weren't that many Jewish All-America quarterbacks starring for Michigan equally adept at running the offense, throwing the ball or kicking it through the uprights. As a matter of fact, Newman was given an early opportunity to show his stuff partly because Friedman's success story was so indelibly remembered. At the end of his freshman year at Michigan, preparing for his try at the varsity in 1930, Harry attended a summer camp in New Hampshire where his game was polished by no less an authority than Benny Friedman himself.

Although only 5'8" and one hundred and eighty pounds, Harry was the sensation of the tough Western Conference as a sophomore. The team had been branded mediocre by the experts that year, and little was expected of the young Wolverines. Sure enough, in the first conference game Purdue scored two quick touchdowns and took a 13-0 lead. But in the third quarter, the coach inserted Newman, and the tenor of the game changed. Harry wasted little time in tossing a touchdown pass and kicking the conversion to close the gap to 13-7. Then, with time running out in the fourth period, he went into punt formation on fourth down; but instead of punting the ball away, he shocked the Purdue defense by hurling another touchdown pass past the deceived secondary. Then he kicked the extra point to give Michigan the upset 14-13 win.

The rest of the season was taken from much the same script, as Newman led the lightly-regarded Wolverines to victory after victory, their undefeated season marred only by a scoreless tie with Michigan State (a game played before Harry became a regular). The week after Purdue, Harry threw a long pass for one score and ran for another as Ohio State was blanked 13-0. A 15-7 victory over Illinois was due to another Newman TD pass and Harry's twenty-three-yard field goal. A tough Harvard eleven was beaten 6-3 only when Harry tossed a touchdown pass, good for twenty-seven yards and the win, in the last quarter. Then Harry organized a drive down to the Minnesota two-yard line and guided his team to a close 7-0 victory over that team as well.

Harry was naturally selected as quarterback of the All-Western Conference, and received All-America mention on the AP's national team. In 1931, Harry's season was hampered by a series of injuries that sidelined him for a substantial portion of the campaign. Still, he played well and Michigan finished with a 8-1-1 mark, good enough to tie Northwestern for the conference championship for the second straight year. In 1932, Newman's senior year, he determined that he was going to win a conference title outright this time — no more ties for the crown. And win it he did, in one of the most extraordinary seasons any college quarterback has ever had.

Under Newman's inspired leadership, Michigan swept through 1932 undefeated and untied. Out of a possible four hundred and eighty minutes in the season, Harry played four hundred thirty-seven. He had a hand in every winning play in every single game. Michigan played eight tough opponents that year, but each in turn fell before the Wolverines and their brainy leader. Harry was everyone's selection as the top quarterback in America, garnering All-America honors on virtually every existing list. He also won the Helms Award as Player of the Year, and the Fairbanks Trophy as the outstanding collegiate player of the season. 1932 was, without question, Harry Newman's year.

The first game was against Michigan State, a powerhouse team which was not to lose another contest all year long. State, captained by Abe Eliowitz — another Jewish gridder himself — knew they had a good squad going into the game, but Newman passed them silly and the Wolves crushed State 26-0. Against mighty Northwestern,

Harry broke a 6-6 tie with a thirty-six yard TD pass, then tore off a fifty-two yard dash to set up a field goal and a 15-6 win.

Favored Ohio State rolled up one hundred forty-four yards from scrimmage and held Michigan to only forty-six; but Newman's uncanny passing undid the Buckeyes and led Michigan to a 14-0 upset. Harry dazzled Illinois by throwing for two scores and returning the second-half kickoff seventy-six yards for another: the final tally was 32-0, Michigan. A brave Princeton eleven held Harry to only one completion — but that one produced the winning touchdown as Michigan edged the fierce Tigers 14-7.

Indiana bowed, 7-0, when Harry ran thirty-four yards to set up a touchdown he carried over himself; then he kicked the extra point. He scored both TD's in a 12-0 defeat of Chicago, racing seventy yards for the first tally and dashing twenty-eight yards with the second. Finally, Harry and his mates faced undefeated Minnesota in a battle that would decide the conference crown, Late in the first half, Newman passed the Wolves into scoring position, and then booted a field goal with thirty-six seconds remaining. That was the only score in the game as Michigan won 3-0.

Crowning Newman the All-American quarterback of the season, Grantland Rice remarked: "From a fine field Newman stood well above the mass . . . He made Michigan's run of eight successive victories possible with his forward passing, his broken field running, and his place kicking. He must be listed as one of the most effective triple-threat backs . . . He delivered fifty-seven of the eighty-three points Michigan scored against Big Ten opponents. He scored all of the points Michigan made in her last three big games.

"Newman had every trick of the great ball carrier: change of pace, cut, pivot, straight-arm, and elusiveness. He had the quickest shift and twist of any Michigan back since Heston, and he could hit a pass receiver in the eye at thirty yards. Newman also was a competitor of the highest type."

The professional New York Giants had developed a large Jewish following with Friedman as their quarterback, and with his career ending they were so anxious to get Newman as a successor that they offered Harry an unusual contract wherein he received a percentage of the home attendance. This made him one of the league's highest paid players.

Harry quickly showed that he was worth every penny. As a rookie, he led the league in passing, and smashed a precedent by making the All-Pro team in his first year. He led the Giants into the first NFL championship game, against the powerful Chicago Bears. Although the Giants finally lost, 23-21, in a game where the lead changed hands six times, Harry was nothing less than heroic in his efforts: he threw touchdown passes and completed thirteen consecutive passes during the game.

In 1934, Newman continued to be as unstoppable as he had been as a rookie. Once again, he led the league in passing. But, in an astonishing display of his multiple talents, he also set a professional record when he carried the ball thirty-nine times, gaining one hundred fourteen yards, in a game against the Green Bay Packers that the Giants won 17-3. But the very next week, at the height of his career, he sustained an injury that was to shorten his playing days. Bill Hewitt of the Bears knocked Harry unconscious with a crunching tackle; Hewitt's knee slammed into the small of

Harry's back, breaking two bones. It was a savage irony that Hewitt, a teammate of Harry's at Michigan, had been the receiver of Newman's first touchdown pass of his college career.

The Giants defeated the Bears in the championship game that season, but the injured Harry retired, unable to play. When he tried to return to the Giants during the 1935 season, his shrewd leadership and marvelous skill was unmistakably evident, but the damaging injury had clearly taken its toll, and he wasn't the same overwhelming player he had been. Still, even a slowed-down Harry Newman was valuable enough to help the Giants to another Eastern Conference title. After the season, Harry retired, for good this time, not wanting to play below the extraordinary standards he had set for himself.

He finished his career as the winner he always was, and will be remembered as he wanted to be: as a triple-threat quarterback of truly giant stature, an immortal passer, runner and leader of men at both the collegiate and professional level. His towering accomplishments mark him forever in memory not as the second coming of Benny Friedman, but as the first coming of Harry Newman.

Acme

MARSHALL GOLDBERG, IN PRACTICE

Marshall Goldberg

Backfield Blaster

A Jewish boy from the hills of West Virginia named Marshall Goldberg was one of the most powerful line-smashers and power runners in football. Playing with the bonecrushing Pittsburgh Panthers during the years when Jock Sutherland's men were among the top gridiron outfits on the college scene, Marshall Goldberg won acclaim as a hard runner, almost impossible to stop once he gathered momentum.

From the very beginning of his football career, Goldberg was a star. When his college days were over, he had twice been chosen an All-American and was one of the most sought after players for professional ranks. And in his years as a Chicago Cardinal he gave yeoman service to a weak team. Like most good runners, Goldberg needed some protection and support from his line. His professional mates weren't good enough to open up holes for him. So Marshall Goldberg's reputation grew a little smaller. But to those who followed the game he remained in professional ranks what he had been in college days — "Mad Marshall" Goldberg, one of football's best running backfield aces.

Born in Elkins, West Virginia, Marshall and his family were heroes in this small hill town of 7,500. His father, Sol Goldberg, an immigrant from Poland, was a prominent man in Elkins, and the fact that he had five sons, all of whom were football stars with the local Davis-Elkins team, didn't hurt his popularity a bit.

When Marshall became a Pittsburgh star, he and his family constituted the town's number one family. Bill Goldberg and Marshall Goldberg were the two best footballers in Elkins. And Elkins was proud.

Goldberg was brought up to believe that the way to score on a football field was to take the ball and smash through the enemy line. Only the professional teams stopped him occasionally. And here's the reason. Because he was so powerful a runner and bowled over the opposition without much difficulty, Marshall never learned how to pass well. In college, his running was enough. But when he became a pro, he found that when a team had no passing to mix up with the running attack, the enemy team is smart enough to know how to stop a ground game. That is why Sid Luckman became even more noted in professional ranks than he was in college. He was a passer who could blend passing with running. He was a threat in both the air and on the ground. Goldberg was a runner. A good one, but not much more. This cut into his over-all effectiveness.

Nevertheless, his college career is studded with heroics and with startling performances. Remember, he played with a great Pitt aggregation. He helped make the Golden Panthers of Pittsburgh a great college team. He broke into the lineup as a sophomore in 1936 and at the end of the season Pitt was chosen to play in the Rose Bowl. Marshall had a lot to do with it.

In Pitt's opening game in 1936, Marshall Goldberg helped beat Ohio Wesleyan, 53-0. A newspaper account started with the phrase, "Goldberg, heralded as the best

Panther prospect in years, starred." He certainly did. In his first game as a Pitt regular, Marshall was the key man in an 88-yard march to the enemy goal, then broke through for a 76-yard run for a touchdown. And later he scored again.

In those days the Pitt-Notre Dame classics were among the top thrillers on the gridiron. These teams were always among the top five in power and performance. Notre Dame, generally a powerhouse, has one of the most noted reputations in football. During Jock Sutherland's reign at Pitt, the Panthers were also a top club. So the games between them were the major clashes of the season. Huge crowds filled ball parks to watch these behemoths smash at each other.

And in Goldberg's first game against the Irish, he really went to town. Pitt beat Notre Dame before a screaming mass of more than 70,000 fans. The two key men for Pitt were Bobby Larue and Marshall Goldberg. Here is how a press association reported the exploits of these two men:

"Rarely could one tackler pull them down and of the two the sophomore Goldberg, who will be eighteen years old tomorrow, was far better. As young and inexperienced as he is the boy stamped himself as positively All-American timber."

Apart from tearing the Notre Dame line into shreds, Marshall grabbed the second half kickoff and dashed forty-eight yards. A few moments later he catapulted for the touchdown.

Later that year he starred against all opposition. Against Penn State, Marshall passed for one touchdown and ran forty-five yards to set up another; against mighty Nebraska he broke through for a 32-yard run. But he really impressed against Fordham that year.

In 1935, 1936 and 1937 Pitt and Fordham played titanic 0-0 games. Fordham was known as one of the best defensive teams in college football. The Ram line was called the "Seven Blocks of Granite." Years later, when many of these linemen turned professional, they ranked with the top pros. For three years in a row, Pitt and Fordham clashed — with Pitt the heavy favorite. The Panther running attack generally tore down all opposition, but against Fordham they didn't score at all in this three-year period.

Nevertheless, Goldberg did everything except score. In 1936 he flashed so much speed that New York reporters named him "glittering Goldberg." He managed to get off an amazing 28-yard run in a game where a 5-yard smash was a long gain. The final score was 0-0, but Marshall proved he could run against any team.

The playing of Goldberg helped Pitt into the Rose Bowl that season. On New Year's day, Pittsburgh met Washington in the Bowl, before 87,196 persons. Pitt was eager to win for this was their fourth appearance in the Bowl and, so far, they had lost all of the three previous games.

All Pittsburgh was excited and, of course, Elkins was under terrific tension. Marshall's father, who ran a movie theater, had been a rabid fan all season and whenever possible, he sat on the Pitt bench during the team's game. Jock Sutherland had said of Sol Goldberg, "Sol Goldberg is my idea of the perfect football player's father. I wouldn't swap him for two good guards and a blocking back." And Sol Goldberg could be given an assist for Pitt's 21-0 victory over Washington.

The Pitt team was tense in the dressing room and none of the brain trusters could break the strain. Then there came a telegram addressed to Jock Sutherland. The good doctor scanned it and then called the boys together.

"Hey, fellas, listen to this. It's from Sol Goldberg."

And Doc Sutherland read the telegram:

"Dear Doctor. Bring home the bacon. And you know how I hate pork!"

The tension was broken. The boys laughed heartily and ran out on the field, loose-limbed and relaxed. They won the game, of course. But there is yet another story here. Marshall's father, remember, ran a movie house. But when the Rose Bowl game was shown that year in the theaters, the competing theater happened to feature the Fox Movietone News, starring Marshall Goldberg. So Sol Goldberg did the natural thing. He wrote a letter to Mr. Fox. This is what he wrote.

"Dear Mr. Fox:

"When you have any more Goldberg pictures, for God's sake send them to Goldberg!"

After his fine showing in 1936, Marshall developed into a real star and in 1937 he made the All-East team (together with Sid Luckman of Columbia) and also made the All-America team for 1937. He couldn't miss, for he starred against all opposition. The Panthers were undefeated and Marshall was their big gun. He was the fifth leading ground gainer in college ranks. Generally stars with the major teams, playing rough schedules against top-notch opposition, seldom chalk up heavy yardage gains. Most often the rushing leaders are men on the small college teams, whose opponents are little-known teams. But Goldberg was a top ground gainer. In ten games he ate up 701 yards. He starred against every team on the Pitt schedule. But it was against Notre Dame that he turned in his best performance of the year.

This time the Panthers licked the Irish, 21-6. Goldberg and Hal Stebbins gave awesome performances of line-smashing. They raced off tackle and around ends. They weren't stopped all afternoon. Marshall crashed through to thirty-nine yards in six plays. And then, in the most neatly-timed play of the day, engineered by Goldberg, Stebbins went over for a key touchdown. Marshall took a reverse around right end, handed the ball to Stebbins, who came from the opposite side, cut toward mid-field and was away for the touchdown. The play fooled the entire Irish team. But Marshall did more than dazzle them; he smashed them. In twenty-five carrying chances he crashed through a tough line for 110 yards.

In the 1937 0-0 tie with Fordham, Goldberg covered himself with further glory. He was the only man to score in all three 0-0 ties. But his touchdown was called back because of a holding penalty on a Pitt tackle. Reporters watching this game called him the "leg-propelling Goldberg."

Here are some of his other 1937 feats:

Pitt: 21; Wisconsin: 0. Goldberg scored two touchdowns. The first came on a series of drives of 14,6 and 29-yard rushes. The second came on a 63-yard run.

Pitt: 28; Penn State: 7. Marshall scored two touchdowns and set up another. He was the key man in 54 and 46-yard drives.

Pitt 13; Nebraska: 7. Goldberg made the longest run of the game, thirty yards. And rushed hard all day.

Pitt: 59; Ohio Wesleyan: 0. On the very first play of the game Marshall intercepted a pass and ran fifty-five yards for a touchdown. This play broke the enemy's back and soon after Marshall left the game.

In his senior year, 1938, Goldberg continued rampaging against the football teams foolhardy enough to face him. When Pitt walloped Temple 38-6, the newspapers said that Goldberg "had to be seen to be believed. He slashed at the tackles, swept the ends, ripped on reverses, pummeled the middle." His power was tremendous, and his blocking was deadly.

Against Duke, Marshall threw two touchdown passes and scored one himself. The score was 27-0. So Goldberg was responsible for three of the four tallies.

In beating Wisconsin 26-6, Goldberg scored a touchdown and continually ripped the Wisconsin line for huge gains.

In licking Southern Methodist 34-7, it was suddenly realized that, with Marshall Goldberg in the lineup, the Pittsburgh Panthers had won twenty straight games.

And then came the climax. It was the Fordham game. In 1935, the year before Marshall joined the Panthers, the Rams and Panthers had played a scoreless tie. And in Goldberg's two previous years there was no further scoring. Now Fordham stood before Pitt, a winner of twenty straight (not counting ties). What would happen now?

Fordham, a power on the defense and proud of its reputation, fought madly to withstand Pitt's attacking power. The teams drove against each other. It was a brutal game, with neither side giving way. The Rams finally scored a touchdown and the Panthers, desperate over their famine against Fordham, tried for a field goal and made it. After a three-year drought, both teams had finally scored. Going into the last quarter the Rams led the Panthers 7-3.

It looked as though a tremendous upset was in the offing.

But Goldberg and Company were not to be denied. Fordham managed to score once more. Then the powerful Golden Panthers of Pittsburgh broke the dam and poured across all their pent-up power. They were not to be stopped. In the last period the Panthers scored three touchdowns. Ripping the Ram line with inexorable strength, the Panthers drove fifty-seven yards to their first touchdown. Then, seven plays later, Marshall Goldberg, bottled up for two years by Fordham (with a penalty nullifying a score a year earlier), smashed across for the second tally. He catapulted over from the 3-yard line, but his sweated body had driven hard up to pay-dirt. By this time Fordham's back was broken. Another good, ripping attack brought the ball to the Ram 2-yard line. Fordham was known for its tenacity and for its amazing goal-line stands. But Goldberg was given the ball. He bent his head forward and ploughed. He disappeared in a mass of struggling bodies. Suddenly the umpire waved his hands signifying another Pittsburgh score. Marshall Goldberg had scored again! Within the last fifteen minutes the Panthers had scored thrice, with Goldberg going over two times. The final score: Pitt: 24; Fordham: 13. It was a wonderful climax to Goldberg's college career.

Marshall Goldberg's professional career was not as amazing as his college feats. Goldberg joined the Chicago Cardinals, the doormat of most of the teams in the professional league. It is difficult to overwhelm teams whose linemen weigh an average of 220 pounds. And when your own team is comparatively weak and you have no passing attack to mix up the opposition, you are under a great handicap.

In Goldberg's first professional game, in 1939, his club was beaten by the Green Bay Packers 27-20. Marshall scored a touchdown and showed that he belonged with the best of the pros. But he was playing a losing game. For example, in losing 14-0 to the Cleveland Rams that year, Marshall carried the ball seven straight times. Apart from the punishment a runner takes in carrying so often, it revealed that Goldberg was the sole hope of the hapless Cardinals. Game after game, he smashed into the huge tackles and guards and although he made yardage, he couldn't bowl them over the way he did college players. His coach said of him that he was a wonderful runner but that he never threw enough passes and that "you can't run over this league."

Now and again, Goldberg made a dazzling play, reminiscent of his days of college glory. He would get off a long run to a touchdown, or would smash an enemy line with awesome power. For years he played with a bad club, uncomplaining, taking a physical beating, doing nothing spectacular. But in the statistical records of the professional game, Goldberg was one of the top ground gainers. He had achieved a silent role. No longer did he win headlines. No longer was he with an all-conquering club. He made the headlines of the team, but who pays any attention to the hard-driving player of a consistently losing squad?

Marshall Goldberg never gave up. In scanning the newspaper report of the hopeless games in which he played, there are these lines: "Goldberg went sixty-six yards for a touchdown in the second period against Green Bay." . . . "Goldberg was the big gun in the Card running attack, chalking up more than one-half the Chicago yardage."

In the All-League choices, Goldberg did not make first team, because he was buried with the Cardinals. But he always made honorable mention, as though it were known that with another club he would be a top star.

Nevertheless, Marshall still had his speed and power and once in a while he pulled another great feat, typical of his Pitt days. In one game in 1942, while his team lost overwhelmingly to the Packer team, he gave a dazzling exhibition of open field running and travelled ninety-five yards to a touchdown. It was one of the longest runs in professional football history.

In losing to the Washington Redskins, 28-0, the Cards had nothing to boast about except Goldberg. Here is how a newspaper described it, and it reveals how well Marshall played:

"Goldberg turned in a scintillating running performance until he was forced to leave the game with a knee injury in the third period."

In 1943 Goldberg played no football. There was a war on, and he was part of it. The Cardinals went from bad to worse without him, as he served Uncle Sam. When the war was over Goldberg returned to football, but once again he took up the chores of unsung line-plunger. In 1947 the Cards finallly emerged as a strong team. Goldberg, however, gave way to Charley Trippi as the top plunger. Luck again turned against him as he found himself eclipsed at a moment when it looked as though he would have a chance to star with a powerful eleven. He continued playing for a few seasons, and then faded from the football scene, a scarred veteran giving way to new stars and new headliners, which is the way of the sports world.

The unusual aspect of the Goldberg career is that in college he was one of the major stars, while Sid Luckman, playing with a poor Columbia team, was second fiddle to Goldberg. And while Goldberg pounded heavy enemy lines for yardage gains in the pro game, Luckman ran wild and became one of the top players in the play-for-pay circuit. But that is another story.

When Pittsburgh won a second successive Lambert Trophy in 1976, Marshall Goldberg was one of those who came to the podium to receive the trophy formally. White-haired but still trim and fit, he was a living reminder of Pitt's first Lambert award in 1936, forty years earlier.

Gordon S. White Jr. of the *New York Times* asked the great runner the secret of winning the trophy. Goldberg's reply was simple and straight-forward. "Win every game," he replied.

SID LUCKMAN LOOKING FOR A RECEIVER

Sid Luckman

Hall of Famer

One of the top football stars during the past four decades has been a trigger-brained quarterback with an unerring passing arm and a hatful of heroic deeds on a gridiron equalled by few players. His name is Sid Luckman, a Jewish boy from Brooklyn who learned the pigskin game at Erasmus High School in 1933 and ran wild for nearly twenty years on both college and pro football fields.

Leonard Cohen, ex-sports editor of the *New York Post,* once wrote: "Far into the night will go any debate as to whether El Sid or Sammy Baugh is the greatest passer pro football has ever produced. We've always taken the stand that Sid has it on Sammy on the long aerials, while Baugh has no equal as a short-pass tosser."

Today it is granted that Sid Luckman, long the brain of the Chicago Bear powerhouse football team, was the man who made that dreaded outfit click. It is remembered that in college Sid was the star of a weak Columbia University team. Lou Little of Columbia had many stars in his time, but none as spectacular, as dependable and as much of a football genius as the keen-eyed passing wizard from Brooklyn.

Oddly enough, Luckman, who was one of the greatest passers in football history, never won real All-American acclaim while he starred in college ball. While playing collegiate ball the same years in which Marshall Goldberg smashed to All-America glory, Luckman passed and led his teams to glorious — but often losing — efforts against teams stronger than the Columbia Lions. The result was that Luckman was known as a good player with a bad team. No one knew how good he really was until he joined the professional ranks. In college, he was just another good passer.

As it happens, Sid was never offered a scholarship by Columbia. The university did offer him an opportunity to obtain jobs to pay his way through college, and he accepted that even though he had done so well in high school that plenty of other colleges and universities wanted him to join their school, and, of course, football team. At Columbia, Sid washed dishes, baby-sat and worked as a messenger around the campus. His father's trucking business had been wiped out in the Depression and Sid did not wish to be a burden to his parents; neither, it seems, did he want to go to any college but Columbia — a break for the football fortunes of that Ivy League university.

Sid was born in Brooklyn on November 21, 1916 and it was when his folks moved to a decent house near Prospect Park, that the young lad began to throw the ball around. Depending on the season, he threw a baseball or tossed a football. When he entered Erasmus High School in Brooklyn, Sid immediately went out for football and soon made the junior varsity, although he was only a freshman. The following season, he became a regular player on the high school team and became the quarterback. Success came rapidly, for, under Sid's guidance, Erasmus won the borough championship. In his last year at Erasmus, Sid earned the McGlue Trophy, given to the outstanding student in the senior class. Now he was ready for Columbia.

To those who followed the fortunes of Columbia, however, Sid Luckman was one of the finest athletes who ever played for Lou Little. Coming to Columbia with a tremendous high school reputation, Sid immediately revealed that college ball was not too fast for him. On October 3 1936 he made his debut with the Columbia Lions. The newspapers of the period stated that he showed ability as a line crasher, an off-tackle runner and as a passer. All of this sounded a bit strange later, for Luckman was acknowledged a kingpin passer, but did little running. In the opening game of the 1936 season, against Maine, the Lions won a 34-0 victory. Sid ran thirty-eight yards for a touchdown, passed for a second one and also threw a perfect 33-yard peg which later was cashed in for another score. In a word, he started off with a bang.

All this was but a debut. The following week, Sid lived up to all his notices as his team was beaten by Army 27-16. Sid, however, showed he could block, run, kick, pass and tackle. At half-time, Army led 15-6. Then Sid went to work. With a cut-back from an off-tackle slant he ran untouched for a score, bringing the game within Columbia's grasp. The Cadets went on to count again but Sid was a dangerous threat all day long. He got off booming punts and whenever he passed there was peril to the opposition. Overwhelmed on this day — as on many others in his collegiate career — Luckman won plaudits as the best player on the field.

At this stage of his career Sid was only twenty years old. He had learned how to throw a football, after years of practice, in Brooklyn's Prospect Park. Lou Little declared after the Army game, "He's just a sophomore but I think he's one of the best passers in the game right now. He's the best I ever had." And Luckman superseded Columbia's Cliff Montgomery as the finest player Little ever had. Years later, Paul Governali starred as a passer for Columbia, but he never accomplished as much in pro football as Sid did.

The rest of the 1936 season Sid was Columbia's major threat. His team had an indifferent year but every Saturday Sid did something unusual. At the season's end he was recognized as a potentially great player.

In 1937 he was good, slowly working himself up to a crescendo of magnificent accomplishments. In beating Penn, Sid had a field day. The score was 26-6 and Sid passed fifty-eight yards to one score, twenty to a second tally and lugged the ball over for a third. The last touchdown came after a series of Luckman passes brought the ball close to Penn pay-dirt. So he was largely responsible for all the points tallied by the Lions.

Curiously, a week later, Columbia lost to Brown, 7-6, and Sid, in a losing game, played one of the finest games of his college career. The *New York Times* reporter wrote that "starting on his own 20-yard line, Luckman gave one of the greatest forward-passing exhibitions ever witnessed." He passed five times in a row. The first toss gained thirteen yards. The second one made fourteen; the next, eighteen; the fourth, fifteen. The final toss netted eight yards. The ball now rested on the Brown half-yard line. Each time Luckman had thrown the ball, the Brown players knew it, but couldn't stop him. Robert Taylor, a Columbia backfield ace, carried the ball for the final half-yard, but slipped in the turf and lost possession of the ball. Columbia's chance was lost. Sid, however, was responsible for the touchdown the Lions did score. He ran back a punt for ten yards, slipped off-tackle for five more, passed eighteen yards to bring the ball closer to the Brown goal and then tossed to Taylor for the tally.

All season Luckman played like that. The *Times* carried this paragraph about Sid in reporting the Navy game: "Once more, Columbia's star halfback, Sid Luckman, covered himself with glory. Although his cause was the losing one, the sharpshooting Lion ace was easily the outstanding player on the field. He did all that could be expected of any back, tossing bullet-like forward passes, punting, carrying . . ."

A few weeks later Sid played a losing game against Dartmouth. The Indians won 27-0 and although the Dartmouth backs led by Bob MacLeod did yeoman work, they did not eclipse Luckman. Years later, Jimmy Cannon, the *New York Post's* sensitive and lyrical sports reporter, told this story:

"On the way down from Hanover, N.H., the Special taking the Columbia football team back to New York stopped at a small town along the way and I went to the movies with Sid Luckman. The Columbia line was light and the Dartmouth guys had no trouble. They broke through when they had to and they were hanging on to Sid and knocking him down and it was astonishing how he got the ball away. It was a weak team but he had greatness that season and with a little help from his club would have made All-America.

"The lights were on in the movies and I started to go. But Sid sat in his seat, struggling to get up and embarrassed by his helplessness.

" 'I'm a little stiff,' he said. 'Give me a hand. I can't get up.'

"I got him up and we walked slowly back to the station. The people with him said he had had a great day and they praised him for his skill and determination.

" 'I didn't have a great day,' Sid said, hobbling along.

" 'The hell you didn't,' a guy said.

" 'How can you have a great day,' Luckman said, 'when your team loses?' "

It was in this spirit that Luckman played football. And in 1937, although Columbia won only two out of nine games, he made All-East, together with Marshall Goldberg, who played with an all-conquering Pittsburgh team. It was Sid's fiery spirit that won him this honor.

In his final college year, 1938, Sid Luckman came into his own as a collegiate star.

In the opener, Columbia licked Yale 27-14. Sid Luckman gave one of his most remarkable performances in leading his team to this notable victory. Allison Danzig, veteran *Times* reporter, wrote a rave story, which said, in part:

"No back in recent memory, neither Frank, Albie Booth nor any other, has given a finer exhibition of all-round ability in the huge saucer (Yale Bowl) than the rugged New York youth put on to win a tumultuous tribute from the 35,000 spectators when he left the field in the closing minutes of play."

Sid passed successfully ten out of seventeen tries, for a total of 146 yards. Two of his passes were for more than fifty yards apiece. Danzig continued to rant about the Jewish boy when he declared:

"Luckman excelled in other departments as well. He

kicked off, punted beautifully, tackled savagely, directed the team, ran back kicks, booted the extra points and took his turn at supplying the scythe-like interference with which the Lions made Yale's blocking seem pitifully weak by comparison."

Danzig concluded his story by saying that "If ever there was a one-man team, Luckman was one today."

John Kieran, in writing of this game, said, "It wasn't luck, it was Luckman." And he added, in a flippant tone:

"They say that once upon a time Illinois was playing Penn on Franklin Field and a fellow named Red Grange turned it into a one-man show. This observer missed that, but saw Sid Luckman in the Yale Bowl on Saturday. He did everything for Columbia except lead the band between the halves."

A week later, Columbia narrowly beat Army 20-18. It was Sid's wizardry which won that one for the Lions. Before 25,000 fans Luckman gave as good a performance as he did the previous week. In the first quarter, the Cadets took a 12-0 lead. At the end of the half, Army retained its lead, this time by an 18-6 margin. But in the third period the Lions scored, with Luckman being the main gun. Thus, at the end of three periods, the count was Army 18, Columbia 13. Then the "modern Frank Merriwell," as the sports columnists called him, went to work. Sid passed three times in the final minutes of the game for a total of fifty-six yards and a touchdown! The final score was in favor of Columbia, 20-18, and the spectators left the stadium limp with excitement and with Sid Luckman's name on everyone's lips.

In his last year as a college star Luckman completed sixty-six out of one hundred and thirty-two passes for eight hundred and fifty-six yards. His efficiency was fifty percent, a phenomenal mark and one which is seldom equalled, no matter how good the passer.

When Luckman completed his college career, he was earmarked for professional ball. There wasn't much else Sid could do. He was a college graduate, yes; but he had been playing football practically all his life, he knew it well and loved it. As a pro he could make good money and win added fame. Besides he had been chosen by the Chicago Bears, one of the strong teams in professional ranks, who had given up their rights to another player, thus winning Luckman. George Halas, Chicago coach, wanted Sid for his T formation attack. He chose Sid over Davey O'Brien because the Jewish boy was taller.

But although Luckman was not an immediate starter or star with the great Bears, he did develop gradually in pro ranks in 1939, his first season. In a game in mid-October against the New York Giants, Sid began to show his stuff to the entire league.

Before more than 58,000 football-mad fans, the Bears were defeated by the Giants 16-13, in a thrilling, up-and-down ball game. Ward Cuff of the Giants gave a wonderful exhibition of kicking and scored nine points by booting three field goals. The Giants added a touchdown for good measure and, entering the final quarter, the New Yorkers led the Chicagoans by a decisive score of 16-0. Relieving Chicago's ace passer Bernie Masterson, Luckman showed that as a passer he took a back seat to no man. He went right to work and began to do magic with the football. Within a few minutes he fooled the powerful Giants by passing sixty-eight yards to a touchdown. The Giants still held a comfortable lead, however, and Luckman had to accomplish even more spectacular feats. Throwing with precision and with poise, Sid began tossing the ball from his own 25-yard line. He threw long, high and accurate passes. Then the Bears scored a second touchdown on his passing, bringing the score to 16-13, the Giants leading. The passes covered seventy-five yards and the fans went wild over the Brooklyn boy's exhibition. But the Giants held, to retain their lead. Luckman had made his mark, even though it was a losing game. And the Bears, for the next three years, averaged less than a loss a season!

Two weeks later, Sid again showed how dangerous he could be. In a thriller-diller with the Green Bay Packers, generally a strong team and the Bears' top opposition throughout the years, the Bears were playing a losing game. The fortunes of both teams see-sawed all afternoon. The Packers held the lead four different times. In the gathering dusk of the afternoon, as time was running out on the Bears, the Packers finally held a 27-23 advantage over the Chicagoans. Then the poised right arm of Luckman began shooting passes. First Sid reared back and tossed a short eighteen yarder to a teammate. But the Bears needed something more than short passes. The clock was ticking on inexorably. So Sid threw a forty-eight yard pass. It was completed and, as darkness came, Bill Osmanski plunged over for the touchdown, giving the Bears a 30-27 victory! It was known now that the Chicago Bears had added a tremendous siege gun to their always powerful and feared attack. The new weapon was called "Sid Luckman, passer extraordinary."

The rest of that year Luckman won his spurs by doing sensational deeds on the gridiron. It so happened that the professional game always boasted of superlative players and even if Sid created a splurge in his first year as a passer, there were many athletes he couldn't overshadow. Nevertheless, he did become a star. He passed to many touchdowns (most of which were caught by his Jewish teammate, Johnny Siegal, who played with him at Columbia), established himself as a fine pro punter and a good defensive football player.

After the 1939 season, Halas said, "In all my years in football I've never seen a player who worked as hard as Luckman. When everybody else left the practice field, he stayed on. He practiced pivoting and ball handling by the hour. He became a great player simply because he devoted about 400 percent more effort to it than most athletes are willing to do."

In 1940, Luckman gradually began to move in on the top stars. He did not achieve the spectacular success first marked up by Sammy Baugh, a passer whose exploits verged on the incredible. Baugh won headlines because his passes were needle-sharp and seldom intercepted. He was also a fine kicker. Luckman was by no means a one-man team. The Bears were too strong for any one man to control their destinies. Baugh, as a one-man club won more plaudits than Luckman. But Sid did well enough.

Against the Giants, on October 27, Luckman became a superstar. The Bears walloped the Giants 37-21. Luckman, with the experience gained in pro ball, called the plays with exceptional shrewdness. He drove his club, in a mixture of passes and power plays sixty-one yards to another tally. The Bears scored again when on the wings of Sid's passes, they went forty-one yards for a touchdown! In the third period, Sid unlimbered his arm once more and passed to a forty-eight yard score. But with all this scoring and passing, he was not the top man in his league. After a month of play he was the fifth leading passer. This indicates the quality of play in this professional circuit.

On November 17, the Bears lost in a stunning upset to the Redskins, who were led by the magical passer from Texas, Sammy Baugh. The score was 7-3, and Luckman was rushed, beaten to the ground and otherwise tied up. Baugh, on the other hand, was a key man in his club's startling victory. There is interest in this game and in the score, because a few weeks later these clubs met again for the professional championship of the world.

The Bears rebounded from the Redskin defeat to beat the Cleveland Rams and the Chicago Cardinals. Sid Luckman greased up his arm and whetted his brain in these contests. Against the Rams he led the Bears to a 47-25 win. His team scored thirty points in a row at one stage of the proceedings and Sid tossed a seventy-four yard touchdown pass. In beating the Cardinals 31-23, the Bears had a lucky escape. Sid passed to a 20-yard tally and then got off a lateral to another touchdown. The Bears scored all their points in the first half. Going into the final period, the Bears led 31-0. Then Marshall Goldberg and Company ran wild. Running with skill and power, Marshall scored one touchdown and helped set up a couple of others. The Cardinals tallied twenty-three points in fifteen minutes; exciting, but not enough to win. So the Bears won the Western crown and qualified to meet the Redskins, winners of the Eastern section of the league.

The game was played on December 8 and it marked one of the most unusual football games ever played. Remember, a few weeks earlier the Redskins had held the Bears in check, to win 7-3. On this day the Bears, in the most fearsome display of power ever revealed on a football gridiron, humiliated and swamped the Redskins in a 73-0 game. This was the highest score ever marked up in professional football competition, the most one-sided game in the history of the sport. And it was supposed to be a championship game between the two finest teams in the land! When it was all over the Chicago Bears were hailed as the greatest football team of all time and Luckman was considered the greatest strategist in the game. The crowd was stunned as they watched the Bears go to work. Within fifty-six seconds the Bears had their first tally, as Bill Osmanski smashed sixty-eight yards for a touchdown. Later, the Bears counted in fifty-four seconds. The Redskins were overwhelmed and the crowd derided them and mocked them. This was a perfect team pounding away at the Redskins. It was football at its best. The Bears scored three times in the first period; once in the second; four times in the third; three in the final quarter. Sid Luckman ran the team, but after the Bears held a commanding margin at the end of the first half, he retired for the rest of the day. The *New York Times* said of Luckman that "no field general ever called plays more artistically or engineered a touchdown parade in more letter-perfect fashion." And George Halas, coach of the Bears, named Luckman immediately, when asked to list the top star of the "contest."

Arthur Daley of the *New York Times* seven years later wrote that in more than twenty-nine years of football reporting this was the "greatest, the best and the most thrilling game I have ever seen."

Here is how the Bears ran wild. After Osmanski ran sixty-eight yards for the first score, Luckman drove the team eighty yards in seventeen plays for the second score. Sid went over for the touchdown. Then Joe Maniaci went forty-two yards for a tally and the score was 21-0 in just one period. But this was only the beginning. Luckman threw a 30-yard pass to Ken Kavanaugh for the only touchdown of the second quarter, and then left the game. In the final half the rest of the Bears went wild. Ray Nolting scampered twenty-three yards to score; George McAfee intercepted a pass and swivel-hipped his way thirty-five yards for a touchdown; even Bulldog Turner, the center, lumbered to a touchdown, on an interception. It was a rout.

Yet notwithstanding his performance, Luckman did not make the professional All-Star team in 1940! He did play in the All-Star game and helped his Bears beat the All-Stars 28-14. He passed to two touchdowns and scored another, just to show that he didn't mind the oversight.

The Bears beat everyone in sight for a while in 1941 and Sid Luckman was the big gun in the victories. The Bears beat the Rams, 48-21. Luckman and Siegal teamed up for a few tallies; in beating the Cardinals 53-7, Sid scored once and threw to two more touchdowns, one of them to Johnny Siegal. Marshall Goldberg tried to stem the tide and was his team's sparkplug. But what can a man do in a 53-7 defeat?

After winning five games and scoring two hundred and nine points to overwhelm the league, the Bears were upset by the Packers. Losing 16-0, the Bears seemed to be in for a severe drubbing. In the last period, however, Luckman got hot. He stood up there against the Packer line, evaded Packer ends and began to throw the ball. First he passed for sixteen yards; then for twelve. The Packers were bewildered as Sid suddenly tucked the ball under his arm and pounded the line. He smashed for twelve more. Uncertain, not knowing what to look for, the Packers were easy victims to Sid's clever mind. He handed the ball to Norm Standlee who went for the first Bear tally.

Getting possession of the ball once more, Luckman played havoc with the enemy, and concluded by passing fourteen yards for a second touchdown. Losing by two points, and in possession of the ball as time was running out, Luckman passed for twenty-seven yards as the game-ending whistle blew. The Bears had lost. But Luckman had starred once more.

When the Bears beat the Rams 31-13 and the Redskins 35-21, the football world became aware of the potent Bear T formation, which was an attack demanding perfect timeing and ball-handling on the part of the quarterback. The beating administered to the Redskins was a T formation win, but now that the Bears were running wild, the T formation became the talk of the football world.

On November 23, the Bears beat the Lions 24-7, and although Billy Jefferson of the Lions ran one hundred and one yards for a touchdown, the headlines went to the Bears who set a record by scoring twenty-five first downs. Despite the defeat by the Packers earlier in the season, the Bears tied the Packers for the Western title when the Luckman-led Chicagoans beat the Chicago Cardinals in a thrilling 34-24 games. The Cards were leading 24-21 up to the last five minutes. Then the great Luckman went to work and the Bears scored twice. Mixing up power plays with his passes, Sid managed to squeeze through to victory.

At this stage of the season, Luckman was finally chosen All-League quarterback and made it nearly every year after that, except toward the very conclusion of his career.

In facing the Packers in the playoff for the title, the odds were about even. The Bears had won one game, 25-17 and the Packers had won 16-14. This was the first divisional play-off in the league's history and 43,425 people came to see the game. It looked like a Green Bay victory when, after less than two minutes, the Packers scored a touchdown on a Bear fumble. Hugh Gallarneau scored for the Bears and the score was then 7-6, in favor of the Packers. But in the second period the Bears inched ahead on a field goal, making the count 9-7. From now on, the Bears were never behind. They completed the rout by scoring twenty-four points in the second quarter. Luckman passed to one touchdown, bringing the score to 30-7. The great Don Hutson, Green Bay's ace pass receiver and the best pass-snarer in football history, caught only one pass all day long!

In beating the Green Bay Packers, the Bears qualified to meet the New York Giants for the title. The Bears were 4-1 favorites and played that way only in the final half. At the end of the first half the score was knotted up at 9-9. Then Luckman went to town and the final score was 37-9. The newspapers the next day said, "Sid Luckman was a passing wizard and a field general beyond compare."

In 1942 the Bears ran wild against all opposition. On November 15, they met the Packers after having won twenty games in a row. The Green Bay boys had lost only once, to the Bears in a ding-dong game after having led 28-27 after three quarters. But the Bears battered Green Bay 38-7, with Luckman running fifty-four yards to a touchdown after intercepting a Green Bay pass.

Curly Lambeau, Packer coach, then said that "Luckman

has beaten the Packers more than any individual in the twenty-seven years I've had a club in the National League."

The twenty-second victory came against the Detroit Lions. It was a 42-0 beating. Sid passed to two touchdowns, one a forty-three and the other a sixty yard pass.

Victory twenty-three was scored against the Cleveland Rams. Score: 47-0. Sid Luckman threw two passes for tallies. The first ended a ninety-yard drive; the second went for fifty-seven yards.

For the first time in eight years the Bears ended a season unbeaten and untied when they won from the Cardinals 21-7. Of course, Luckman threw a pass for a score.

Unbeaten in twenty-four games, winning thirty-nine out of forty games, the Bears faced the Redskins for the professional crown. Chicago was seeking its third title in a row. They had beaten the Redskins 38-14 in a pre-season game and the fans still remembered the 73-0 walloping of 1940. Heavy underdogs, the Redskins got their revenge. The final score was 14-6, in favor of the Washington Redskins. The Bears were completely outplayed and Luckman wasn't given a chance to do anything. It was one of his most miserable days on a football field.

But in 1943, Luckman finally wrested the passing laurels from Sammy Baugh, his most persistent rival. The war against the Axis was in full swing and Luckman, who later joined the Merchant Marine and saw dangerous service on an oil tanker, took advantage of the quality of play to do incredible things on the gridiron.

Here are some of his feats:

In beating Brooklyn 33-21, Luckman completed fifteen

passes, passes for sixty-four yards, forty-two yards and twenty-six yards.

Luckman scored his sixth and seventh touchdown passes when he helped beat the Cardinals 20-0.

The Brooklyn passing wizard tossed three touchdown passes in a 48-21 victory over the Steagles (a combination of Philadelphia and Pittsburgh teams), making it nine touchdown passes in four games. He threw one for a sixteen yard tally, two passes for forty-one yards, gained fifty-one yards in three tosses and threw seventeen yards for another score.

In beating the Lions 27-21, Sid threw passes for a total of two hundred and thirty yards. Two were for touchdowns, bringing his scoring passes to eleven!

The Bears licked the Lions 35-14. Sid threw passes for scores. They were thirty-eight yards, fifty-one yards and twenty-five yards. He completed nine out of twenty for two hundred and forty-one yards. This brought his total to fourteen touchdown passes.

Luckman made his fifteenth touchdown pass against Green Bay when the Bears won 21-7.

On November 14, 1943, Sid Luckman had the greatest football day of his life. He gave the most outstanding exhibition of passing ever seen on a gridiron when he threw seven touchdown passes in one game, against the Giants, always a top-notch team. It was the worst beating ever suffered by the Giants. Sid established or assisted in establishing six new records. Only a few weeks earlier Baugh had set a new record of six touchdown passes in one game. And as though to spur him, Baugh only fired Luckman to beat this mark. He added 120 yards to his pass total to break Cecil Isbell's record by thirty-three yards, for so far his grand total was the highest ever compiled. He gained four hundred and fifty-three yards and completed twenty-three out of thirty passes. He had twenty-three touchdown passes for a season — one from the record, so far that year.

Leonard Cohen of the *New York Post* called this game "one of the highlights of our twenty-five years of attendance at football contests." And the *Times* story went as follows:

"As a Columbia undergraduate and since he joined the Bears to make them what they seem today — one of the greatest if not the greatest aggregation in football history — Sid has had many a field day, but none to compare with yesterday . . . His was passing artistry of a kind probably never before witnessed on any gridiron, and although his wizardry sent the Giants down to depths they never had explored, the fans gave the black-haired star a tremendous ovation when he trotted from the field after chucking his final toss to Hampton Pool a trifle more than five minutes before the game ended."

Of that great day, Luckman said, "It just happened to be one of those days that come to a player once in a lifetime."

Here is what happened.

Soon after the kickoff, Sid set his sights for the Giant goal. He wound up and threw a 30-yarder for his first pass. The Bears were beginning to flex their muscles and the Giants hardly knew what hit them when Sid went to work. Luckman saw his end, Jim Benton, floating free, so he threw a 19-yard pass to the lanky Benton who scampered thirty-five more to the Giant eight-yard line. Always canny, Sid called for a ground play. Then, standing on the Giant 4-yard line, Luckman faded back and rifled a short pass to Benton for a touchdown. He showed that he could also toss longer ones by passing fifty-four yards to Connie Berry.

For a brief moment it seemed the game wouldn't be a runaway, when the Giants scored, to make the score 14-7. But Luckman hit Hampton Pool in the end zone from twenty-seven yards out for another tally. Later Sid mixed up his receivers. Throwing perfect strikes to three different receivers, Sid ended another drive by passing to Pool for a twenty-yard touchdown pass. He got his fourth touchdown pass on a fifty-five yard toss to Harry Clark, and his fifth on a toss to Jim Benton. At this stage of the game, Luckman was withdrawn from the game.

Neither Luckman nor his coaches were aware of the fact that he was close to Baugh's record, but as soon as Luke Johnson, one of the co-coaches, realized it, he called Hunk Anderson, the other coach, and told him about it. The fans, meanwhile, were cheering for Luckman and chanted, "We Want Luckman, We Want Luckman, We Want Luckman." Liking and admiring Luckman, his own teammates and coaches wanted that record for him, so he finally was sent back into the game.

Immediately he began to throw the pigskin. On a series of three passes he threw the tying touchdown pass. George Wilson was the receiver.

But the fans were aware of the great day and wanted to see the incredible. Here is how the *Post's* Leonard Cohen saw it:

"The Giants kicked over the goal line and the Bears started from their 20. Once again Luckman swung into action. His right arm went back, the ball went sailing down the field to McLean for a 40-yard gain. A line buck netted two yards. The ball was snapped to Luckman, he faded back, watched the potential receivers go down the field. Hampton Pool, another wingman, now co-coach of the Miami Seahawks, was thirty-eight yards away, guarded by two Giants.

"But with unerring accuracy Luckman hit his target. The crowd tore the roof off the Polo Grounds as Pool, after a fine catch, put the ball on the ground; Luckman had broken the pro record with seven T.D. passes. That was a thrill in sports those 56,000 will never forget."

It was, as Sid Luckman so aptly called it, "the thrill that comes once in a lifetime."

But his great work for the season was not done. When the regular season was over, Luckman had broken all passing records, with twenty-eight touchdown passes and a one-season record of a total gain of 2,194 yards on passes.

Naturally, Sid made the league All-Star team and he proved his greatness once again in the playoff for the title. Again the Redskins were the opponents. They had beaten the Giants to get into the title fight. A year earlier the Redskins had won 14-6 and Luckman had had a very bad day.

Sid set a new playoff record when he threw five touchdown passes to lead his Bears to an overwhelming 41-21 victory. The Redskins were knocked out by Luckman, as one sports scribe put it. Playing what he considered was his last game of pro football (Luckman entered the Maritime Service on January 3, 1944), Luckman capped an illustrious five-year career by completing thirteen out of twenty-four passes for 276 yards. What is more remarkable is that of his twenty-four passes not a single one was intercepted. But Sid himself broke a record by intercepting three enemy passes.

After the Redskins scored first, Sid threw Harry Clark a screen-pass for a thirteen-yard touchdown. He did more than pass in this game, however, and ran often and hard. He set up the second touchdown by running twenty-four yards and then getting off to a fifteen-yard gallop. The ball then rested on the Washington three-yard line. Bronko Nagurski went over for the tally. Luckman's interception of a Redskin pass helped the Bears score their third touchdown. He threw a sixty-six-yard touchdown pass to Dante Magnani and tossed twenty-nine and sixteen-yard passes to rout the Redskins.

In 1944 the Bears were no longer formidable without Luckman in the lineup. But he managed to get shore leave when his tanker was in New York and he played with the Bears whenever he could. In his first game he helped beat the Packers, 21-0. He showed that war service had not rusted his trusty right arm. Completing eleven out of twenty-three passes, Sid threw to one score and ran for another tally himself. Nevertheless, the Bears were no longer the terrors of the league. They had Luckman, luckily, but not much else. He managed to do amazing things, but couldn't offset completely the weakness of the wartime Bears. He threw an eighty-six yard pass, the longest of the season, and completed fifteen tosses for 247 yards against the Boston Yankees and helped his team win. But the next week the Bears lost to the Lions by the unheard of (for the Bears) score of 41-21. He passed to all three Bear touchdowns.

One of his better days was against the Eagles. The Eagles were heavily favored, but in less than four minutes, Luckman threw a touchdown pass to ruin the enemy. His club won 28-7. Sid was also responsible for the third score.

In 1945, Luckman, still managing to play while on leave, starred with the weakest Bear team in years. The Bears lost often, but each time Luckman's feats kept them in the game. For example, in losing to the Cardinals, Sid completed thirteen passes and played with a broken nose and an injured foot. In every game Sid Luckman passed often and successfully. But his club was a bad one.

In 1946, with the war over and the big bad Bears back in circulation, the Chicagoans won the championship once more, for their eighth crown.

The Bears opened the season by whipping Green Bay 30-7. Luckman passed to two touchdowns.

And here is how the Associated Press reported the next game: "After trailing throughout the game, the Chicago Bears broke loose for three touchdowns in the final quarter to smother their arch city rivals, the Cardinals, 34-17, before a crowd of 39,263 in Comiskey Park and remain unbeaten in the National Football League.

"The Bears' great quarterback, Sid Luckman, passed for two touchdowns, set up another with his aerials and contributed greatly to a fourth with a twenty-eight yard gallop."

A huge crowd of 68,381 saw Luckman play brilliantly against the Los Angeles Rams on November 10. The newspaper lead read as follows: "Sid Luckman, Mr. Quarterback in person, led the Chicago Bears to a thrilling 27-21 victory over the Los Angeles Rams before 68,381 spectators, largest pro crowd of the season here (Los Angeles)."

Here is what Sid accomplished. He threw three touchdown passes to shade Bob Waterfield in a passing duel and clinched the game by intercepting a pass thrown by Waterfield in the waning minutes of the game, to choke off a Ram rally deep in Bear territory.

With the score 7-7, Luckman really went to work. He threw a thirty-eight yard touchdown pass to Ken Kavanaugh to put the Bears ahead 14-7. In the second quarter he sparked an eighty-yard march with four passes, the last one a thirty-four yarder to Kavanaugh for a score. In the third quarter Sid climaxed a sixty-nine yard drive with a twenty-eight yard touchdown pass, again to Kavanaugh. Sid completed twelve passes for two hundred and fifty-four yards.

A week later Luckman was the major factor in a Bear victory over the Redskins when he pitched a forty-two yard pass in the last moments of the game to win for the Bears, 24-20. With less than four minutes to go and losing 20-17, the Bears began to move forward from the Chicago nine yard line. Luckman threw a thirty-four yard pass to Jim Keane and two plays later tossed a twenty-two yarder to Keane who ran unmolested the rest of the way for the winning tally.

By this time in Luckman's career, he was acknowledged as the man who made the Bears run. He had 197 plays clearly outlined in his brain and, as George Trevor of the *New York Sun* once wrote, "If you go into permutations and combinations, it could be claimed that the Bears have five hundred plays in their repertoire, but these involve slight variations in blocking technique." And then he added, in admiration, "Luckman has a play at his fingertips to fit every type of enemy defense and every style of individual technique. For example, the same pass play, with subtle variations in the key blocks, can be modified for use against a defensive end who crashes, or waits, or floats, or pinches."

Bob Snyder, once Sid's understudy and later a coach, said, "Sid knows exactly what every teammate is supposed to do, whether the assignment is against a five, six or seven man line."

It was with such subtlety that Luckman ran his Bears. And in the championship game against the Giants, the Luckman magic held good. But there is a background story to this finale of 1946.

Just a few days before this game a scandal broke wide open in professional football ranks. Two Giant players had been accused of dealing with gamblers who were attempting to bribe them to throw the game to the Bears. It was one of the most shocking stories to come out of sports ranks in years. And while Merle Hapes, one of the two players, was declared ineligible for the game, the other one, Frank Filchock, was permitted to play. After the game became history, it was revealed that neither player was blameless and both were banned, and never played professional football again in the U.S.

The Bears, however, needed no help from dishonest athletes. The bruisers from Chicago won from their ancient rivals by a 24-14 score. Naturally, Sid Luckman was the star of the encounter.

Aware of the scandal in their ranks, the Giants took the field determined to do-or-die in an effort to lick the Bears. In the opening period the Bears scored twice. Once, when Luckman passed for a touchdown to Kavanaugh and the other time on an interception and thirty-nine yard dash by Dante Magnani. Fighting their hearts out, the Giants came back with twin touchdowns on passes by the suspected

Filchock. Going into the final period the score was all snarled up at 14-14. In the final period, the Bears brought the ball up to the Giant thirty-four, mainly on Sid's passes. Then Luckman threw an incomplete toss, but a penalty on the Giants for unnecessary roughness brought the ball to the Giant nineteen-yard line.

Luckman, who seldom carried the ball, took the pass from center, faked beautifully and raced through a hole in the Giant left side. He went all the way for the marker. Hit by two Giants on the five-yard line, Sid kept his feet and went over for the clincher. Although the Giants rallied after that, their last chance was snuffed out when Sid intercepted a pass on the Bear thirty-yard line.

After the game was over, Luckman talked to reporters in the dressing room and described his playing in the game. He called his passing the worst of the season, but he passed to one touchdown, set up his own tally and completed nine passes for one hundred and forty-four yards, which isn't bad.

Discussing his nineteen-yard "bootleg" run, Sid declared, "That was the first time I had carried the ball this year. About the ten-yard line I saw some red shirts moving in on me; I was hit, lost my balance, but stumbled on across the goal line."

A record crowd of more than 58,000 saw Luckman star in this triumph and when they left, they talked as much of Luckman as they did about the gambling scandal. It wasn't only that Sid passed and ran, although his power drive was a shock to those who forgot that Sid used to be Lou Little's top runner. He also punted like an expert. He didn't kick very long ones, but he booted forty-five-yard and fifty-yard slow "floaters" that enabled his ends to nail the Giants before the ball could be fielded. In all, as one reporter put it, Luckman had been more spectacular, but seldom more valuable, in a game which had to be an honest and bruising one.

In 1947 Sid was as brilliant as ever. He passed with the same deadly effect and was the Bears' sole big gun. He threw three touchdown passes to beat the Detroit Lions, 33-24, completing eighteen tosses for three hundred and forty yards. A week later he made twenty-two passes for two hundred and seventy yards to beat the Redskins 56-20. Again he threw three touchdown passes. The next week Sid tossed four touchdown passes against Boston, to lead his club to a 28-24 win. So it went all year. In the first nine games of the year he passed to twenty-one touchdowns. In all, he tossed twenty-four touchdown passes.

In 1948, when Johnny Lujack came from Notre Dame to spell Luckman, Sid continued to play at his former brilliant best. He threw eighty-nine complete passes in one hundred and sixty-three tries, but he saw the handwriting on the wall, and prepared to earn a living off the ball field. He went into business in Chicago and, while there had been rumors that he would become a coach, Luckman was satisfied to allow his football stature to be measured by the work he did on the gridiron. He played a few seasons longer, but by the time the early 1950's rolled around Luckman was a name of the glorious football past.

In 1965, Luckman was elected to the Football Hall of Fame, to the satisfaction of sports writers and fans who remembered his achievements with admiration and felt he was a true football immortal.

He was a Jew who was aware of his background, and in

a fine story about him in *Sport* magazine in 1949, Ed Fitzgerald asked him whether he was a religious man.

"Well, yes," Luckman replied. "I go to the temple regularly and I observe the high holidays and I never go to bed at night without saying a little prayer." He was slightly embarrassed as he spoke, but he did speak out and the reporter was grateful for this insight into the man.

There have been few players in the history of football as spectacular and as good as Sid Luckman. It is entirely likely that many decades will come and go before there is another like him.

Beguiling Basketball

The dazzling speed, accurate ball-handling, flashing set shots and breathtaking stamina of its players, made basketball, a once-humble sport, into one of the most popular games in America.

Relegated to half-demolished gymnasiums a few decades ago, the game leaped into the forefront of the American sporting scene and is now, both professionally and on the high school and college level, played by hundreds of thousands of youngsters in urban centers, small cities and even farms.

For some inexplicable reason, the hoop game was dominated for a long time by Jewish athletes. Now it has become a truly national sport and, in the professional ranks, it is dominated by black players.

Pete Axthelm, in writing about basketball in New York, with emphasis on playground ball and the New York Knicks, has written a lyric book on the game, its players and the pressures of the big city on black athletes. The book is *The City Game,* and in it, Axthelm writes: "Basketball is the city game. Its battlegrounds are strips of asphalt between tattered wire fences or crumbling buildings; its rhythms grow from the uneven thump of a ball against hard surfaces. It demands no open spaces or lush backyards or elaborate equipment. It doesn't even require specified numbers of players; a one-on-one confrontation in a playground can be as memorable as a full-scale organized game. Basketball is the game for young athletes without cars or allowances — the game whose drama and action are intensified by its confined spaces and chaotic surroundings."

He insists that basketball belongs to the cities, that it is "more than a sport or diversion in the cities. It is part, often a major part, of the fabric of life. Kids in small towns — particularly in the Midwest — often become superb basketball players. But they do so by developing accurate shots and precise skills; in the cities, kids simply develop 'moves.' Other young athletes may learn basketball, but city kids live it."

Axthelm points out that the game has moved in phases in New York City; that Irish athletes made good playmakers, that "tough, aggressive Jewish youths grew into defense-minded, set-shooting stars" and that finally the "hunger" vanished from the white players and black athletes filled the gap, some making it big and others succumbing to the poverty of the streets and turning to drugs.

Red Auerbach, who played the game, led the Boston Celtics and then became the president and general manager of the team, has written much and spoken much about the game. He recalled that when he was a member of the George Washington University team, he was one of six Jewish players on the team. He told a reporter of an Anglo-Jewish newspaper in 1977, "Jewish boys at one time played in the cities, on the playgrounds. That's where we got them." There were a lot of Jewish kids playing in small towns more recently. He then said more or less what Axthelm wrote. "There are only a few left playing football and basketball. The rest want to be doctors, lawyers and businessmen. They have cars and they're not hungry any more."

Nevertheless, the history of the sport sparkles with countless Jewish names. Perhaps the greatest of them all was Nat Holman, who was a legendary player with the Original Celtics and for more than thirty-seven years basketball coach at CCNY. There are, however, too many Jewish stars to name them all. Some, of course, must be listed in any account of Jews in basketball. Barney Sedran was both a college and a professional star, although he seldom weighed more than one hundred and ten pounds. The best team of the 1935-1936 season was the LIU Blackbirds. There were three Jews on this squad: Ben Kramer, Jules Bender and Leo Merson. The NYU 1935-1936 team, one of the top quintets in the land, had four Jewish regulars: Willie Rubinstein, Milt Schulman, Len Maidman and Irwin Klein. The national champion of 1938-1939 was the LIU team, which included three Jewish stars: Irv Torgoff, Danny Kaplowitz (whose brother Ralph later starred with NYU) and Ossie Schechtman. The following year's champ was Temple, led by its captain, Mike Bloom.

Possibly the finest of all college teams was St. John's quintet of 1927, 1928, 1929 and 1930, called the "wonder team." These boys won sixty-four out of sixty-eight games! Of the starting five, four were Jews. They were Mac Posnack, Allie Shuckman, Mac Kinsbrunner and Rip Gerson. Two years later, this same outfit won the championship of the American Professional League. In later years, St. John's had Harry Boykoff, about whom there is a chapter in this volume.

Rudy La Russo came out of Dartmouth to play pro ball and excelled as a rough, aggressive performer. Bob Kauffman played with Buffalo for a while, made the All-Star team and then became general manager of the Detroit club. Neal Walk, a very tall athlete and Dave Wohl, a comparatively short player, were among other pros in the National Basketball Association.

However, it is important, in discussing basketball, to go a bit afield and to devote some space to coaches as well as to athletes because they have had a great deal to do with the changes in the game, in setting styles, in influencing players and in establishing patterns of performance.

Holman was the first great Jewish coach. When he learned how to play basketball, few people thought that any basketball player could win national fame at this sport. But Holman became involved in the game when it was far from a major sport in the United States. He attended Commerce High School in New York and learned the game there. In 1917, he became the coach at City College in New York, at the age of twenty-one. He was the youngest man ever to become coach of a college basketball team. Years later, the college's 3,500-seat gymnasium was named for Nat Holman. Robert E. Marshak, president of City College, said, "Nat Holman has made historic contributions to the game of basketball and to City College basketball in particular. It is altogether fitting that this magnificent facility, where new chapters of City College basketball are being written, should be called Nat Holman Gymnasium."

He played pro ball as he coached at City and he was the best player on the Original Celtics and the Whirlwinds. From 1920 to 1928, the Celtics travelled across the country, showing how basketball should be played. They played as many as one hundred and thirty games a season and lost perhaps ten. They disbanded in 1928 simply because they were too good and nobody could win from them. The team included Joe Lapchick, later a famous coach at St. John's and the coach of the New York Knicks; Dutch Dehnert; Johnny Beckman; Chris Leonard and Dave Banks (who was another Jewish star). Unfortunately, there was a basketball scandal, on the issue of point-shaving, in the early 1950's. Holman's team was involved and in 1959, Nat Holman resigned as coach of City College, upset and disturbed by the turns in contemporary basketball. Nonetheless, his way of teaching the game carried forward in the pro style of Red Holzman, who learned from Holman. That is, to pass the ball, find the open man and play the game in a disciplined fashion. Holzman, who brought the New York Knicks to two world championships, introduced what was known as "New York basketball" to the pro sport. It was a line that directly followed the teachings of Nat Holman.

Red Auerbach, on the other hand, won national fame as the man who built and led the most successful team in the annals of the pro game, the Boston Celtics. He played high school and college ball and became a gifted teacher of the hoop sport. He organized and coached Navy teams during World War II and, after the war, created a new team made up of his former Navy stars. They were the Washington Capitols, and soon finished first in the Eastern Division of the Basketball Association of America, the forerunner of the NBA.

In 1950 he came to the Boston Celtics, after a career of coaching on the high school and college level. He was an NBA coach for twenty years, sixteen with the Celtics. In ten years, his Celtics won nine NBA championships. He instilled in his players a sense of pride that they were playing for the Celtics. He stressed the individual's contribution to the team, not individual statistics or glory. When a man played defense and didn't score many points, it really made no difference to Auerbach. He knew what the man's value was to the team. This sense of pride and unity were instilled by Auerbach more than by other coaches. It was what made him the most successful coach and basketball executive in the history of the game.

Holman, Holzman and Auerbach were the top Jewish coaches in the game, but there were others. Larry Brown coached the Denver Nuggets while his brother, Herb, was the coach of the Detroit Pistons. Larry played for the University of North Carolina and for the United States Olympic team in 1964. He also was an All-Star in the American Basketball Association. He started his coaching career with the Carolina Cougars. Herb played college ball at the University of Vermont, coached at C.W. Post and at Stony Brook and became a coaching assistant at Detroit before he replaced Ray Scott there. Competitive men, Larry and Herb have not always got along, but they have faced each other on opposite sides of the court in pro basketball and it was the first time in history that brothers were both coaching teams in the NBA. Another odd statistic involving Jews in sports.

The predominance of Jews in basketball in an earlier period has been the subject of learned articles and scientific treatises which attempted to prove that Jews are so constituted that they can best stand up under the tension, strain and stamina required by the game invented by Dr. James Naismith.

Now that the entire country is on an equal basketball footing, it has been demontrated as hokum that Jews can play the game particularly well because (1) they are short, and short men have better balance and more speed afoot; (2) they have sharper eyes and (3) they have sharper minds than others.

Jews starred on the basketball courts of America for one reason, the reason spelled out by Axthelm in writing about blacks and basketball. Basketball, because it requires little space and paraphernalia, has been a popular city sport. Just a ball, a court, two hoops, enough boys, and you can play the game. Well, most of the Jews in the United States live in the big cities. That is the simple answer. But it goes beyond that. As the pro game had been taken over by extremely tall young men from the ghettos, the game has been influenced, in style as well as personnel by black athletes. The dunk shot, the dazzling moves, the brilliance of an Earl Monroe as against the pure moves of a John Havlicek, have led sports writers to analyze the "white" game as against the "black" game. Some white players play the "black" style game of basketball and it works the other way around as well. But it no longer is, if it ever was, the "Jewish" game.

Jews, however, have made a substantial contribution to the sport and no doubt will continue to be drawn from college ranks, for Jews do attend college and schools of higher learning to an uncommonly high degree.

HARRY BOYKOFF, WHEN HE STARRED AT ST. JOHN'S

Harry Boykoff

Big Man

One of the most fantastic basketball players in modern times has been a tremendously tall, deadly shooting Jewish boy named Harry Boykoff. At nine-and-a-half inches over six feet, he towered over all opposition during a half-dozen year period in most spectacular fashion.

Once upon a time there were few very tall men in basketball. The game requires perfect coordination, speed afoot, no awkwardness. And most tall men, that is men inordinately tall, lack the speed required of this court game. Some of the finest players in history have been way under six feet tall; on the other hand, some of the silliest-looking basketball players have been the bean-pole athletes who were put into a game merely because of their size — and they found the little men literally ran rings around them.

During the past few decades tall men have become a major factor in the game. Astute coaches in high schools have taken the gangling giants and have taught them some of the tricks which give an athlete coordination. By the time these overgrown boys get to college, they have learned how to keep off other people's feet. Within a year or two they learn to move around like an average-sized basketball player. And when they do that, their height becomes a great advantage in the game.

Now coaches look for tall men, knowing that careful

handling will make stars out of them. If you get a man tall enough and skilled enough, he seldom fails to become a star. A tall man can score points, he can steal the ball from smaller opponents and, most important, he can act like a goalie under the basket. Not only does he control the backboard, but he can knock out of his own basket perfectly accurate shots made at it by dead-eye sharpshooters! The basket is ten feet up. It is simple arithmetic to figure out that a man close to seven feet tall, with a long reach and a short jump can knock shots out of his basket. And this factor has kept the rule-makers awake nights. The game of basketball has become a tall man's game.

One of the best of the tall men has been Harry Boykoff. His size attracted Coach Mac Hodesblatt of Thomas Jefferson High School, in Brooklyn, where Harry was brought up and educated. Mac saw great possibilities in the tall, awkward player. Not that Harry was talented when he first began. It was his size that was the potential "talent." In the beginning Harry was extremely gawky and knew nothing about the game. For many months the shrewd high school coach worked with Harry, teaching him the basic fundamentals of the game . . . training him . . showing him how to move . . . how to pivot . . . how to take the set shot . . . how to handle himself in every way.

For Harry to play for many hours each day was a sacrifice, as he came from a working-class family and life was difficult for them. Harry told me* of his early life. "My father and mother both came to America from Russia," he

*H.U.R.

said, "and met and married in New York City. I have two sisters, one older and the other younger than myself, and all three of us were born on the Lower East Side. Both my parents work, and had to, in order to give me the proper education they wanted me to have."

Harry did not delve into the hardships involved, but in outlining his educational background, it was evident that his parents were interested in instilling within him a good and honest Jewish spirit. "At the age of six," Harry said, "I began to go to Hebrew school and had a Bar Mitzvah." He didn't say any more, because he was interested in relating how he became a basketball player, but it is obvious that throughout his career he had to bear in mind that as he played, his parents worked. Perhaps that is why he tried so hard to become outstanding. Maybe that is why he finally became a great star and signed a contract, years after he learned how to play, with a top professional team.

Harry's best friend in high school, another Jewish boy who became a star, was little Hy Gotkin. Although Hy was only five feet six, it was he who pushed Harry and encouraged him to play the game. They went to the gym together all the time and together they learned how to play this complex, razzle-dazzle game called basketball.

A good high school player, Harry was still far from being a polished court man. But his practice was beginning to pay off. He and Hy received scholarships to St. John's, a good school, with a fine scholastic rating and a good basketball tradition.

"Things were not up to par at home," Harry said, "when I was lucky enough to receive a scholarship to St. John's." So the hours of practice had paid off to the extent that

Harry was going to get a free college education. That was something!

But it was only the beginning. Under Joe Lapchick, Harry really learned the game. Here is what he had to say about Lapchick:

"I thought I knew something about basketball when I came to St. John's. But I soon found out that I didn't know much. Sure, I was all-scholastic in high school and was a top scorer, but my height had a lot to do with it. In college it was different. There were other tall guys around. Lapchick showed me how to roll on a pivot play . . . he taught me how to move around . . . how to draw out my guard . . . how to feed the other boys on the team."

Whoever gets the credit, Harry did very well in the beginning. As a sophomore Harry scored better than sixteen points a game, 326 all year and in the National College Invitation Tournament he scored fifty-six points in three games. When the season was over, he was one of the most famous players in the game.

Here is how the season went for him.

Against Oklahoma, in Madison Square Garden, Harry helped his team win, 51-43. The game was broken wide open within the first ten minutes, when the Johnnies took a 21-4 lead. Boykoff was the big gun. Good at handling the rebounds, batting two sure Okie baskets out of the hoop, and scoring eighteen points himself, Harry was Mr. Big this night.

A week later, St. John's faced Tennessee before 18,334 frenzied Garden fans. Unbeaten, Tennessee led at the half by a 35-22 margin. But St. John's never quit trying. In what the *New York Times* reporter termed "one of the greatest rallies in Madison Square Garden basketball history," St.

John's began to pull up. St. John's scored fourteen points in a few minutes, to Tennessee's two. And then Boykoff was given two free throws. The tall boy walked up to the foul marker and threw the first one up — and in! Calmly, as the spectators looked bug-eyed and tensely, Harry tossed the second one in. The score, for the first time, favored St. John's, 38-37. And from that crucial moment on, St. John's pulled ahead. Harry scored only nine points, but they were highly important ones.

On January 6, 1943, St. John's and CCNY hooked up in another of their traditional and bitterly-fought games. The rivalry between the two clubs was immense. The two coaches, close friends throughout their entire college careers, were foes in the coaching game. Few victories were as satisfying to Nat Holman, or to Joe Lapchick, than wins against each other. But in Boykoff's tenure in college, Nat Holman had a miserable time. The Holman teams seldom boasted of tall men and Harry's reach often was fatal to the Lavender of City College.

In the first game between City and St. John's in which Boykoff played, Harry played a major role. Starting early, he was never stopped. Intercepting passes, feeding his mates, shooting with deadly accuracy, Boykoff scored more points in the first half than the entire City team. At halftime the tally was 29-13, in favor of St. John's. Boykoff himself had scored seventeen points. In all, Harry scored twenty-three points and his team won, 50-42. This was only the first of the traditional games which he broke up. Holman had plenty of rough nights because of this huge Jewish lad who ran wild against City in the Garden.

On February 9, 1943, Harry Boykoff had one of the best nights that ever came to a basketball player. In whipping

St. Joseph's the Redmen of St. John's were spectacular — but Boykoff was the best man on the court. Here is how the *New York Times* correspondent wrote about Harry's night: "In all the nine and a fraction years that college basketball has been played in Madison Square Garden there never was a more spectacular performance than the one Harry Boykoff gave last night." Harry played thirty-nine minutes and twenty-nine seconds of the game. He received a thunderous ovation. His pivot playing and his set shots bordered on the miraculous. He had twenty-four points at halftime. He broke two Garden records and tied a third. His team won 76-46 and Harry Boykoff scored forty-five points! Only one less than the forty-six made by the entire St. Joseph team! His spree broke the Garden high of thirty-seven set by Bob Gerber of Toledo. His eighteen goals beat by one the number made by Gerber when the Toledo star ran wild. And Harry's nine fouls were also tops for a single night. Nevertheless, Hank Luisetti's fifty points, the all-collegiate record, was still safe.

Five days later, Boykoff was still red-hot. The Redmen went to Convention Hall in Philadelphia to play Temple, always a good club. St. John's won 62-40 and Harry scored thirty points, to break the Hall's record. In two games, then, Harry Boykoff scored seventy-five points!

On March 3, St. John's faced NYU, one of the nation's top basketball teams, year in, year out. That year, however, the Violets could not stop Harry. Before 18,163 fans, Boykoff helped his club sew up a berth in the National Invitation Tournament by scoring twenty-two points in a 57-53 victory.

St. John's first opponent in the championship tournament was Rice. The game was a thriller. The score was tied eleven times. Two minutes from the end of the game the tally was 49-all. Harry Boykoff had been playing a tremendous game, scoring twenty-one points but his buddy Hy Gotkin was the real star up to the final minutes. He was the outstanding floor man and everyone knew it. The minutes and seconds ticked off. It looked like this wild game would be forced into overtime. And then little Hy got the ball, shot and sank a basket! The clock had ticked off the moments and now only one second remained. It wasn't enough time for a comeback, and the Redmen of St. John's were the winners by a 51-49 count.

On March 27, five nights later, St. John's faced Fordham. Earlier in the season these clubs had clashed and the Rams had been beaten 63-47, with Boykoff being held to only eleven points. This game, however, was a lot more important, the semi-final match in a national tournament. Again the Redmen revealed their superiority over the Rams. The score this time was 69-43, with Harry Boykoff doubling his score of the previous game, with twenty-two points.

Two nights later, with an opportunity to wrap up the Invitation Tournament and face Wyoming, winners of the NCAA (National Collegiate Athletic Association) title, St. John's faced Toledo.

Moving speedily and with deadly precision, the Redmen overwhelmed Toledo by a score of 48-27. At the half the boys from Brooklyn led by 22-16. But an eleven point rally by St. John's set the game on ice, Boykoff helping with thirteen points for the evening. He was the top man in the championship tourney, with fifty-six points.

This victory won St. John's the right to face Wyoming for the mythical national crown. Up to this game Harry

Boykoff had scored 382 points for the season. The Wyoming game paired Harry against Milo Komenich, star of Wyoming. The duel went in Milo's favor, for he scored twenty points to Harry's seventeen and the Westerners won.

Although the season ended sourly on this note, Harry experienced his major thrill when he scored the forty-five points against St. Joseph. "It was my greatest thrill," he told me. And yet he had many more.

Before he played big time basketball again, Harry spent his share of time in the Army. In April 1943 he was drafted. For a month he twiddled away his time at Fort Dix as Army tailors worked to fit him properly. As a matter of fact, Harry was rejected for service because the Army had a regulation which didn't permit men taller than six feet six to don a uniform. But after a lot of wrangling, he managed to get himself a 1-A classification. His first assignment was to help guard President Roosevelt at his home in Hyde Park. "After six months," Harry said, "I was transferred to West Point as a GI Field Artillery instructor." When Harry was discharged from the Army after the war, he returned to St. John's to continue with his studies in accounting and to whip himself into basketball shape. He hadn't played ball in two-and-a-half years and was badly out of condition. The years had befogged many memories and a great number of court fans had forgotten the great Boykoff record and asked to be shown once again how good Harry really was.

Harry's junior year in college included the 1945-1946 season. He worked his way into condition slowly. Although he scored twenty points against Utah in the

Garden, the writers acknowledged that Harry was not really sharp; he could have, or should have, scored more often.

Against Ohio University, on December 22, Harry began to shine as he did in his pre-Army years. At the half St. John's led 42-8, and Boykoff scored twenty-one points in only thirty minutes. A week later St. John's lost to a great Kentucky quintet by the overwhelming score of 73-59. The writers raved about the marvelous Kentucky team, but Boykoff was not outshone by any individual. He scored twenty-seven points.

At this stage of the season Harry Boykoff was the star of old. In whipping St. Joseph's Boykoff scored fourteen points in a few minutes and retired for the rest of the night. After fifteen minutes the Redmen led 29-9. This was merely a tune-up for the City game. And once again Boykoff made things rough for Holman's boys.

The final score was 75-50, marking the worst beating taken by the Beavers in the twenty-five-year-old rivalry. It was a great night for Harry. He didn't beat City all by himself, but he scored twenty-seven points, which helped considerably.

It should be stressed at this point that the St. John's team was a comparatively bad one that season. The Redmen had an indifferent record, and Boykoff was carrying an inexperienced club. On nights when he was especially hot, the team clicked. Otherwise it didn't. Harry didn't get much support from the rest of the boys a good part of the time, mainly because they were green and also fresh from service — where the major sport was not basketball.

In facing Temple on the night of January 26, the Redmen were the underdogs. But St. John's turned in a major upset by vanquishing the Owls by a tight 57-54 count. Harry, who was the key player for his team, scored twenty-eight points, his high for the year.

And then Boykoff began to roll.

St. John's beat Boston College 69-44. Harry counted twenty-one tallies.

In losing a return game to Temple, Harry continued to be the pacemaker for his club by scoring eighteen points in a 55-51 loss.

In dropping a 58-54 decision to NYU, Harry did his level best to win the game for his mates. Seven minutes before the end, St. John's led by fourteen points. At half-time the tally was 24-24 and then Harry went to town, helping his mates score eleven points in a row to give the Redmen a heavy lead. It wasn't good enough and as St. John's crumbled, the Violet snatched the game out of the fire.

Against Manhattan, Harry got thirteen points; against Brooklyn College, fourteen; in the game against St. Francis, eighteen. His feats led the Redmen into the Invitational Tournament, but they were beaten in the opening game by West Virginia, 70-58, thus ending an indifferent season, with Boykoff revealing that he could still play basketball. His feats won for him the same kind of recognition he had before he entered the Army. In 1943 he was chosen for the annual All-Star game in Chicago, and at the end of the season he was picked once more.

In his last season, 1946-1947, Harry Boykoff played some of his most spectacular basketball and revealed the form that had won for him the acclaim of experts who considered him one of the best of the college stars.

Playing under constant pressure, aware always that he was the man the opposition had to stop, Harry scored heavily in nearly all his games. In losing to Nevada 55-49, he tallied twenty-two points. In beating Loyola 58-43, Harry counted twenty points, and twenty-six more in helping to whip Iowa. In losing once more to that fine Kentucky team, Harry was the only New Yorker to stand up to them and play as well as the best of them.

St. John's, however, was experiencing another bad season. Coming up to the CCNY game, the Redmen had lost three in a row and were underdogs once again. Boykoff had been showing flashes of his great form, but, again, he wasn't capable of sparking the entire team. Against City, however, he came through with his usual aplomb and skill. The Redmen upset the Lavender by a 46-41 score, and Harry scored twenty-one points. The Redmen were never better. Agile and opportunistic, they were accurate as well. Dick McGuire, a new young player, attained real stardom in this game. He was the key floor man, but the real key was the condition of Harry Boykoff. If he held up, the Redmen would give City a battle. Harry did his share — and his team won.

On January 16, 1947, Harry Boykoff had a great night but it was not enough to carry the club. He scored twenty-four points against Temple, and yet his team lost. The season moved along without too much excitement, until March, when the climactic games were scheduled. Facing a super-charged NYU team, St. John's, a short-ender in the betting, played the NYU Violet to a standstill in a thriller. More than 18,000 fans went limp with excitement as the lead changed hands six times. It was the best game of the year seen at the Garden. It was fast and had incredible finesse. Boykoff was a big man as he chalked up seventeen points. With two-and-a-half minutes left and with the

Redmen leading by a single point, the men from St. John's elected to freeze the ball; that is, they tried to keep possession of the ball, not giving NYU a chance to score. As the clock ticked off the seconds, the crowd went mad, but the Johnnies, desperate and skilled, held the ball until the final whistle blew. It was a tremendous victory.

A week later, however, Harry Boykoff had one of the greatest days he had ever experienced. It was the "greatest one-man basketball act ever presented on the Madison Square Garden floor," a *Times* man wrote. Indeed it was. In overwhelming St. Francis by a 71-52 score, Harry Boykoff scored fifty-four points, beating George Mikan's record of fifty-three made on the same court. He scored when the game was fifteen seconds young. In all he shot twenty-one goals and was voted the most valuable player on the court. "The big fellow was defending brilliantly, intercepting passes and capturing rebounds," the *Times* story said. It was a memorable way to end a college career. It ranks among Harry's top thrills, and no wonder.

After his college career, Harry Boykoff played professional ball beginning at $10,000 a season. But, Harry said, "I don't want to be an athletic bum. I'll have to support myself and my family long after my playing days are over and I'll only be able to do it if I can make something of myself." Therefore, he also worked as an accountant.

As far as being aware of his Jewish heritage is concerned, Harry was a good Jew, sensitive and ready to fight those who maligned him for his faith. "About anti-Semitism," Harry told me, "I can go into great detail and probably could not express myself as clearly as I would like to." He added, "I feel the same as any Jew feels when his people are humiliated or attacked." Big Harry had his share of being called names because of his faith.

Harry Boykoff's college and professional career established him, together with the younger Adolph Schayes and Max Zaslofsky, as one of the major hoop stars of his time. It is no wonder that he ranks as a star in a game which had its difficult moments but which, as a professional sport, achieved new status and prestige and is today one of the most popular games in the world.

ADOLPH SCHAYES, POISED FOR A SHOT

Adolph Schayes

Pro Star

Professional basketball has leaped from fumbling obscurity to national importance and in the process the great hoop stars have become as famous as baseball players and heavyweight boxing champions. In the days when the Original Celtics, with Nat Holman and other Jewish stars, played basketball for money, there was no television, there were no glowing newspaper reports and no large arenas where many thousands could come to watch the wizardry and ballhandling of the famous quintet. Nightly stands in grubby towns kept the professionl game obscure. Today, it is different. TV has invaded the pro game and basketball stars, extraordinarily tall, limber and lithe, are national heroes.

In the emergence of the game as a big-time sport, it seems odd that Jewish players are most notable by their absence. When Harry Boykoff was a professional star, Jewish basketball players were prominent in college ranks. But at that time the professional game was of minor importance. In recent years, however, there have not been many Jewish courtmen, either in college ranks or in professional circles.

There is one athlete who will go down in history as one of the finest in the annals of professional basketball and at this writing ranks as the best of all Jewish basketball players. He is Adolph — usually called Dolph — Schayes. He was a pretty good college player and, after fifteen full years in the pro ranks, gained recognition as one of the outstanding men in the sport.

When he ended his career in 1963, he had played in more league games than anyone else (1,035) and had scored more points than any other player in the sport (19,115). He also held the record for free throws (8,216) and was acknowledged to be a deadly foul shooter. A rugged man, Dolph also established a new record for playing the greatest number of consecutive games in the National Basketball Association, 765 between February 17, 1952 and December 26, 1961. The streak ended when he collided with another player and broke his own jaw. He required surgery and sat on the bench for a few weeks.

January 11, 1958 was an important date in the life of Dolph Schayes. He scored twenty-three points in a game against the Detroit Pistons and reached the total of 11, 770 points. This made him the highest scoring player in professional basketball, replacing huge George Mikan, whose record had been 11,764 points. This record also made Dolph the best player ever to perform for the Syracuse Nationals for whom he starred throughout his career.

I* remember Dolph Schayes when he was a gangling New York University player, big, but with little else to recommend him. He was an important cog in the NYU machine only because any college boy who is six feet, eight inches tall must be reckoned with by his coach. But students at NYU recalled how much better the earlier NYU key players used to be, and we smiled sardonically when we

*H.U.R.

heard Schayes' name mentioned in the same breath with theirs. "Pop" Auerbach, Ralph Kaplowitz, Bobby Lewis and Irv Resnick, we thought, were excellent ball-handlers and true basketball players. In those days, when a team scored fifty points, it was reaching high. Today, many college teams pour that many points through the basket in half a game. So Schayes, to us, was just another big guy, making the grade because the trend was toward the goons in the game, who had size without ability.

Yet for a dozen years Schayes was one of the best hoop men in history. He had been elected to more All-Star squads than any other player in the National Basketball Association. He was a set-shot artist, an excellent foul shooter and a key rebounder. He *was* the Syracuse National team for a very long time.

How did Dolph get this way? What changed him from an awkward player into a great one? Howard Cann, Dolph's coach at NYU, had stated that in college, "Dolph was all adolescent arms and legs. He was a good player — no more that that." But Dolph wanted to improve. "His mind," Cann said, "was set on being great. He was in the gym practicing every spare minute. We had to chase him out." So well did Schayes work at improving himself that in 1961 he was chosen (together with Sam Mele, later manager of the Minnesota Twins baseball team) by the Varsity Club of NYU as the first annual winner of the NYU "Alumni of the Year in Sports" award.

As a professional star, Schayes did not ease up. He haunted the Syracuse gym to perfect his game. He explained his compulsion for perfection in this way: "It's only forty-eight minutes, I say, only forty-eight minutes I've got to deliver. Most of those people watching me have to deliver for eight hours every day on their jobs. I've got forty-eight minutes. That should be easy. I tell myself how lucky I am to be getting paid for playing a game."

To a sports reporter who asked him why he was still so enthusiastic about the game and worked so hard at it, Schayes replied, "I feel I can still improve. Where? Defensively, for one thing. And you can always become a better shot, can't you?"

As late as 1961, when Dolph was thirty-two and not too far from the end of his career, his hustle was the talk of the league. A former coach of the New York Knicks, Fuzzy Levane, said, "Schayes never stops. He's always moving and he keeps the other guys moving. Without him they haven't got a franchise. But it's still a long season. At his age, I don't know if he can keep putting out that way."

Carl Braun, who was the Knick coach in 1961, also praised Schayes, but along different lines. "What sticks in my mind," he said, "is that every night he puts on his sneakers and he plays to the best of his ability — whether it's for 18,000 here at the Garden or 800 in Syracuse, he knows only one way."

Again, in 1961, when it appeared that Schayes was slowing down, Alex Hannum of the Syracuse Nationals, reminded himself and a reporter: "When I broke into pro ball here with Dolph thirteen years ago, Dolph was always one of the first on the court for practice, but most often, he was the last off. And that's what I immediately noticed when I returned as coach here last year. That Dolph was still one of the first on the floor, and almost always the last one to leave. I believe that this self-discipline in practice is what has made Dolph so great." And Hannum added, "Dolph lives basketball the year around. He has 100 per cent both physical and mental dedication to the game. Few players can stay in the game as long as he, for he knows when to relax, too."

There was good reason for Schayes to keep bearing down for his career, in spite of its success, had some pretty rough edges. And he never forgot them. Here is how Vince Boryla. former star at Notre Dame and later coach of the Knicks, reported on his experiences with Schayes:

"Schayes had to close in on Mikan's record to remind people that he's one of the game's all-time greats. He's always been underrated. He can lick you more ways than anybody I've ever seen. He's come so far it's hard for me to believe he's the same fellow I once outplayed in college."

It happened on the night of February 10, 1945, when Boryla led Notre Dame against NYU in Madison Square Garden. Schayes was only sixteen and was playing in his second varsity game for the Violets. In the first half, Boryla outscored Schayes by sixteen points to three and then the Irish coasted to a 66-60 victory. The game was particularly painful to Dolph's high school coach, Nat April, who told Stanley Frank (author of a fine article on Schayes in the *Saturday Evening Post*), "You could almost hear the tattoo Boryla's elbows were beating on Dolph under the basket. Making due allowances for Dolph's inexperience and stage fright, I still was shocked that he didn't fight back against Boryla. Frankly, I wondered then whether Dolph had the guts to make the grade in the big time."

In 1948, Dolph was graduated from NYU, receiving a degree in aeronautical engineering, and Cann suggested he forget about professional basketball. Some years later, when Cann selected an All-Star team of men who played under him, he omitted Dolph. "I suppose," he admitted, "that makes me look like a bum judge of talent. Dolph unquestionably is the best player ever turned out at NYU, but I picked the men on the basis of what they had done in college and Dolph was not particularly outstanding while he was here. I didn't think he was rugged or aggressive enough to survive in pro ball."

Cann was wrong, of course, as so many have been about Schayes. I myself can recall seeing Schayes play against the Boston Celtics, with the spectacular Bob Cousy and the clever Bill Sharman opposing him. The fans would concentrate on the two Celtics, brilliant ball-handlers and passers. They were dazzling. Schayes would seem to lumber along, run up and down the court and occasionally steal a ball or grab a rebound. But when the half-time scoring was anounced, more often than not Schayes would be the top man. And if the game would go down to the last second, somehow or other Dolph would be making the key play. It happened too frequently to be accidental.

Schayes began to play basketball at DeWitt Clinton High School in the Bronx, N. Y., with his father's rooting support. The elder Schayes was a sports fan who nearly became a professional fighter. He used to take his three sons to Madison Square Garden for sporting events and was happy when Dolph made the high school basketball squad.

But even then, Dolph had his troubles. He was a six-foot-five-inch tall player, but he was a bad one and, in spite of his enormous height, was dropped from the team within a week. Only at midyear, after five of the regulars had graduated, did Dolph make the team. He improved somewhat and when he entered NYU he found himself a regular, but far below a high level of excellence. Cann remembered that "he proved to be beyond his depth whenever he met a top-notch opponent."

Still, when he finally was graduated from NYU — following a mediocre college career in basketball — Syracuse and the Knickerbockers bid for his services. Syracuse made the better offer and so that is where Schayes went. Years later, Ned Irish of the Knicks said that "our failure to win a championship can be traced to our not getting Schayes." And then Irish praised Schayes as one of the few real powerhouse men in the league and said he did not wonder that Syracuse could not afford to trade him (Irish had wanted to give up three first-string stars for him) because Dolph was their entire team.

In 1952, Schayes broke his right wrist, later claiming it was a useful accident. "Losing the use of my right hand was the best break I ever got. I developed a left-handed shot that made me twice as effective," he said. A few years later, he had another, more painful, injury. In 1954, during the final game for the Eastern Division title, in Boston against the Celtics, Schayes jumped high for a shot and was hit by a Celtic. Dolph landed heavily on the floor and suffered a deep gash under an eye. Five stitches were taken to sew up the cut, as Syracuse kept calling for time-out after time-out, or as long as was legal. But when play was resumed, Dolph realized that something was wrong with his left wrist. Somehow, his team managed to win and get into the championship playoffs. Dolph was rushed to a hospital to have his eye treated and his wrist placed in a cast. At four in the morning he left the hospital and eight hours later was working out with the team.

The Syracuse Nationals met the Minneapolis Lakers in a best four-out-of-seven series. The Nats won three times, just one short of the title. Dolph played poorly in the early games, but was his efficient self in the remaining championship games.

From that point forward, the Boston Celtics seemed to take a stranglehold on championships and the headlines veered away from Schayes to men like Bob Cousy, Wilt Chamberlain, Oscar Robertson, Elgin Baylor and Bill Russell. But the Celtics appreciated Schayes as much as any fans did, and after Dolph had been a top star for a dozen years, he was given a "Day," or more accurately, a "Night." It did not happen at Syracuse, but in Boston and that night the Nats beat the Celtics 142-134.

When Dolph was in his fourteenth year of play, he had moved to the very top of his profession. He had scored some 2,800 more points than anyone else; he was scoring at an average of twenty points a game; his foul shooting average was .841 and for twelve of the fourteen years he had been named to the All-Star team. The owner of the Nats, Danny Biasone, said of his star player, "Dolph is the greatest all-round basketball player of all time. Maybe there are better shots . . . or better rebounders . . . or better playmakers . . . and so on. But overall, believe me, nobody is a better all-round player than Dolph."

In his fifteenth year with the Nats, Dolph was an old veteran. He attained a landmark when he performed for the 1,000th time in a Nat uniform, but he no longer was a forty-minute man and it was clear that the end of the road was in sight. Then the Philadelphia Warriors went to the West Coast and the Syracuse National franchise filled in and became the Philadelphia 76ers. Hannum, who had been the Syracuse coach, decided he did not want to move to Philadelphia and in 1963 Dolph Schayes became the coach of a top professional team, and lasted until 1966. Dropped from his job, he became a League official.

It was perfectly natural and normal that Schayes should move up the ladder, for basketball was the biggest thing in his life. Yet curiously, he has belittled his size and height as major factors in his success, although in later years seven-foot players quite obviously used their advantage quite effectively. In discussing how he broke George Mikan's scoring record, Schayes said, "I'd get a bigger boot out of the record if Mikan didn't hold it. He epitomized the type of player I never admired. I've always resented strong-arm guys who are effective just because of their size."

And Dolph added, "Even when I was half a head taller than the other kids, I refused to play the pivot [which is where Mikan scored most of his points throughout his career]. To me, basketball is a game of movement and finesse.

"The emphasis should be on teamwork and skill, not on size as it is today. Maybe I'm an ingrate for criticizing Mikan. He helped to turn my height into an asset by proving that all big men weren't goons. He was a tremendous competitor who took as much punishment as he dished out. I wonder, though, how good he would've been if he was only six feet tall and had to depend on cleverness to get by. That's the real test of a player."

In 1977, Schayes made a sentimental return to the game he knew and loved so well. After careful consideration he agreed to make a brief return to the coaching ranks to manage the American squad that would compete in Israel's Maccabiah Games.

"A lot of people asked me why I did it, why I'm coaching the Maccabiah team. I thought it would be exciting, the experience of a lifetime," said Schayes. Then he cheerfully acknowledged his ulterior motive. "I thought my son had a chance to make the team and I wanted to be there if he did."

Danny Schayes had just graduated high school, but he already stood 6′11″ as he planned to enter Syracuse University. He made the team, all right, but he had to work for it. "I might be his kid off the court," he remarked after the coach had run everyone through another exhausting workout, "But I'm just another player while I'm in there."

Under the demanding guidance of their Hall of Fame coach, the young squad learned to play an unselfish, passing, hard-working game where teammates looked for each other rather than just for their own shots. They learned their lessons well.

"It's going to be something," Dolph said optimistically as the team prepared to go to Israel. It was. Led by Danny Schayes, the U. S. entry swept to the finals and defeated the tough Israeli quintet to win the Maccabiah championship. When the father and son combination returned to America, it was with the gold medal.

Dolph Schayes is very much like Hank Greenberg and Al Rosen in baseball. All three reached the heights in their sports profession mainly through drive and work and the realization that nothing came easily to them. Schayes was an overgrown youngster and an awkward athlete for years. It would have been simple for him to give up on himself. Certainly the temptation was there. His college coach belittled him and constantly said that he had little talent. Instead of succumbing to defeatism, he literally made himself into a great player. He became aggressive on the court; he practiced even when he was a star; and he always felt there was room for further improvement. As a result, he became the highest scorer of his time. Feared, respected and admired, he won fewer headlines than some other basketball players. But when the history of this game is finally written, Adolph Schayes will have to be ranked with the very best. This has been a tremendous feat, for it is not too difficult for a brilliant player to dazzle the opposition and the fans. It is much harder to start as a fair player and make yourself into a great one. That is Schayes' major accomplishment.

The Tennis Court

The story of the Jew in tennis was, until the early 1950's, similar to that of the progress, or lack of it, of the Jew in golf. Of all the major sports played in America, tennis boasted fewer Jews than all of them, with the exception of golf.

The reason was not that Jews were incapable of tennis ability or that Jews could, for example, box and play football and hit a baseball (or throw it) but not hit a tennis ball accurately within a proscribed area. The role of the Jew in tennis was similar to the status of the Jew in the country in which he lived as a Jew. And it is in tennis that there has been a real revolution.

When earlier editions of this book were written or brought up-to-date, tennis was, without any serious argument, a "social" sport. It was played by wealthy people, for most tennis courts and clubs were supported and sponsored by the so-called upper classes. Like golf, tennis was most frequently played by the "idle rich." For every boy who came up the ladder of poverty in tennis, there was the background story of a patron, or a break, which permitted him to jump into the hitherto forbidden area.

How things have changed! Tennis was once relegated to exclusive clubs and there were few tournaments and all of them were of the amateur persuasion. Then, with television, with many corporations sponsoring events, tennis opened up. It really became "open." Amateurs and professionals played in the same events. Purses became enormous. Tennis stars, like Jimmy Connors and Bjorn Borg and Manuel Orantes and Guillermo Vilas, became international stars of superstar stature. Billy Jean King and Chris Evert opened the game to women in a way previously unknown. Where a Pancho Gonzales or a Pancho Segura were once uncommon in that they represented minorities, the game became enriched when players from all walks of life and ethnic groups started to find that tennis clubs and tournaments were now open to them.

For example, Harold Solomon and Brian Gottfried, whose stories are included in this book, had not yet been born when the first edition of this work was published!

Until the 1950's, there really were no major American Jewish tennis stars until Dick Savitt and Herb Flam came along. Savitt's career is outlined in the following pages. Herb Flam reached the quarterfinals in six Nationals and became the first Jewish star to reach the finals when he did so in 1950. Just to show what an achievement that was, Jewish players had a hard time being allowed to play at Forest Hills in the era when Flam made the finals. And the following year he played for the United States Davis Cup team; that was 1951.

Probably the best Jewish tennis star, until the advent of Flam and Savitt, was Dr. Daniel Prenn, the champion of Germany in 1930, 1931 and 1932. He also was a member of the German Davis Cup team in 1932, but when the Nazis took power in Germany, the German Tennis Federation passed a resolution barring Jews from the Davis Cup team and membership in the Federation. In addition, the resolution specifically barred Dr. Prenn from the 1933 German Davis Cup team. Prenn settled in England and never again was as good as he had been at his peak. His son did, however, star briefly on the English tennis courts.

To understand why Jews did not emerge as stars of the tennis courts until fairly recently, one must understand the way in which a tennis star used to be made in the United States. By and large, the good players came from college ranks. To some degree, this still holds, but obviously it was not the case with Jimmy Connors and many of the younger players. Tennis camps opened within the past two decades and the stress on junior tennis has helped many youngsters emerge without the aid of college competition.

But if a Jewish boy learned to play the game in college, he generally avoided concentrating on the game after his college days. Otherwise, he would have been called a "tennis bum" or a "tennis tramp," if he played as an amateur and took money under the table for "expenses." In time, these players had to perform in many amateur tournaments to earn a semi-illicit living. They had to become social butterflies, play up to local tennis bigwigs. It is no wonder that such athletes won the appellation of "tennis bum."

This was not the sort of environment which either attracted or wanted Jews. The overall picture improved with the years. Pancho Gonzales, a Mexican-American, became National champion. Later, Arthur Ashe became the first black on the American Davis Cup team. There had been progress through the 1950's and 1960's and today there are Jewish players coming up with a degree of regularity.

In the past, there were Jewish players of more than average ability and achievements. In the 1920's, Julie

Seligson of Lehigh University was probably the best Jewish player of that era. He was intercollegiate champion in 1928 and ranked ninth nationally. Eddie Jacobson of Baltimore was a National junior champion, as Seligson was before him. Izzy Bellis of Philadelphia won the same title. Joey Fishbach created a temporary stir but never went very far. Other players included Len Hartman; Henry Prusoff, who ranked eleventh once in the National ratings; and Seymour Greenberg, who went as high as fifth. Sam Match and Pablo Eisenberg were fairly prominent in the Savitt-Flam era. Julius and Gladys Heldman started a remarkable tennis dynasty. They themselves were pretty good players. He won the National Junior Outdoor Championship in 1936 and years later the Senior championship. His wife also was a rather good player, who competed at Wimbledon and was the first ranked woman player in Texas. She founded *World Tennis Magazine* and the Heldmans remain prominent in the sport. Their daughter Julie ranked high as an amateur and did well as a professional. Another daughter, Carrie, became a tennis writer as well as a player.

Finally, tennis became another sport finally opened to and enriched by the Jewish athlete. An earlier edition of this book predicted that it would have been difficult to guess that a time would come when Jews would be talked about in tennis circles. Then Savitt came along. Most recently Harold Solomon and Brian Gottfried emerged as stars on the pro circuit. Who knows what the near future will bring in terms of new Jewish tennis stars?

DICK SAVITT, SMASHING THE BALL

Dick Savitt

Wimbledon King

The rise of the Jew in tennis in recent years is a most interesting gauge of growing American tolerance and democracy. It was long recognized that tennis, because it was a "social" sport, was reluctant to accept members of minority groups with the same eagerness that it embraced Protestant white Americans. Arnold Forster, in the Anti-Defamation League report on democratic trends, *A Measure of Freedom* (published in 1950), wrote that "in tennis 'the best man wins' — if he is free, white and Gentile." Forster further explained that many ranking tennis clubs throughout the United States practice discrimination against minority groups, although this fact does not prevent these groups from producing an occasional star.

According to Forster, "the Anti-Defamation League believes that the West Side Tennis Club, 'the capital of the tennis world,' has practiced a policy of discrimination," and that the Los Angeles Tennis Club, too, keeps out Jews and Negroes. The ADL pointed out that Jews, Negroes, Mexican Americans, etc., "are discouraged from making tennis their careers simply because they are unable to obtain the expert instruction required for a player of championship caliber." The report also stated that in smaller tennis clubs, bias is as strong as it is in the larger clubs.

Nevertheless, in spite of the bias reported by the ADL,

Jewish names have cropped up with pleasing regularity in tennis tournaments during the past few decades. Two Jewish court stars, Herb Flam and Dick Savitt, were among the finest tennis players in America — and the world — for many years, and Dick Savitt, during his tenure at the top of the tennis world, was ranked as the greatest player of his time, which was a sweet triumph for those who had believed that Jews were capable of producing top-grade tennis, and had been blocked only because of bias. Later, of course, Brian Gottfried and Harold Solomon came along.

In 1951, Dick Savitt won two major championships, the Australian and the most valued Wimbledon championship. He lost in the U.S. nationals in the semi-finals to Victor Seixas only when he pulled up lame with a boil on his leg. He was sufficiently dominating in tennis to gain a *Time* magazine cover story, prior to the playing of the nationals in 1951, and he was a constant subject for articles in other national and sports magazines. Savitt was the first Jewish net ace of major proportions. Herb Flam, the only other Jewish player of that time to win high national rating, was a fine tactician and he proved his ability when, at the age of twenty-one, he reached the finals in the nationals in 1950. But Flam never had the powerful game which wins not only matches but headlines. Savitt did, and he became an international personality.

Raised in Orange, N.J., Savitt was an only child of well-to-do parents. He was athletically inclined, but took no games particularly seriously, not until former national champion Don McNeill moved to Orange and began to play with Savitt. In 1941, Dick Savitt entered a tournament in Orange but realized that tennis was difficult to master, when a 6-0, 6-0 defeat in the New Jersey boys' championship impressed that fact on his mind.

But tennis continued to remain comparatively minor to the young man. The Savitts moved to El Paso, Texas, and Dick, now sixteen, started to play basketball. By 1945, Savitt was El Paso High's co-captain and all-state choice at forward. Tennis was only a casual game to him at this point in his athletic career. In 1944, he had come East to compete in the national juniors, but was beaten in the quarter-finals. He also entered the U.S. national and was overwhelmed in the first round by another Jewish player, Seymour Greenberg.

In 1945, Savitt joined the U.S. Navy, where he interested himself primarily in basketball. In late 1946, he was discharged from the service and returned to his family, again living in New Jersey. Now he entered Cornell University and, naturally, tried to make the basketball squad. He succeeded, but a badly wrenched knee sent him back to tennis. Savitt began to reveal the dogged determination that led him to the top within a few years. He practiced with intensity and soon became the Number One player on the Cornell team. He entered many tournaments and won against many name players. In 1947, he won a national ranking of twenty-sixth. In 1948, he had not raised his rank at all, although in 1949, he was sixteenth best in the land. He was a good college player, eager to compete in all tournaments. He had yet to win from any of the truly outstanding players.

In 1950, still an average tennis player, Savitt began to improve. He won the Eastern Intercollegiate, East Clay Court and New York State tournaments. But in the Pennsylvania championship at the Merion Cricket Club, Savitt started to gain attention. He won from Harry Likas and Vic Seixas. In the semi-finals he lost the first two sets to Earl Cochell, but fought hard to retrieve the victory. In the finals, against canny Ed Moylan he again lost the initial two sets. Once again, he dug into his reserves and pulled even and then ahead to win the championship.

This victory gave him the confidence he needed in himself and from that point forward, Dick Savitt was on the spectacular rise.

Although he did not go as far as Flam in the 1950 nationals, Savitt played impressively and added to his store of confidence. In his first match, he won easily from Australian ace Mervyn Rose. His second-round opponent was the brilliant Australian veteran John Bromwich, who knew more than most players the intricacies and tactics of the game. Bromwich held a lead of 3-0 in the fifth and final set. Allison Danzig, tennis expert for the *New York Times,* described this match in an article for *Sport* magazine, saying, "Bromwich was bringing screams of delight from the crowd with the baffling cleverness of his tactics as he trapped Savitt with drop shots and lobs, disguising his stroke so effectively each time that his opponent couldn't guess what was coming. Savitt should have been finished — but he wasn't. He proceeded to take six games in a row for the match."

Following this splendid victory, Savitt proceeded to win in a beautifully played match from Sidney Schwartz. But in the semi-finals, he lost to Art Larsen, who, in turn, went on to defeat Flam for the championship. Savitt had never before played in front of so many people, and when this experience was over, he was convinced of his own ability to beat anyone in the world. He traveled to Australia where he once again licked John Bromwich and then faced Frank Sedgman in the semi-finals of the Australian championship. It was a tense match. Sedgman took a 4-2 lead in the fifth set, usually an insurmountable edge. But then Savitt, a nervous player, relaxed. "When I'm winning," he said, "I get tense. If I'm losing, I relax." Against the Australian star, Savitt relaxed himself into victory. This is how he told it: "I thought Sedgman had me at 4-2 in his favor and I relaxed. But I didn't quit. I started hitting winners all over the place. When I broke his serve for four-all, I knew I had him. When I had beaten their champion, I felt nothing could stop me. I never had any doubts in the final." Apparently not, for Savitt beat Ken McGregor 6-3, 2-6, 6-3, 6-1. One American had beaten the entire Australian Davis Cup team!

Then came Dick Savitt's greatest tournament and no matter what happened later, this was his week and the manner in which he triumphed placed him among the immortals of the game.

Wimbledon is perhaps the greatest single tennis tournament in the world. All the outstanding court aces try to win the Wimbledon championship and, usually, only the truly talented players come away with the crown.

Savitt, who seldom had easy matches, was pressed in the third round by Denmark's Kurt Nielsen, whom he beat in five sets, 6-4, 1-6, 6-3, 8-10, 6-4. In the fourth round, Savitt won from the Hungarian Asboth in straight sets, overpowering his opponent all the way. It was, however, in the quarter-finals that blood was spilled on the Wimbledon courts. Herb Flam beat Sedgman, the top-seeded player in the tournament and Savitt upset the American champion,

Art Larsen, in an easy match, 6-1, 6-4, 6-4. Savitt jumped into stride at the very outset of his match and had his backhand working well. Again and again he drove Larsen's service out of reach or on the baseline. The U.S. champion was completely overpowered and overshadowed.

Flam, who had beaten the great Sedgman after spotting him two sets, was America's Number Two player and Savitt was ranked sixth. For the first two sets, it appeared that Flam would duplicate his victory of the previous day. Again the soft-hitting player was beating the man with the power. Flam won the first set with ridiculous ease and reached 5-1 in the second set before Savitt rallied. Neville Deed, reporting from Wimbledon for *American Lawn Tennis,* said that "it was refreshing to see a young player using his head. Flam was out to break up his opponent's game and he succeeded beyond his wildest dreams. He gave Savitt absolutely nothing to hit. Soft returns of service, made with a turn of the wrist, became semi-lobs that landed within inches of the baseline. Hitting deeply on every shot, Herb kept Dick away from the net and, when Savitt did get there, a perfect lob sailed over his head, or an innocuous looking passing shot dropped at his feet."

Utilizing these tactics, Flam won eleven of the first thirteen games. Then Savitt relaxed, as he usually did when losing. He began to clown and hit one of Flam's semi-lobs high into the sky, ridiculing Herb's style. According to Deeds, "that gesture certainly won the second set for Savitt and very likely the match, for Flam immediately dropped the brainy game he had been playing and returned to normal driving and at just the pace that suited Savitt."

The Associated Press was more realistic in its report.

Savitt, behind 1-5, held his own service, winning four straight points to do so. Flam then served and, with the help of a double-fault, Savitt broke his service. Still leading 5-3, Flam reached set point against Dick, but Savitt at this time playing recklessly, rushed the net and hit a winner to avert defeat. He kept up the hot streak until he drew even at 5-5. Flam regained his touch to break Savitt's service and take a 6-5 lead. Then Savitt went back to even terms when he won Flam's service on four straight points. That is how the two men played for sixteen more games. Flam staved off two points in the eighteenth game, one in the twenty-sixth and one in the twenty-eighth. When Savitt finally won the set, 15-13, with a cross-court pass, Flam never again regained the offensive. Savitt was now holding service with regularity and broke through Flam with far less difficulty than previously. He won the third set 6-3 and swept through the match when Flam dropped service three times in the fourth and final set.

The next day, Savitt, who never took a tennis lesson in his life, emerged as the top player of the year when he won in straight sets from Ken McGregor in less than an hour to capture the Wimbledon title. The United Press reporter said that Savitt won with "the finest array of volleys and passing shots seen in this 65th staging of the game's best-known tournament." He won by scores of 6-4, 6-4, 6-4.

McGregor had three real chances to win the match, but each time Savitt lifted his own game to the necessary heights to thwart McGregor. In the first set, Savitt was leading 5-4 and serving. McGregor forced the game to deuce and then to his advantage by charging the net for perfect stop shots and cross-court smashes. Savitt held firm. He utilized a perfect drop shot to get the score back to deuce, took the advantage with a volley from the net and then passed McGregor at the baseline for the decisive point.

In the second set, McGregor again needed only a single point to break Savitt. But Dick beat him with a forehand cross-court pass. In the final set, Savitt held a 5-1 lead before McGregor made a desperate but futile stand. The Australian pulled the score up to 4-5 and twice held off Savitt at match point. But finally, Dick drove a placement past McGregor and was the winner of the most important match of his career.

This was the peak moment of Savitt's tennis life. What happened later was less glamorous and less successful. But it must be recorded as part of his accomplishments. In September, in the U.S. nationals, Savitt attempted to complete the cycle of great tennis wins. To sweep the major championships, he had only to win this tournament, to add to the Australian and Wimbledon championships. Favored to pull off the "grand slam" of tennis for the first time since Don Budge accomplished the feat in 1938, Savitt was ranked Number One in the 1951 tournament. But he picked up a boil infection and played under severe handicaps. Nevertheless, he fought hard. In his quarter-final match against Budge Patty, who had won at Wimbledon in 1950, the year before Savitt triumphed on the same court, Savitt stumbled but rallied to win a tremendous match. Allison Danzig of the *Times* grew lyrical in his account of this tense match. "With one of his typical demonstrations of his unsurpassed fighting qualities," he began, "Richard Savitt of Orange, N.J., tottered seemingly on the brink of defeat and then came on to stir 11,000 spectators to applause yesterday as he defeated Budge Patty of Los

Angeles in the national tennis championships at Forest Hills. The score was 6-3, 1-6, 4-6, 6-1, 6-4."

Savitt was outmaneuvered by the clever Patty in the second and third sets, and his infected leg was bothering him more than ever before. "As the Californian trapped him with lobs and ran him all over the court," Danzig reported, "Savitt looked to be a thoroughly beaten man." After the intermission period, however, Savitt made a blazing comeback. This time he was able to control his first serve, and consequently, his powerful serving weapon was behaving for him. He played with such fury and speed that Patty was unable to mount his tactical attack any longer. Savitt's comeback indicated that, at the peak of his form, he was too much even for the finest tennis ace in the world.

But the constant draining of his infection left Savitt with a marked limp, and exhausted him as well. In the semifinals he hobbled about as best he could, but was an ineffectual player against Vic Seixas and was defeated. Nevertheless, he had already been named to the Davis Cup squad and the Cup captain, Frank Shields, said, a few months before the Cup matches, "All I know for certain right now is that Dick Savitt will play singles."

When Savitt and Flam were named to the Davis Cup team. it marked the first time that Jewish players made the squad. And what happened later led some to believe that Savitt was mishandled by Frank Shields. For Savitt did play against Japan, but he did not play against Sweden or Australia in the big matches. Instead, Ted Schroeder, who had played no grass tournaments in two years and who had been beaten in three of his 1950 assignments, was substituted for the best player in the United States!

The reason for Savitt's being left off the Davis Cup in

the key matches was discussed by sports writers all over the world. Savitt did not behave with the quiet aplomb of the Davis Cup player — and it was no wonder. He felt badly that he was not given the chance to win the Cup for the United States. What actually happened was best reported by Al Silverman, in an article in *Sport* magazine on Dick Savitt. Silverman, who talked with Savitt soon after Dick's actions had won front-page headlines, wrote as follows:

"What hurt Savitt most was not so much the fact that he had been left off the Davis Cup team, but by the continuous controversies stirred up by Australian newspapers at his expense. The bitterest and most widely publicized of these came in the Australian national championship tournament when he was accused of staging a sit-down in protest against the use of spikes by his semi-final opponent, Ken McGregor.

"Before you pass judgement on Savitt, you should know of an occurrence which took place at the Victoria Tennis Championships in Melbourne — just before the United States players who would meet Sweden in the Interzone finals were to be picked. It goes a long way toward explaining Savitt's subsequent conduct in the Australian nationals. Savitt was a finalist in that Victorian tournament, held at Adelaide, and his opponent was Frank Sedgmen, the most feared tennis player in the world today. Late in the opening set of their match, when the footing became especially slippery from an earlier rainstorm, Sedgman switched from sneakers to spiked shoes. Savitt made no objection to the move. He lost the match 8-6, 6-0, 6-4. Thirty minutes later, the American captain, Frank Shields, named Schroeder, not Savitt, to face the Swedes. If you can conceive the psychological blow dealt Savitt by

Shield's trigger-like decision, you may get a better idea why Dick later was to protest so violently McGregor's use of spikes in the Australian singles test. It was that defeat by Sedgman which, to all intents and purposes, cost Savitt any chance he might have had of playing in the Davis Cup."

Having offered this background information, Silverman went on to quote Savitt as saying that "At no time did I stage a sit-down strike. In fact, McGregor sat down before me while we were waiting for Sir Norman Brookes, who is president of the Australian Lawn Tennis Association, to hear my complaint. When Sir Norman reached the court, I told him I thought it wasn't fair to allow Ken to wear spikes. I wanted him to stay in tennis shoes to keep it even." Later, Sir Norman Brookes said that as far as he was concerned, it was sporting of Savitt to continue to play. It was a close and brilliant match, nonetheless, and when it was over, the Australians cheered Savitt as he and McGregor walked off the court arm in arm.

The defeats of Schroeder in the matches made both Schroeder and Shields the goats of the tests. In an attempt to justify his choices, Shields came back to the United States and delivered a personal attack on Savitt. He was so unfair, as a matter of fact, that Russell B. Kingman, president of the United States Lawn Tennis Association, stated that Shields' statements were "purely personal remarks and were most unseemly coming from the captain of the Davis Cup team."

No matter what caused the friction between Shields and Savitt, Savitt grew embittered over the fact that he did not play in the matches against Australia. He continued to compete in tennis tournaments for a few more years, never regained his past heights, and went into business.

During the peak of his popularity as a national tennis figure, Savitt made a number of references to his Jewish background. Once he played in Germany and was asked whether he had any trouble in Berlin. "Oh," he asked, "Because I am Jewish? . . . No, I never had any trouble that way. I know some clubs are prejudiced because they don't have any Jewish members . . . I don't think about it much."

Yet in the summer of 1951, both Savitt and Flam played at the Louisville Boat Club, which had no Jewish members and which, it was understood, barred Jews from membership, according to a report in the *National Jewish Post* of July 27, 1951. In the same issue of this newspaper, Frank Free, a correspondent for the *Post,* queried both Savitt and Flam on their Jewish affiliations and Savitt, although the grandson of the late Issac Hoberman, one of the pioneer Jewish leaders in Bayonne, N.J., said that his Jewish affiliations were slight. He and Flam emphasized that sports took up most of their time.

Commenting editorially on the interview with the tennis stars, Gabriel Cohen, editor and publisher of the *National Jewish Post,* said, "It would have given us much satisfaction to report that Savitt and Flam, although all their spare time has been devoted to tennis, were well aware of their obligations to organized Jewish life and were knowledgeable Jews. But wherein does the college life these two portrayed in the interview differ except in minor details from that followed by most Jewish students, many of whose parents not only are strictly Orthodox, but often officers of congregations of all three wings of Judaism . . . Savitt and Flam may have learned for the first time by the interview that something has been lacking in their Jewish attitude when they began to be asked questions about Jewish affiliations and interest."

At the close of the interview, Savitt said, "I'm sorry if you're looking for a special angle; there just isn't one." Cohen saw Savitt's attempt to apologize to the reporter as a sign that he was a nice young man and typical of contemporary American Jewish youth.

No doubt that was one way of looking at Savitt; another was to realize that here was a sensitive athlete who, at the top of his form, was one of the finest tennis players in the world, and that when he was rebuffed and slighted, lost just enough of his efficiency to plunge out of the championship grade. But while he held his form, there were no better tennis players.

Nevertheless, Savitt remained a highly controversial personality even after he became a semi-retired tennis player. Year after year, he would emerge from the business world, whip the top-ranking net stars — and win new invitations to represent the United States in the Davis Cup matches. Just as regularly, Dick would reject the invitation, remembering always how he had been left off the team in Australia.

Finally, the United States, in 1958, recaptured the Davis Cup, with the help of a transplanted Peruvian, not Dick Savitt.

Another opportunity had slipped by. Savitt would be remembered now only for his Wimbledon triumph and not for any Davis Cup victories.

For him, this was more than enough.

HARRY SOLOMON, CONCENTRATING ON HIS RETURN

Harold Solomon

True Grit

The game of tennis has altered radically in recent years. Once a stately, even staid, gentleman's game played elegantly before respectfully hushed crowds at country clubs, it has become a mass sport played by millions on city courts all over the country, and watched by tens of millions on television extravaganzas. Big money, endless worldwide tours and international attention have revolutionized the sport; and the game itself has changed. Only Wimbledon of the world's major tournaments remains a competition on grass; all the circuit competition is dominated by slower clay or synthetic surfaces.

In this age when strategy and cunning are as crucial as a powerful serve-and-volley game used to be, and when canny hustlers dominate the game once peopled by polite gamesmen, perhaps no one is more representative of the "new breed" of tennis player than Harold Solomon. By sheer determination and tenacity, Solomon has clawed his way to recognition as one of the world's top-ranking players.

At 5'6" and one hundred thirty-eight pounds, he is the smallest player in major tennis. He has an unimpressive first serve, a weaker second serve, and rarely goes to the net to put away a flashy winning stroke. At the beginning of most matches, he can easily appear to be overmatched.

There is virtually nothing that Solomon can do on a tennis court that one top player or another can't do better. Except win.

There has never been any way to measure guts in any sport, or any endeavor, except in the heat of the crucible itself. Countless times in competitive sports, a seemingly less talented player has emerged triumphant because he had a better brain and a deeper heart than his gifted foe. Solomon's trademark on the court is that he never gives up, never concedes defeat on any shot, let alone any game. Give him any less than your very best effort, and he'll find a way to beat you.

"We call him 'The Mole' because he's a little guy who just keeps digging," says Erik van Dillen, an American colleague. "Everybody knows Solly has the worst serve-and-volley in the world, but he's a great competitor and a terrific match player and has unreal ground strokes that compensate for his lack of ability at the net. He wins. We've seen it time and time again."

"Jesus, nobody wants to play Solomon," moans tennis star Arthur Ashe. "He runs after *everything*. On a slow court, he runs you into the ground." Tom Okker, the Dutch ace, knows all too well that "when you go out there against him you've got to work for every point. He doesn't give any easy points away, he just hits the ball back. There are ways to beat him, but you know it's going to be a long match. You're going to be tired whether it's 6-0, 6-1 or 7-6 in the third set."

There is no question that Solomon's game is to wear down his opponent. On clay, points out Barry Lorge in an admirable and perceptive article in *Tennis* magazine, "He can do what he does best — run and grind opponents into the ground until the drab courts are soaked with their sweat, sometimes their blood, frequently their tears.

"You can see the determination in his face," Lorge says. "When he hits a shot, he is a portrait of concentration — eyes riveted on the ball, teeth clenched, matted brown hair flying. Even when he crouches, waiting to return a serve, he looks as if he is in a private trance — lips pursed, eyes straight ahead, attention focused, both hands on the handle of the racquet he holds out straight in front of him. He grips it manacingly, as if it is a club he expects to use against a guy trying to mug him. That's the way he plays, too — with the ferocity of a man battling to save his life and property from a mugger."

That's the way he has always played. As a schoolboy, Harold won the National Interscholastic championship while attending Springbrook High in his home town of Silver Spring, Maryland, just outside the Capitol in Washington, D.C. His father Leonard, a successful businessman and avid tennis player himself, encouraged his children to play the game; Harold's brother and two sisters have all played competitively. Leonard even had a court built in the back yard so that his tennis prodigies would have the opportunities they needed to perfect their games.

When Harold went to Rice University in the fall of 1970, the college had two star players with national reputations, Zan Guerry and Mike Estep. Rice coach Sam Giammalva, by his own admission, expected little of his new addition. "He looked pretty bad — like a public parks pusher," he admits. "I never thought he'd get higher than No. 4 on my varsity." But what Giammalva didn't count on was Solomon's relentless determination. Solly played both stars, and he beat them both by simply refusing to lose. "There was almost blood on the courts when he went out there," the coach recalls.

In 1972, he dropped out of college after two years, feeling that if he was going to be able to compete against the best he had to start facing them without delay. He had already won the U.S. Amateur Clay championship, the Orange Bowl International three times, and been a collegiate All-American. So he set out to seek new horizons.

He found them, fast. Selected for the American Davis Cup team, Harold represented his country in matches against Chile and Spain in 1972, and both times won key matches in thrilling fashion. In Santiago, he fought fiercely against Chilean star Patricio Cornejo to fashion a 9-7, 4-6, 6-1, 3-6, 6-2, triumph that helped America to victory. Even more impressive was his win in Spain, where he defeated Juan Gisbert, thought to be almost invincible on his home court in Barcelona. American ace Stan Smith had been upset in the opening singles match, so Harold's tough win was crucial to the Americans' tight 3-2 defeat of Spain.

Gisbert played well in front of his adoring fans, but Solomon, with steely concentration, swept the first two sets. But then Harold was struck by agonizing cramps in his right hand; hardly able to hold the racquet, let alone hit the ball, he played the third set in terrible pain and was demolished 6-0. Darkness had set in, and play was postponed until the next day. Solomon spent much of the night writhing on the floor, trying not to scream in agony. The next day, beset by throbbing, vicious pain, he started shakily and lost the fourth set 6-1. But he clenched his teeth and made a supreme effort; the crowd cheered Gisbert wildly on against the injured American, but Solomon "toughed it out" and somehow managed to win the final set, 6-4.

"That was the most impressive effort I've ever seen Solly make," says Dennis Ralston, the U.S. Cup Captain. "I can't think of any gutsier player. As far as a guy who never gives up, I'd have to rank him No. 1 on my list."

Playing against top competition, Harold made steady progress. After having won only $38,245 in prize money in 1972 and 1973, he amassed $96,003 in 1974 and $113,425 in 1975. In 1973, he won two tournaments; the next year he won one but was a finalist in two others and a semi-finalist in another pair. In 1975, he was a finalist at Melbourne and South Pacific, and champion at Perth and World Championship Tennis events at Memphis and Toronto. That same year, he won perhaps the biggest victory of his career by taking the title at the South African Open. That victory against Brian Gottfried, another rising young Jewish star, was a characteristic win for Solly, as he wore Brian down with his relentless pursuit of every ball in play. He had defeated Gottfried in the French Open that year with a marathon four-and-a-half hour, five-set struggle when Solly saved two match points and won, so Brian knew what he was in for.

Solomon did a good job, and won much attention, during the 1977 open championships at Forest Hills. Jimmy Connors, Guillermo Vilas and Bjorn Borg were the major names. And Brian Gottfried was No. 3. For some reason, many of the experts thought well of Vitas Gerulaitis, a flamboyant and streaky player. But when Solomon met Gerulaitis, it was not Harold who yielded. Instead, Vitas broke. Jack Wilkinson of the *Daily News* in New York reported that Solomon said to him, "I didn't fell like an underdog, especially on clay. Going into the match, I thought the key was getting my first serves in and it paid off. I got every first serve in in the tiebreaker. I kept the ball deep. Then, when Vitas came in, I passed him."

Solomon won the match, 7-6 (7-3 in the tiebreaker), 6-3. It was a "bitter defeat" for Gerulaitis, according to Neil Amdur of the *New York Times*. Amdur observed that "Solomon forged his victory with patience and persistence, his trademarks. He also got seventy-six percent of his first serves in, compared with only forty-eight percent for Gerulaitis." Solomon told Amdur that he was very nervous in this match. "You play," he said, "in the French championships, before fifteen to sixteen thousand people, but it's not the same as playing before a home crowd."

Yet when Solomon met Vilas, the Argentinian won, as he had been winning from almost everybody in that year of success for him. To reach the semi-finals, Solomon had to win from Dick Stockton, a fine player and a longtime rival of Solomon's. Stockton had power, pace and speed afoot. But once again Solomon served well and played with consistency. Whenever Stockton had a chance to break Solomon, Harold fought back and won. In the end, he beat Stockton, 6-4, 6-4, 6-2. Amdur wrote that "Solomon was hitting with depth, moving to the ball well, and is competitively keener than last year when he was ousted in the first round after having exhausted himself in reaching the final of the United States Pro championships."

Following his victory over Stockton, Robin Herman of the *New York Times* wrote a feature on Solomon, in which she stressed Harold's stamina and ability to play long hours. She quotes his father Leonard as saying, "We don't feel Harold has played a good set unless he makes it last an hour. I don't care what the score is." At this time, Harold had won his first set against Stockton in forty minutes.

Before meeting Vilas at Forest Hills, Harold Solomon and his father both talked about the Argentinian. Solomon said that while Vilas was big and strong, "He gets tired like anyone else. I've never lost to him in three out of five sets. I beat him twice."

Leonard Solomon remembered the matches well. Both Vilas and Harold Solomon were nineteen years old when they met in the French open. Solomon won 3-6, 8-10, 6-2, 6-4, 6-4. His father recalls that "they literally had to carry both those kids off the court; they were dissipated." Leonard Solomon confided in Robin Herman by saying, "You have to understand this about Harold. He's a little guy. His forte is his strength. Tennis today has become physical, and he's reaching out to be as physical as the game demands." He pointed out that when two men walk on a court, "one's stronger and bigger" so Harold had to acquire the necessary stamina to win — and he had to develop patience.

However, at Forest Hills, Vilas played his hot hand and continued to win. He beat Solomon in the semi-finals and won from Connors in the finals to take yet another championship. By this time, he had won forty-six matches in a row on clay. Vilas took Solomon in straight sets, 6-2, 7-6, 6-2. Many of the games were long, and well-played, but Vilas was the better player that day.

"Solomon has the knack of disintegrating opponents," Lorge says, "tantalizing and mesmerizing them with soft stuff, then stinging them, destroying their legs and minds by hitting everything back until their shots go awry . . . The wear and tear on both him and his foes is considerable;

he lost at least four matches last year (1975) because of cramps, and won many more than that because his opponents were worn to a frazzle. Solomon has been called the Marquis de Sade in short pants. Just the thought of playing him leaves some of his colleagues glassy-eyed."

"Solomon at tennis," says Bud Collins in *The Boston Globe*, "recalls that great but unspectacular belly puncher, Carmen Basilio, who eroded the opponent on the inside, delivering the knockout tap only after his foe was hollowed out."

Despite his emergence as one of the world's top players, generally seeded in the first sixteen of any given tournament, Solomon's style, or apparent lack of it, has been known to draw choruses of disbelief or even contempt from fans and occasionally players. Solly has aggravated criticism with the use of one of his patented shots, the "moonball," a high, looping lob that more resembles a foul popup in baseball than a tennis stroke. Solly explains that he lofts it sometimes to break up his opponent's rhythm, but the technique so stunned Rex Bellamy of the *London Times* that the Englishman called Solomon "a danger to low-flying sparrows."

"Those who are charitable describe Solomon's technique as 'unorthodox,' " says Lorge. "Other descriptions range from 'inelegent' to 'grotesque.' He uses an open-faced, Western forehand that several coaches have tried to change, and that shovel-stroke, double-fisted backhand." And, of course, there is his weak serve. "It's improved, but not enough," says Ralston. "It's still a big deficiency . . . it hasn't got much on it and he doesn't get a very high percentage in. He tries to give a little kick on the second one, but it just sits up there like a piece of toast."

But no matter how untraditional his form, Solly knows how to win. "Even if his strokes are eyesores," Lorge points out, "Solomon knows how to get the most mileage out of them. He studies his opponents' strengths and weaknesses, knows his own capabilities and limitations, and plans his strategy accordingly. He realizes that only quickness and dogged pursuit of the ball can make up for his lack of reach and muscle. So he trains meticulously and stays in as good condition as many of the pros. Tactically, he is very astute, his hustle complemented by good brain-power."

A shrewd strategist on the court, Harold works hard to improve himself at practice, and realizes fully that he must take proper care of himself physically to be able to play an effective game. He neither smokes nor drinks. "You can't be out getting drunk or taking dope," he says flatly. "It's ridiculous for an athlete to do anything that might be bad for his body."

"The kid tries like hell," writes Larry Shane, sports columnist for the *Jewish Week* of Washington. "He's not strong, he can't hit with those guys. He would get murdered. He is a fancy boxer in with a blockbuster slugger. If he tries to play their game he gets his head knocked off. Harold is a defensive player."

Ralston does not entirely agree; he feels that Solomon's game, however awkward it may sometimes appear, is a lot more effective than many people would like to believe. "He can come in and hit an overhead," observes the Davis Cup Captain, "his volley's not as weak as everybody thinks, and his passing shots are as good as anybody's. He really belts the ball from the backcourt."

But whatever his technical skills, or lack of them, there is no question in anyone's mind that what makes Solly one of the best is the total effort that he puts into his game. In the course of a televised thrashing that Solly administered to Phil Dent, NBC broadcasters admiringly referred to Harold as "Little Dynamite . . . the man with the battery charge . . . the human backboard," and other, similar appellations. Don Drysdale, the Dodger pitcher turned commentator, summed it up: "He beats your brains out."

Ralston explains succintly why Solomon consistently beats players who may be endowed with greater natural talent. "You know Harold's never going to quit, that to beat him you have to be prepared to stay out there all day. Psychologically, that's demoralizing. You'd rather play somebody who's more emotionally inclined to throw in the towel — like some of the Europeans. You know if you win the first set they're finished. Harold's never finished until you've won the last point."

The truth of Ralston's observations could be noted in one of Solomon's finest exhibitions, his victory over the legendary Ken Rosewall in the final of the WCT Shakey's Tournament of Champions. The winner — Solomon — took home a $60,000 check. The finalists reached their eminence by surviving a long and difficult competition. They played in New York's Madison Square Garden.

Rosewell was forty-two and Solomon was on the eve of his twenty-fifth birthday. When Solomon was ten, he was a ballboy for Rosewall, but time alters men and this time Solomon won, 6-5, 6-2, 2-6, 0-6, 6-3. Rosewall, a master of the courts, lost the first two sets, and then began to move Solomon around, catching him off balance and confusing him with drop shots. "I got a little tired," Solomon admitted, and in the fourth set, he suffered leg cramps. If he were less determined, he could have quit right there. But he is tough. Losing 0-4 in the fourth set, he gave away the last two games, hoping he would regain his strength and lose the cramps. He held service in the opening game. For the next five games, neither player could hold service and then Solomon managed to hold his service in the seventh game and took a 5-2 lead. Rosewall was now exhausted and Solomon grimly held on to win. It was a remarkable match between two players who have the same philosophy of playing tennis; the positional game, the clever game, the brainy game.

If Solly never advanced further than he already has, he would have accomplished a great deal; but no one knows how bright his future may be if he continues to hone his technique on the court, improving his serve and adding new refinements to his game. One thing is certain: he will never lose for lack of heart.

What drives him to play so fiercely? The same force that drives artists, writers, and anyone who broods about the brevity and purpose of this short life on earth: a desire to be rememberd, a need to have made his mark.

"When I was a kid," confesses Solomon, "I would often lie awake at night and think about dying without anyone ever knowing I ever existed. Now, I think people would know I lived."

Yes, they will know. And they will remember him for the guts and courage on the court. A match that represents Solly as well as any other was the one at the 1975 Masters Tournament in Stockholm. He and Raul Ramirez faced each other after both had been effectively eliminated from advancing in the round-robin structure. The match was a meaningless one, yet Solomon exhausted himself in a tremendous effort and managed to overtake Ramirez, coming from behind to edge Raul and win the match. He was asked afterward why he had tried so hard when the result was of no consequence.

"People pay to watch us," was his simple answer. "We owe them our best effort every time out. A pro should have pride in his performance, whether it counts or not."

With Harold Solomon, it always counts; and consequently, so does he. There have been and will continue to be other players with stronger serves, flashier forehands, more dazzling shots, a finer net game; but there will be none with any more heart, or with any more of the gritty determination that characterizes the true champion.

BRIAN GOTTFRIED DISPLAYS HIS BACKHAND

Brian Gottfried

Reliable Star

As the game of tennis had been revolutionized in the 1970's, so had the men and women who play it. No longer is tennis the preserve of a ruling clique of Australian amateurs; the open era, in which professionals and amateurs alike compete together, has combined with huge financial opportunities and televison coverage to alter the game irrevocably. In 1972, a collection of young, ambitious athletes, most of them American, began to make their presence felt on the international scene. By the late 1970's, this new wave of players was dominating almost all of the countless tournaments being held all over the world on a year-round basis; four of the young stars, each in his mid-twenties, had clearly emerged as the cream of the crop. They were Bjorn Borg, the blond Swede with nerves of steel and consecutive Wimbledon titles; Jimmy Connors, the abrasive but gifted American winner of Wimbledon and Forest Hills; Guillermo Vilas, the Argentinian clay-court master with a poetic nature and deadly backhand; and Brian Edward Gottfried, an American Jew whose blend of natural talent and untiring effort made him one of the biggest winners on the international circuit.

As a young boy in Miami in the early sixties, Brian was seen playing by teaching pro Nick Bollettieri, who took the youngster under his experienced wing. Brian spent six summers working intensely with the pro on the fundamentals of the game they both loved. "I'd be out on the court with Nick every morning about seven,' says Brian. "It constructed the entire foundation of my game."

Gottfried learned quickly and well. In 1962, he won the national 12-and-under doubles championship (his partner was little Jimmy Connors) and the next year repeated his feat with a different partner (this time, Dickie Stockton, later a teammate and rival at college). In 1964, he added the singles title.

Brian's parents realized that their son's athletic prowess was something quite special. For his last two years of high school, they sent him to the Baylor School in Chattanooga, Tennessee, which boasted a magnificent year-round tennis complex and a professional emphasis on that sport. One of Brian's classmates was Roscoe Tanner, also a leading star of the future. In Brian's first year, Baylor was runner-up in the National Interscholastics; in his senior year, they were champions.

But Brian was far from happy at the tightly disciplined atmosphere that characterized Baylor; the militaristic aura was so different from the affectionate Jewish home life to which the young man was accustomed. "My whole life," Brian says, "had been spent in a warm, liberal-thinking, closely-knit Jewish family pattern where nothing was especially structured and an atmosphere of relaxed enjoyment prevailed. Now, suddenly, here's all this Mickey Mouse coming at me. I found it hard to cope."

He also discovered girls and the pleasure of partying, both novelties to the intense young athlete. "Why, I never even dated before I was sixteen," he told Shepherd Campbell of *Tennis* magazine. "How could I? I was always on a tennis court." He left school before graduation, but still took his final exams after the school year had ended. He was admitted to Trinity College of Texas, says Campbell, "with an interesting status: on academic probation but with a full tennis scholarship."

"Truthfully," Brian admits, "ever since my younger years in Florida — my bar-mitzvah and all that — I'd lost interest in academics. Even my choice of college was almost solely dictated by where I could best improve my game. I hit the books primarily just to maintain grade eligibility, but tennis was the only thing I ever truly studied."

He studied it well. Trinity coach Clarence Mabry spoke with his young charge, explaining that Brian would have to make a choice between playing around and having a good time, or devoting himself towards the goal of becoming a really good tennis player. Brian's choice was unhesitating. He played tennis, he practiced, and then he practiced some more. As an eighteen-year-old freshman, he won the 1970 National Junior Outdoors crown (defeating, among others, Jimmy Connors and Sandy Mayer), added the National Indoors (beating Mayer and Harold Solomon) and received the USLTA's Junior Sportsmanship Award.

As a sophomore, Brian was selected as an All-American, and played singles for a Trinity team that came in second in the national NCAA tournament. He returned to Trinity in 1972 and with Stockton, Bob McKinley and Paul Gerken formed one of the greatest college teams in history. That year, Trinity won twenty-seven straight dual match wins, and the NCAA championship with a record-breaking point total. Brian made it to the finals in both singles (against teammate Stockton) and doubles (with Gerken, against Tanner and Mayer of Stanford).

Even after later professional victories, Brian was still able to say that "the whole team effort still ranks as the most emotionally satisfying moment of my life. Even with some of my successes as a pro so far, there's still been nothing yet that compares to being on a spirited championship college team." Having achieved all he could at a collegiate level, and convinced that the only way he would improve his game was to confront world-class players every week on the professional WCT tour, Brian left college after his junior year and turned pro.

Brian rapidly impressed the experienced veterans of the tour. The twenty-one-year-old Jewish newcomer enjoyed a sensational first season, winning a remarkable $90,000 in prize money and playing on even terms against virtually everybody. He whipped Ilie Nastase in a startling upset to advance to the semi-finals of the U.S. Pro Indoor Championships, then won the WCT tournament in South Africa. His most astonishing feat came at Las Vegas, in the King Classic, which included virtually all the top male players of the time. To the amazement of most, Brian swept to the finals, where he met Arthur Ashe; and Brian stunned Ashe and the audience by routing Arthur, 6-1, 6-3. Clearly, a star had been born.

At the end of the season, Brian was selected by *Tennis* magazine as its Rookie of the Year. This feat was even more impressive, the magazine observed, because "the 1973 tennis season produced a number of exceptional rookies. Among them were Dick Stockton, Gottfried's hard-charging Trinity teammate, Roscoe Tanner, who has the most feared serve in the game, Harold Solomon, the doughty little Davis Cup star, and Vijay Amritraj, the brilliant and engaging young Indian. It was not easy to single out one of them as the best."

But even in that fast company, Brian was clearly something special. The great veteran Ken Rosewall remarked that "he has that natural ability. He swings loose and easy. He's a very under-rated player right now, but keep your eye on him. He looks like he's going to be a big winner." Rival Phil Dent observed that Gottfried's game had "no major weaknesses. He has solid ground strokes from either side, a notable smash and an outstanding volley."

What Gottfried also possessed was a quality as rare as talent, and that was complete dedication to his game. He developed a well-earned reputation as a devotee of grueling practice sessions. Neil Amdur of the *New York Times* remarked that Gottfried "holds the unofficial record for hours spent on the practice court." Campbell makes the point that "if practice made perfect, Gottfried would probably already be there. He thrives on practice, to such a degree that sometimes players he seeks out try to duck him because they know it's going to mean an extra-demanding workout."

Indeed, one of the most popular anecdotes about Gottfried is that he put in his practice time on the courts on the day of his wedding; and then atoned for missing his afternoon practice by putting in a double workout on the next day.

Once, when asked what he enjoyed doing, Brian answered, "Well, I enjoy playing matches." Asked to think of another pleasure, he responded, "Well, I like to practice a lot."

Brian's own comment is simple and deceptively modest: "I work hard because I think I need it the most. I wouldn't like to believe I lost a match because I wasn't in shape or well-prepared." Regarding his superb rookie campaign, he adds that "I learned a lot by playing against all those veterans. It meant not only building up my game but also building up mentally. I think that in tennis, developing mentally sometimes takes longer than developing your game."

For the next three years, Brian did well, but still seemed to be playing somewhat below his enormous potential. Technically, his game was a more aggressive serve-and-volley attack. But there were three areas of his game that needed sharpening: consistency, confidence, and imagination. His own personality was quiet, even phlegmatic, and his endless practice contributed somewhat to the seeming predictability of his game.

Sandy Mayer, an opponent of Brian's from the age of nine, says that "Brian just wanted to be a purist. He could put the ball where he wanted to anytime, anywhere, and it really didn't matter so much to him whether he won or lost." Sometimes Brian would drop a game to a player of lesser quality, and his style was accused of being "too fixed." Brian himself noted that confidence and consistency came together in a kind of cycle, and when he achieved one it would feed the other.

Always an excellent doubles player, Brian became half of the world's best combination when he teamed with Mexican Raul Ramirez in 1974. In 1976, they won the Wimbledon championship, and in 1977 the French Open. But Gottfried recalls the turning point of his singles career as coming during a match he had with Bjorn Borg during the U.S. Open at Forest Hills in 1976. It was in the round of 16, and Brian had not lost a set in the entire tournament. Though known for his slow starts, Brian flashed out to a quick two-set lead and was ahead 2-0 in the third. But Borg fought back, aided by a key double-fault of Gottfried's and Brian could only win eight games in the rest of the match.

"It was ridiculous," Brian confessed to Frank Deford of *Sports Illustrated.* "Here I was, up two sets and a break, four games from the match, and I honestly didn't think I could win. Whenever I'd get in a big match like this one, I just played to make it close. But losing that time had a big effect on me. Never again have I gone in against anybody thinking I couldn't win."

From that point on, Brian emerged as one of the best players in the world. He won his next tournament, defeating Eddie Dibbs, Connors, Nastase and Ashe in that order. The next time he played Borg, he beat him — and that was in Bjorn's home turf of Stockholm. As the calendar turned into 1977, Brian went on a winning rampage that made some people wonder if there was anyone anywhere who could beat the sizzling Gottfried. He whipped Vilas in Palm Springs to win one tournament, and went on to rack up other championships. By the time of the Italian Open, he had won no fewer than four Grand Prix tournaments, playing in seven finals, and an AP report said that "many have the feeling this could be his year."

In March, at a tournament in La Costa, California, Brian met Borg in the semi-finals and crushed the brilliant Swede, 6-1, 6-1. Fred Tupper of the *New York Times* started his story by observing that, "There is reason to think that at this moment Brian Gottfried is the No. 1 tennis player in the world . . . in 1977 he has taken three tournaments — at Baltimore, Palm Springs and Washington. He has won 32 of 35 matches . . . Gottfried was devastating today. Borg was unable to cope with the shots that thundered by him, baffled by the accuracy of Gottfried's placements."

"I feel that Borg was overpowered," said canny old-timer Pancho Segura, Connors' mentor. "He gave up hope . . . he lost to a better volleyer." In the finals of the tournament, Brian obliterated Marty Riessen, 6-3, 6-2, for yet another championship. "All of a sudden," wrote Tupper, "Brian Gottfried is the man everybody has to beat." Riessen rated him the world's best. With his fourth tournament crown of 1977, and his 33-3 record, he had earned almost $100,000 in prize money and stood in first place in the Grand Prix standings of tennis. But when Brian was told that he was now "the man," he responded with characteristic modesty: "Really? I just try to play tennis matches."

In April, Brian defended his Pacific Southwest Open championship, having won the previous year. In the semi-finals, he started slowly against the hard-serving Tanner, and Roscoe took the first set 6-3 and led 4-3 with a service break. Brian seemed out of the match, but he fought back gamely to break Tanner's serve and came back to win the second set, 7-5, and the third, 6-3. As he stroked a winning backhand for match point, the roaring crowd rose in tribute and cheered Gottfried's impressive exhibition.

As 1977 came to its final months, Gottfried's intensity seemed to lessen and he went far in each tournament he entered, but not quite far enough. In the United States open championship at Forest Hills, probably the most important single championship in this country, Gottfried fell short. He was ranked third, a tribute to his all-round excellence and steadiness. When he beat Wojtek Fibak of Poland, it was, as of that moment, the best-played match of the tournament. But then he lost to Corrado Barazzutti without much opposition, the scores being 6-2, 6-1, 6-2 in favor of the foreigner. Later, Gottfried reached the finals (as he usually seems to do), in the Southern California open tennis championship. He beat Eddie Dibbs to get to the finals, 6-2, 3-6, 6-4. But then he lost to his old doubles partner Raul Ramirez. It appeared that Gottfried was playing too much tennis and his own coach said, after he was upset by Butch Walts, that Brian was a slow starter who needed a great deal of practice to be at his best. Perhaps he was simply playing too much and too frequently. This may be true of many of the top tennis stars. Instead of entering a handful of tournaments a year, they seem to play every week. The human body cannot keep up this pace. Gottfried, then, was in a slump.

Throughout his mercurical rise to the top of world tennis, Brian has remained the same quiet, low-keyed individual he had always been. Comfortable in jeans and loafers, neither smoking nor drinking, he is content to constantly improve his imposing game, play steadily, and travel to tournaments around the world with his wife Windy, whom he met at Trinity University. Gottfried is already one of the brightest stars in the game, but he knows full well that it is just as hard, or even harder, to stay at the top as it is to get there.

In an interview with Amdur, Windy summed up her husband's dedication and tenacity. "I'll sit with other wives during matches," she explained, "and they'll be watching their husbands and say, 'Oh, he just gave up, that's it.' I know Brian won't quit. He never gives up, because he's worked so hard to get where he's at."

Scattered Stars

There are so many Jews in sports, that in choosing the outstanding ones, a sports fan has to be aware of many curious and sometimes little-known areas of sport. For example, what impression does bullfighting make on the American public? The answer is probably, "No impression at all." Yet Sidney Franklin was a Jewish star in a Latin sport.

The section that follows is devoted to outstanding athletes who participate either in minor sports, or those who are the only notable Jews in major sports. For instance, golf is one of the most popular games in the country, or the world for that matter, yet Herman Barron, who won the most important tournament in the world in 1946, is about the only Jew who really excelled in golf.

For that matter, soccer has been the most popular of international games but it won a following and appreciation in the United States only in 1977. I* remember meeting Erno Schwarcz years ago. He was a leading important soccer organizer in the United States, after he retired as a player. Now a forgotten figure on the American sporting scene, Schwarcz tried, but failed, to bring soccer to the

*H.U.R.

American people, who remained indifferent to the sport, until decades later when Pele came on the scene.

In hockey, for instance, there have been very few Jewish stars, the most recent one being Bernie Wolfe, a good and competent goalie for the Washington club. The most outstanding Jewish hockey personality was Cecil Hart, who managed the Montreal Canadians to the Stanley Cup in 1930 and 1931. There were a handful of others: Alex Levinsky, burly defenseman of the Chicago Black Hawks of the 1938 Stanley Cup winners; Sam Rothschild of the old Montreal Maroons; Max Kaminsky of the Boston Bruins; Maurice Roberts of the now-gone New York Americans; Hy Buller, who played with the Detroit Red Wings and New York Rangers.

Why so few?

The answer may be found in the fact that hockey is a cold country game, a Canadian sport, where there is lots of ice and one can play much of the year. In addition, there are comparatively few Jews in Canada and the best players start as juniors and work their way up at an early age. Most are uneducated men, and Jews do not generally fall into that category.

Soccer is another matter and its phenomenal rise is described in the chapter on Shep Messing. Nevertheless, one might, in passing, point out that the history of soccer is part of the history of Jewish sports activities. Among the most notable soccer squads of all time have been a number of all-Jewish teams. Teams from Palestine and, later, Israel have also come to the United States. In the late 1940's, the Palestinian Hapoel arrived on a goodwill tour and attracted 40,000 persons into Yankee Stadium. Many of the players had escaped from German concentration camps and the sports pages were full of human interest stories about the athletes. When Hapoel returned to what was then still Palestine, American sports fans cheered the athletes heartily. After the establishment of Israel, other soccer teams visited America and received a warm welcome on these shores.

Then there was the Hakoah team, originally called Hakoah-Vienna, for this all-Jewish team was the championship team of Austria in 1924-1926 and 1928-1929. Hakoah toured many lands, including Palestine in 1923 and the United States in 1926. The appeal of Hakoah in the United States was startling. Until Hakoah arrived, not more than 16,000 people came to see a soccer game in the United States. Hakoah attracted crowds of 26,000 and 46,000 to put soccer on the big time map — for a short time. Only fifty years later did soccer come into its own in the United States, with the aid of professional teams, international stars and the financial backing of major American business corporations.

The Jewish team toured the country and drew great crowds everywhere. Hakoah played ten games in the United States and won most of them. Their style of play, their speed and skill won them great acclaim. Among the Hakoah stars were Alexander Fabian, Alex Neufeld, Moritz Haeusler, Leo Drucker, Ziggy Whortman, Bela Guttman and Erno Schwarcz. They were so admired that the following year Hakoah returned to America and stayed permanently. The stars were grabbed up by various American clubs. Needless to say, these teams were immeasurably strengthened by the addition of the Viennese Jews.

Erno Schwarcz was the top soccer personality in

America, and how he would have rejoiced over the present eminence of the game on these shores. He managed the New York Americans for more than twenty years and was the premier figure on the major soccer circuit in New York.

Soccer has been part and parcel of Jewish sports life and it is almost a matter of justice that Shep Messing, one of the key players on the championship New York Cosmo team, should have been a Jewish player who attended Harvard University and had a great deal to do with the popularity of the game after years of indifference to it in the United States.

There are many fields of sport which hold a tight but small audience of fans and admirers. Probably in proportion to the number of players, these sports have a numerically high number of Jews. But the literature and sports coverage of these games is not full; too few fans follow the games and, as a result, many of the heroics are carried out in near privacy.

For example, how many people in the United States pay much attention to fencing, to ice-skating, to wrestling or swimming, except in Olympic Game years? Take bowling. It is true that it is one of the most popular participation sports in the land. But bowling does not win newspaper headlines and — but for an exception or two — who knows the names of top bowlers?

One was Max Stein, who in 1937 won national recognition when he won all the events at the American Bowling Congress. He made a record-breaking score of 2070. In 1919, Mort Lindsey became a top-notch bowler and was one of the original eleven men named to the American Bowling Congress Hall of Fame in 1941. A woman named

Sylvia Wene was the "Woman Bowler of the Year" in 1955 and 1960.

Ice-skating is, of course, a seasonal sport, and one does not belittle it in saying that it is truly a "minor" sport. Nevertheless, Irving Jaffee, who was an Olympic winner and made a professional living out of his skating magic, attained major prominence, for a while, on the American sporting scene. His story, told within these pages, is exciting and inspirational.

Professional wrestling has never been taken seriously as a sport in the United States. In the 1920's and 1930's, when Jim Londos cavorted on the mat, it was a popular "exhibition." Amateur wrestling, on the other hand, is a skill and an art. It is not flamboyant, but it is a tough sport which makes enormous demands on the body. Henry Wittenberg was the best of them all and deserves special attention in this book. There have been other wrestlers, but none as overwhelming or as impressive as the former New York City policeman who demonstrated awesome strength and skill as a wrestler.

The history of track and field has been replete with Jewish names. Harold Abrahams, a British Jew, won a gold medal for Great Britain in the Olympic Games of 1924 in the 100-meter race. Lillian Copeland four years later won a silver medal for the United States for throwing the discus and in 1932 she won the gold medal in the same event. As long ago as the 1906 Olympics, Hugo Friend brought home to the United States a bronze medal for the long-jump and Gary Gubner, who attended New York University, was a remarkably successful shotputter and discus thrower. He represented the U.S. in many international meets and, while he won many impressive victories, injuries made it difficult for him to compete at his best during the Olympic year of 1964 and Gubner had no chance to set records or win medals for the United States.

Two American Jews have been legendary track personalities and, while they scored their victories quite long ago, their names continue to crop up in track histories. According to the *Encyclopedia of Jews in Sports,* Lon Myers "was the greatest runner of the nineteenth century." Apparently, he ran at a wide range of distances. He held American records from fifty yards to the mile. He won fifteen national titles, ten Canadian championships and three in Britain. He ran in the United States, in England and in Australia. In time, when all challenges had run out, he became a professional and was just as dominant as he had been as a great amateur runner.

The other notable athlete was Abel Kiviat, a middle distance runner who won a silver medal in the Olympics of 1912. He developed into a great indoor racer and consistently set records when he ran. He had shattered many records by the time the Olympics came around in 1912, but somehow he faltered in the big race and came in second, when an Englishman stormed to the tape ahead of him. He continued running until World War I cut short many track and field competitions. But Kiviat kept running when he served in the American army and in the early 1920's was a college track coach.

Another city game is handball, which gets little attention in the sports pages, although its competitors are intense and very serious about the game. Just as basketball became an urban sport because it was easy to play the game in schoolyards, so did handball become a big city game, with Jews in the forefront of the sport. Two of the biggest names in handball have been those of Vic Hershkowitz and Jimmy Jacobs. It is said that Hershkowitz was the finest player the game had ever seen. And the records bear this out, for Hershkowitz won at least thirty national championships. Jacobs, who later became famous as the man who exhibited documentary films of the great prize fights, followed Hershkowitz as the best handball player in the world.

Of course, there are no Jewish horses. Nevertheless, there have been quite a few Jews connected with the turf sport. Because horse racing is mainly a gambler's game, one cannot write about it in the way one can describe a match between two baseball teams, or football teams, or boxers. Still, much is worth noting.

Two of the best trainers in the sport were Jews, and their names were nearly alike. One was Max Hirsch and the other was Hirsch Jacobs. Both men saddled more winners than anyone else, and many of the most famous horses in turf history were trained, coaxed and built up by these two men. In 1947, Stymie, which became one of the top money winners of all time, was originally bought by Hirsch Jacobs for $1,500, which is only an indication of what a smart horse expert he was.

Another oddity is that in 1936 the Kentucky Derby was, in effect, a Jewish "sweep." Bold Venture was the winner, owned by Morton Schwartz, trained by Max Hirsch and ridden by Ira Hanford. All the human beings involved in this horse racing victory were Jews. Sometimes we suspect that Bold Venture was Jewish that day, too!

There also have been a number of important, victorious Jewish jockeys. Willie Harmatz, who rode for twenty years, was inducted into the Jewish Sports Hall of Fame.

Upon his induction, reporters talked with him about his career, in which he brought home some nineteen hundred winners. He reflected that, "I don't know why there have been so few Jewish jockeys. In recent years I guess Walter Blum and I were the only successful ones." Blum won the George Woolf Award in 1964, an honor given to the rider who has reflected credit on the profession. Harmatz won the same award a few years earlier and had the exciting experience of riding the Preakness winner — Royal Orbit — in 1959. Other Jewish jockeys included Sammy and Joie Renick, Charley Rosengarten and Eddy Litzenberger.

The best Jewish jockey of them all was Walter Miller, a member of Jockey's Hall of Fame and considered one of the best riders of all time. While Miller is now more or less forgotten, he has entered the record books of racing as a remarkable jockey. During one four-year period, he mounted more than a thousand winners, while most jockeys did not get half as many rides in that same four-year stretch. He worked the tracks in the early years of this century and in 1906 became the first jockey to ride more than three hundred winners in a given year. He hit a smashing mark of three hundred and eighty-eight winners. The next year he almost repeated that astonishing record with three hundred and thirty-four winners. A Jockey Hall of Fame official is quoted in the *Encyclopedia of Jews in Sports* as saying, "The incredible thing about Miller's records is that they were accomplished in the days of six and seven race cards and abbreviated racing seasons."

Of course there have been many Jewish race horse owners but as they were themselves far from athletes, no space need be given to them, except to mention that the name of August Belmont is a major name in racing annals.

He was the first president of the American Jockey Club, founded various racing parks and Belmont Park and the Belmont Stakes are named after him. A banker, Belmont had little to do with the Jewish community in which he lived.

Obviously, swimming is an amateur sport, for there is hardly any way in which speedy swimmers can translate their skills into commercial importance. So the history of swimming revolves around the Olympic Games. As most swimmers mature quickly and fade just as rapidly (and their records vanish just as quickly), few make a major impact on the American or world sports scene. One phenomenal swimmer became, overnight, a world-famous swimmer. He is Mark Spitz, winner of seven Olympic medals in the Munich Olympics of 1972. It is ironic that as he set all sorts of records, he also was a center of controversy in an Olympic competition remembered far longer for the massacre of eleven Israeli athletes by Arab terrorists than for the achievements of any one, or group, of athletes. Also, Spitz had been the focus of anti-Semitism throughout his brief sports career. Yet under enormous pressure, in the shadow of international murder and tragedy, he managed to break all Olympic swimming records. It is worth devoting an entire chapter to the man and his feats, which *were* exploited commercially.

Close followers of the world of sports will notice that personalities in many sports fields are omitted. To write a full history of Jews in sports is beyond the aim of this study. The intention here is to write about leading athletes who gained attention, if only for a brief span. Thus a Jewish ping-pong player (and there are Jewish stars in this speedy and demanding sport) could be included for the record — but too few readers are interested in reading about people they never heard of, in sporting events they barely know about. The individual athletes in these volumes, taken together, form a substantial and fascinating segment of Jewish sports history in America.

Press Association

SIDNEY FRANKLIN ON A HOLLYWOOD LOT

Sidney Franklin

Bullfighter from Flatbush

"Of course I like bullfighting immensely, and feel a kind of voluptuous pleasure in fighting quietly, seeing the danger close at hand. I would not change that for any other sensation in life."

The speaker was Sidney Franklin, a thin, studious Jewish boy from Brooklyn, who became one of the topflight athletes in one of the most dangerous, spectacular and cruel sports in the world — bullfighting.

Always considered a Latin sport, bullfighting is curiously un-American. It is a colorful sport, the national pastime of Spain and Mexico. Champion bullfights in these lands are worshipped by excitable and noisy fans. Men like Juan Belmonte become legends and their feats are related in song and story. They make fortunes. Belmonte used to get $7,000 for a single performance in the bull ring and a smart bullfighter, if he promoted his own shows, sometimes made as much as $40,000 in a single afternoon. For example, Belmonte, about whom lyrical books of praise have been written, made more money in his career than Jack Dempsey and Gene Tunney combined. Rodolfo Gaona, the star matador in Mexico, made four million dollars in six years. This is enough to indicate the hold of the sport on millions of people. But bullfighting has fascinated many Americans as well. Ernest Hemingway, the famous novelist, has written a book called *Death in the Afternoon,* which is actually a handbook of bullfighting. And in many of his novels and short stories his heroes are bullfighters.

Writing in *Death in the Afternoon* on Sidney Franklin, Hemingway said, "Franklin is brave with a cold, serene and intelligent valor but instead of being awkward and ignorant he is one of the most skillful, graceful and slow manipulators of a cape fighting today . . . He is a better, more scientific, more intelligent, and more finished matador than all but about six of the full matadors in Spain today and the bullfighters know it and have the utmost respect for him."

Why is the sport so fascinating? For one thing it offers sudden death in the ring. It is said that a matador has a six-year career. For two years he is on his way up to the top ranks. For two more years he is at his peak and then he goes downhill. This process also takes about two years, and often the end is death. The bulls are rough and tough and they play for keeps. In America auto racing is the only sport which offers death as one of its possible thrills. And the major races are always jampacked with people. It seems that danger in sport is always attractive to an audience which remains out of peril while watching daring men play for high stakes with their lives in balance.

Sidney Franklin attended Columbia University and studied commercial art. He went to Mexico to study Mayan history and managed to see his first bullfight in the land south of the border. He was drawn to it and the attraction never ceased. He decided to make the sport his life work. His Brooklyn famliy must have been amazed, but apparently they got used to it, all six brothers and his two sisters.

In his own autobiography, *Bullfighter from Brooklyn,* Franklin wrote, "I have often been asked how I came to be a bullfighter; what there was in my background that led me into such a unique profession. Frankly, when I try to review my early life I am puzzled to find an answer to that riddle."

But this is how Franklin explained it elsewhere:

> "Bullfighting is just as dangerous as prize-fighting, but more interesting and more honest. There can be no crooked work in the bull ring, because you can't talk to the bull. You can't tell him to lie down, and you will divide the purse with him. You either get him or he gets you."

Before one can appreciate the feats of Sidney Franklin in the bull ring, one must know something about the sport itself. Here is how Sidney told it to an American correspondent, in the years when he was the sensation of the sports pages of the world:

"Armed only with the *capote de brege,* or large working cape, made of silk, lined with heavy duck, the matador attracts the attention of the bull, which charges. The matador waits until the bull is only a few feet away. Then he slowly extends the cape to one side and draws the bull by with it. Man and cape have been as one object to the bull at the beginning of the charge, but here is something moving, and that is the thing to be destroyed. So suddenly that the eye can hardly follow the change, the bull's charge is deflected toward the cape.

"Then comes a series of charges back and forth, on either side of the matador. A bull can turn more quickly than a race horse, so the matador must be ready for the reverse attack. But there must be no undue hurry on his part. Misjudgment of the speed of the bull's charge, or of distance between man and animal, may translate itself into disaster for the matador."

This is only a brief statement. The corrida, or bullfight, is much more complicated. Because the sport is traditional, Latin and full of the breath of death, it is loaded with superstitions and with customs. The critics and writers of the sport indulge in fancy words and write of bullfighting as though it were an art. Some of them consider the corrida a religion. And if you would stop to study all the terms in the sport and were to watch how things were done, with the marching and strutting of the athletes before the huge crowds, you would think that there is a very strong tie-up between religion and bullfighting.

Sidney Franklin, whose background is so different from the background which gave birth to bullfighting, overcame all obstacles and became a top man in the sport, after years of training. He made his big-time debut at Chapultepec, Mexico. This was like starting a baseball game at the Yankee Stadium. The break came to him after tedious years of fighting in small towns throughout Mexico. And then he fought in Spain, the big league of the corrida. He paid a heavy price, for he nearly was killed in his attempt to prove that a Yankee could make good at the Latin sport.

He faced a big, black wicked bull and after a few parries and thrusts, the bull's horn caught his gold-trimmed cape. In a few moments Franklin lay wounded on the sandy floor of the ring. The bull snorted and attempted to finish off the beaten man, but a swarm of men rushed in and saved Sidney. This, however, was only the beginning of the show. A short while later Sidney Franklin reappeared, bandaged up, woozy and hurt, but eager to fight again.

With a new sword and the cheers of the crowd ringing in his ears, he killed a bull and revealed that he had the kind of guts appreciated all over the world.

Although this was a bloody performance, Sidney did better later on, even if he was not cut up and wounded. In his first appearance in Seville, 10,000 fans idolized him and, when the fighting was over, carried him through the main gate. This is the sort of an honor paid only to great matadors and the performance which preceded the honor was indeed a great one.

Sidney knew that he faced a cynical audience, a crowd which had to be shown. After all, you can't easily convince a Spanish crowd at a bullfight that an American, a North American that is, can compete with Latins at an age-old Latin sport. But Sidney dispatched his first bull with a single stroke. That showed courage and skill and the audience sat back in their seats to see what else the young American had to offer. And Sidney showed them. He gave them a real performance with the second bull. He parried and sidestepped and generally displayed enormous knowledge of the game. A critic wrote, after the fight:

> "It is astounding the way he tackles the bulls, calling them with phlegmatic serenity, letting them rush into his cloak and pass along his body, without the slightest concern. This mastery he demonstrated, putting his cape behind his back when playing with the bulls with an art unequalled."

But this judgment came in the heat of excitement. It took many more years before Sidney Franklin became a real star, a fellow who could rank with the few top bullfighters. After many years of hard fighting all over the bull rings of the world, Franklin made his debut as *alternativo,* or main attraction, in 1945 in Seville. He killed two bulls with artistry, with coolness and with courage.

The spectators roared their approval in the Spanish manner. They called "Viva tu madre (Long live your mother!). Viva America!"

This must have been music to the ears of the long-legged Brooklyn boy who had come a long way to reach this point in a rough career. For Franklin learned, as all bullfighters must, that killing the bull is not the really important thing: it is that the killing must be done in style. It is not important to the general reader to know the difference between matadors, picadors and banderilleros, except that a picador fights the bull from a seated position on a horse and that banderilleros put harpoon-tipped shafts into a bull's neck to infuriate him and make him a more formidable foe. To Americans the sight of killing a bull, or the sight of seeing an angry bull gore to death a helpless horse is no fun. The fine points of the bullfight (like knowing if a bull favors using its left horn or its right horn, or observing if a bull rushes in a straight line or swerves while rushing at the cape) don't mean much to the North American who knows only that bullfighting is an odd sport which seems not only dangerous but cruel.

The preliminaries, the colorful trappings all seem like part of an ancient ritual which has outlived its day. Sidney Franklin often said that he hoped that the sport would become as popular as baseball in America. But it never will, for its elements are too basic and too cruel to win many Americans. It is interesting, however, that even in such a sport, which is a closed circle insofar as Americans are concerned, a Jew had become outstanding. It is difficult to understand why a Brooklynite who studied at

Columbia should become a bullfighter. But he has, and his story is one of the oddest in sports history and certainly one of the most peculiar tales in this book. The Kid from Brooklyn is now the Kid from Spain and the history of the bull ring is enriched with a new and strange legend.

IRVING JAFFEE, OLYMPIC SKATER

Irving Jaffee

Olympian Speedster

Speed skating on an ice rink is not the best-known or most popular sport among aspiring young American athletes. Traditionally, many of the great racers come from Europe, especially the Scandinavian and Slavic countries with their cold climates. Those Americans who do take up this specialized pastime are often from the West or Midwest, and are almost always All-American types from small towns. In this context, the achievements of Irving Jaffee were particularly remarkable. The Jewish boy from the sidewalks of New York fought his way past numerous obstacles, including racial prejudice, to become one of the great speed skaters of all time, a two-time Olympian and record-setter.

Ironically, Jaffee, like so many other young American boys, originally dreamed of being a hero not on an ice rink but on a baseball diamond. "I had my heart set on becoming a major league baseball star," he said in looking back at his life and career. "I was brought up in the Crotona Park section of the Bronx, the same section that spawned Hank Greenberg.

"We used to go to the park and play baseball. Hank's parents would look at him and say, 'there he goes, with his *shtickel holtz,'* his piece of lumber, his baseball bat. They didn't think much of what he was doing and my parents felt the same way about me then. We were good Jewish boys, supposed to be doctors, lawyers, and instead we were involved in sports."

Much to his disappointment, however, Irving did not have the extraordinary baseball skills that his buddy Hank possessed. But he made a determined effort before conceding that he was just not cut out for big-time hardball.

"As a kid I was ninth assistant batboy for the Giants," he recalled. "I ran errands for the regular batboy. That's how I got tickets for the Polo Grounds. I also pitched for P.S. 42, the same school Al Schacht pitched for. When I graduated I went to DeWitt Clinton High School. After two months I quit. I couldn't make the baseball team."

While the young boy worked on developing his athletic ability, he did his best to help out at home. The Jaffee family came to the U.S. from Russia in 1896. Irving's father sold cotton goods from a pushcart. Irving, born in 1906, was the middle of three children. When he was old enough, he helped the modest family income by working as a newspaper delivery boy.

The young lad did a great deal of walking, bicycle riding and roller skating, all of which built up strength in his legs that was to come in handy when he skated in later years. But it wasn't until he was fourteen that Irving developed an interest in speed skating. He began to spend time at the Gay Blades, a rink that later became the Roseland Ballroom, at Broadway and 52nd street. After he quit school, he became, in his own words, "a rink rat," hanging around the ice at every opportunity.

"I couldn't afford the seventy-five cents to get in so I cleaned the ice," he remarked. "Without even knowing it, I was developing a strong back and legs pushing the tons of scrappings off the ice.

"Actually, I was a freak," he explained. "They called me the 'Hothouse Champion.' That's because my background in skating was on artifical ice. I came to the sport at a relatively late age and had virtually no racing experience before I got to the Olympics. Another thing, I was a trail blazer. No Jew had ever made much of a dent in speed skating until I came along. As a matter of fact, few have followed me. In most countries where speed skating is popular, the Jewish community is small. And where the population happens to be big most of the Jews are in urban areas and not exposed to ice."

Not that Irving became an instant star right away. He found that as in other sports and endeavors, it took a lot of hard work to achieve a high performance level. At the Gay Blades of Iceland, he entered the weekly speed races and lost twenty-two in a row. Then he was noticed by Norval Bapte, one of skating's greatest stars.

"Bapte took a shine to me," Jaffee remembered. "I guess maybe he felt a little sorry for me, too, losing all the time. Anyway, he took one look at the skates I bought from Sears Robuck and said that the shoes were about four sizes too big. He got me a good pair of second-hand skates for six bucks and I was on my way."

Jaffee entered the Silver Skates competition in 1924. He lost decisively. Undeterred, he tried again in 1925, and was whipped again. But with gritty determination, he refused to be discouraged, and kept on practicing and working to improve himself, learning something from every defeat. Finally, the hard work paid off. In 1926, Irving won the Silver Skates two-mile senior championships. The next year, he went to Lake Placid and broke the world record for the five-mile event!

Jaffee's extraordinary performance at Lake Placid made him an obvious choice for the 1928 Olympic team. But prejudice reared its head, and Jaffee was at first denied certification for Olympic competition. He was not only an Easterner but a Jew as well, and those in the West who controlled the sport tried to keep the doors closed to him. "I was heartbroken," admitted Jaffee, "but I stayed in shape just the same."

The day before the Olympic team sailed, Jaffee was suddenly told that he could go along. With just twenty-four hours given him, he had to scramble to straighten out his passport and prepare his trip. As it was, his poverty had almost worked to disqualify even this haphazard opportunity. To support his skating efforts, he had at times been forced to pawn some of the medals he won in various competitions.

"The pawn shop put my medals in the window for advertising," he recalled wryly, "and the representatives of the skating organizations saw them there. I was given a chance to redeem them but I had to borrow the hundred dollars from my folks, and that took food off their table."

Free at last to compete against the overwhelmingly favored Scandanavians, Jaffee boarded the boat for Europe. But before he did, some former Olympians looked him up and told him that since he had no chance at all to win against the powerful competition, he should make sure to at least have a good time.

The remarks bothered the proud New Yorker. "I remember saying to myself that if I got this far I wasn't going to have a ball," he said grimly. "I was out to win."

He started with a world record in the mile at Oslo in a pre-Olympic meet; but when the Olympics themselves began, the competition proved sterner. Jaffee came in fourth in the 5,000 meters, which was the best finish ever recorded by an American at the distance. Then, having had to quickly adjust to the different techniques and rules of European racing, Jaffee entered the competition for the 10,000 meter prize.

The major difference in European racing was that instead of having the entire field go at once, racers were matched in pairs and competed against the clock. The man with the fastest time at the end of the competition was declared the winner.

In the 10,000, Jaffee was matched against Bernt Evensen, Norway's great defending world champion. For six miles, the two men matched strides; then, incredibly, Jaffee pulled away and won!

But bureaucracy found a way to deny the American the gold medal he so richly deserved. After a half-dozen races had been held, the weather became warm and the ice began to melt. The remaining races were cancelled. They were not re-scheduled, since the 10,000 meter race was the last event on the program.

Jaffee had posted the fastest time, and the best of the skaters had competed before the cancellation. He should have been awarded the gold medal. But the referee, a Norwegian, ruled the competition no contest, a decision that was without precedent. Jaffee protested, as did the International Olympic Committee; but the referee refused to reverse his decision.

That night, skaters from all over the world picketed the referee's hotel, demanding that Jaffee be declared the gold medalist. The outrage was so universal that Bernt Evensen himself was among the demonstrators at the hotel. American newspapers made the event a major news story, and U.S. citizens reacted with fierce indignation. Papers carried front-page healines that cried: NORWEGIAN REFUSES AMERICAN JAFFEE CHAMPIONSHIP and WORLD CHAMPION PROTESTS IN JAFFEE'S FAVOR.

Ironically, the injustice dealt Jaffee at St. Moritz brought him the support and attention he had never before received. Jimmy Walker, the popular Mayor of New York, gave him an official reception; and he was offered a job on Wall Street with the Curb Exchange that helped him support his family while providing him with the opportunity to perfect his skating. The Curb Exchange sponsored a skating team, and Jaffee vowed to win an Olympic gold medal in 1932.

But once again, hardship struck the Jewish skating star. His mother became gravely ill, and Jaffee stopped training and stayed by her for nine months. When the trials were held for the 1932 Olympics, he was seriously out of shape, and lost his first three qualifying races before finally succeeding in his final attempt.

"Actually," Jaffee said, "I skated myself into shape by losing the first three races. I remember a lot of people who were sorry to see me on the 1928 Olympic team yelling, 'The King is Dead,' before I won the 10,000."

The 1932 Olympics, held in Lake Placid, gave Jaffee the advantage of familiar surroundings and American rules. But the period of time leading up to the competition proved to be more grueling an experience than the races themselves. Some of his teammates hounded his training by taunting him with anti-Semitic remarks. When Jaffee ignored the vicious slurs, his teammates stole his mattress and spilled water on it. When he tried to sleep at night, they shone a light in his eyes.

But the tough skater from the streets of the city did not crack under this ugly harassment; instead, Jaffee's resolve only hardened. He stepped up his own training schedule, and promptly aroused the ire of the U.S. officials, who claimed he was a showoff not following the coach's instructions.

Two days before Irving was to skate for a medal in the 5,000 meter competition, one of his teammates forced a fight with the Jew. They agreed to square off in the ring. "It was the suggestion of Bill Taylor, the manager, who apparently thought I was going to take a beating," Jaffee recalled. "But I had spent a lot of time around Lou Stillman's gym as a kid and after two minutes I drew blood. Taylor stopped the fight immediately."

The night prior to the race, Irving slept not at the camp but at the home of a friend, to make sure of a least one solid night's sleep. The next day was the race. For the first time, the Winter Olympics were broadcast over radio. While countless Americans listened at their radios, Jaffee skated to victory in the race. He had finally won his undisputed gold medal, but he didn't stop there. Competing in the 10,000-meter event, he won at that distance as well and achieved a second gold medal. He was the only American who ever swept both events in a single Olympics.

In winning the second event, Jaffee triumphed in one of the most spectacular finishes in the history of competitive ice racing. Through most of the race, he established his own commanding pace, but not far behind were his two strongest rivals: Frank Stack of Canada and Norway's famous star, Ivan Ballangrud. The three men seemed to be in a dead heat as they entered the stretch run, and as they rapidly approached the finish line, it was unclear which would surge ahead at the last moment. Ten feet from the tape, the three were still dead even when Jaffee left his feet and hurled himself, diving, at the finish line. He slid across his stomach, barely ahead of the other two, and double champion of the world.

He came home in the full flush of victory. But after the parade on Broadway and the flood of congratulations, he found that glory by itself was not enough to live on. He struggled to find ways to make money from his achievements, but it proved to be rough going.

"There was some talk of professional racing but nothing came of it." he said later in an interview with Vic Ziegel of the *New York Post*. "I got $450 from Wheaties and $600 from Gillette. Their ad said, 'Be Sharp,' something to do with skates. I gave exhibitions at the hockey games between periods, skating around the rink five times for $25. I had no commercial outlet and I had no job. I had to bring some money home to my family."

The Great Depression swept America at the same time that Jaffee swept the Olympics, and money was tighter than ever for the new champion. So he did the only thing he could: he took his gold medals, which represented so much hard work and glory, and took them to a pawnshop. Together with all his other medals — about three hundred and fifty in all — he pawned them for $3500, money he desperately needed to survive.

Over the next few years, he kept thinking about the day on which he would have enough money to buy them back.

"In my mind," he explained, "I was getting a loan." Finally, with a job on Wall Street, he saved the money and went searching for the pawnshop in Harlem.

But he found, to his despair, that the building had been torn down. The gold medals, for which he had endured so much and struggled so long, were gone. He never saw them again.

He continued to skate, of course, for his own pleasure as much as for competitive purposes. In 1934, he smashed a thirty-year-old record for a twenty-five mile marathon race. Over the years, he has helped to train no fewer than ten U.S. Olympic competitors. "But the thing that still bothers me," he says today, only half-kidding, "is that I never made it as a big-league baseball player."

But he made it as a great American athlete, a courageous Jewish kid from the city streets who fought his way past poverty and prejudice in a sport not accustomed to his kind. And he made it in the biggest possible way.

Henry Wittenberg

Lord of the Mat

Mention wrestling to many people, and you will evoke images of the carnival shenanigans that characterize professional wrestling. This pastime is as much show business as it is sport, with huge men wearing masks and freakish costumes and comporting themselves in exaggerated fashion. There is a carnival atmosphere to these follies, and the competitors go through contorted acrobatics to make all their attacks look cripplingly fierce.

But real wrestling, in the Graeco-Roman tradition of the sport, is a sensual, complex sport. Competitors grapple for takedown and escapes, testing their stamina by going three grueling periods at full intensity. At the U.S. national championships, or at the Olympics, fans are given a taste of the power and excitement that can personify a tough,sincere match between two men who are out to outwrestle each other, not impress an audience.

Perhaps no sport is more primal, and more traditional, than wrestling, the most honored of the Greeks' manly arts; as long as the competitive urge has existed, men have wrestled. One of the most famous stories in the Bible tells of Jacob wrestling with the angel. But through the long history of this honorable pastime, few men have so thoroughly dominated their weight class as a Jewish cop from the East, who competed for a dozen years without ever losing a match.

Born in New Jersey in 1918, Henry Wittenberg never wrestled at all until he reached college, an amazing fact in view of his prowess in the sport. In high school, his passion was not the sweaty physicality of combat on the mat, but the cerebral concentration of chess. As captain of the team, he led his high school chess group to a state championship. But when Henry enrolled at City College of New York, he made a decision to engage in more physical sporting events.

"There are a lot of stories about how I began to wrestle," says Wittenberg. "The most famous is that I went out for the swimming team and the coach told me to wrestle in order to build myself up. That's not exactly true. What really happened is this: there were only two sports open to me at CCNY — swimming and wrestling. Both were winter sports and I had to choose one or the other. I swam a little but picked wrestling. I weighed only one hundred and fifty pounds at the time and had never wrestled before."

In his first competitive match, Henry demolished his foe and in the process broke two of the man's ribs. It was instantly apparent that the Jewish novice had a special gift for the demanding standards of wrestling. He learned and improved as he went along, and when he graduated CCNY with a B.S. in Education, he came in second in the national NCAA 174-pound championships. That was in 1939. It was 1952 before Henry Wittenberg ever lost another match.

"Everyone talks about Henry's incredible streak of never losing in National AAU Championship competition," says Walter Steinhilber, one of Wittenberg's early coaches. "But the thing I remember best is his first AAU title. I was coaching the West Side Y in New York and packed Henry, four other kids and myself into an old, beat-up car and headed West for the meet. It took us three days to get there. The boys were dirty, tired and hungry. We must have looked like gangsters. Anyway, we won the team championship, but it was Henry who drew the big crowds. He had to be carried out of the ring, and it wasn't in celebration. He hurt his back during his last match.

"There's no question but that Henry was the best," he continues in considering Wittenberg's entire incredible career. "He brought intelligence to wrestling. He could think ahead of his opponents. He was a planner. I know he once turned down a $60,000 offer to turn pro. He had too much dignity for that kind of thing. Wrestling today isn't even a shadow of what it was during the era of Hackenschmidt."

The Hackenschmidt to whom Steinhilber refers is George Hackenschmidt, one of the top three or four wrestlers in the entire history of the sport. George was one of the greatest of all professional grapplers, a legend in his own time, an athlete who commanded respect, even awe, in his chosen sport. And what did this giant in the field have to say about the Jewish amateur who never touched a professional dollar, who wrestled only for sport and the competition? Hackenschmidt's comment was simple and to the point: "Henry Wittenberg is the greatest wrestler I ever saw, amateur or pro."

Indeed, by the time he retired in 1953, Wittenberg had compiled a record that was hardly less than unbelievable. He won two Olympic medals in freestyle wrestling, a gold in 1948 and a silver in 1952; an unprecedented eight national titles, two at 174-pounds and six at 191-pounds; and two gold medals in the Maccabiah Games. In 1941, he was selected by the AAU as the Wrestler of the Year. In 1947 he was the runnerup for the Sullivan Award, given to America's outstanding amateur athlete. In 1949, he was named America's best Jewish athlete.

His exploits as undisputed lord of the mat won him a place in the Helms Wrestling Hall of Fame and the National Wrestling Hall of Fame, but Wittenberg had other accomplishments to his credit. He spent two years in the U.S. Navy, received an M.A. degree from Columbia University, and joined the New York City Police Department, where he remained for thirteen years (while still wrestling), rose to sergeant's rank, won five citations for bravery, and married a policewoman.

But first and foremost, he was Henry Wittenberg, the wrestler. "I got into wrestling almost by accident," Henry observes. "But once I got involved I had a great compulsion, a drive to win an Olympic title. My parents didn't like the idea at first. My family had no athletic background. But once I started to wrestle my father became my greatest fan."

In 1948, Henry at last achieved his dream of winning a gold medal in the Olympic games. He competed in the light-heavyweight division, and his alternate and understudy was Vern Gagne, who went on to an illustrious professional career.

"I'll never forget the final match of the London games," says Henry. "I was ahead for almost three-quarters of the bout. Then I ripped some tendons in my chest. I was in agony. But I knew I could win if I hung in there. I was lucky. I did."

Although Henry announced his retirement after collecting his gold medal, having achieved the pinnacle in his sport and wanting to devote himself to his police work, he was still tempted out of that retirement to compete in the 1950 World Maccabiad, where as usual he pulverized the competition.

"And then," he recalls, "a couple of months before the 1952 Olympics in Finland, my wife suddenly began a campaign around the house for a trip to Helsinki. She said it was a lovely place to spend a vacation. What else could I do? I went back into training. I won the national championship and then was injured and lost to Dale Thomas in the Olympic trails. It was my first defeat in more than four hundred matches. However, I reversed the decision and beat Thomas in the final tryouts and earned a trip to Finland."

In a gesture of admiration and respect for the gritty Wittenberg, he was chosen captain of the U.S. wrestling contingent. In the course of winning a silver medal, Henry whipped the fearsome Russian champion, August Englas, in a match that many felt was the highlight of the competition.

"Englas was the reigning world champion," Henry observes, "and I had never been able to compete in the World Championships. I just couldn't get away from my police work. A victory over him meant a great deal to me. Anyway, I was relaxed. I already had lost to a Swede on a decision. I had nothing to lose. I beat Englas and it was the first time an American had ever defeated a Russian in international competition."

After winning yet another gold medal in the 1953 Maccabiah Games, Henry retired from active competition. But he became a successful wrestling coach at Yeshiva University, and guided Steve Friedman of the New York Athletic Club to a 1961 national championship and a Maccabiah gold medal. Henry also wrote a book on physical conditioning, *Isometrics,* and had the pleasure of seeing his son Mike follow in his footsteps, winning two Maccabiah gold medals in 1961 as a wrestling star from Cornell University.

Wittenberg's colossal achievements remain on record for all to see: the Olympic triumphs, the astounding thirteen-year winning streak, the praise heaped upon him by the greatest of his contemporaries. While he reigned, Henry Wittenberg was truly the lord of the mat.

World Wide Photo

MARK SPITZ, WHEN HE WON HIS SEVENTH GOLD MEDAL

Mark Spitz

Seven-Medal Olympian

The irony was richly bittersweet. The 1972 Summer Olympic Games were held in Munich, Germany: and just as a black American, Jesse Owens, had humiliated Hitler's race of "supermen" the last time the Germans had hosted the games, this time the brightest of all the athletic stars was an American Jew. And in a tragic twist of fate, Mark Spitz and his phenomenal performance shared the spotlight with the brutal Arab terrorist massacre of eleven Israeli athletes in the Munich Olympic village.

After the murder of the Israelis, Spitz was whisked home to the U.S. under armed guard. Before he left, he stated, "As a human being and as a Jew, I am shocked and saddened by the outrageous act in Olympic village." But the vicious, senseless assassination, a cruel reminder to the world that hatred of the Jews is far from obsolete, did not entirely dim the dazzling and unprecedented achievements of the dark-haired, mustachioed marvel of the swimming world.

At twenty-two years of age, Spitz was rather old by the standards of competitive swimming in 1972; but from the very beginning of his life, he had always had a natural affinity for the water. His parents introduced him to swimming almost as soon as he could walk. Born in California, he was only two when his family moved to Honolulu.

"We went to Waikiki every day," Mark's father Arnold reminisced to a *Time* magazine reporter in 1968. "You should have seen that little boy dash into the ocean. He'd run like he was trying to commit suicide."

The Spitz clan moved back to California and Mark, at age eight, took his first formal swimming lessons at the Sacramento YMCA. At nine, he worked with Sherman Chavoor, who would later coach the women swimmers at the Munich Olympics, at the Arden Hills Club in Carmichael. By the time he was ten, Spitz held no fewer than seventeen national age group records, and practiced seven days a week, ninety minutes a day. When he skipped Hebrew classes to practice his strokes, his father explained to the rabbi that "Even God likes a winner."

Arnold, the prodigy's father, constantly urged the boy to greater feats. "Mark," he would ask, "How many lanes in a pool?"

"Six," came the reply.

"And how many lanes win, Mark?"

"One."

Mark's sister Nancy denies any excessive pressure on her father's part. "Dad didn't push him," she insists. "Mark did it on his own will. My Dad was just behind him all the way, helped him along."

"If I pushed Mark," Arnold Spitz said two years after his son's triumph in Munich, "it was part of his development — and you know why I pushed him? Because he was so great, that's why . . . Swimming isn't everything, winning is . . . I never said to him, 'You're second, that's great.' "

Mark's progress continued to be remarkable. In 1964, after three years of frustrated development due to his family's moving to another town, he came under the guidance of George Haines, the legendary coach of Santa Clara Swim Club, and qualified for the National Championships. The next year, at fifteen, he won four gold medals at the Maccabiah Games in Tel Aviv. By 1967, he was emerging as the dominant man in the sport. In a California meet, he set a new world's record for the 400-meter freestyle; and a month later, dominated the quadrennial Pan-American Games with five gold medals and two more world's records. He set three more new records before the year had ended, and *Swimming World* magazine cited him as the Swimmer of the Year.

Approaching the 1968 Olympics in Mexico City, Spitz was confident to the point of brashness. Entered in six events, he boldly predicted six gold medals for himself. But the meet turned into a disaster for the cocky Californian; although he did pick up a pair of golds as part of two relay teams, his individual performances were lackluster. His three individual events resulted in a second place, a third and one dead last finish. Spitz later told *Sports Illustrated* that "I had the worst meet of my life." In truth, the fact that an Olympics which resulted in two gold medals, a silver and a bronze could be widely regarded as a failure for Spitz clearly indicates how great a swimmer he had already become.

Many factors were speculatively raised to account for the star's disappointing performance, among them a bad cold, a lack of rapport with his teammates, and the pressure of high expectation. But Chavoor, four years later, spoke of one major element not widely discussed at the time: the problems of an aggressive, ambitious Jewish outsider competing in a sport long dominated by well-off, competitive Gentiles.

"Mark ran into a lot of anti-Semitism from his teammates at Colorado Springs after the Olympic trials," Chavoor conceded. "Some of the older guys really gave it to him. They tried to run him right off the team. It was 'Jewboy' this and 'Jewboy' that. It wasn't a kidding type of thing either. I heard it with my own ears. I remember one particularly brutal day on a golf course out there when it *really* got brutal.

"He didn't know how to handle it. He tried to get ready for a race and he'd get so wound up he'd come up with all sorts of imaginary sicknesses: sore throat, headache, like that. He was psyched."

After his misfortune in Mexico City, Spitz, having graduated from high school in Santa Clara, enrolled in predentistry at Indiana University, a collegiate swimming powerhouse under the canny coaching of Jim "Doc" Counsilman. Fully aware of the potential problems that might be caused by Mark's presence, the Indiana coach called his team together and asked them all to judge Spitz on the basis of present performance,not past reputation. Accepted by his new teammates and encouraged by Counsilman, Spitz rapidly regained his confidence and coupled it with a new-found maturity.

At the same time, Mark found himself increasingly at odds with his old mentor, Haines. Spitz felt that the Santa Clara coach treated him as though he were still an adolescent, and was more interested in scoring points in meets than in the development of the individual swimmer. They parted ways in August, 1969, when Spitz refused to compete for Santa Clara at the national AAU meet in Kentucky.

Less than a month earlier, though, Spitz had given evidence of his development both as a swimmer and as a person. In the 1969 Maccabiah Games, Spitz pulverized the competition and collected six gold medals. He could easily have had a seventh, but he asked the coach if he could withdraw from the final event to give his teammate, Paul Katz, a chance to win a gold medal. Spitz withdrew, and Katz won his gold.

At the 1970 AAU championships in Los Angeles, Spitz broke his own world record in the butterfly event, and Frank Litsky of the *New York Times* observed that Mark seemed to be "making a comeback at the age of twenty." Under Counsilman's shrewd guidance, the comeback culminated in 1971 when Spitz smashed seven world standards and two American records, won four national and two collegiate championships, a second *Swimming World* award and even the coveted Sullivan Award as America's outstanding amateur athlete of 1971.

All of this, of course, was preparation for Munich. The 1972 games presented Spitz with the opportunity to prove, once and for all, that he could beat the best in the world in the one meet that counted most. He qualified in seven events, but this time he avoided the reckless predictions that had helped his downfall in 1968. More mature at twenty-two, an inch taller at six feet and fifteen pounds heavier at one hundred and seventy pounds than he had been in Mexico, Spitz was ready this time. "In 1968 he was a young colt," remarked Don Gamril, an assistant U.S. coach. "Now Mark's a stud."

Spitz was the center of attention when he arrived at

Munich, as the world waited to see whether he would choke again in the face of Olympic pressure or fulfill the seemingly impossible expectations of his supporters. He cut a striking figure as the events got under way: he wore his dark hair longer than most of the closely-cropped swimmers, and his dark mustache made him easily recognizable, a "Jewish incarnation of Omar Sharif," according to a fanciful *Sports Illustrated* reporter.

As his competitors gloomily noted, Spitz was also blessed with the perfect body for a swimmer. "Did you ever look at Spitz's legs?" a reporter was asked by Jerry Heidenreich, Mark's American teammate. "He's so hyperextended that he can kick six inches deeper than anyone else. His legs are like a bow. When he puts on a pair of pants, the stripes on the seam go in different directions." Larry Merchant of the *New York Post* described Mark's "great body" as being "sleek as a fish," and *Life* reporter Bill Bruns referred to his "outsized hands dangling like sugar scoops" and "feet resembling built-on fins."

His first event was on Monday, August 28. Competing in the 200-meter butterfly, Spitz demolished his doubters by smashing the world's record and establishing a new standard of 2:00.7 in what the AP characterized as "an astounding triumph." Just minutes later, he anchored the U.S. 400-meter freestyle relay team to another gold medal and another world's record.

"I feel great!" Spitz exulted after his spectacular start. "I did my best tonight, I'll do my best tomorrow and the day after that — and the day after that."

Sure enough, on Tuesday he returned to pick up a third gold medal and a third world's record in the 200-meter freestyle. On Thursday, he set a new standard for the 100-

meter butterfly with a time of 54.7 seconds; and within an hour, he had anchored the U.S. relay team to victory again, this time in the 800-meter freestyle, as yet another world record fell by the wayside.

Spitz had now done what only three athletes in history had accomplished: won five gold medals in the Olympics in a single games. But Nedo Nadi, an Italian fencer in 1920, Willis Lee, an American shooter of the same year, and Anton Heide, a U.S. gymnast in 1904, were all about to be surpassed. For on Sunday, September 3, Mark Spitz won a sixth gold medal in what had been considered his most vulnerable event, the 100-meter freestyle.

On Friday, Spitz had hurt his back while frolicking in a mini-car at the Olympic village amusement area. During Saturday's preliminary and semi-final heats of the race, he managed to qualify, but was whipped both times by Australian Mike Wenden, the defending Olympic champion. Spitz admitted afterwards that "the back has been killing me. I knew what I had to swim to qualify and I did it — no more and no less."

In the championship final, Spitz rose to the occasion like the champion that he was. He set a sixth consecutive world record; his time of 51.22 seconds shattered his own former standard by almost three-tenths of a second. America's Heidenreich finished second, and Wenden could manage no better than fifth.

On Monday, Spitz completed his awesome achievement by winning a seventh and final gold medal, this one as part of the U.S. relay team in the 400-meter medley. Realizing full well that this moment of glory could not conceivably be surpassed, he retired from swimming after the Olympics.

Before collecting his last two medals, he had charcteristically given the assembled reporters one more flurry of excitement by speculating aloud that if he did manage to win the sixth medal, he might not even try for a seventh. "If I win the 100," he remarked casually before the race, "I might not swim in the 400. I'd rather win six of six than take a chance on six of seven."

Whether this was a serious thought or a passing comment aimed at throwing his competitors off-balance was never established. When the remark was quoted to Sherm Chavoor, who was Spitz's counselor at Munich as well as the women's coach, Chavoor replied simply, "If he drops out of one, I'll break his damned neck." Needless to say, Mark stayed in the final relay race, adding the seventh gold medal to the six he already held.

In retrospect, his achievements are truly staggering. Prior to Munich, he had set world records twenty-three times and American records thirty-five times. His seven Olympic gold medals still stand as an unapproached standard. Mark Spitz is considered by many followers of the sport to be the greatest swimmer who ever lived.

And all this, as *The New York Times* pointed out, "in a sport that generally attracts conservative, polite, middle-class Anglo-Saxon teenagers with the shortest haircuts in their schools. Spitz has for years been a standout, in the pool and out. He is the first Jewish athlete to make it big in the sport and his bushy mustache and his outspokenness don't fit the 'swimmer's image.' "

Indeed, it seemed that there were always people willing, even eager, to find flaws in Mark's character. Two incidents at Munich sharply illustrate the kinds of problems with which he was constantly confronted. Both revolved around Tuesday night's 200-meter freestyle event.

One of Spitz's teammates and rivals was American Steve Genter, a six-foot Californian who swam with a shaven head and a burning frustration at his inability to overtake Spitz in a race. Only a week before the Olympics began, Genter was taken to a Munich hospital and underwent surgery for a partly collapsed lung. The doctor, as Genter himself conceded, told him that the "worst thing I could be doing now was swimming." When Spitz went out of his way to speak to both Genter and his coach, expressing concern that Steve might risk permanent injury unless he withdrew from the competition, Genter was enraged.

"He may be the world's best swimmer, but he can't be my friend," said Genter bitterly, convinced that Spitz was trying to "psych him out."

"As soon as he found out that I was in the hospital here and still might swim, he went to see my coach and told him that if I tried to come back it might endanger my life. He talked to him for about two hours. It was really ridiculous," Genter insisted. "I couldn't believe it. Then he talked to me in the morning (before the trial heats) and said he didn't think it would be a good idea for me to swim because I might hurt myself again. Then in the evening he came along and told me he didn't think it would be wise for me to swim hard in the final.

"I just don't believe in this guy at all. Nothing would have pleased me more than to beat him," remarked Genter after his second-place finish in the race. "But I just couldn't do it."

The younger Spitz might have become moody or angry at the unpleasant incident, but Mark had grown up since

Mexico City. He spoke to his teammate again after the feud had been trumpeted all over the papers, and Genter emerged from this conversation with an altered viewpoint.

"I didn't know Mark's side of the story," Steve said apologetically. "I know now he was looking after my interests, but I was suspicious at first. Spitz is going to medical school — dental school — and has some knowledge of anatomy and he though it was foolish for me to go out at the risk of a recurrence of the illness. But he repeated it so often that I thought it was a psych job."

The upshot of the whole affair was that Genter, after winning the second-place silver behind Spitz on Tuesday, turned in a gritty performance on Thursday as part of the 800-meter freestyle team, giving Mark a 15-meter head start after heroically wiping out a seven-second lead held by West Germany halfway through the race. "His 200-meters today," Spitz declared afterwards, "was one of the most outstanding swims I've ever seen. Steve has to go down as pretty tough, especially after what he went through."

Genter wasn't the only person ready to assume the worst about Spitz. A second misunderstanding, of a different nature, directly followed that same freestyle race on Tuesday. On his way from the victory stand, Mark happened to be casually carrying a pair of old track shoes he hadn't yet had time to put on. As the crowd roared their appreciation for his latest record-breaking performance, Mark happily acknowledged the cheers by waving back, first with his bare hand, then with the one holding the shoes.

Reaction was quick and furious when pictures were printed that showed Spitz holding the shoes. "The scandal-mongers tried to have Spitz indicted today for innocently waving a pair of shoes." said *The New York Times,* remarking on the pettiness of the incident. One German paper blared that it was "impossible to advertise on the victory stand in a more obvious way." And Karl Schranz, the Austrian skier who had been barred from the Winter Olympics as a professional, was caustic. "I'd like to see whether Avery Brundage has the guts to go against an American," he sneered.

Silly as the incident seemed to many, the Olympic Committee felt it necessary to summon the startled swimmer for a hearing. Showing up in his U.S. parade uniform, Spitz explained that he had not been paid to promote anyone's shoes. No one ever explained clearly why a swimmer should have been asked to promote track shoes at all, let alone a scuffed and faded pair Mark had bought in Sacramento for a discount. Actually, Spitz had been signing so many autographs after the race that he simply didn't have time to put the shoes on before the medal ceremony.

He was, of course, cleared. "I'm already a Jesse Owens," he remarked lightly. "Now they're trying to make a Jim Thorpe out of me." All of this pressure, as *Sports Illustrated's* Jerry Kirshenbaum dryly observed, came from an Olympic Committee that had authorized the sale of Olympic postcards bearing the likenesses of various athletic stars. Ironically, the hottest seller was the one of Spitz.

Spitz also observed that when Swedish swimmer Gunnar Larsson waved his track shoes (a Swedish brand) at the crowd after winning the 400-meter individual medley, no one complained. "You know why they didn't make anything of that?" asked the American rhetorically. "Because he's not Mark Spitz."

But Mark took the whole incident with good grace. After collecting his fifth world record, Mark headed to the victory stand to receive his gold medal. As he walked towards the stands in his bare feet, someone in the crowd yelled, "Hey, Mark, where's your shoes?" Spitz just grinned and shot a "V" sign to the applauding spectators.

These two incidents demonstrate how marked a man was Spitz; but he let none of it interfere with his concentration, and his moment of glory remained untarnished. People could distrust, dislike or envy him, but no one was able to beat him in any of the races.

Looking back at his career during the summer of 1977, Spitz reflected on his identity as a specifically Jewish American swimmer. "I feel that being a Jewish athlete," he said, "has helped our cause. We have shown that we are as good as the next guy. In mentality, we have always been at the top of every field. I think Jewish people have a more realistic way of looking at life. They make the most of what's happening in the present while preparing for the future."

Whatever the future brings for Mark Spitz, his place in the annals of sports history is totally secure: as the greatest swimmer of his, or perhaps any, day.

BERNIE WOLF, HOCKEY GOALIE

Bernie Wolfe

Hockey Netminder

Bernie Wolfe was the only Jewish player in professional big time hockey as of the end of 1977. A competent, popular goalie for the Washington Capitals, Wolfe showed moments of brilliance with a weak club — and won consistent attention on the sports pages of the country's newspapers, with particular emphasis on the English-Jewish press, which found him good copy.

In June, 1974, the Capitals sent out a press release which read like this: "The Washington Capitals have signed All Canadian goalkeeper Bernie Wolfe of Sir George Williams University to a multi-year contract . . . The 5′9″ 165-pound finance major starred four years on the collegiate team which finished second this year in the Canadian CIAU competition, i.e., second in the nation. In addition to being named to the All Canadian first team, Wolfe was the Most Valuable Player in the CIAU tournament and was a four-time conference all-star. The twenty-two year old Montreal resident played international hockey against the USSR, Czechoslovakia and Sweden, for Quebec all star teams and an all star team from Ontario. As a senior, he had a 3.41 goals against average and a.910 fielding average (saved 91 per cent of all shots against him)."

This is how his professional career began. Clearly, he

was a fine prospect for the tough game of hockey and the toughest position on the team — goalie.

Wolfe worked his way up into the big leagues, following an impressive college career. The property of the Washington Capitals, he did not start with them immediately. Instead, the Caps sent him to the Maine Nordiques of the North American League for "seasoning." At the time, the Nordiques were probably the least effective hockey team in the pros. They had won only once and lost eighteen games. But Wolfe demonstrated that he had the ability to play the game and stop the pucks, no matter how frequently they were shot in his direction. In some games, sixty shots were taken against him, an enormous number. Yet he managed to maintain a winning record with a hopeless club. He won nineteen games, lost eighteen and drew one. He had begun with the Richmond Robins, but didn't play with them. It was with the Nordiques that he got his start. After his good showing in Maine, Wolfe was sent back to Richmond and again gave evidence of his talents in goal. As in Maine, he quickly became a favorite of the fans — a gift that trailed him wherever he performed.

The cry became "Bernie, Bernie" wherever he was playing. Early in the hockey season of 1975, Wolfe was a notable figure with the Robins. Jerry Lindquist, writing in the *Richmond Times-Dispatch,* started one story with this lead, "From the moment he joined the Richmond Robins last year, Bernie Wolfe became an instant hit with the gallery. The fans loved him, and at first you had to wonder why. What made Wolfe so special?"

Lindquist himself wondered. The team had had goalies just as good and perhaps better. He had a loose, floppy style, but so did others. He was small, but he wasn't the only small goalie the team had. Wolfe himself, in a lengthy interview with Lindquist, thought it was, in part, his style. Also, "I've always given one hundred and ten percent. That's the reason I'd like to think I've caught on with the fans." He added that "they always feel sorry for the little guy. They think 'geez he's out there with six-foot three guys and everything' . . . but I never felt little until I came to Washington."

When the regular goalie for the Caps, Ron Low, was injured late in October, 1975, the club called up Wolfe and in his first game, against the Kansas City Scouts, another poor club, Wolfe received the primary credit for a 6-2 Caps victory. A local Washington columnist, Alan Richman, wrote after Wolfe's debut, "Bernie Wolfe is 1-0. That wraps up the good news. He is not tall. He is not gifted. He is not fast. He is not coveted. But he is 1-0." Bob Philip, who coached him in college, remembered that "The thing about Bernie is that he's a clutch goaltender, he handles pressure." Michel Belhumeur, the other Washington goalie, had a 0-24-4 record in two years with the unimpressive Caps, so a victory had more meaning than it usually does for a professional team.

Although Wolfe lost his next start, the Caps decided to retain him, a decision understood by his coach, Larry Wilson, of the Richmond Robins. "He won't see Richmond again," Wilson predicted, when the Caps called up the diminutive netminder. Wilson said, "Everyone who sees him the first time says what a lucky goalkeeper he is, but he's more than that. He's got a lot of spunk, that kid. He'll stop the puck with the back of his head if he has to." Cap fans took to him as rapidly as the fans of the Robins.

Another man who took credit for discovering Bernie Wolfe was Billy Taylor, who was a scout for the Caps. He was accustomed to watching hundreds of games a season and he said it took him less than a full game to see the potential of Wolfe. The best Canadian youngsters develop in the junior leagues and those with college potential usually go to the United States. Taylor attended a collegiate championship game in Toronto one night and he liked what he noticed. "Bernie was in goal for Sir George Williams," Taylor said, "and by the end of the second period I had him on our negotiation list. There were other scouts there, and I didn't want to miss out."

Wolfe lost that second big league game to the Los Angeles Kings, 3-1. But Robert Fachet, writing in the *Washington Post,* said that the fans "saw two marvelous goaltending performances, by highly touted Rogie Vachon of the Kings and by rookie Wolfe." He added, "Wolfe, only 5-foot-9, made saves while lying on his stomach, sitting on his pants, diving to the left, right and bearings in between. He was given a standing ovation after just seven minutes, and more were to follow. Afterward, hundreds of fans gathered around the Telscreen interview area, cheering interviewee Wolfe so loudly that announcer Marv Brooks was forced to request quiet."

The *Washington Star* reporter, J. Russell White, felt that Wolfe's teammates played with more intensity and effect when he was in the nets. "It shouldn't really surprise anyone," White reported. "Special performers in all the games of sport have had a certain something extra that became infectious to others on the team . . . Wolfe's alert play has rubbed off on his teammates, who seem anxious not to let him down. If he makes the stops that are expected and adds a half dozen of the spectacular variety, the Caps figure they can help him clear rubber and protect him from the cheap rebound scores . . ."

After a few months in the big time, Wolfe realized that he was with a poor club and victories came extremely seldom. He performed well and kept the scores down, but the Caps remained a losing team. Nonetheless, he remained cool and continued to do his best. Some days, he couldn't keep the puck out of the net, but his teammates and coach knew that he remained steady in the nets, and, in spite of the high scores against him, was actually keeping those scores down with his agility.

They returned to Washington after a long road trip and, Russell White wrote, "Their constant heroes were their goaltenders, Bernie Wolfe and Ron Low." Coach Tom McVie said, "The Caps are the kind of team that makes their goaltenders the stars. Our two guys are always going to be busy, stopping shots." White said that Wolfe and Low were an "odd couple." This is why. "Wolfe, a rookie, is a Jewish boy from Montreal, college educated, articulate . . . Low is a farm boy from Birtle, Manitoba, with a strong back and large hands that have handled mud, muck and manure!" He also called Wolfe "the most articulate and well-read of the Washington players."

By the time the season ended, Wolfe had made himself a solid National Hockey League player. He had stopped eighty-eight per cent of the shots against him and recorded victories in some important games. He set the team record for consecutive scoreless periods and best goals against average (4.16) during his rookie year. During that year, Wolfe also became active in the Jewish community affairs in the Washington area and became the subject of frequent columns in the English-Jewish press.

After the season ended, Wolfe was selected as Washington's most valuable hockey player, but the 1976-1977 season started uncertainly for him. He won his first game of the year but then trouble developed in the course of a game with the Cleveland Barons. "One of the goals the Barons scored made me aware that something was wrong with me," he told Russell White. "I saw the puck coming all the way and I knew that I could stop it with a routine save. My eyes twitched and suddenly the puck had gone behind me. They had scored. I kept thinking about that goal for the next few days. What happened? How could I have missed the save? The next thing I realized was that my legs were giving out and my fingertips were becoming numb. There was something terrible going on. At first, the doctors didn't know just what when I went to them. The tip-off was when my eyes went. I began having double vision. The doctors knew then that I wasn't just tired. That I had to have something other than the flu."

Hospital tests revealed that Wolfe had an inflammation of the nerve ends. Complete rest was ordered and slowly he came back into shape and condition, but it was frightening, especially for an athlete. But he did come back, to continuing applause by Washington fans. In March, Wolfe again won the most valuable player title, this time in a contest sponsored by the CYO and the official presentation was made to Wolfe at a game with the New York Rangers which was attended by three thousand CYO members, coaches and adult advisors.

That same month, Wolfe gave an interesting interview to the *Buffalo Jewish Review,* in which he said only Jewish newspapers asked him about being a Jewish athlete; that "I don't think of myself as a Jewish hockey player," although he knew he was the only one then in captivity. He also tried to explain why there are so few Jewish players. It is, he said, "the way Jewish people are brought up. Jewish parents try to keep their kids away from contact sports. A mother doesn't want her son to go out and get knocked around. My parents let me do as I pleased." He reported that half of his fan mail came from Jewish fans and that he frequently had been asked to speak at Jewish functions. He said also that he did not face any anti-Semitism. That, he declared, is "kid stuff."

Wolfe told Abby Mendelson of the *Jewish Chronicle* of Pittsburgh the same thing about anti-Semitism. No, he said, there was no such problem. "Everybody's a professional athlete. You've got a job to do when you're out on the ice, and that's to win hockey games. Here everybody has winning on their minds and there are no problems at all."

Hockey is a fast, rough, violent sport and players do not last very long. Wolfe managed to be popular and good while performing for a weak expansion club that was working its way up to respectability. Such respectability as the Washington Capitals had came because Bernie Wolfe guarded its nets with skill, courage and fast reflexes. As the sole Jewish hockey player of his period, Bernie Wolfe has earned his niche in this volume.

HERMAN BARRON AUTOGRAPHS A PICTURE

Herman Barron

Links Master

Herman Barron has been the only top Jewish golfer in the ancient Scot-invented sport, which is one of America's major athletic crazes. On the surface, golf is a quiet game for middle-age players. Nothing could be farther from the truth. Golf is one of the most nerve-wracking sports in the world. As "Jug" McSpaden, a well-known golfer, once wrote, "The pressure is almost unbelievable. No other competitive sport holds a man under constant strain for six hours on end, as frequently happens during tournament play."

For a Jew, golf holds an even greater strain. Golf is a social sport. The golf "pro" is, frankly speaking, a hired expert, a man who must cater to his rich clients, on the one hand; and on the other, he must hit the tournament trails, play well, and win some crowns so as to gain prestige both for himself and for his club members who can then boast that they are taught by a champion.

Under such conditions, it is extremely difficult for a Jew to become a star personality. The fact is that Herman Barron was the only Jew to emerge as a golf star.

More or less brought up near golf courses, Herman Barron was a teacher of golf for more than half his life. When he was twenty years old he decided to look for glory. He remembered his years as a caddy around his home town of

Port Chester. He recalled his hopes and dreams for golfing fame. And so, in 1930 he entered his first National Open championship. This was the year Bobby Jones won everything in sight. Herman Barron did not stop him. The youngster finished nineteen strokes behind the great Jones.

For years Herman tried to win. He traveled all over the country. No golf course was foreign to him. His search for fame took him everywhere, but to no avail. For more than a decade, Herman Barron pounded the tournament trails. He had everything except those long drives which add distance to a golfer's strokes and lower his score to a winning margin. Barron was a clever player who knew his way around; but he didn't have distance.

Meanwhile, the old stars faded and new ones rose to take their places — and their glory. Herman Barron continued to teach at Fenway Country Club, in White Plains, New York. He was an admired instructor and he remained at Fenway for years. Nevertheless, the magic of tournament play continued to elude him.

In 1940 Barron, although long a teacher, was himself taught how to overcome his weakness. Byron Nelson, one of the great golfers of all time, and "Jug" McSpaden went to work on him and showed him how to increase the distance of his drives. This was something he needed, if he was going to win titles. He practiced and worked like a slave in perfecting his new swing.

In two years the work paid off. In 1942 Herman Barron won his first major title, the Western Open. His fine putting now stood him in good stead as he added long shooting to his arsenal of golfing weapons. He also brought to bear all the knowledge he had stored up while watching such golfers as Bobby Jones, Gene Sarazen, Mac

Smith and other top-notchers against whom he played in the 1920's.

In 1946, Herman Barron became one of the best golfers in the land. One of the major money winners of the tournament season, Barron was also the most improved tournament player of the year. He proved, in 1946, that you can be a Jew and star in golf, even though Sandy Kertes, Eddie Gayer and a few other Jewish golfers couldn't attain the top rank. Herman won more than $30,000 in prize money. He captured the Philadelphia *Inquirer* tournament and nearly won a tremendous prize when he came close to grabbing the United States Open crown in 1946. He blew up on the last two holes and lost. He played those holes in a thunderstorm and three-putted the short 17th hole and fizzed on the final hole.

In July, 1946 Herman won his greatest title, the $50,000 Tam O'Shanter, All-American Open. Everybody who was anybody entered this tournament. It took place in Chicago and more than 150,000 enthusiasts came to see the champion golfers play. The prizes, totalling more than $50,000 represented the largest cash prize ever offered in golf's history. It was played up as a grudge match between Ben Hogan and Byron Nelson, the two leading money winners and the stars who had both won this tournament twice before.

Paying no attention to the noise and fanfare, Herman Barron smacked a 68 to take the lead on the opening day. Nelson soared to 74 and Lloyd Mangrum, the Open champ, who beat out Barron in the Open tournament, straggled home in 79. Most of the big shots were far behind Herman. His golf was so hot that experts claimed he could have had a 65, if he would have been just a little more accurate in putting on the greens. But 68 was enough to lead the field.

The next day the competition grew warmer. Herman slipped to 71, one under par, yet retained his lead. The margin, however, was only one stroke. Ellsworth Vines, the former tennis champ, closed in when he managed to shoot a 69. Ben Hogan, whose opening day mark was a horrible 76, also came closer with a 70. Barron made the first nine holes in 34, which is good, but returned in 37, a bit off his own pace. He sank a ten-foot putt and made other good shots. Three times he stroked the ball into the cup in an under-par pace. His consistency won him headlines because in golf one bad day is enough to ruin a player. At this stage Herman held a one-stroke lead over Vines, 139 to 140, and seven players were from three to four strokes behind.

The tournament moved on and Barron held his lead with the desperation and tenacity of a man who saw fame before his eyes. At the end of the third grueling day Barron was further ahead than ever before, although Ben Hogan nearly caught up with the field. At the beginning of the final round, Barron had 208 strokes, Vines, 212; Hogan, 213 and Claude Harmon, a dark menace, 211.

Here is how Kerr N. Petrie of the *New York Herald Tribune* described the events of the final day:

"In dire danger of defeat today when he reached the turn in 38, two over par, and was overhauled by Ellsworth Vines of Chicago, the former tennis champion, Herman Barron of Fenway Country Club came back brilliantly and courageously in 34 and captured the first prize of $10,500 in the annual All-American professional championship at the Tam O'Shanter Country Club . . . Barron knew what was required of him as he began the torrid grind of the inward journey with what was undoubtedly the greatest gallery in the history of golf, 52,000, hemming in every inch of the fairways, tees and greens."

By the time the Jewish golfer had reached the 12th hole, he was all even with Vines. Although Barron was now playing brilliantly, Vines had also done well. At the 16th hole, Barron regained another stroke, but Vines' excellent play at the 17th hole was too much for Barron and the pressure remained with Barron at the 18th and final hole. Herman needed four strokes on this hole to win the title. He drove his first shot into the rough on the right side of the hole. He was left with his ball in front of a group of trees. Unperturbed, Barron played the next shot to the left, hoping to fade his shot around. Instead, the ball hit a tree and came back diagonally to the right as the crowd moved back from the path of the ball. The next shot was worth more than $10,000. If Herman brought it within striking distance he had a good chance to make the par four necessary for victory. He carefully studied the terrain. He measured with his eye the various possibilities. He lined up to the ball and hit it. The ball rolled slowly up to the cup and stopped within four feet of it. So far he had three strokes. Now he was four feet away and one more shot — if the ball went in — would clinch matters. Putting the ball unerringly, Barron dropped it in! He had won his greatest triumph. He withstood the terrific pressure which beat him in the Open, and here, with a great opportunity before him, he did not miss out.

The final count was 280 for Barron, 281 for Vines, 284 for Sam Byrd and 285 for Ben Hogan. Byron Nelson was sixth with 287.

This was Barron's greatest golfing victory. But from now on he was a rough man to lick. He did well in the PGA tournament a month later, but he was finally ousted by Nelson, although he broke par himself. In a two-day invitation tournament, with only five players, Sam Snead, Hogan, Nelson, Barron and Mangrum — all champions — Barron was behind winner Snead — but shot the best golf of the two days, with a 67, which was an improvement over Snead's pair of 69's.

In 1947, in the Westchester Open Barron shot an opening day 67 which was sensational golf. He played a near-perfect round and seemed to be well on the way to another major triumph. The second day Herman managed to garner only 68 strokes, to take a two-round lead of 135, three strokes ahead of the field. But at this point a spectator pointed out that Herman was carrying sixteen clubs, two over the number allowed by the PGA, and Barron was disqualified.

Herman was a member of the 1947 American Ryder Cup team, which completely overwhelmed the British. Playing with Bryon Nelson against Dai Rees and Samuel King, Barron and Nelson won 2 and 1. For some vague reason, when singles matches were played a day later, Barron was dropped and an American alternate took his place.

This, however, was part of the game. Barron had his ups and downs and a few years after he won the Tam O'Shanter, he quit playing the circuits, limiting himself to exhibition and match play around his native Westchester. Now and again, he broke into the headlines after having completed a fine round of golf, but it was obvious that he was satisfied to rest on his past accomplishments. They had, indeed, served to make him the greatest of Jewish golfers. When, on June 11, 1978, he died at Pompano Beach, Florida, at the age of 67, his contributions to the sport were recalled with respect and appreciation by all those who remembered watching his triumphs in the glory of his prime.

SHEP MESSING, SOCCER GOALIE

Shep Messing

Goalie of the Cosmos

No sport in the United States during the 1970's enjoyed a more phenomenal rise than soccer. The North American Soccer League, a pro circuit formed by sports entrepeneurs hopeful that their pastime might eventually make a major impression on the public consciousness, struggled through the early 1970's with minimal attention and straggling attendance. The American teams imported talented foreign stars, but the sports public greeted them with massive indifference. Even when the New York Cosmos team signed Pele, the greatest player in the game's history and the most famous athlete in the world, there was no immediate rush to the stadium; indeed, the team still struggled to fill Randall's Stadium on the outskirts of the city, a strangely tacky setting in which to display Pele, the crown jewel of the sports world.

Then, in 1977, something happened. Seemingly overnight, soccer was a booming, major sport, drawing huge crowds and national television exposure. The presence of Pele was certainly a factor, as was the rising popularity of the game among youngsters, who could play anywhere with only a soccer ball (needing no equipment, baskets, bats, sticks or arenas), and the hunger of television for another sports product to present to a willing public. But the truth is, no one really knows why tens of thousands of spectators poured into stadia in 1977 to watch a game they had always been able to ignore in the past.

In a sense, though, the suprise may have been not soccer's popularity, but the time it took to achieve acceptance in this country. In most nations of the world, soccer is easily the most popular game. The World Cup, held every four years (actually, the three intervening years are filled with elimination rounds to narrow the field to the final group) is the most closely followed sports event on the planet, and victory in even an elimination round can cause jubilation on a national scale in many places. National feeling runs so high in this sport that riots are quite frequent at games, and two Latin American countries even staged a brief war once that was sparked by a controversial game between their two countries. American citizens may have wondered whether the rest of the world was crazy, but the rest of the world marveled that a people could care about something called the World Series or the Super Bowl and not about the World Cup.

When soccer in general, and the NASL in particular, did soar in popularity in 1977, the league's flagship team was clearly the New York Cosmos. In most sports in the United States, a strong franchise in New York is considered important to the overall strength of the league, because of the enormous publicity generated out of that city; in soccer's struggle for recognition, a good team in New York was absolutely vital. After all, the initial natural audience for the game would be immigrants from other countries who already loved soccer, and where better to start than the great melting pot of the New York metropolis?

The tremendous attention given to the game in 1977 was

clearly related to the fact that the Cosmos were strong contenders for the league championship. Actually, they had won an earlier crown in 1972, but that was in the days when Pele was in Brazil and no one cared much about U.S. soccer results. But in 1977, the Cosmos squad boasted not only Pele, the nonpareil, but also Georgio Chinaglia, the tempestuous Italian star and prolific scorer; Franz Beckenbauer of Germany, the outstanding player in all Europe and the world's premier midfielder; Steve Hunt, the gifted and gritty English forward, and a number of other stars from various nations. But as the powerful team swept through the season and the playoffs towards the championship itself, they were sparked and sometimes saved by an unlikely addition to the group of established foreign stars: an American Jew from Long Island with a Harvard degree and no professional experience outside the NASL. Shep Messing was the goalie of the Cosmos.

Though a soccer game offers ninety minutes of continuous action with constant movement and no time-outs, goals are usually scarce and low scores are the rule rather than the exception. The skill of the goalie is crucial to the result: much of the time, he can personally make the difference between winning and losing. As the Cosmos marched to glory, Messing emerged as a true star.

As a schoolboy growing up in Roslyn, Long Island, Shep's athletic feats were registered not in soccer, but in more familiar American sports. As a trackman, he set a state record in the pole vault and could run the 100-yard dash in very fast time (both his speed and leaping ability contribute to his soccer prowess). He also played football before switching to soccer. He entered college first at New York University and then at Nassau Community College, but found himself dissatisfied; he transferred to Harvard, where he majored in social psychology (he claims he still uses psychological theories to outguess onrushing attackers in a game), kept exotic pets (including a boa constrictor), made the Dean's List and was twice an All-American goalie for Harvard's strong team. He was, incidentally, the first transfer student ever admitted to venerable Harvard.

Testing his soccer skill at an international level, Shep continued to distinguish himself. He starred for the U.S. Maccabiah team in Israel, and when he competed in the Pan-American Games in 1971 he was selected Most Valuable Player.

The experience of the Pan-American Games was an enlightening one for the Jewish boy from New York. Typically, Shep had as much trouble from his own staid, stiffly old-fashioned coach as he did from opposition scorers. Despite his excellent play, the American coach persistently chided Shep about the length of his sideburns, and his distaste for coats and ties. But the actual experience of playing in Latin America was eye-opening for Shep in a very different way as well. The astounding poverty, the manic enthusiasm of the soccer fans, the barbaric viciousness of some of the games, all left an enduring impression upon the young American collegian.

In the game the Americans played against the skilled and ruthless Cubans in Colombia, Shep found himself, along with many others, feeling the kind of chauvinistic rage he used to laugh at as the Cubans tried to physically intimidate and even injure the young Americans. Shep himself describes the scene vividly:

The same athletes who had nodded amiably at each other

> in the dining hall now lunged at each other with murderous intent. By some insidious psychological process, we had been transformed from players into soldiers, staunch defenders not of a small white net, but of the American Way. It was frightening.
>
> Had anyone told me beforehand that I'd end up shrieking "Viva Americana" like some jingo crazy, I'd never have believed it. But by the time the whistle blew at half time, I found myself clenching a raised fist and grinning at a guy on the sidelines who screamed, "Get their commie asses." That's what blood can do to a suave young liberal.

Shep's shoulder was ripped open in that game, but he had it stitched up at halftime and held the veteran Cubans to a hard-fought 1-0 win. Later in the tournament, the U.S. upset El Salvador in a tiebreaker when Shep distracted an El Salvador player by ripping off his goalie's jersey and waving it wildly over his head while screaming and ranting in Spanish and English, causing the unnerved opposition forward to miss the game's last shot.

Shep was not only selected as the MVP in the Pan-American Games; he was awarded the same honor in the American NCAA Championships when he returned to Harvard and led the Crimson to the championship game in Miami's Orange Bowl.

While still an undergraduate, Shep was considered so highly as a player that he was selected to the United States Olympic soccer team. Thus, he was a member of that team during the tragedy of the 1972 Munich Olympics, when eleven Israeli athletes were brutally butchered by terrorist murderers. Like the other eleven American Jews in the U.S. contingent, Shep had a guard posted by his door after the massacre. The event obviously shadowed his enthusiasm and excitement at being an Olympic goalie, and he recalls the period as being "both the high and low point of my life until then." In the competition itself, Shep was outstanding, and again had more problems with his own coaches than with his opponents. For a while Shep, as determinedly individualistic as ever, was benched because he would not cut his hair or wear a tie. But when he was finally inserted into the lineup against West Germany's powerhouse team, Shep played with brilliant flair, setting a record for saves.

Though technically amateurs, the West German team, which would win the gold medal that year, included the very finest players from the German national team, itself one of the world's strongest. The game was a hopeless mismatch from beginning to end, but the one player who caught the imagination of the awed crowd was Shep Messing. While Germany set an Olympic record with seven goals, Shep set his own with no fewer than sixty-three saves, an unbelievable number. He saved point-blank shots with his hands, feet, arms, chest and head. He stopped one with his face. He even stopped one with his back. Even afterwards, he admitted that he had trouble absorbing the magnitude of his achievement, and the staggering number of saves he had made in setting his record.

Five dozen and three. That comes to one every ninety seconds.

> It didn't matter that my hands were raw, my body bruised, my nose broken. I had set an Olympic record with sixty-three saves in front of eighty thousand people who understood soccer. Amidst the rubble of defeat, I found my own high at the Munich Olympics.

Then, a few days later, Shep was awakened by a thick, German-accented voice asking, "You are Jewish?" Shep related the incident:

I looked up into the face of a uniformed guard and for an instant, my blood froze, I was terrified.

It was, of course, the kidnapping and subsequent horrifying murder of the Israeli athletes that had roused security in Olympic village. Like so many of his fellow Jews, or fellow Americans, Shep felt waves of rage at the seeming indifference of the Olympic organizers — who insisted the games proceed as planned — and the lack of response even by some of his fellow athletes. One of the Russian soccer goalies whom Shep reproached for suiting up as if nothing had happened looked away at the ground and repeated softly, "Orders. We have orders." Shep left Munich shaken and disillusioned with the Olympic ideals. Every year since, he has attended a benefit dinner in memory of the eleven slain Israelis.

In 1973, Shep turned pro and joined the Cosmos. The young soccer league was struggling for attention, and a home-grown star was a welcome addition. In his first pro game, Shep made nine saves and allowed only one goal. He played well in 1974, too, but he also established himself as a controversial athlete. Shrewdly recognizing that a colorful personality was required to help sell an unknown sport to the American public, Shep comported himself with flair both on and off the field.

"You have to be a little nutty to want to be a goalie," Shep observed. "Who else would want to face a free kick at ninety mph?" Once, faced with an opponent taking a penalty kick, Shep abruptly ripped off his shirt, waved it frantically in the air and screamed at the top of his lungs. His startled attacker kicked the ball far over the goal. In an earlier game against Guatemala, he had torn off his jersey and tossed it over the head of an enemy forward. He showed up for some games wearing solid black, and spent a season wearing skin-tight shorts. He once even engaged in a glass-chewing contest with a football star named Mike Battle. "Goalies are always doing something weird to hang on to their sanity," Shep explained.

But behind the occasional wildness of his behavior was another factor in addition to individualism — and that was the grueling pressure placed upon a goalkeeper. A goalie has to be relentlessly alert at every moment of a game, but unlike his fellows, he cannot release his tensions by racing up and down the field. On the contrary, he must keep himself wound and coiled at all times, ready to spring instantly in any direction, all his energy taut and disciplined. Shep's antics provided at least a partial outlet for letting off steam; and some sort of outlet is necessary to avoid cracking under the endless pressure of being a semi-helpless target. In addition, soccer can be a rough game sometimes, and opposing teams are quick to physically intimidate a goalkeeper if they think he will wince at hard contact. Battles around the goal, which Shep calmly characterizes as "brutal," have resulted in surgery on his thigh, his knee, his elbow and his shoulder. But he continued to unhesitatingly stand his ground against his hardcharging attackers. "A goalie has to be fearless," he says simply. "If you flinch, you're lost."

Despite his evident talent, the Cosmos management had mixed feelings about their flamboyant young goalkeeper. In his first year with the team, he was fined no less than $1800 for varied offenses — an amount which happened to equal the total sum of his salary. After the 1974 season, the Cosmos traded Messing to the Boston Minutemen. "Talented but controversial," was the analysis of Boston coach Hubert Vogelsinger. "He'd show up at a press conference in a turban, in a lady's hat, in any kind of crazy getup."

The Cosmos were now aware of the mistake they had made in parting with the gifted goalie, and they labored to arrange a trade that would return Shep to New York. "Maybe they realized I was just independent and not an anarchist," Shep speculated wryly. Messing played the first part of the 1976 season with Boston, playing nine games with seventy-seven saves and an average of 1.30 before the Cosmos managed to steal him back on the 29th of June. Shep rejoined his old team with a flourish, registering four shutouts in the ten games he played. Against Toronto in one contest, he was bombarded by enemy forwards and chalked up fifteen saves, preserving a 3-0 shutout with his spectacular play. "He is the most improved player on the team," said New York coach Gordon Bradley.

Going into the 1977 season and the Cosmos championship drive, Messing had clearly arrived as a star in his own right. "A standout goalie . . . very steady on crosses," wrote the *1977 Handbook of Soccer.* "Messing relies on quick reflexes," said the *New York Post* during the season. "His play of late has been superb, especially in shootouts." *People* magazine observed that "his sixty-yard kicks and ferocious attacks on every round object that approaches the goal have made Shep one of soccer's most valuable players."

The Cosmos made the playoffs, and prepared for the first round against the Fort Lauderdale Strikers. Much emotion was involved, for Eddie Firmani, the new Cosmos coach, had been the Striker coach at the start of the season. And Pele announced that this would be his last season of active soccer, and his only wish now was to go out a champion.

In the pivotal game at Fort Lauderdale, the contest ended in a tie, and so did the first overtime; and so, in accordance with NASL rules, the next phase was a shootout. This innovative method of settling deadlocks reduced soccer to its most fundamental aspect — shooter against defender. Each team selects five attackers, and each of them in turn has a free kick with only the goalie in his way.

"The shootout . . . a phenomenon peculiar to the NASL, designed by someone who hates goalies," is how Paul Zimmerman of the *New York Post* describes the process. "Best out of five wins, when everything else is tried. You give a hotfoot forward the ball thirty-five yards from the goal, allow him five seconds to beat the goalie in any manner he chooses. The odds are 3-1 on the shooter. Except when Messing's in the goal. Lunacy evens it up."

"I do my yelling and screaming," Shep says, "my crazy stuff, when the guy first gets the ball. You've got to distract him, make him hesitate and use up some of those five seconds. Shake your head, wave your arms, yell at him — anything." While three of his teammates were booting the ball past the opposing goalie, Shep faced the attacking Strikers. Zimmerman describes what happened.

"The first shooter was Norm Piper, a nervous kind of guy. Messing made him hesitate and change his mind. Then he cut off the angle on him and the shot went wide. Next came George Nanchoff, a power guy, a gunner. Messing clapped his hands twice and charged. Foot, ball and chest all together. Then came David Proctor. He threw a fake. Messing didn't take it. The shot was deflected. Oh-for-three, which is like hitting the number three straight times at roulette."

The experienced Beckenbauer, experienced World Cup champion, raced over to the goalie and happily thumped him on the back. The legendary Pele led his charging teammates towards the goal, and the Brazilian immortal hoisted Shep into the air, publicly proclaiming him the hero of the hour. "When Pele ran out and grabbed me like that, I cried," Messing confessed later. "I mean here he was, running out there in his bare feet, like a teenager."

Having gotten past the Strikers, New York next faced the formidable Rochester Lancers. The first game of the two-game set was held at Rochester and nationally televised on a Sunday afternoon. Millions of enthralled viewers across America saw Shep spark the Cosmos to a tense 2-1 victory. Playing with a 102-degree fever, he stymied Rochester throughout the game and broke their spirit with three magnificient saves to quell their last desperate rush at the end of the game.

"There are a number of people on the Cosmos who believe the team has won its last two playoff games, both away from home, because of Shep Messing, Shep Messing, and Shep Messing," wrote Alex Yannis in the *New York Times* after the contest. "Having made three spectacular saves in the shootout victory over the Strikers . . . Messing was even better in Rochester and was named the outstanding player of the game. Messing's three superb saves toward the end of the rough game preserved the triumph for the Cosmos."

For his part, Messing was pleased that his teammates had displayed the grit to make up a 1-0 deficit against the tough home team. "We showed plenty of character in coming back, didn't we?" he asked rhetorically. "We have done that for two games in a row now. Don't tell me this team doesn't have the makings of a championship team." His mates were even more appreciative of Shep. "Shep is the best goalkeeper, no doubt about it," was the firm verdict of the seasoned star, Chinaglia.

But to qualify for the championship game, the Cosmos still had to beat Rochester in the return game in New York — and win the Cosmos did, thanks in large part to the cool, inspired play of Messing. After New York's 4-1 victory, Shep was voted the Most Valuable Player of the series. "Another fine game in goal by Shep Messing, allowing Rochester only one goal," marveled John O'Reilly of NBC-TV, and Shep confided to Marv Albert of that network, "Nothing will stop us now."

There now remained only one obstacle between the Cosmos and the coveted crown, and that was the Seattle Sounder squad they were to meet in the championship Soccer Bowl game. The game, described by many as "a classic," was a fiercely played, taut contest from beginning to end. It was shown over national television and to ten other countries, and played before a record crowd for a title game.

The first goal was scored by New York's Steve Hunt in the 19th minute, and four minutes later Seattle's Tommy Ord blasted a low shot just past Messing to tie the game at 1-1. That was the only time the Sounders were able to score on Shep. He made eleven saves while Seattle dominated play for a good deal of the game. With only thirteen minutes remaining in the contest, Chinaglia headed in a goal on a lovely pass from Hunt and New York led, 2-1. Moments before, Messing had made "a spectacular save," noted the *Times* in a front-page story the next day. After Chinaglia's goal, Seattle threw caution to the winds, and attacked Messing in goal with all their force and fury. "Seattle had several excellent chances," remarked Lawrie Mifflin in the *Daily News*, "but Messing made at least three spectacular saves." Again and again, Seattle was stopped by Shep. Then, with 7:10 remaining, Seattle's Steve Buttle muscled past the Cosmos defense and faced Messing at point-blank range from eight yards out. He blasted a shot at the right corner, but Shep dove at it and somehow touched it; the sound of the ball striking the post and bounding away was nearly as loud as the frustrated wail of the disbelieving Sounder supporters in the stadium. The game ended with the Cosmos still ahead 2-1 and Seattle still unable to kick the ball past Messing.

"Championship games sometimes are decided on key breaks," Shep observed after the match. "Today we created these breaks in a game that could have gone the other way. We proved that we can respond to the pressure." Like the rest of his teammates, Shep was excited more by giving Pele his crowning championship than by attaining one himself. "Right now," he confessed in a lockerroom roaring the Brazilian's name, "I don't even care that I won a championship, or that the Cosmos won a championship, but that Pele did. It's such an honor to be part of giving him this championship."

Shep summarized all his feelings about winning the crown and sharing it with Pele by saying simply: "I've never felt emotion like this in my life."

But while Shep's play on the field was outstanding, the prim officials who ran the team remained uneasy with his honest outspokenness and iconoclastic lifestyle. Coach Eddie Firmani, a capable tactician but a man notorious for his inability to communicate with his players as human beings, wanted a clause in Shep's contract that would forbid the popular American star to speak freely to reporters. Management made it clear they were looking for another goalie. Dick Schaap, the respected sports commentator on NBC television, addressed the issue on his show one evening:

> I'm angry because there's a report that the New York Cosmos are going to trade Shep Messing. Now outside of Pele and maybe Beckenbauer for his ability, no one has done more for Cosmos soccer than Shep Messing . . . He has done everything he could to make the game a success in New York and now that the game seems to be a success and was going to pay off, it looks like the Cosmos want to get rid of him and I think this is an outrage . . . Write the Cosmos, call the Cosmos and keep them busy talking so that they can't trade Shep Messing.

In alarm, the team's executives quickly shut down the switchboard in anticipation of the angry reaction they were likely to get from their fans. They did sign another goalie, and Shep, a free agent, signed to play with the Oakland Stompers.

"I reached the point where I achieved everything with Pele and the Cosmos," he remarked in an interview during the summer of 1978. "It's not like I wanted to leave, but I'm glad I made the decision to go."

While continuing his distinguished career, Shep also became an author. His own account of *The Education of an American Soccer Player* (written with David Hirshey) is a sensitive, perceptive, frequently hilarious account of an intelligent, gifted athlete who finds in soccer an opportunity to express his own individualism. He deals not only with the fascinations of the game itself, but with the experience of being an American Jew in a diversified international sport; the feeling of playing in local ethnic leagues where opponents occasionally tried to maim the goalie while screaming anti-Semitic epithets; and the sociological gaps between soccer players of radically differing cultures and countries.

Joining the Oakland franchise, Shep Messing was chosen as captain of the team. He became the first American ever to win a $100,000 contract in soccer. He joined Oakland with the best lifetime goals-against average (1.29) of any active goalkeeper in the entire league. He had emerged as a major star and fully fledged sports celebrity in a newly popular American pastime, an athlete whom rock music impresario Bill Graham described as "the Bob Dylan, the John Lennon of soccer . . . the first radical-hip sports hero."

The Bronx-born Jewish Ivy Leaguer had become more than a successful professional athlete. Shep had fully earned his place as an international figure who steadfastly maintained his own unique style and integrity in a sports world controlled by men quick to resent both. He had become not only the most famous, and perhaps the most skilled, of native American soccer players, but also one of the most engaging and interesting figures in the sport.

NANCY LIEBERMAN, A GREAT WOMEN'S BASKETBALL STAR

Nancy Lieberman

They Call Her "Fire"

In the decade of the 1970's, women's athletics penetrated the consciousness of the American sports public as never before. The enhanced opportunities newly available to women in various professions and walks of life were powerfully reflected in the arena of sports. Chris Evert and Billie Jean King, the tennis stars, were as well known as their male contemporaries, establishing an interest in women's tennis that enabled Tracy Austin to become a millionairess while still a high-school teenager. Olga Korbut's mesmerizing appearance at the 1972 Olympics almost single-handedly made women's gymnastics a popular national sport in America. Nancy Lopez became as popular as any man in the world of professional golf. Greater national recognition, as well as increased financial rewards, proved formidable lures to young girls growing up with dreams of balls, rackets and gyms instead of doll's houses.

A vivid illustration of the new opportunities afforded the female youth of America is the case of Sharon Shapiro, a Jewish coed at the University of California, Los Angeles, who not only won the all-around gymnastics championship of the AWIA (Association of Women's Intercollegiate Athletics) national competition, but also achieved the astonishing feat of capturing individual championships in every single one of the five separate categories. Sharon was, after all, a student at the same U.C.L.A. which was a perennial national power in collegiate football, and a virtual legend in basketball; in an earlier era, her accomplishment, stunning as it was, might not have received its proper acclaim. But with the rising interest in women's athletics, her feats were televised on national networks, where the nation had a chance to see this gifted young woman.

Those who benefited most immediately from the women's sports boom, were the stars of individual sports like tennis, golf or gymnastics. Certain team sports, especially those known for their rough contact, like football and hockey, were still considered largely the domain of the men. Basketball — a fast, tough game dominated in the male ranks by physically gigantic specimens — was no exception. Sure, there was women's basketball; but it was perceived as a slow, gentle, ladylike game, not to be compared with any seriousness to what the hardcore American sports fan knew as the game of basketball. Until the arrival of Nancy Lieberman.

Nancy Lieberman is a great player, but she is also much more than that. She is that sports rarity — a player who by her presence and skills has changed the nature of the game she plays. In a long feature article on her contributions to women's basketball, *Sports Illustrated* observed: "Nancy *is* women's basketball — the pioneer, the leader, the superstar, the finest all-round player of her game in the land . . . a case can be made for Nancy Lieberman as the most dominant player in basketball. At the women's level there is nobody close."

There are several elements that make Nancy uniquely special. First and foremost, of course, is her undeniable ability. She can do virtually anything on the court, and do it all well; she has played with outstanding distinction in both the frontcourt and the backcourt. U.C.L.A.'s coach, Billie Moore, who coached her on the 1976 Olympic medal-winning team when Nancy was a high-school teenager, calls her a "model player," and adds: "She is quick, very smart on the court, a good shooter, excellent jumper, very, very strong rebounder, aggressive, hard-nosed, very strong on defense. She just doesn't have a weakness. She does everything you can ask a player to do."

Perhaps as important as her natural skills, though, is her intensely fearless, competitive attitude. When her admirers claim that she plays "like a man," they are paying tribute to her considerable ballhandling skills, including the ability to throw a variety of flashy, tricky "blind" passes; her physical, intimidating defense; and her willingness to drive to the basket with a reckless abandon customary in the New York schoolyards of her youth but unprecedented in the previously genteel universe of the ladies' game.

The intense dedication with which she has honed her abilities has ultimately resulted in her being showered with virtually every award given in her field. A 1980 graduate of Old Dominion University in Virginia, she led the Lady Monarch team to two consecutive national championships. She was awarded the Wade Trophy for the outstanding women's basketball player in America in both her junior and senior years, seasons in which she led her team to AIAW crowns with records of 35-1 and 37-1. She won the Broderick Cup, presented annually to the top AIAW athlete of the year. She was the recipient of the Maccabee Award for the Jewish athlete of the year in both 1979 and 1980. She was named to every All-American squad throughout her college career, and was an integral part of United States teams that have won medals at the Pan-American Games and at the Olympics. The fledgling professional Women's Basketball League waited eagerly for her to graduate and become eligible for the pro ranks, in the expectant hope that her electric presence and reputation would help establish the widespread appeal of women's basketball.

All of this astonishing and unprecedented success is, of course, the result of untold hours, days and years of long, hard work. Raised by her mother (after her parents' marriage broke up) in Far Rockaway on New York's Long Island, Nancy found the tough demands of playground basketball a perfect outlet for her energies and ambitions. She played at the local YMHA, and all the playgrounds, often taking the subway to Manhattan to play some more against sterner competition.

She played and practiced, not only days but also nights: "radar ball," as she calls it, because when you couldn't see the ball go in the basket, you had to hear it. And always, she played against boys. In fact, she didn't play against other girls until her sophomore year in high school; and she acknowledges that that head-to-head competition against the men was the best possible experience.

"Just go out there and play every day in the schoolyard," she advises any young girls who might dream of following in her already fabled footsteps. "And if you've got a kid who looks good, then send her to an all-boys basketball camp. It will be hard — really hard — but she'll learn to play."

Nancy learned to play by playing — as often and as hard as she could. "That was the time of my life," she says now.

"The guys were always bigger and rougher, so I had to be mean and hard-nosed. I had to learn to maneuver around that pole in the schoolyard. I had to learn to take elbows and give them back. When I got better, I'd get chosen over the boys for five-on-five. When they lipped off about that, I gave them lip right back. I got in a lot of fistfights that way. I had to show them I could play and get respect, so they didn't ease up on me. It took me about two times playing against new guys before they realized I could handle myself. I learned all aspects of the game. When basketball season ended each year, my life ended too."

In season or out, though, she continued, always, to practice. When there was no one else to play against, she would dribble around the house, or practice jump shots with such abandon that she left palm prints on the ceiling. And she would watch and imitate the moves of her favorite players, notably New York Knick stars Willis Reed and Walt "Clyde" Frazier.

"I tried to imitate them all the time," she confesses. "I wore the same sneakers they did. I practiced lefthanded layups and hooks because Willis did them. Oh, and my backhanded dribble — I got that from Clyde."

And all the countless hours she worked, it never occurred to her that what she was doing was anything but the greatest pleasure. "I didn't know I was practicing," is the way she puts it. "I thought I was having fun."

When she started competing against other girls, her pace was as fierce as her competitive drive. On occasion, she would play a high school game in the afternoon, watch or play in another game later, then play in yet another team game at night (she was simultaneously in at least three different leagues at the time). It was in Harlem, while playing for an AAU team called the New York Chuckles, that she got her nickname: the redheaded white girl who always played with such burning intensity was dubbed, appropriately enough, "Fire."

"Nancy was the queen of Harlem," said LaVozier LaMar, who coached the Chuckles. "She would roar down the court left, right, turning, spinning, flying in the air. You know, getting it all done. Once the Chuckles scrimmaged some high school guys, and the guys were yelling 'face job, face job' at each other every time she did something. Everybody got to know the Fire right away, so nobody messed with her on the streets. I can't even remember everywhere she played up there. I'd have to look on the trophies."

All of this was a bewildering puzzle to Nancy's mother, who tried to discourage her daughter's basketball fixation by any means available, including the unsubtle one of once puncturing Nancy's basketball with a screwdriver. "She just went out and got more balls," admits Renee Lieberman.

"She was so pretty, gosh. People would call to me, 'Hey, get her out of the tree,' " Nancy's mother told *Sports Illustrated's* Curry Kirkpatrick. "I'd get her dolls, she'd want balls. My kid and sports, you wouldn't believe. I yelled. I screamed. 'I'll murder you. Stop it already. Sports aren't for girls. Why don't you be a secretary? A nurse? Put on a dress?' Nothing worked. She thought it was a challenge having everybody against her. She'd fight the world if she had to."

Nancy always thrived on challenges, and indeed it is in pressure situations in important games that her game rises to its highest peak, one of the marks of athletic greatness.

When I* asked her whether growing up as a *Jewish* female athlete had posed any additional pressures on her, she laughed and said, "Not really. It was enough of a rarity being a girl playing basketball." Still, she takes particular pride in being named the Maccabee Athlete of the Year, and pointed out with pleasure that there is a large Jewish community in Norfolk, the Virginia city in which she attended college at Old Dominion University.

Her initial arrival at the campus posed some predictable problems. It took a while for the brash, outspoken, self-confidently talented New York Jewish girl to gain her new teammates' full acceptance, but gain it she ultimately did; partly by her own sense of increased maturity, and partly by willingly sublimating her extraordinary individual skills for the sake of whatever would be best for the team.

"It's very hard when one person is getting all the recognition that a lot of people work together for," Nancy says now in perceptive retrospect. "I was never close to my teammates. Then at ODU I hadn't set foot on the court, and people were already retiring my jersey. All the girls had read that stuff. It wasn't fair. I didn't know how to react to them, or them to me. When we won, my picture was in the papers. When we lost, my picture was in the papers. It was awful. The first year the girls and I were just polite, the usual consideration teammates have for each other. But that was all."

Though a new set of increasingly skilled teammates joined her at ODU, and her first coach was replaced by a successor, Nancy came through the pressures of the team and of adjusting to life at a southern college, and did

*M.Z.R.

whatever was asked of her. In her first year, as a guard, she averaged more than twenty points a game and led ODU to a 23-9 record and a national ranking.

In her next year, the new coach asked her to switch positions and play forward, so she did — and again averaged twenty points in helping compile a 30-4 record. Shifting back to guard for her last two years, she sacrificed her prolific scoring to take on the job of quarterbacking the team, concentrating on playmaking, assists and defense instead of driving the lane for her swirling layups; and her success in this additional role was reflected in the team's two straight national championships and the two-year composite record of 72-2. The Lady Monarchs of Nancy Lieberman had become, almost certainly, the finest basketball team in women's collegiate history.

Nancy still continued to be one of the team's top scorers; but she led the squad in assists and steals, and by a huge margin in both categories. Every so often, when she was called upon to take total charge, she did, and with flair. When she finally achieved her long-time dream of playing at New York's Madison Square Garden, home of the Knicks, she scored thirty-three points, garnered ten rebounds and passed for five assists as ODU set a Garden women's scoring record, 106-53. But for the most part, she concentrated on raising the level of her teammates' play; and her efforts did not go unnoticed or unappreciated.

"Nancy is a super person, on and off the court," one teammate said of her. "She gave up a lot of her game to help the team from the guard position. And she was very unselfish, always looking for the open player."

"Nancy's quickness excites everybody watching a game," added another. "She really brings out most of the fans, especially to the good games where we have sellouts."

"She is a total court leader," summed up her coach, Marianne Stanley. "She controls the offense and plays great defense. And she is very unselfish."

"You can't put a dollar value on what Nancy Lieberman has meant to this university," ODU Athletic Director Jim Jarrett said, and his point is well taken. With Nancy's exploits gaining recognition and respect, the university was able to more than triple the cost of season tickets, and still sell four times as many as the previous year. Women's basketball started to be as popular an event as the men's games. The sport — thanks in large part to Nancy — had begun to arrive.

"The important word is PR," says Nancy, explaining that she enjoys her role as a representative of the women's game. "I know the media exposure I get reflects on the sport. The individuals have been accepted; the sport as a whole has not. Someone has to step in and be the representative."

Because of her dominating ability, her outspoken charm, and her gregarious good humor, the attractive redhead would seem to be an ideal ambassador for her sport. Certainly, if increased media attention and larger and more enthusiastic crowds are a criteria, she has been succeeding splendidly. In concluding her college career in a storybook blaze of glory, she anticipated with relish the new challenge that loomed ahead in the form of the professional Women's Basketball League.

"I think the WBL is fantastic," she says enthusiastically. "I would very much like to be a part of it." No more than the league would like her to be a part of it. Her charismatic personality combined with her consummate talents are just what any league most relishes. Nicknamed "Lady Magic" for a while, she was compared to the Los Angeles Lakers' Earvin "Magic" Johnson because of her crowd-pleasing passing skills and personal appeal.

"I'm flattered to be compared to Magic Johnson," she says, "but I don't do anything fancy deliberately. I don't play to the crowd. I'm not a hotdog; simply a fundamental player who thinks the art of passing makes the game more exciting. People think it's a flair. I believe it's just a part of the game that's just catching up to men's basketball."

To fully understand the value that Nancy Lieberman can have to her team on a basketball court, it is instructive to examine any given contest carefully to see the tremendous effect she has on the outcome, not only in obvious ways like scoring points, but in the kind of subtle court nuances that sometimes don't appear in a box score at all. Her final college game provides an excellent example.

The AIAW national championship game between defending champion ODU and second-ranked Tennessee was nationally televised. The game was close until about midway through the first half, when Nancy began to assert her presence. With ODU leading only 16-14, she grabbed an offensive rebound and scored her first basket. Shortly thereafter, she garnered another rebound at the defensive end and was fouled on the play; she hit both free throws. Taking another rebound off an opponent's miss, she drove the length of the court, only to pass off to an open teammate. Then she made a beautiful pass inside under the basket, her alert teammate quickly snapped the ball right back to her, and Nancy, now open, hit an outside jump shot. Two more Lieberman free throws gave the Lady Monarchs a 26-20 lead. She followed this with a spectacular driving rush past virtually the entire Tennessee squad, passing off to an open teammate for a spectacular assist at the last second. A perfect lob pass to center Inge Nissen provided Nissen with an easy layup and ODU with a 30-20 margin. Nancy's aggressive defense then forced her opponent to throw the ball out of bounds.

When Nancy finally went to the bench for a rest with her third foul, the television commentators were quick to notice how severely the Lady Monarchs missed her ball-handling, penetration and court mastery. Suddenly, ODU had trouble handling and holding onto the ball. Plays that had looked routine, almost easy, when Lieberman orchestrated them suddenly stopped working. Suddenly struggling, ODU managed only two more points, and the half ended 32-24.

After halftime — which featured Nancy, having been chosen to represent the AIAW, give a little speech on television on behalf of women's sports programs — Lieberman took total charge of the game, once again rising superbly to the occasion when the stakes were highest. The score when the second half started, remember, was 32-24. This is what happened.

Nancy got possession off the opening tip-off, drove to the basket, and missed — but, following her own shot, fought successfully for the hotly contested rebound, got it and scored. 34-24. After a Tennessee basket, Nancy stole the ball, drove downcourt, and executed a beautiful assist for any easy layup. 36-26. Again she passed to Cotman (the same teammate) for an open layup; this time Cotman missed the shot, but the rebound was put in by ODU's Donovan, who was fouled and completed the three-point play. Officially, Nancy registered neither a score nor an assist on the play; but, typically, it was her penetrating pass that set up the entire play and opened the ODU lead to 39-26.

The next play is also one that box scores do not count, but players and spectators note: a teammate lost the ball, but, as it was heading out of bounds, Nancy sailed right with it, saved the errant ball and recovered control for her team. Another textbook pass resulted in another layup underneath for Donovan. It was now 41-26, and Nancy was turning the contest into a rout. She grabbed another offensive rebound. She fought off a double-teaming defense, found Nissen for the open shot, and the lead mounted to 43-28. Fighting taller Tennessee players for a rebound, she managed to tip the ball to an open teammate. Two more crisp, slick passes to Cotman and Nissen resulted in two more easy baskets and a huge 49-32 lead.

With 13:15 left in the half, Nancy was charged with her fourth foul (five means expulsion). She left with the score 49-32. ODU promptly turned over the ball four consecutive times. "Now she's out of the game, you can see how much she was doing," observed TV commentator Kathy Rush, herself a noted coach.

Tennessee's press, ineffective while Nancy was in the game, was suddenly giving ODU fits. With about seven minutes remaining, Lieberman came back. She changed the tempo of the game as soon as she entered, breaking the pressing defense consistently without difficulty. She hit two more free throws, stole the ball off an inbounds pass, snatched another rebound, passed for another pretty assist, then stole the ball again. By the time she fouled out with 1:42 to play, the game was long over; the score was 65-49.

When Nancy went to the bench, the spectators exploded in appreciative, loud applause.

The final score was 68-53, and at the end, Nancy was carried off the court on the shoulders of her teammates and fans. Her final statistics included twelve points, nine rebounds, six assists and three steals. Impressive enough, perhaps; but as we've seen, figures that do not begin to suggest the degree to which she dominated the game.

"She's the most tenacious player I've ever coached," said a delighted and impressed coach Stanley, paying well-deserved tribute to her graduating star. It was, in many respects, a typical Lieberman game. All she did was do everything conceivable, in every aspect of the game, to guarantee her team victory.

"You don't find many guards that'll rebound the way she does," coach Stanley continued. "You don't find many players who can completely control the tempo and complexion of the ball game as Nancy does. I don't think I've seen many people who have her confidence. You can't teach that. Nancy probably had that when she was born. She probably came out of the womb swinging."

As impressively as she has honed and refined her basketball skills during her magnificent amateur career, Nancy has also taken full advantage of her opportunities to mature and develop off the court. Exposure to different kinds of people and her ball-playing travels to foreign countries made her far more aware of the universe that existed beyond her formerly single-minded dedication to basketball.

"I've changed," she says freely. "I've learned. Of course I've grown up. Isn't that what college is all about?

"There is so much more than just basketball," she adds

reflectively. "I've enjoyed seeing different cultures because it makes me realize that in the United States we have so much that these other people don't have. And unfortunately, we want, want, want. These people need. They lack for the necessities. We ask for more, while they fight to survive."

One of the most traumatic, and unexpected, developments in Nancy's brilliant career was directly caused by the political international universe well beyond her control: the American boycott of the 1980 Moscow Olympics. Ever since 1976, when Nancy — then a high school senior — helped the U.S. Olympic squad to a silver medal with her fiercely competitive skills, Nancy's great dream had been to win an Olympic Gold medal.

"Since I was a little tomboy, I've always had three goals," she said. "I wanted to play basketball, play on a college championship team, and on an Olympic championship team."

She had turned down substantial amounts of money offered to her if she would forfeit some of her college eligibility and turn professional; but she was determined to remain an amateur so that she could win that Olympic medal. "That's what I'm playing for. That's what I'm living for. That's the whole deal. When we beat the Russians . . . well, wow, that will be really something.

"You can't believe the feeling of lining up and bowing your head so they can put the medal around your neck. Thousands of flags are waving and the national anthem is playing. It's the ultimate."

But after the Soviet invasion of Afghanistan, President Carter declared that U.S. policy would be to boycott Moscow in 1980. Many American athletes, understandably depressed about seeing four long hard years of training and preparation suddenly voided, complained unhappily, expressed bitterness, or tried to work out some way to attend anyway. But Nancy, who had dreamed and worked as hard as anyone towards the same Olympic goal for four years, chose to sacrifice her own personal interests in favor of supporting her country's diplomatic efforts. Having been selected for the 1980 American team, she voluntarily left the training camp, expressing the view that there were larger, more important issues in life than the advancement of athletes' interests, and that as an American she wanted to support her country, even though she freely conceded that it meant the end of her personal long-cherished dream.

Once again, Nancy Lieberman had done what she had always excelled at doing — leading the way. When the history of American sports is written, and the development of women's athletics is considered, Nancy Lieberman's name will loom large in the records: as a pioneer trailblazer, the greatest basketball player of her era, and a glowing standard by which subsequent generations of female athletes will be measured. Countless little girls who right now are practicing jump shots, ground strokes or floor exercises, and other girls who will some day succeed them, will owe more than most of them will ever know to the redheaded basketball dynamo whom they called "Fire."